SOUTH CAROLINA NEGROES, 1877-1900

NEGROES IN POLITICS

Robert B. Anderson, I. R. Reed, Robert Smalls, William J. Whipper, James Wigg, and Thomas E. Miller *were the Negro members of the constitutional convention of South Carolina of 1895.*

South Carolina

NEGROES

1877-1900

By   George
Brown
Tindall

COLUMBIA

UNIVERSITY of SOUTH CAROLINA PRESS

1952

To

BLOSSOM

FOREWORD

South Carolina Negroes, whether actively or passively, have been for well over two centuries a central factor in the political, social, and institutional life of the Province and State. Considerable research has been directed to them during the period of slavery and during Reconstruction. South Carolina, leader in the ante bellum sectional controversies and home of secession, was also the State in which the rule of the Radical Republicans was most prolonged after the Civil War. The attention that has since been focused upon South Carolina by historians of the postwar period has made it a classic example of Reconstruction. Since that time it has been repeatedly in the fore of sectional controversies centering on issues of race.

South Carolina is therefore a fertile field for the investigation of Negro history, but comparatively little attention has been devoted to that phase of the State's history in the period since Reconstruction. Yet it was in this period, Professor E. Franklin Frazier has said, "that the pattern of race relations in the South was established . . . that the Negro was disfranchised through State constitutions; that discrepancies in educational facilities and the system of racial segregation known as Jim Crow were established by law in the Southern states." In South Carolina the process described by Professor Frazier had progressed far toward completion by the end of the nineteenth century. Negroes were almost completely disfranchised in 1895 and were segregated on railway cars by 1898. The last Negro to sit in the legislature of the state was defeated in his bid for re-election in 1902.

This book is an effort to fill in for one Southern state the gap in our knowledge of the history of American Negroes. Its objective is to trace the post-Reconstruction developments, in Negro life and institutions and in race relations, that are pregnant with meaning for the present day.

This study grew out of an earlier essay on the South Carolina Constitutional Convention of 1895. It was begun under the direction of Professor Fletcher M. Green of the University of North

Carolina, whose courses in the history of the South and whose suggestions and criticisms are responsible for much of whatever merit it may have. Professors J. Carlyle Sitterson and Hugh T. Lefler of the University of North Carolina and Professor Arney R. Childs of the University of South Carolina read the manuscript and made valuable suggestions for improvement. Financial and secretarial assistance was made available by the Institute for Research in Social Science, Chapel Hill, North Carolina.

Grateful acknowledgment is also given to Professor Howard K. Beale, whose courses at the University of North Carolina were fruitful sources of knowledge and interpretation. Background information without which this study would have been much more difficult has been found particularly in the pioneering works on Reconstruction history by Alrutheus A. Taylor, Francis B. Simkins, and Robert H. Woody. The research of Vernon L. Wharton on the Negroes of Mississippi has blazed a trail that is followed here.

Those who assisted in the process of research are too numerous to list. However, particular gratitude is expressed to the following: Professors John Hope Franklin and E. Horace Fitchett, and Mrs. Dorothy B. Porter of Howard University; Dr. Elizabeth McPherson and Dr. Percival Powell of the Library of Congress; the staff of the University of North Carolina Library, especially Mr. J. Isaac Copeland, Miss Georgia Faison, Mrs. Louise P. Newton, and Mrs. Carolyn A. Daniel of the Southern Historical Collection; the staff of the Duke University Library; Miss Virginia Rugheimer and the staff of the Charleston Library Society; the staff of the Charleston Free Library, especially the Dart Hall Branch; Dr. Anne King Gregorie and Miss Elizabeth Jervey of the South Carolina Historical Society; Dr. Robert L. Meriwether and the staff of the South Caroliniana Library, University of South Carolina; Dr. J. Harold Easterby and the staff of the Historical Commission of South Carolina; President S. R. Higgins and the staff of the Allen University Library; Miss Mabel Runette of the Beaufort Township Library; and Dr. Henry D. Bull of Georgetown, South Carolina.

Many thanks are also due to the people and organizations who helped the author to procure illustrations which would be completely authentic. Either furnishing pictures or aiding in locating them were the following: Dr. J. A. McFall, Mr. W. S. Noisette, Mrs. Susan Dart Butler, Mr. A. J. Clement, Jr., and Mr. Preston W.

Robinson (International Bricklayers, Masons, and Plasterers Union), Charleston, S. C.; the South Caroliniana Library, the South Carolina Historical Commission, Prof. C. A. Johnson, and the family of the late Mr. and Mrs. Robert C. Nelson, Sr., of Columbia, S. C.; Mrs. Janet Smith and Mrs. Charlotte Garrett, Greenville, S. C.; and the Prints and Photographs Division of the Library of Congress, Washington, D. C.

For permission to use quotations, I am obligated to the following: the Association for the Study of Negro Life and History for material in the *Journal of Negro History* and the *Negro History Bulletin;* the *Journal of Southern History;* the *South Carolina Historical Magazine;* the *Atlantic Monthly* for use of the articles on "The Political Condition of South Carolina" published in 1877; Jane Edna Hunter, *A Nickle and a Prayer* (Cleveland: Elli Kani, 1940); William Pickens, *Bursting Bonds* (Boston: Jordan and More, 1923); Arthur W. Page, son of Walter Hines Page, for permission to quote from *The Training of an American: The Earlier Life and Letters of Walter H. Page* (Boston: Houghton Mifflin, 1928), edited by Burton J. Hendrick; the University of North Carolina Press for material from Francis B. Simkins and Roberty H. Woody, *South Carolina during Reconstruction* (Chapel Hill, 1932); Hilda June Zimmerman for use of her unpublished Ph.D. dissertation at the University of North Carolina, "Penal Systems and Penal Reforms in the South Since the Civil War;" and Mrs. Rupert S. Holland for material from *Letters and Diary of Laura M. Towne* (Cambridge, Mass.; The Riverside Press, 1912), edited by Rupert S. Holland.

Typing of the final manuscript was done by Mrs. Wilma Finlay of the University of Mississippi. For guiding the book through the last stages I am indebted to the editorial staff of the University of South Carolina Press. Especial acknowledgment is due to my wife, Blossom McGarrity Tindall, who assisted in the process of gathering material, functioned as a patient critic during the process of composition, and helped to prepare the index.

G. B. T.

CONTENTS

[xi]

ILLUSTRATIONS

Note: The illustrations are all from photographs taken during or shortly after the 1877-1900 period. With two exceptions, they were reproduced from the originals by the Munn and Teale Studio, Columbia. The Neptune Volunteer Fire Company was reproduced by the Globe Photo Service, Greenville, S. C., and the picture of the Charleston peddlers comes from the Prints and Photographs Division of the Library of Congress.

SOUTH CAROLINA NEGROES, 1877-1900

1

SLAVERY AND RECONSTRUCTION

THERE has been speculation that the dark-skinned Yemassees, one of the many small Indian tribes of South Carolina, were descendants of immigrants who came from Africa before the European discovery of America.[1] There is no substantiation for the story, but it would be one of the curiosities of history if Negroes first occupied the area of what is now Beaufort County, where they were later to be concentrated as slaves of the white man, and after emancipation were to control the politics of the county for nearly three decades.

The first Negroes in South Carolina of whom there is definite record were three who came with the first settlers in 1670.[2] After that, Negroes were imported in great numbers from both the West Indies and Africa, so that during most of the colonial period they formed the most numerous portion of the population of South Carolina. Although conflicting, the estimates of population in the colonial period show clearly that Negroes outnumbered the whites during most of the eighteenth century.[3] However, in the first census of the United States (1790) whites outnumbered the Negro slaves 140,178 to 108,895 and Negroes did not again constitute a majority until 1820, by which time the growth of the cotton plantation system had fixed slavery as the state's chief source of

[1] State Board of Agriculture of South Carolina, *South Carolina: Resources and Population. Institutions and Industries* (Charleston, 1883), pp. 366-67. Harry Hammond is generally believed to have been the editor of this volume. Hereinafter cited as *Handbook of 1883.*

[2] David Duncan Wallace, *The History of South Carolina* (3 vols.; New York, 1935), I, 81.

[3] Evarts Boutell Greene and Virginia Draper Harrington, *American Population Before the Federal Census of 1790* (New York, 1932), pp. 173, 176.

labor. After 1820, Negroes composed a majority of the state's population until the census of 1930 showed them in a slight minority.[4]

The predominance of Negro population, as well as the institution of slavery itself, played an important part in shaping the conditions under which Negroes lived. Intermittent fear of servile insurrection was a perennial source of repressive measures during the period of slavery. The first statutory provision with regard to slaves in the province, passed in 1686, demonstrated white fears by inhibiting direct trade with Negroes and by making it unlawful for a Negro slave to go abroad without a note or ticket from the master, mistress, or overseer.[5]

Other laws on the matter of slavery followed in abundance, but the first elaborate slave code was not adopted until 1712. Like the first slaves themselves, the code was imported from Barbados. With a significant revision in 1740, following hard on the Stono Insurrection of 1739, the Barbadian Code remained throughout the period of slavery the basic slave law of South Carolina. More moderate than the Virginia code, which grew up piecemeal as various occasions for repression occurred, the Barbadian Code as modified in South Carolina seems harsh enough to the contemporary reader. Since the code was written by white men and designed to serve their purposes, it emphasized controls which would facilitate the exploitation of black labor. Only secondary consideration was given to the protection of slaves against mistreatment and overwork.[6]

Under this system there was, of course, ample opportunity for the practice of cruelty. Corporal punishment was generally accepted as an appropriate means of discipline, and cases of mistreatment by masters and patrols can be cited.[7] County slave patrols, under the influence of high spirits and low sensitivity, sometimes assumed

---

[4] United States Bureau of the Census, *Negro Population, 1790-1915* (Washington, 1918), pp. 43-45.

[5] *Statutes at Large of the State of South Carolina* (Columbia, 1836-_____), II, 22. Hereinafter cited as *Statutes at Large*.

[6] For general discussions of the slave code, see Edward McCrady, "Slavery in the Province of South Carolina, 1670-1770," *Annual Report of the American Historical Association for the Year 1895* (Washington, 1896), pp. 648-54; Howell Meadoes Henry, *The Police Control of the Slave in South Carolina* (Emory, Virginia, 1914), pp. 1-78.

[7] Henry, *The Police Control of the Slave*, pp. 66-79, cites cases of unnecessary cruelties to slaves.

the aspect of lynching bees, whipping and even killing inoffensive slaves. A white South Carolinian, writing after emancipation, said:

> I have heard Southerners . . . in moments of jovial conversation relate with great gusto anecdotes of how in the good old times they used to hunt down runaway negroes with hounds and guns, brand them, beat them till senseless, and while patrolling at night flog negroes who had passes "just to hear them beg and hollo."[8]

The moral effect of such escapades on the whites was equally as damaging as their physical effect on the Negroes.

At first concentrated on the Low Country rice and indigo plantations, the slave population spread across the state with the development of the cotton plantation system. The slave system came to be so generally prevalent that there developed in South Carolina a homogeneity, remarkable even for the South, both in population and in attitudes. Unlike North Carolina which had a considerable mountain element without slaves and hostile to slaveholders, South Carolina had no concentration of non-slaveholding white population. The yeoman farmers and poor whites were scattered along the fringes of the plantation economy, chiefly on poorer lands to which they had been crowded by the encroachments of successful planters. Generally they fell under the influence of their wealthier neighbors.[9]

Within the homogeneous social pattern of South Carolina, criticism of the institution of slavery became taboo. The slaves were not only considered indispensable in the growing of cotton, but became more and more valuable with an expanding demand for slaves in the Southwest. When wholesale attack on the institution began, the "Hotspur state" was at the front of the propaganda and

---

[8] A South Carolinian, "South Carolina Morals," *Atlantic Monthly*, XXXIX (April, 1877), 471. This is one of a series of three articles by Belton O'Neall Townsend on South Carolina morals, politics, and society.

[9] An anomalous racial group not fitting into the social pattern were the outcasts of indefinite origin, referred to variously as brass ankles, Croatans, red bones, Turks, and yellow hammers. They were predominantly Caucasoid in features, but apparently descended from the numerous independent Indian tribes of the coastal regions who had received an intermixture of the blood of white traders and adventurers and probably also of runaway slaves and free Negroes. They were found chiefly in the coastal pine barrens. Brewton Berry, "The Mestizos of South Carolina," *American Journal of Sociology*, LI (July, 1945), 34-41.

political battle in its defense. Writers like William Gilmore Simms, William J. Grayson, Richard Furman, William Harper, John Bachman, and James Henry Hammond joined the issue. John C. Calhoun formulated a theory of minority rights in the federal union that would leave Southern whites free to control the slave population as they saw fit, and in time, under the expert political manipulations of Calhoun and his followers, South Carolina became as solidly Democratic in the last decade before the Civil War as it was again to become after Reconstruction. The unanimity of conservative sentiment that was built up in the pro-slavery argument had an important and persistent influence on race relations after emancipation.

Yet, even in the dark tapestry of servitude and repression it is possible to trace a bright thread of Negro progress. The institution of slavery, especially where tempered by paternalism, was in a very real sense a school of Western civilization, and successive generations of Negroes learned well their rudimentary lessons in agriculture and industry.

From the early part of the eighteenth century, white missionaries of the Anglican Church, operating through the Society for the Propagation of the Gospel in Foreign Parts, labored long and hard in the work of Christianizing and educating Negroes. From 1702, when agents of the Society first entered South Carolina, they recorded distinct progress in proselyting and educating Negro slaves.[10]

The Charleston Negro School, begun in 1743 by Alexander Garden, was one of the earliest colonial efforts to recognize and develop the potentialities of the Negroes for enlightenment. It was closed in 1765, but as late as 1819 there were Negroes in Charleston who had been taught to read and write in this school.[11]

Not only Episcopalians, but later Presbyterians, Methodists, and Baptists worked assiduously among the Negro race, the last two

---

[10] Frank J. Klingberg, *An Appraisal of the Negro in Colonial South Carolina* (Washington, 1941), is devoted chiefly to the work of the S. P. G.; *see also* Carter G. Woodson, *The History of the Negro Church* (Washington, 1921. Second edition, 1945), p. 6.

[11] Klingberg, *An Appraisal of the Negro in Colonial South Carolina*, pp. 102-22.

with greatest success.[12] In Charleston, there was at least one church organized by Negroes themselves. Affiliated with the African Methodist Episcopal denomination, it increased from one thousand members in 1817 to three thousand in 1822, including both slaves and free Negroes, but in the latter year was forced to disband after the disclosure of the Denmark Vesey plot for a slave insurrection.[13]

Another significant aspect of Negro progress came with the growth of a free Negro population, centered chiefly in Charleston.[14] "Free persons of color," as they were designated, occupied an anomalous position in the ante-bellum social structure, yet one decidedly above the status of slaves. Many of them achieved economic success, and a student of their development reports that in 1819 they were engaged in at least thirty branches of work in Charleston.[15]

Within the free Negro group of Charleston a number of successful organizations were formed for social, educational, and mutual benefit purposes. The Brown Fellowship Society, oldest of the Negro friendly societies in the state, was founded in 1790 and showed a discretion that permitted it to be maintained intact even through periods of strain when other Negro organizations were disbanded by the whites. It was a mutual benefit burial association, but also had the objective of maintaining schools for Negro children. Other societies of the same nature were formed in abundance. At least two of these, the Brown Fellowship Society and the Humane and Friendly Society, continued their existence beyond the end of the nineteenth century.[16]

Despite a law of 1834 to prohibit the education of slaves and restrict closely the education of free Negroes, a number of Negroes learned to read and write and some went on to more advanced training. The law requiring the presence of whites in classes conducted for free Negroes was generally ignored in Charleston, and

---

[12] Woodson, *The History of the Negro Church,* pp. 98, 139-40.

[13] *Ibid.,* p. 67. The Morris Brown Church in Charleston is named for the pastor of this congregation.

[14] E. Horace Fitchett, "The Origin and Growth of the Free Negro Population of Charleston, South Carolina," *Journal of Negro History,* XXVI (October, 1941), 421-37.

[15] Fitchett, "The Traditions of the Free Negro in Charleston, South Carolina," *Journal of Negro History,* XXV (April, 1940), 143.

[16] C. W. Birnie, "Education of the Negro in Charleston, South Carolina, Prior to the Civil War," *Journal of Negro History,* XII (January, 1927), 15-16.

there is record of at least fifteen schools operated by free Negroes between 1800 and 1860 without interference from the authorities.[17]

Many persons later to become leaders of the race received a rudimentary education during the period of slavery from lenient masters or in these schools. Bruce H. Williams, a slave of Dr. J. D. Magill, on Waccamaw Island, was taught by his master to read and write, despite the law. He later became an African Methodist minister and was elected in the eighties to the state senate. Thomas Ezekiel Miller, born in 1849, and destined to serve in the state legislature and Congress and as the first president of the state college for Negroes, attended a school operated by free persons of color. Daniel Alexander Payne, later a bishop, received instruction in the school of the Minors Moralist Society in Charleston. Thus, even behind the façade of slavery, a Negro leadership was developing.

Early in the Civil War, November, 1861, federal forces attacked and captured the island of Port Royal at the southern tip of the state with the towns of Beaufort and Port Royal, and several other sea islands in the area were quickly occupied by the federal army. Agencies for the education and aid of the "contrabands," later freedmen, were formed in the cities of the North, and numerous agents of these societies were sent into the Port Royal area to establish schools for the freedmen. They set up institutions that exerted a healthful influence for many years after the war and trained a nucleus of experienced educators for the wider problems that came with general emancipation. The most famous of these institutions, the Penn Normal and Industrial School founded by Laura M. Towne and Ellen Murray, had a continuous independent existence until 1948, when it was taken over by the state school system.[18]

At the end of the war there was considerable uncertainty on the part of both victor and vanquished, as well as the slaves themselves, as to the precise status to be occupied by the freedmen.

---

[17] *Ibid.,* pp. 17-21; *see also* Josephus R. Coan, *Daniel Alexander Payne: Christian Educator* (Philadelphia, 1935), for the life of a teacher in one of these schools who later became a bishop in the African Methodist Episcopal Church.

[18] Columbia *Record,* May 6, 1948; Rupert Sargent Holland (ed.), *Letters and Diary of Laura M. Towne Written from the Sea Islands of South Carolina, 1862-1884* (Cambridge, 1912); Rossa Belle Cooley, *School Acres, an Adventure in Rural Education* (New Haven, 1930).

While the institution of slavery had introduced Negroes to the basic features of Western civilization, it had not prepared them for the responsibilities of freedom. To many, freedom meant the opportunity to wander around the countryside without the necessity for written passes. To many, it also meant being raised to the status of the whites, and since to innocent minds it seemed that the white master and mistress never labored, freedom meant the absence of labor. This was merely a transitory situation and it was not long before the Freedmen's Bureau, established by Congress, began to bring order into the postwar chaos. Distrusted by whites who wanted no interference in the working out of new social and economic arrangements, it brought relief to suffering masses, persuaded both whites and blacks of the value of labor contracts, and encouraged the signing and enforcement of such contracts throughout the South.[19]

President Andrew Johnson appointed as provisional governor of South Carolina a former Unionist, Benjamin Franklin Perry of Greenville, and under Perry a constitutional convention was convened in September, 1865.

Civil rights for Negroes received little attention in the conservative convention of 1865. However, the convention authorized a commission to report to the first legislature elected under the new constitution a proposed program for the regulation of the black population. At a special session of the legislature in September, 1865, the so-called "black code" was passed.[20] This code was the first effort by the whites of the state to redefine the relations of the races under the new conditions. The nature of the black code indicates that white South Carolinians could not conceive of Negroes as truly free agents in their relationship to the economy of the state. Granted new legal rights, Negroes were still hedged about with restrictions that relegated them to an inferior caste.

To a large segment of the Northern public this and similar codes in other states appeared to be an effort to perpetuate the restrictions of slavery as much as possible under the guise of freedom. Congress, convinced of a tendency in the South to maintain the slavery system in disguise, determined upon an independent course,

---

[19] Laura Josephine Webster, *The Operation of the Freedman's Bureau in South Carolina* (Northampton, Mass., 1916).

[20] *Statutes at Large*, XIII, 245-85.

and proceeded to carry out Reconstruction on a more radical basis than that proposed by President Johnson. It immediately passed over his veto two significant bills. One expanded the powers of the Freedmen's Bureau and extended its life. The other was the Civil Rights Act of 1866, the purposes of which were to make Negroes citizens and to establish equality for all citizens in the enjoyment of legal rights. The purposes of the Civil Rights Act were later embodied in the Fourteenth Amendment. The provisions of the black codes were thus superseded, and the work of establishing a new subordinate caste for Negroes had to follow somewhat more subtle methods once the Radicals were ousted from power in the state.

The provisional governments established by President Johnson were also doomed by Radical control of Congress after 1866. The Johnson governments were overturned, the states were again placed under military rule, and provision was made for the reorganization of state governments on the basis of universal suffrage.

Under Radical direction, an election in which the freedmen voted was held in November, 1867, for delegates to a new constitutional convention. Most were Republicans, and 76 of the 124 delegates were colored. Of these, according to one authority, 57 had only a few years before been slaves.[21]

This convention wrote a constitution that was to stand for nearly three decades, and sizable portions of it are still included in the constitution of the state. Elected on the basis of a bi-racial suffrage, the convention readily acceded to the congressional requirement that it place no racial restriction upon the suffrage. This was its most radical innovation, but there were others. A measure was adopted to annul all debts incurred for the purchase of slaves. Another relief measure provided a homestead exemption from debts of $1,000 and a personal property exemption of $500. The convention inserted into the constitution a requirement that the General Assembly establish a system of public schools.

Numerous changes were also made in the machinery of government. Popular election was provided not only for the governor, but for eight other state officers, circuit solicitors, and county commissioners.

---

[21] Francis Butler Simkins and Robert Hilliard Woody, *South Carolina During Reconstruction* (Chapel Hill, N. C., 1932), p. 91.

Two historians of the Reconstruction period have described the work of the convention as follows:

> The learning of the leaders bore fruit in a constitution written in excellent English and embodying some of the best legal principles of the age. In letter it was as good as any other constitution the state has ever had, or as most American states had at that time. This assertion is supported by the practical endorsement which a subsequent generation of South Carolinians gave it; the Conservative whites were content to live under it for eighteen years after they recovered control of the state government, and when in 1895 they met to make a new constitution, the document they produced had many of the features of the constitution of 1868.[22]

The turn of events in South Carolina brought rapid development by the state's Negroes in many directions. The most obvious of these was the entry of Negro leaders into politics. At various times before 1876 eight Negroes were elected to Congress. Two became lieutenant governors, another a justice of the state Supreme Court, another secretary of state, and great numbers of them entered the state legislature. Negro members for six years predominated in the lower house of the state legislature, but they never had a majority in the upper house. The whites constituted a majority in each house from 1874 to 1876, although enough of them were Republicans to give that party a majority.

There were adventurers, both native and alien, who were attracted after the war by the prospects for gain not only in legitimate activities, but also in the illegitimate activities of political manipulation. Many of the prominent white members of the Republican party and many of the Negroes were drawn into the meshes of widespread corruption, to be exposed by investigations undertaken during the Chamberlain administration of 1874-1876 and continued under the Democratic administration that succeeded him.

However, the eight year period of Republican control, long denounced by partisan historians as an era of unparalleled corruption and abuse, has in the third and fourth decades of the twentieth century been subjected to re-examination in the light of cooling partisanship and found to have been also a period not only

---

[22] *Ibid.*, pp. 93-94.

of constructive social and economic progress, but also of substantial governmental achievement.

The social and economic adjustments, brought about during the Reconstruction period, were extremely important. The growth of independent Negro churches marked a departure from ante-bellum practices, and the systems of land tenure and agricultural labor that grew up during the period have continued with slight modification to the present day.

Corruption in government, it may be suggested, has been exaggerated to the neglect of important accomplishments.[23] Chief among these were the establishment during those eight years of the principle of the equality of all men before the law and the right of all citizens to attend public schools supported by the state. In principle these accomplishments were never afterward seriously attacked. The structure of government established by the Republicans has not been altered in the fundamental matters of the terms and manner of election of public officials, the organization of the courts, county governments, and until very recently in the public school system.

The brief, though dramatic, period of Republican control was brought to an end in the aftermath of the election of 1876. This date is usually cited by historians as marking the end of the period of Reconstruction. It does not lie within the scope of this study to narrate the twice-told tale of the election of 1876 and the lengthy struggle of the dual governments that followed.[24] Some generalizations, however, will be pertinent to the story that is to follow.

---

[23] Alrutheus Ambush Taylor, *The Negro in South Carolina During the Reconstruction* (Washington, 1924), pp. 1-4; Simkins and Woody, *South Carolina During Reconstruction*, pp. vii-viii.

[24] For accounts of this election, see John Schreiner Reynolds, *Reconstruction in South Carolina* (Columbia, 1905); Simkins and Woody, *South Carolina During Reconstruction;* Taylor, *The Negro in South Carolina During the Reconstruction;* Henry Tazewell Thompson, *Ousting the Carpetbagger from South Carolina* (Columbia, 1926); Alfred Brockenbrough Williams, *Hampton and His Red Shirts: South Carolina's Deliverance in 1876* (Columbia, 1935); Walter Allen, *Governor Chamberlain's Administration in South Carolina: A Chapter of Reconstruction in the Southern States* (New York, 1888); *Recent Election in South Carolina: Testimony Taken by the Select Committee on the Recent Election in South Carolina* (House Miscellaneous Documents, 44th Congress, 2d Session, No. 31); and *South Carolina in 1876: Testimony as to the Denial of the Elective Franchise in South Carolina at the Elections of 1875 and 1876,* 3 vols. (Senate Miscellaneous Documents, 44th Congress, 2d Session, No. 48).

The last Republican governor, Daniel Henry Chamberlain, had come into office in 1874 with a reputation not untarnished by Radical corruption, but had immediately become a reform governor. This was quite pleasing to the economy-minded white landowners, who wanted lower taxes. Not only that, but Chamberlain was already showing tendencies toward his later conversion to white supremacy, although he remained correct, from the Republican standpoint, on the question of racial equality before the law. There was widespread sentiment, vocally supported by the Charleston *News and Courier,* for a coalition to support Chamberlain's re-election.[25]

On the other hand, the unreconstructed white supremacists would not rest until the state should be delivered completely into the rule of its white citizens. With Martin Witherspoon Gary of Edgefield as their chief spokesman, they favored a "Straightout" Democratic campaign to secure control of the state government, and events during 1876 played into the hands of the men who had an aggressive program for the complete overthrow of the Radical government. Two incidents were of greatest importance in this development: one involving chiefly the issue of Radical corruption, the other involving the all-important issue of race.

The first incident arose from the election by the legislature on December 16, 1875, of W. J. Whipper (Negro) and F. J. Moses, Jr. (white), as circuit judges. Both had been repeatedly charged with corruption, and the action of the Republican legislature was seized upon by the opposition as proof that the Republicans were totally unregenerate. Chamberlain's effort to undo the damage by refusing to sign commissions for the men did not serve to stop the cry among the Democrats to "Organize! Organize! Organize!"[26]

However, there was still considerable sentiment for a coalition behind Chamberlain. But this situation was changed by the Hamburg Riot of July 8, which set the tone for the bitter campaign that was to follow. The riot grew out of an incident between two white men passing through the village of Hamburg and a company of colored militia who blocked their path. Six Negroes and one white were killed. An early reaction of moderate whites was that the "men who thus appease their wrath at being detained on the

[25] Charleston *News and Courier,* July 5-9, 12-15, 18, 1876.
[26] *Ibid.,* December 21, 1875.

street by the parading of negro militiamen . . ." were guilty of "the grossest outrage ever perpetrated in the State."[27] Negro mass meetings in Charleston and Columbia passed resolutions that attributed to the affair a motive of political intimidation, and requested national protection from this sort of mistreatment.[28]

The Hamburg affair quickly took a political turn, and in the mounting fury moderate voices were drowned by the uproar of agitation and vilification. One Democrat who had earlier supported Chamberlain complained that "the unhappy affair at Hamburg will be made such use of in the canvass that no alternative would probably have been left us than to 'take it straight.' "[29]

The Democratic convention in August voted 88 to 64 to make nominations for all state offices and quickly named Wade Hampton, a Confederate hero, for governor and a complete slate composed entirely of white men. The platform promised honesty and economy and in one significant portion said: "We declare our acceptance, in perfect good faith, of the thirteenth, fourteenth and fifteenth amendments to the Federal constitution."[30] It was a plank that was to arouse much controversy and no little soul searching among Democrats in the future.

Neither the Democratic state committee nor Wade Hampton followed the straightout policy to the extent of adopting Gary's program of violence and intimidation. In the campaign Hampton consistently endorsed the platform pledge to accept the postwar amendments. He promised at Darlington: *"Not one single right enjoyed by the colored people to-day shall be taken from them. They shall be the equals, under the law, of any man in South Carolina.* And we further pledge that we will give *better facilities for education than they have ever had before."* On another occasion, in Sumter, he predicted a time when "every colored man will be a Democrat, because they will find that their rights will be better protected by that party."[31]

---

[27] Yorkville *Enquirer*, July 13, 1876.

[28] Charleston *News and Courier*, July 18, 1876; *South Carolina in 1876*, III, 489-96.

[29] Joseph B. Kershaw in Charleston *News and Courier*, July 28, 1876.

[30] Columbia *Daily Register*, August 18, 1876.

[31] Wade Hampton, *Free Men! Free Ballots!! Free Schools!!! The Pledges of Gen. Wade Hampton, Democratic Candidate for Governor to the Colored People of South Carolina, 1865-1876* (Charleston, 1876), pp. 6, 7.

The upshot of the disagreement between the moderate Hampton and the fanatical Gary was that the Democratic party waged a dual campaign, with Hampton and the state committee appealing to Negro support, and Gary and the extremists practicing intimidation. A long and indecisive argument has been waged by the participants in the struggle and by subsequent historians as to which policy was responsible for Democratic success.[32] It would seem that neither policy alone would have carried the election. The promises of Hampton were regarded by Negroes with a wary eye. One Negro asked a meeting of the Richland Democratic Club in Columbia,

> Whilst I know that if the men that you have nominated had their way, none of our rights would be endangered, yet what guarantee have I that their opinion will be regarded? I will agree with you that I and many like myself are not competent to run this government, but you must not draw a line and exclude all of my race. Give us representation and we will go together and reform the state together and we can then have good government.[33]

In Beaufort, where Wade Hampton appeared at the last meeting of the campaign, Laura Towne overheard a Negro man say, "Dem says dem *will do* dis and dat. I ain't ax no man what him *will do*— I ax him what him *hab done*." "Pretty hard on the Democrats, that . . . ," commented Laura Towne.[34] It was difficult to move Negro voters into support for a party whose leaders merely promised not to undo what had already been done for them, while it was clear that great numbers, probably a majority of that party, disagreed with the moderate approach of their leaders. On the other hand, it probably would have been impossible to carry a campaign of intimidation without serious interference from the national authorities had not that campaign been tempered by the moderation of Hampton.

At the same time it was difficult to arouse enthusiasm among Negroes for Chamberlain. He was renominated by his party, but

---

[32] William Arthur Sheppard, *Red Shirts Remembered: Southern Brigadiers of the Reconstruction Period* (Atlanta, 1940); Hampton M. Jarrell, *Wade Hampton and the Negro: The Road Not Taken* (Columbia, 1949).

[33] Richland Democratic Club Minutes: Scrapbook, 1876-1880, October 5, 1876. The South Caroliniana Library, University of South Carolina.

[34] Holland (ed.), *Letters and Diary of Laura M. Towne*, p. 254.

not until Robert Brown Elliott, a Negro leader, had warned the convention that Chamberlain was not to be trusted by the Negroes.[35] The initiative seized by the Democrats could not have been wrested away by half-hearted Republicans who were now on the defensive. Hampton moved through the state from the Up Country to the coast on a wave of enthusiasm. Adopting a policy labelled by a latter-day Hamptonite as "force without violence,"[36] groups of Red Shirts invaded Republican meetings, and though remarkably well disciplined, gave the impression of trigger-happy toughs who might easily be tempted to homicide.

The election itself, according to Belton O'Neall Townsend, "was one of the greatest farces ever seen."[37] Terror and fraud were used on both sides wherever one or the other had the upper hand, and the vote was so affected by these tactics that no one will ever know what the outcome would have been in a fair and honest election. It was followed by a tense period of confusion, compounded by uncertainty as to the presidential election, with both sides claiming victory and inaugurating their gubernatorial candidates. Because of the presence of federal troops the Republicans were able to retain control of all the state offices until April, when the new President, Rutherford B. Hayes, announced his intention of withdrawing the troops, and the Republican claimants shortly thereafter vacated their offices.

The great irony of the campaign of 1876 was that the protagonists in the most bitter and violent political campaign ever waged in the state, Chamberlain and Hampton, were both essentially moderate men whose avowed aims were conciliation, pacification, and reform. Hampton, it was later demonstrated, could not control the extremists in his party, despite his great prestige. Those who had followed Gary in 1876 during the eighties found a leader in Benjamin Ryan Tillman, who carried to completion in the nineties their program for the complete elimination of Negroes from politics and the more stringent definition of their social and economic subordination. That development is at the center of the story to which this study is devoted.

---

[35] Columbia *Daily Register,* September 13, 1876.

[36] Jarrell, *Wade Hampton and the Negro,* pp. 63-85.

[37] A South Carolinian, "The Political Condition of South Carolina," *Atlantic Monthly,* XXXIX (February, 1877), 187.

2

THE TWILIGHT OF RECONSTRUCTION

AT NOON on April 10, 1877, in accordance with the decision reached by President Rutherford B. Hayes, United States soldiers marched out of the State House in Columbia. Later that day D. H. Chamberlain, on the advice of six Republican state officials, decided to abdicate the office of governor because, as he later wrote William Lloyd Garrison, "the uneducated negro was too weak, no matter what his numbers, to cope with the whites."[1] He then issued to the Republicans of the state a bitter address in which he claimed legal title to the office of governor and expressed disappointment at the failure of the new administration in Washington to give him support. In praise of the effort of South Carolina Republicans, he said:

> By heroic efforts and sacrifices which the just verdict of history will rescue from the cowardly scorn now cast upon them by political placemen and traders, you secured the electoral vote of South Carolina for Hayes and Wheeler. In accomplishing this result, you became the victims of every form of persecution and injury. From authentic evidence it is shown that not less than one hundred of your number were murdered because they were faithful to their principles and exercised rights solemnly guaranteed to them by the nation. You were denied employment, driven from your homes, robbed of the earnings of years of honest industry, hunted for your lives like wild beasts, your families outraged and scattered,

---

[1] Daniel Henry Chamberlain to William Lloyd Garrison, June 11, 1877, in Allen, *Governor Chamberlain's Administration*, p. 504.

[15]

for no offence except your peaceful and firm determination to exercise your political rights.[2]

Nevertheless, he expressed the hope that the state might henceforth enjoy "peace, justice, freedom, and prosperity."[3]

One of the first acts of Hampton, now undisputed governor, was to call for a special session of the legislature on April 24, to which he dispatched a message presenting general observations on the state's finances, recommending investigation into the state debt, and urging reorganization of charitable and penal institutions, and of the state university. The message also called for support of a public school system that would place the means of education "within the reach of all classes in the state." Turning to the task of conciliation that was to be the primary objective of his policy as governor, Hampton expressed hope that the legislators would "forget the animosities engendered by political strife, and rise superior to the petty considerations of partisanship."[4]

The legislators, however, had in mind more pressing business than conciliation. With the senate still controlled by the Republicans and the house so constituted that Democrats would have only a bare majority should the members of the defunct Republican house be admitted, the Democrats turned first to the consolidation of the victory that had been won. A formula was evolved in a house committee whereby members of the "Mackey House" could appear before the bar of the Democratic house, present their credentials, take an oath "purging themselves of contempt," and be seated as members in order that the house might "carry out the broad, just and liberal policy of the administration, and proscribe no one, as far as they can do so consistently with the dignity of the House of Representatives and the majesty of the law."[5] Under this arrangement thirty-three Republicans were eventually seated in addition to four who had already deserted the Mackey house. Fifty-five Republicans presented their credentials, but of these, two members resigned, two were expelled, one white Republican refused to "purge himself of contempt," and the seventeen seats from Charles-

----

[2] *Ibid.*, p. 480.

[3] *Ibid.*, pp. 480-81.

[4] *Journal of the House of Representatives of the General Assembly of the State of South Carolina* (1877, special session), p. 15. Hereinafter cited as *House Journal*.

[5] Columbia *Daily Register*, April 26, 1877; Yorkville *Enquirer*, May 3, 1877.

ton County were arbitrarily declared vacant. All of the vacated seats were filled by Democrats, leaving 37 Republicans in a total membership of 124.[6]

At the first meeting of the senate R. H. Gleaves, Negro claimant to the office of lieutenant governor, announced his decision to step down as presiding officer because of the recognition of Hampton as governor. "In reaching this conclusion," he said, "I desire to place on record, in the most public and unqualified manner, my sense of the great wrong which thus forces me practically to abandon rights conferred on me, as I fully believe by a majority of my fellow citizens of this State."[7] Immediately upon his departure, W. D. Simpson, the Democratic claimant, was sworn in as lieutenant governor and proceeded to swear in four Democratic senators whose seats were being contested.[8] This gave the Democrats fifteen seats to the Republicans' eighteen. Before the end of the special session, Republican resignations gave the two parties an equal representation in the body, with a deciding vote, in case of a tie, held by the Democratic lieutenant governor.[9] When the regular session of 1877-1878 convened in November, eight additional Republicans resigned, giving the Democrats complete control over both houses.[10]

During the special session of 1877 a committee was appointed by the house to inquire into the activities of Negro Justice Jonathan Jasper Wright of the state Supreme Court, with the obvious purpose of seeking some pretext for removing him. After taking secret testimony for two weeks the committee submitted to a secret session a resolution impeaching Wright for drunkenness. With a great deal of vacillation the house first decided to continue the committee report to the next session, then considered a resolution requesting Wright's resignation, and finally passed the resolution of impeachment.[11] Thomas E. Miller reported that witnesses before

[6] Charleston *News and Courier,* June 11, 1877; *House Journal* (1877-1878), pp. 5-7. The "Mackey" house consisted of those who remained loyal to the Republican cause after the disputed election of 1876 in contradistinction to the "Wallace," or Democratic, house—each taking its name from that of the speaker.

[7] *Journal of the Senate of the General Assembly of the State of South Carolina* (1877, extra session), pp. 5-6. Hereinafter cited as *Senate Journal.*

[8] *Ibid.,* pp. 9-11, 18-19.

[9] Charleston *News and Courier,* June 11, 1877.

[10] *Senate Journal* (1877-1878), p. 6.

[11] *House Journal* (1877, special session), pp. 31, 39, 92, 137, 182, 194, 210, 226, 227.

the committee had been offered pay by Representative C. S. Minort to testify that Wright had been found drunk in the gutter, and when a special committee was appointed by the house to investigate Miller's charges, it reported that Miller had sufficient *prima facie* grounds to make the charges, but that the committee thought Minort in fact not guilty.[12] A motion by Hastings Gantt, another Negro Representative, to have the injunction of secrecy removed from testimony in the case of Wright was overwhelmingly voted down.[13] However, Wright decided to resign, and later reported that "Governor Hampton said, in accepting my resignation, that he placed no belief in the charges, and that as a jurist I was one of the purest."[14]

Meanwhile, some of the Reconstruction legislation was repealed or altered, and expenditures were drastically reduced. An act originally intended to aid victims of the Ku Klux Klan, requiring counties to grant relief to the widows and orphans of persons killed because of their political beliefs, was repealed, as was an act to provide free scholarships in South Carolina University.[15] The scholarships had been established chiefly to assist Negro students and to assure an income to the college in the face of decreased revenues after many white students had ceased attending upon the admission of Negroes in 1873. The chief immediate purpose of the revolution, however, had been accomplished with the transfer of political power into the hands of the whites. No drastic change in the governmental machinery was considered necessary.

In accordance with Governor Hampton's recommendation, a joint committee was established under the chairmanship of Senator John R. Cochran, a white Republican, to investigate alleged corruption in the previous administration and the election of United States Senator John J. Patterson.[16] Although the committee was headed by a Republican and although it carried forward a movement of investigation into corruption that had been begun during the Chamberlain administration, it was inevitable that its disclosures should be interpreted by the Democratic press as a blanket indict-

----

[12] Columbia *Daily Register*, May 24, 26, and June 7, 1877.

[13] *House Journal* (1877, special session), pp. 211-12.

[14] *Senate Journal* (1877-1878), p. 17; Columbia *Daily Register*, August 21, 1878.

[15] *House Journal* (1877, special session), pp. 103, 250.

[16] *Senate Journal* (1877-1878), p. 10.

ment of all things Republican. It was an attitude of which a Negro member of the legislature had complained in 1876 when he said that the white opposition "gave them no credit for their honest efforts at reform, but attributed base and corrupt motives to the best intentioned measures, and indulged in indiscriminate and insulting taunts and ridicule . . . , confounding the pure and the corrupt, the honest and the dishonest, the statesman and the demagogue, and pouring obloquy on all alike. . . ."[17]

It is not the purpose here to analyze the disclosures of the investigating committee, but much of the testimony and much of the evidence concerning fraud in the Reconstruction governments could not be gainsaid. The chief accomplishment of the committee, aside from bringing to light undeniable evidence of corruption, was the production of a spate of Democratic propaganda.[18] Fewer than twenty-five persons were eventually indicted, and of these only three were convicted: Francis L. Cardozo and Robert Smalls, Negroes, and L. Cass Carpenter, a white Republican.[19] All three were later pardoned by Governor W. D. Simpson, in pursuance of a mutual agreement between state and federal officials to drop charges in state and federal courts, a number of white Democrats having been charged in the federal courts with election frauds and Ku Klux atrocities.[20]

Thus the Democrats succeeded in securing complete control of the state government and in marking the Republican party in the public mind as hopelessly corrupt and degraded. It was a burden of which the Republicans were unable to rid themselves.

Negro leaders watched carefully the development of Wade Hampton's policy on racial issues, being not so much doubtful of his intention to carry out his pledges to the Negroes as fearful of his ability to restrain the Negrophobe elements of his party. In

---

[17] "A Southern Visit," *The Friend* (Philadelphia), XLIX (March 11, 1876), 237. The legislator was not identified.

[18] For reports of investigations into public frauds, see *Reports and Resolutions of the General Assembly of the State of South Carolina* (1877-1878), pp. 626-94, 803-26, 949-1004, 1013-1780. Hereinafter cited as *Reports and Resolutions.*

[19] *Reports of Cases Heard and Determined by the Supreme Court of South Carolina,* XI, 195-261, 262-75.

[20] Jarrell, *Wade Hampton and the Negro,* pp. 175-86, reprints correspondence between Hampton and Hayes on this subject. The book is an excellent study devoted to a vindication of Hampton's racial policies.

his public statements they found him clear and unequivocal. Arriving in Columbia on April 6 with news of the forthcoming withdrawal of federal soldiers, he had reiterated the pledge that he would "know no race, no party, no man, in the administration of the law." He further pledged himself to fulfill his promises to the letter, and promised that if the Democratic party should ever go back on its program and seek to take away "any of the rights now enjoyed by the colored people" he would resign rather than become the instrument of such a program. Further urging good will upon the people of the state, he said:

> I appeal to the colored men to recognize the Government which is now firmly established, to trust us for a while, and as they are still in the majority, if the government I have established does not carry out the pledges I have made, then throw out all the men in office at the next election, and put in anybody you please.[21]

Speaking several weeks later at a celebration sponsored by the Washington Light Infantry of Charleston, he revealed that several Republicans in high position in Washington had consulted him as to the best method of restricting the vote of Negroes. He had replied that the Democrats did not want the Negro vote restricted because it gave the South thirty more votes in Congress, "and when peace comes we are satisfied that the best men in both races and parties will vote together for the common weal. We don't want to take that right away. (Great applause.)"[22]

Hampton worked steadily toward the objective of conciliation. "The dominant theme of the two years of his administration," says a recent student of the Hampton program, "one too slightly noticed by historians of this period, is his struggle to end discord in the state—between parties, between the two races, and between the North and South—and to redeem his pledges in a political atmosphere that made such redemption extremely difficult, if not impossible."[23]

The liberal nature of the Hampton program, however, should not be exaggerated, nor on the other hand, should it be condemned in the light of contemporary programs for Negro advancement. It

---

[21] Charleston *News and Courier*, April 7, 1877.
[22] Yorkville *Enquirer*, April 26, 1877.
[23] Jarrell, *Wade Hampton and the Negro*, p. 122.

was largely negative in approach, merely promising that certain rights already gained by the Negroes would not be taken away by the Democrats; and it was also, as the all-white personnel of the Democratic state ticket elected with Hampton indicated, basically a program of white supremacy. But there was in the Hampton view no necessary correlation between white supremacy and black proscription. His program did not carry the connotation that latter-day white supremacists included of the complete elimination of Negroes from public life, even to the point of removing the constitutional right to the ballot. It was, in great measure, a program of *noblesse oblige*, a program of paternalism. "The old slave owner," said a white editor in Columbia, ". . . feels no social fear of negro equality. He feels no desire to maltreat and browbeat and spit upon the colored man. He feels no opposition to the education and elevation of the black man in the scale of civilized life. . . ."[24] While the editor's generalization included too many white men, it characterized the attitude of Hampton and those who, like him, gave not only lip service to the pledges of 1876, but also active effort in carrying them out.[25]

Hampton, explaining his program to a group of Negroes in Greenville, lectured them in a manner of tolerant superiority,

> You must stand upon your own footing. You cannot be put upon any better one merely because you are colored men. We propose to protect you and give you all your rights; but while we do this you cannot expect that we should discriminate in your favor, and say because you *are* a colored man, you have a right to rule the State. We say to you that we intend to take the best men we can find to represent the State, and you must qualify yourselves to do so before you can expect to be chosen. Proper qualification is necessary in all cases, and the white man who is afraid to enter the race upon such terms, does not deserve to be called a white man.[26]

Under a regime of white supremacy Wade Hampton saw room for the talented and trained Negro and left open the door of advancement for the whole race, trusting that a sufficient number of Negroes would support his program to make it possible for the

---

[24] Columbia *Daily Register*, October 15, 1879.

[25] It should be remembered, however, that when Tillman secured the Democratic nomination in 1890, Hampton refused to bolt the party.

[26] Yorkville *Enquirer*, September 26, 1878.

white minority, with their assistance, to govern the state. Given the situation in which he found himself and the dominant spirit of the times, with both Northern and Southern white opinion accepting as axiomatic the innate inferiority of the Negro race, the Hampton program marks him as a generous and constructive statesman with regard to race relations. Unfortunately, although his fame has survived the test of time, it has until recently been left to rest upon his leadership of the movement to overthrow the Republican government.

During his administration Hampton carried out the announced policy of naming the "best men" to office without regard to race by appointing a number of Negroes to minor offices. It is significant, however, that in no case was any Negro appointed to an important state office. The *News and Courier* said that the Negroes " . . . were so appointed because they are equally capable with white applicants of filling, with credit, the offices in question and not because of their color," but added significantly, "Of course the endeavor is made to avoid putting colored persons in positions where they would, or could, be peculiarly offensive."[27]

Negroes were named trial justices, jury commissioners, and in at least one case to a county board of election commissioners, and by August, 1877, ex-Governor Scott was telling a newspaperman in Ohio, "Hampton is honestly carrying out the promises he made during the campaign. He has already appointed more colored men to office than were appointed during the first two years that I was Governor. . . ."[28] R. H. Gleaves of Beaufort and Martin R. Delany of Charleston were appointed trial justices by Hampton.[29] Sir George Campbell, traveling the state in 1878, found Delany "a pure negro and notable character. He has been in England and in Africa, and has seen the world. . . . He seems a very characteristic, pleasant, amusing sort of person, and talks well. He was educated in the North. He is in favour of Wade Hampton, who, he says, appoints black men when they really are educated and fit. I hear he quite holds his owns as a justice."[30]

------

27 Charleston *News and Courier,* April 14, 1877.

28 Columbia *Daily Register,* August 28, 1877. A recent survey by the staff of the Historical Commission of South Carolina indicates that at least eighty-six Negroes were appointed to minor offices by Governor Hampton.

29 *Ibid.,* April 5, 1878.

30 George Campbell, *White and Black: The Outcome of a Visit to the United States* (London, 1879), p. 327.

In Georgetown County, Jonathan A. Baxter, a Negro Republican, was appointed to the board of election commissioners.[31] A white Republican was appointed in Beaufort, but beyond this, there seems to have been no effort to give representation to Republicans in the election machinery.

In Columbia Hampton named Charles McDuffie Wilder, the Negro postmaster, to the board of the state orphan asylum and the board elected him its chairman.[32] Meanwhile he permitted T. W. Parmele, a white Republican appointee, to retain his position as superintendent of the state penitentiary and told him that employment policy "depended on a man's competency and his conduct, if he was capable and did his duty faithfully to retain him, black or white."[33]

In the Democratic convention of Charleston County, called in 1877 to name candidates in the special election to fill the seats declared vacant by the legislature, James Conner announced that Hampton "anxiously desires that the colored citizens should have their fair representation in the delegation." "It is due," Conner said, "not only to the pledges he has made, but it is due as a matter of simple justice. They are a part of the community, to be affected by the laws made and entitled to representation to make known their wants or their grievances, and to advise on matters peculiarly affecting their interests. . . ." On a ticket of seventeen, Negro Democrats were given three places.[34] This policy, first adopted in Colleton County during the campaign of 1876, was afterwards adopted at various times in Orangeburg, Sumter, and Barnwell counties.

Thomas E. Miller, a Negro Republican, later claimed that Hampton had worked with him to establish a new county with the objective of electing a Negro Democrat to the state senate. N. B. Myers of Gillisonville had deserted the Republicans and joined the Democratic house because, as Miller put it, "he had confidence in the promise of Hampton . . . that the intelligent Negroes would be recognized." This act had destroyed Myers' influence in Beaufort County, but Miller asked Hampton to support a scheme to

[31] Charleston News and Courier, December 1, 1884.

[32] The New York Age, May 9, 1885, gives a sketch of Wilder's career by T. McCants Stewart, former Negro resident of South Carolina.

[33] T. W. Parmele in Columbia Daily Register, November 1, 1878.

[34] Charleston News and Courier, June 20, 1877.

cut off a portion of Beaufort County and name it Hampton, "so that Myers could come to the State Senate." Upon Hampton's approval of the plan, said Miller, "I worked hard and secured the new County," but the Democratic organization in the new county adopted a resolution barring from the party any Negro who had not voted for Hampton in the election of 1876. "Hampton regretted this move," said Miller, "but he was powerless. Myers was prevented from joining the Democratic Party and the resolution . . . made it impossible for men of Myers' stamp of the Negro race to join the Democratic Party."[35] The outcome illustrates the grass roots opposition that plagued the Hampton program.

In other places, however, there was evidence of amelioration at the grass roots. On July 7, 1877, a public meeting was held in Ellenton, where there had been a serious race riot in 1876, "for the purpose of restoring harmony and good feeling between all classes of the community." It was attended by large numbers of both races.[36] A subsequent meeting, several days later, resolved that all prosecutions in both state and federal courts in connection with the Ellenton riot of the previous year should be dropped.[37] The following year, when two Negroes applied for membership in the Agricultural Society of Newberry the group "met the color question promptly and fearlessly. . . . The society, on motion of Mr. Johnstone, one of its members, immediately adopted a resolution providing that they should be admitted to the privileges of membership upon complying with the usual terms of admission."[38]

The efforts of Hampton began to attract the attention of the nation. Early in 1878, E. P. Clark, managing editor of the Springfield *Republican,* visited the state and wrote an account of his observations. He found political turmoil gone and the financial condition of the state improved. In race relations he found a remarkable improvement, although the bright picture was unconsciously dimmed by the revealing statement that "the universal testimony of all employers is that they have never had so little trouble with their hands since the war as during the past years."[39]

---

[35] Thomas Ezekiel Miller to Theodore D. Jervey, December 19, 1927, Carter Godwin Woodson Papers, Manuscripts Division, Library of Congress. The late date of Miller's account should be noted.
[36] Charleston *News and Courier,* July 12, 1877.
[37] *Ibid.,* July 16, 1877.
[38] *Ibid.,* August 26, 1878.
[39] Columbia *Daily Register,* April 19, 1878, quoting correspondence from Columbia dated April 10, 1878, source not given.

Testimony of Republican leaders, white and black, Clark found to be "the most sweeping commendation of Gov. Hampton's course," showing implicit confidence in the man. Benjamin A. Boseman, Negro postmaster of Charleston, testified, "You may quote me as expressing absolute confidence in Gov. Hampton and entire satisfaction with his course. We have no complaint whatever to make. He has kept all his pledges." Negro postmaster C. M. Wilder of Columbia said, "Governor Hampton has done everything that we could have asked. He promised to protect us, and he has kept his word." Both were reported as adding in almost the same words, "I can't help regarding it as Providential that Wade Hampton became Governor of South Carolina. God only knows what would have become of us if things had kept on the way they were going."[40]

Additional evidence of Hampton's success in his efforts to establish interracial good will can be seen in the comments of other Negro leaders. Ex-Justice Jonathan J. Wright, speaking to a reporter before the election of 1878, said: "He has kept every pledge he has made, and on the seventh of next November he will be re-elected Governor almost unanimously. He will get nine-tenths of the colored vote. I speak advisedly on that point. There is not a decent negro in the State will vote against him."[41] At a Republican meeting on St. Helena Island, Beaufort County, Negro Representative Robert Smalls referred to the "just and liberal course of the Governor which had recommended him to the confidence of the people."[42]

Years later Thomas E. Miller wrote: ". . . it is impossible . . . to express in words the great worth of that very distinguished, faithful, patriotic, self-sacrificing humanitarian, Governor Wade Hampton. He is in a class by himself and if the people of our State had taken his advice after he was elected Governor, the politician [sic] tension between the races would have been destroyed. He was sincere when he said that he intended to make a part of the government of our State mixed as to race."[43]

---

[40] *Ibid.*

[41] Columbia *Daily Register*, August 21, 1878, quoting Philadelphia *Times*.

[42] Charleston *News and Courier*, July 17, 1878.

[43] Thomas E. Miller to Theodore D. Jervey, December 19, 1927, Carter G. Woodson Papers.

White Republicans, too, had good words for Hampton's course. In Columbia, T. W. Parmele, Republican superintendent of the state penitentiary left in office under Hampton, created a sensation with the announcement to a group of Negroes that *"Governor Hampton is as good a Republican as I want to see."*[44]

President Hayes, hearing of disagreement in the Democratic party with the Hampton policies, predicted that Hampton would have to separate from "the Bourbons" and might even become the Republican candidate for governor in the subsequent election.[45] Although the immense popularity of Hampton eliminated any such unlikely possibility, once the campaign of 1878 started, opposition to the Hampton program made itself manifest, though not in any direct attack on the man himself.

The Democrats in 1878 found themselves faced with a new problem, the Negro vote in the Democratic clubs and primaries. Although state candidates were still chosen by the convention method, as they were to be until 1896, some counties had already adopted the primary as the method of nomination for county candidates. In the Democratic precinct clubs, which chose delegates to the county conventions, a similar problem presented itself. Attracted by the Hampton policies, some Negroes demonstrated a desire to join the Democratic party, and even in Edgefield were reported as desiring admission *en masse* into the party.[46]

The issue was thrust into the forefront by the Democratic convention of Edgefield County, which passed early in June a resolution excluding Negroes altogether from the Democratic primary. In addition to proscribing the Negroes completely, the Edgefield convention, after hearing a "straightout Edgefield speech" by Martin W. Gary, resolved "That we regard the issues between the white and colored people of this State, and of the entire South, as an antagonism of race, not a difference of political parties;" and further "That . . . white supremacy is essential to our continued existence as a people."[47] These were favorite themes of Gary.

The white press, generally loyal to Hampton, took issue with the Edgefield program. The *News and Courier* expressed confidence

---

44 Columbia *Daily Register,* November 1, 1878.
45 Charleston *News and Courier,* May 10, 1877.
46 *Ibid.,* June 4, 1878.
47 *Ibid.*

that the views incorporated in the resolutions did "not express the sentiments of the people of the State, or in other words, of the Democracy in general." White supremacy could be maintained without complete proscription of the Negro and colored people could be educated to the point of voting for proper candidates, "and this can be effected more readily through the Democratic party than by making a political pariah of the negro."[48] Later the same paper urged that all Negroes who had voted Democratic "should be admitted to full membership of the party, and enjoy all its privileges, including the right to vote at primary elections."[49] An Up Country paper, the Spartanburg *Spartan,* however, expressed fear that the Negro vote was being brought into the party so that it might be manipulated by unscrupulous politicians. In this it saw a weapon for Low Country planters in the old intrastate sectional controversy. The Negro vote, said the *Spartan,* "will not only destroy the controlling influence of the white man, and endanger his institutions and civilization, *but will put the up-country of South Carolina under the control of the low-country, where the great negro vote lies.*"[50] In the absence of a statewide primary it is difficult to see how the Negro vote within the party could have given the Low Country counties greater influence in the party, and the *News and Courier* reminded the *Spartan* that the Negro vote would be more dangerous outside the party because it would be a constant temptation to candidates who had independent leanings.[51]

Outside of Edgefield the extreme policy was not adopted in 1878. Instead, many counties adopted the slightly less stringent policy of admitting to the Democratic precinct clubs Negroes who had voted with the party in 1876. In Charleston it was required that one must have voted Democratic in 1876 or would have voted Democratic had he been old enough.[52] In other counties the policy was more liberal. In Orangeburg the county committee recommended a policy of dividing offices with the Negro Democrats in proportion to their numbers, the Negroes to choose their own

---

[48] *Ibid.*
[49] *Ibid.,* July 20, 1878.
[50] *Ibid.,* June 4, 1878, quoting Spartanburg *Spartan.*
[51] *Ibid.*
[52] Columbia *Daily Register,* October 31, 1878.

candidates. They named one candidate for the legislature and one for the board of county commissioners.[53] In Bamberg as early as April a club of fifty Negro Democrats was reported to be organizing to "put themselves in trim" for the electoral fight of the year.[54] Abbeville adopted a policy of excluding Negro Democratic clubs as such from representation in its county convention, but admitted Negroes to the various precinct clubs on the same footing as the whites, where they were able to vote for delegates to the county convention. The Abbeville *Medium,* in praise of this policy, said: "The color line has been obliterated, and we are all moving along together upon a higher and better platform of equal rights and equal justice to all, 'without regard to race, color or previous condition.' "[55] The Greenville Democratic Club passed a resolution inviting "colored people who confide in the Democratic party" to become members.[56] The Kershaw *Gazette* urged "every good Democrat to put down the enunciation of race antagonism." "We want every good colored voter," it said, "to join our party and help swell our majority in each county. The buga-boo of social equality has never disturbed our equipoise. . . ."[57]

Wade Hampton himself delivered a telling rebuke to the men who wished to proscribe Negro Democrats when he went to Blackville on the fourth of July and was called upon for impromptu remarks. In words clearly directed at the Edgefield extremists he said:

> If you listen to demagogues, if you listen to men who subordinate everything to office, to wealth, to place and to power; if you will hearken to extreme men, who will tell you that the glorious platform of 1876 was very well as a promise to be kept only to the ear and broken to the heart; if you listen to those men, then I say *you may as well at once relinquish the fight,* for South Carolina will soon pass again under the rule and to the ruin from which she has just emerged, and in the great Presidential contest of 1880 we shall not only lose our own election but we, the people of South Carolina,

---

[53] Charleston *News and Courier,* August 12, 1878.
[54] *Ibid.,* April 9, 1878.
[55] *Ibid.,* June 8, 1878, quoting the Abbeville *Medium.*
[56] *Ibid.,* June 10, 1878.
[57] Columbia *Daily Register,* September 6, 1878, quoting Kershaw *Gazette.*

will be the cause of breaking down the national Democracy.
(A voice: "We will never do it!")[58]

The election of 1876, he said, had been carried "because you
came before the people, white and black, . . . saying, 'You shall
all be equal under the law.'" Negroes came by the hundreds to
support that platform and yet some leaders in the party would say
that now they could not even vote in the primaries and clubs.

> If this be the policy of South Carolina, then am I sadly mis-
> taken in the people of South Carolina and the people are
> mistaken in me, because *I can carry out no such policy as that.
> I stand where you put me in 1876.* I have not deviated one
> iota, and despite the criticism against me, I defy any man to
> place his finger upon one single act of mine that is not in
> strict accord with the policy of the Democratic party in con-
> vention assembled in 1876.

The election of 1878, he said, could be won only by supporting
the platform of 1876, and by that means it could be carried overwhelmingly. But on any other platform he would not accept the
leadership.

> If you are to inject into it any new and abhorrent principles—
> if you are to go back upon all pledges that I have made to
> the people—if you are to say that the colored men that have
> sustained us are no longer to be citizens of South Carolina—
> if you require me to go up and give my allegiance to a plat-
> form of that sort, then, my friends, much as I would do for
> you and for South Carolina, earnestly as I would desire to
> spend or be spent in her service, willing as I am to give even
> my life for my State, I should have to decline. I would give
> my life for South Carolina, but I cannot sacrifice my honor,
> not even for her.[59]

When the state convention met in August it was found that
Hampton was still the undisputed leader of his party, and while
the campaign later revealed that he was as helpless as in 1876 to
restrain its extremists, there was no opposition to his renomination.
Along with the renomination of Hampton the convention included

---

[58] Columbia *Daily Register*, July 7, 1878. The account of Hampton's other
remarks is based on this source.
[59] *Ibid.*

in its platform a reiteration of the 1876 pledge to accept the post-war amendments.[60]

In the face of the immense personal popularity of Hampton, only one man dared to give articulation to the undercurrent of opposition to his policies—Martin W. Gary. As early as June, 1877, when a reporter of the Cincinnati *Gazette* questioned Hampton as to his opposition within the party, he had said "with a twinkle," "I believe the opposition includes at present only one man, and he is a gentleman of somewhat eccentric political qualities."[61] This eccentric and bitter man, speaking at Edgefield in August, 1878, said:

> As far back as 1874, I announced . . . that in my humble judgment the mistake that our leaders were making was in considering the differences between the negro and white a difference of politics, instead of a difference in point of fact of *race;* that whenever the Caucasian united upon this issue the negro had to go to the wall, as the Ruler of the Universe had made the white race the dominant race of all the races.[62]

After Gary uttered similar sentiments in a speech at Greenville, pro-Hampton leaders arranged a military review and a speech by E. W. Moise, state adjutant and inspector general, to counteract the effect of his remarks. The review included the Mountain City Guards, a Negro group, and the Neptune Fire Company, an organization of Negro firemen, together with white military and fire companies, as well as a number of "mounted clubs" from the countryside. Moise reminded his audience that sixteen thousand Negroes had voted Democratic in 1876 because of Hampton's guarantee that "they would receive every right and privilege guaranteed them by the constitutions of the United States and of this State."[63]

Meanwhile J. W. Gray, a Hampton supporter in Greenville, wrote to the press that Gary "did not express my sentiments towards the colored race, nor, in my opinion, those of the Democracy of the State." Gary's speech was pronounced by Gray "unwise, impolitic, and in violation of the avowed policy and tenets of the Democratic party." General Gary replied that he would not dispute with Gray

---

[60] Charleston *News and Courier,* August 2, 1879.
[61] Yorkville *Enquirer,* June 14, 1877.
[62] Charleston *News and Courier,* August 15, 1878.
[63] Columbia *Daily Register,* August 20, 1878.

the honor of having brought about the first instance of colored troops marching in line with the white militia, a reference to the demonstration arranged to hear Moise, and concluded that since Gray claimed the event "a natural result of Hampton Democracy," he supposed "we shall next hear of '*dining*' or *dancing* with the colored brothers and sisters as events the natural result of Hampton Democracy."[64]

This was perhaps an oblique reference to an incident that had covered the state in rumor. During the summer of 1878, when Hampton and the state superintendent of education, Hugh S. Thompson, were invited to the home of President Cooke of Claflin College in Orangeburg for dinner, they found upon their arrival that ex-Judge J. J. Wright and Professor Sasportas, both Negroes, were present. After a moment's hesitation they had both sat down and eaten.[65] Even Gary, however, did not mention the incident out of fear that it would hurt the Democratic campaign or perhaps that Hampton would openly defend his action.

Meanwhile Republican leaders were making an effort once again to breathe life into their organization. At the state convention of August 7-9, however, there was an expression of a great amount of support for Hampton and a resolution to endorse him for governor failed only by a small majority.[66] It was recognized by the convention delegates that it would be futile to attempt the election of a state ticket with the election machinery in the hands of the Democrats. In addition to other factors there were new election laws, enacted by the Democratic legislature with the objective of restricting the Negro vote.[67] The party platform arraigned the Democrats for enacting a law "whereby numerous voting precincts in large Republican counties were abolished, so that thousands of Republican voters are virtually disfranchised, or else compelled to walk twenty miles or more in order to vote, and in some places to cross rivers in order to reach a polling place."[68]

---

[64] *The Nation* (New York), XXVII (September 5, 1878), 140.

[65] Wallace, *The History of South Carolina*, III, 329.

[66] Charleston *News and Courier*, August 8, 9, 1878.

[67] Separate boxes and ballots were provided for state and federal elections so that Congress would have no authority to intervene in state elections. *Acts and Joint Resolutions of the General Assembly of the State of South Carolina* (1877-1878), pp. 565, 632-33. Hereinafter cited as *Acts and Joint Resolutions*.

[68] *Appleton's Annual Cyclopaedia*, III (1878), 771; Charleston *News and Courier*, August 8, 1878.

A sizable element in the convention, led by Whitefield J. Mc-Kinlay, a Negro delegate from Charleston, proposed the nomination of a "straightout" Republican ticket, but the majority of the delegates determined instead to concentrate upon electing Republican members to the county offices and to the legislature, where, said the Republican platform, only the presence of a sizable Republican minority had made it possible for Hampton to keep his pledges.[69]

The Republican party tried in its various county nominations to take advantage both of disaffections in the Democratic party wherever they existed and of the increased good will that had been brought about in some places by Hampton's policies. When the Republican party of Laurens County included on its ticket the incumbent Democratic judge of probate and school commissioner, the Columbia *Daily Register* called it "a high compliment to the fairness and justice of Democratic officials, both these gentlemen having given entire satisfaction in their official duties to all classes and conditions of persons."[70] In Union the Republicans named three white Republicans, three Negroes, and three white Democrats on their ticket.[71] In Marion the county ticket carried five Democrats.[72] But in most cases of this sort the Democrats refused to permit the use of their names on the Republican tickets. In Darlington County, W. J. Lockheart, an aged white man, accepted the Republican nomination for county commissioner, but when he visited the county seat he was surrounded by a crowd beating tin pans, ringing cowbells, and abusing him for permitting his name to be used on the Republican ticket. He got away to Timmonsville, but was there stopped by another crowd and after he had drawn his knife in an attempt to get away was badly beaten and received several injuries, including a skull fracture.[73]

The Republicans in naming Democrats to their tickets also attempted in some counties to take advantage of a new phenomenon, the Independent Democrat, the white man willing to appeal to Negro votes against the regular party candidate. Although rumors

[69] Charleston *News and Courier,* August 8, 9, 1878.

[70] Columbia *Daily Register,* October 2, 1878.

[71] *Ibid.,* October 10, 1878.

[72] *Ibid.,* October 3, 1878.

[73] Julius Faaborg to R. M. Wallace, October 23, 1878, National Archives, General Records, Department of Justice, Source-Chronological Files, South Carolina, Box 650, Document 232. A letter from the deputy marshal in Darlington to the United States marshal in Charleston.

of such candidacies became rife early in the year, the Democrats were generally able to prevent them, either by violence or by the severe strictures of the Democratic press.

In Charleston County, when James B. Campbell, a Democratic member of the state senate, found himself eliminated from the race as a result of the primary from which all Negroes were excluded except those who had voted Democratic in 1876, he announced as an independent candidate in the general election. He was immediately placed at the head of the Republican ticket and was accused of having been in agreement with the Republicans when he announced.[74] Reaction in the press illustrates the opprobrium that was heaped upon any white politician who attempted to act independently. Accusing Campbell of "selfish ends and implacable prejudices," the *Daily Register* said:

> Let the welkin ring with the name and the foul blot cling to his memory. Out upon the policy of treating him with tenderness, because he has once occupied an honorable position in the community! His fall is akin to that of Lucifer, and should be as damning and eternal![75]

After his defeat in November, Campbell told a visitor that he had been beaten by means of ballot box stuffing because "he represented the principle of Conciliation against those who would not yield anything."[76] Such candidacies, however, were rare and universally unsuccessful. Unlike Georgia with its Felton, and Virginia with its Mahone, South Carolina never saw the development of strong independent candidacies, nor later of a Populist organization. Francis W. Mackusker, elected to the legislature from Georgetown in 1884 by the defection of Negro voters from the fusion ticket in that county, was the only successful independent in the post-Reconstruction period.[77]

The campaign of 1878 followed much the same dual development as that of 1876. It was afterward described by a Northern correspondent in all its irony.

> Negroes sit on juries and hear evidence for and against their own color. There is moderation toward them at the State House,

---

[74] Columbia *Daily Register*, October 27, 1878.
[75] *Ibid.*, November 1, 1878.
[76] Campbell, *White and Black*, p. 330.
[77] *House Journal* (1884), p. 4; Charleston *News and Courier*, November 9, 1884.

in the executive chamber, and in the General Assembly. But what does this moderation mean? Wade Hampton, as governor, said that the negro should enjoy all rights as the white man's political equal. But does he, can he, enjoy any of these rights? When it comes to an election or to any exercise of the right of suffrage, the party steps in and takes charge of things. The negro is bulldozed and intimidated, and his vote is thrown out of the ballot-box after he has contrived to get it in. This done and the object attained, the Butlers and Garys retire, and all is once more moderation and conciliation.[78]

As the election approached its climax, Laura Towne of St. Helena wrote in her diary: "Political times are simply frightful. Men are shot at, hounded down, trapped, and held till certain meetings are over, and intimidated in every possible way."[79] The white editor of the Beaufort *Tribune*, boldly writing in the midst of a Republican area, said: "In order to prevent our county from falling into such hands (Republican), *any* measures that will accomplish the end will be justifiable, *however wicked* they might be in other communities."[80]

Negro Congressman Robert Smalls was hampered in his campaign by the interference of Red Shirts. At a meeting in Blackville there were only three hundred Negro supporters of Smalls and an approximately equal number of Red Shirts, some of whom were Negroes.[81] In the new county of Hampton he attempted to make a speech at Gillisonville. When he arrived at ten in the morning he found about forty Negro men gathered at the meeting place and groups coming up the street to attend the meeting when suddenly a large group of Red Shirts rode into town, giving the "real rebel yell," or as Smalls described it, "whooping like Indians." They drew up on the outskirts of the crowd and remained still, except that every few minutes a squad of three or four would set off down the street and "lick off the hats" of the colored men and slap the faces of the women coming to the meeting, "whooping and yelling and scattering the people on all sides." Smalls with some difficulty restrained the Negro men from counterattacking. Then

---

[78] Edward Hogan, "South Carolina To-day," *International Review*, VIII (February, 1880), 109.

[79] Holland (ed.), *Letters and Diary of Laura M. Towne*, pp. 288-89.

[80] *Ibid.*, p. 289.

[81] Charleston *News and Courier*, October 12, 1878.

the leader of the white group insisted that he be given halftime at the meeting. Smalls refused to speak at all on the grounds that it was a Democratic meeting, but the Democrats insisted that there should be a joint session and gave Smalls ten minutes in which to make up his mind to hold the meeting. During this time he withdrew with some of his supporters into a nearby storebuilding, where they were surrounded by Red Shirts who fired several shots into the building and threatened to set it afire. However, as the alarm was spread in all directions, Negroes from the countryside, armed with guns, axes, and hoes, began to converge on the town and the Red Shirts galloped away. A major riot was narrowly averted.[82]

On the day of the election Sir George Campbell entered the state on his tour of the South and found that the first station he came to "was full of people dressed in the famous red shirt, which we also saw continually at all the stations as we came along." He saw no evidences of "bulldozing" but noticed a "good deal of talking and shouting and galloping about on horseback, and some few symptoms of whisky." Upon his arrival in Columbia he talked with several men in the State House who readily admitted that the election was an "utter farce."[83] Hampton himself later admitted to a Northern reporter that there had unquestionably been election irregularities, and he welcomed the investigation of them by the Teller Committee. He blamed them, however, on the "terrible moral obliquity visited on our people by the Radical rule," and added: "No one can regret this more than I do, and no one could have striven harder to impress its wrongfulness and absolute impolicy upon our people than I have. And I now hold, as ever, its utter impolicy."[84] Unfortunately for the state, two days after the election Hampton met with a serious accident that finally made necessary the amputation of a leg. It has been suggested that he might have brought his influence to bear against election irregularities if he had not been completely incapacitated at the crucial moment.[85]

The election was of course carried by the Democrats. The only county carried by the Republicans was Beaufort, where they had

[82] Holland (ed.), *Letters and Diary of Laura M. Towne*, pp. 289-91. The account of this incident is taken from the story as told by Robert Smalls and recorded by Laura Towne, who was strongly pro-Republican.

[83] Campbell, *White and Black*, pp. 312-13, 316.

[84] Yorkville *Enquirer*, January 23, 1879.

[85] Columbia *Daily Register*, November 9, 1878; Jarrell, *Wade Hampton and the Negro*, pp. 151-52.

overwhelming strength.[86] In the new legislature there were only eight Republicans, five in the senate and three in the house, all Negroes with the exception of two white senators, holdovers from the election of 1876. Some fruit of the Hampton program could be seen in the fact that six Negro Democrats were elected to the lower house from Charleston, Colleton, Orangeburg, and Sumter counties.[87] Hampton was reelected by a vote of 119,550 to 213.[88]

Immediately after the election it was widely assumed that the candidate to replace John Patterson in the United States Senate would be Wade Hampton, and a movement was soon under way in the legislature to elect him. While there does not appear to have been any conscious effort on the part of the extremist element of the party to put him out of the way by sending him to the Senate, it was recognized by clear-headed observers that the effect of his removal from the state would be the weakening of the conciliatory racial policy that he represented. An anonymous correspondent to the Columbia *Daily Register* wrote a series of trenchant letters signed "Cato" pointing out the possibility of unfortunate results from the election of Hampton to the Senate. In the first of a series of five letters he urged that Hampton was the most potent cohesive force in the Democratic party of the state. The second letter urged the candidacy of James Conner for the Senate.[89] A third letter came to grips with the race issue, classifying the whites into three groups according to their outlook. The first group, "happily the smallest in numbers of the three," he said, regarded the Negro as unworthy of any consideration. The second group, perhaps the most numerous, "look upon the negroes as human beings of an inferior order or grade." They would favor a limited suffrage for the Negro, based upon qualifications of education or property or both. They argued that the Negro, in his condition of "ignorance and vice," was unworthy of the suffrage and not capable of using it wisely; and "they honestly believe that they are justified, before God and man, in defeating candidates of the colored people by any device, however disreputable, by any fraud, however transparent." The third group, or Hampton party, Cato said, believed that "the unfortunate colored race, thrown unprepared into the attitude of

---

[86] *Reports and Resolutions* (1878), p. 404.
[87] See Appendix.
[88] *Reports and Resolutions* (1878), p. 436.
[89] Columbia *Daily Register*, November 23, 1878

freemen and citizens, have conducted themselves better, under the circumstances, than could have been expected. They have not committed to any extent, the outrages upon the whites which have marked emancipation elsewhere." The Hampton party adopted the reasoning of their leader that the Negro masses were not responsible for the troubles that had come to the white people of South Carolina after the war, and that the whites must accept the duty of educating Negroes to their responsibilities under freedom.[90]

In his fourth letter Cato continued this line of reasoning, and urged the retention as governor of Wade Hampton, "the representative, in the eyes of the world, of justice to the colored man." The Hampton party was a minority and, "to make this minority a majority . . . we need the inestimable services of *Governor* Hampton." If removed from the state, "He would not have the opportunity to speak the 'fitly spoken' word, nor to interpose his powerful moral veto when the occasion required it."[91] In a fifth letter Cato replied to a critic who had contended that the whites were in full accord with the political convictions of Wade Hampton, by saying that "none but a blind man, seeking to lead the blind, can believe that our people have risen to the heights upon which the colossal figure of Hampton stands and beckons them upward."[92]

On the date of the publication of Cato's last letter, Hampton dispatched a letter to the General Assembly in which he stated that the decision was up to that body as to whether he could most profitably serve as governor or senator. The legislature promptly elected him to the Senate.[93]

Thus the moral influence of Hampton was removed from the scene at the crucial time when it seemed possible to at least two observers, E. P. Clark and Cato, that he was within reach of his objective of establishing inter-racial good will on such a permanent basis that it would become the standing policy of the state. Although Hampton continued until the end of his career to speak publicly as he had spoken in the campaign of 1876 and during his administration as governor, it was with weakened influence. His passing from active participation in the state government did not

[90] *Ibid.*, November 28, 1878.
[91] *Ibid.*, November 30, 1878.
[92] *Ibid.*, December 10, 1878.
[93] *Ibid.*, December 11, 1878.

completely remove his influence from the state; Democratic governors through the eighties continued to give expression to the
Hampton doctrines. Johnson Hagood was supported for governor
in the Democratic convention of 1880 against Martin W. Gary by
Hampton who was reported to have threatened to resign and run
against Gary if he were nominated.[94] In his inaugural address
Hagood repeated the pledge he had made during the campaign
"that in the discharge of this high trust, I shall know neither white
man nor colored man, but only citizens of South Carolina, alike
amenable to her laws and entitled to her protection."[95] Governor
Hugh S. Thompson, who like Hagood had been closely associated
with the Hampton administration, in his second inaugural address
in 1884, said:

> The fact that in South Carolina all departments of the State
> Government are controlled by one race of the same political
> party, but adds to our responsibility. Without the wholesome
> check which strong minorities in a government oppose to the
> abuse of power, we should be the more careful to act with
> scrupulous justice and fairness. . . .[96]

And as late as 1889 Governor John P. Richardson said, "We believe
that the whites must dominate, but at the same time we do not
refuse local offices to the blacks."[97]

Meanwhile, however, the momentum of the Hampton party
rapidly ran out. Martin R. Delany, Negro trial justice of Charleston,
was removed from his post, which he said "I lost as soon as they
got rid of him [Hampton] by sending him to the U. S. Senate,
as he was too liberal for the rank and file of the party leaders."[98]
After the election of 1878 Negroes were not given any representation in the election machinery. That the policy of Negro appoint-
ments was not completely scrapped, however, is indicated by a
notice published in Charleston in 1889: "Northern and Western
papers of the Republican type are requested to take notice that
a colored man, Mr. Ingliss, has been appointed jury commissioner

---

[94] Sheppard, *Red Shirts Remembered*, p. 279.

[95] *House Journal* (1880), p. 112.

[96] *Ibid.* (1884), p. 137.

[97] Columbia *Daily Register*, May 7, 1889.

[98] Martin R. Delany to William Coppinger, August 18, 1880, American
Colonization Society Papers, Library of Congress, Manuscripts Division, Letters
Received, Vol. 210, No. 130.

for Charleston County. He has been in office for a number of years. His predecessor, Mr. Holloway, was likewise a colored man. . . ."[99] The number of Negro Democrats dwindled with successive elections, so that only Charleston and Orangeburg counties were consistent through the eighties in sending at least one Negro Democrat each to the legislature at every election. Orangeburg dropped the practice in 1890 and in 1892 no Negro appeared on the Democratic ticket in Charleston.[100]

Appearing at Abbeville in 1879, Hampton made a speech commending recognition of the rights of Negroes and was hissed and booed by his white audience. It was his first taste of the treatment that he was to get a decade later from the supporters of Ben Tillman who were to force his retirement from politics an embittered man.[101]

Why was the Hampton program a failure? First and foremost, because it was a policy opposed by the majority of the whites and upheld only by the immense prestige of Hampton. Second, because Hampton perhaps wearied of the struggle and was willing to move on to Washington where the terribly difficult responsibility of his pledges would be left behind. When in 1882 he was called upon to speak out against a new registration and election law designed to disfranchise Negroes he remained silent. Third, because the program rested entirely on the good will of the whites and their willingness to carry it out. With the passage of time and the perfection of the methods of disfranchising Negroes there was less pressure upon white politicians to give attention to their desires. Fourth, and perhaps most serious, because the program was subject to the ancient ambivalence of the Southern white on the race issue, the constant gulf between his theory and his practice, his ability, so striking to Gunnar Myrdal in the early 1940's, to rationalize the race problem out of existence and to magnify out of all proportions the concessions that he makes to the Negro.[102] Hampton himself was not immune to this difficulty, and near the end of his senatorial career argued that every Negro entitled to vote could do so if he

---

[99] Charleston *News and Courier,* January 12, 1889.

[100] See Appendix.

[101] L. C. Northrop to Charles Devens, November 25, 1879, National Archives, General Records, Department of Justice, Source-Chronological Files, South Carolina, Box 651, Document 182. A letter from the district attorney to the attorney general. The incident was not reported in the state papers.

[102] Gunnar Myrdal, *An American Dilemma: The Negro Problem and Modern Democracy* (New York, 1944), pp. 30-36.

desired, but that the rank and file of Negro voters had lost their registration certificates.[103] Fifth, because Hampton had come into office dragging in his wake the inarticulate forces of Negrophobia and their extremely articulate spokesman, Martin W. Gary, who did not even make the pretense of lip service to liberalism.

D. H. Chamberlain contended that he could have carried out the Hampton program more wisely and more effectively, for under an honest Republican administration "no man's civil or political rights would have been abridged or denied."[104] It would seem from their utterances that Hampton and Chamberlain were not far apart in their attitudes toward the race issue, and it is ironic that the bitter campaign of 1876 was waged between men who were apparently so close together in their policies. It is a greater irony that Wade Hampton should become the advance agent for the rise to power of Negrophobia as represented in Martin W. Gary and Ben Tillman, and should be canonized in the white folklore not as a man of generous sentiments and great moral courage so much as the leader of a violent campaign to remove the Negro from the government of the state.

---

[103] *Congressional Record* (Washington, 1873-_____), XXII (51st Congress, 2d Session), 1419-20.

[104] Columbia *Daily Register,* May 22, 1877.

3

THE DECLINE OF THE REPUBLICAN PARTY

ALTHOUGH W a d e Hampton was able to make some converts among the Negro voters by his moderate program, the politically active Negroes generally remained loyal to the Republican party. Not only had that party been the agency of their liberation and enfranchisement, but it had been the agency through which the Negro masses had been organized into an effective political force in the South.

Those who were converted to Democracy by threat or by the hope of gaining favor with the white community were frequently regarded with contempt even by white Democrats, and it was generally felt that the more independent and more intelligent Negroes remained loyal to the Republican party. In the campaign of 1876, William Watts Ball said, "The few dozen or hundred that voted the Democratic ticket in Laurens were, as a rule, trifling, lazy, and careless fellows, who lived by tips from their white friends rather than by labor."[1] June Mobley, a Negro Republican, warned the whites that they would have to watch the colored Democrats constantly or they would steal everything in sight.[2] A traveller, when introduced to "Democrat" Riley, a prosperous Negro livery-stable keeper in Charleston, found his story "a little too much as if it had been rehearsed. He tells very fluently how he was a slave, and how he was educated by his mistress; and how after emancipation his master and mistress, being reduced to poverty, he sup-

---

[1] William Watts Ball, *A Boy's Recollection of the Red Shirt Campaign* (Columbia, 1911), p. 15.

[2] Abbeville *Press and Banner,* May 5, 1880.

ported them both, and eventually buried them both—he lays great stress upon the *burying*."[3]

A disgusted Democrat observed that "in such districts where the numbers of the colored people largely preponderate over the whites, . . . they have been swayed in their choice and political belief by evil and designing men, or by the ignorant and prejudiced of their own race, who have assumed their leadership; it has been difficult to wean them from the Republican fold and draw them into the ranks of the Democracy." Complaining of the Republican counterpart to Democratic intimidation, he noted that "the apprehension of violence, and social and religious ostracism prevent them from changing."[4]

A Charleston Negro wrote in 1889, ". . . we are strongly Republican. The party that rocked the cradle of liberty is the black man's party. . . . Upon this rock we have built our political faith, and neither the assaults of Democracy nor the treachery of Republicans shall prevail against it."[5] A Negro resident of Orangeburg wrote in similar vein:

> . . . I declare that no honorable colored man, uninfluenced by fear or boodle, is or can be a Democrat, so long as that party fails to protect him in his full rights as a man. To my thinking, the alarm about "carpetbag rule" and "negro supremacy" is anachronistic. . . .
>
> We want no more reconstruction, if reconstruction means a holiday for illiteracy, a carnival for vice. We do not want negro supremacy. Such a thing this State has never seen, even in the years from '68 to '76. We want an honest Government, a Government based on no race or class lines, a Government neither plutocratic nor paupercratic, neither aristocratic nor kakistocratic or plebian, but purely Democratic in the strict sense of the word, a Government of the people, for the people and by the people.[6]

One of the most potent factors in keeping the Negro masses loyal to the Republican party, aside from the fact that the Demo-

---

[3] Campbell, *White and Black*, p. 327.

[4] Mary Doline O'Connor, *The Life and Letters of M. P. O'Connor* (New York, 1893), pp. 203-4.

[5] New York *Age*, July 14, 1888.

[6] William L. Bulkley in the Charleston *News and Courier*, December 5, 1888.

crats offered only negative enticements, was the fear of reenslave-
ment. "Their fear of being reenslaved," said one observer, "offers
a means by which dexterous politicians can often impose on them.
If you can prove to their satisfaction that any measure will tend
to give the whites any advantage over them, it is instantly quashed
and its opposite forthwith carried, *nem con.*"[7] The persistent influence of this sentiment could be seen after the election of Grover
Cleveland in 1884 as the first postwar Democratic President, when
a wave of rumor swept the state that the Democrats intended to
reestablish slavery. It became so general that the press felt it
necessary to publish a series of interviews with Negro ministers,
all of whom assured the readers that the Democratic administration
would not reinstitute slavery.[8] At a Democratic rally in Columbia,
held to celebrate the Cleveland election, there was a mammoth
parade in which transparencies were carried reading "Anglo-Saxon
Supremacy" and "The Republican Party is Dead," and one carried
by the white college students with a representation of a Negro and
the words "Chairman of the G. O. P.," but Wade Hampton on this
occasion once again assured Negroes that the Democrats would
respect every political right which they enjoyed, and promised
again that he would quit the party if they did not.[9]

The Republican party did not put up a state ticket in 1878. The
party organization, however, was held together under the chairmanship of Robert Brown Elliott, an outstanding Negro leader of
the Reconstruction period, and after 1878 biennial conventions were
regularly held in election years. But not until 1884 did a party
convention feel sufficiently strong to nominate a state ticket, and
when it did nominate such a ticket, headed by Daniel T. Corbin
and with four Negroes in a total of eight candidates, every candidate withdrew from the race before the election except Daniel
Augustus Straker, Negro candidate for lieutenant governor, who
accepted the nomination "even though in result it be an empty
honor" because it was the duty of the Republican party "to nominate candidates to represent its party principles" in the hope "by
perseverance in the right to get justice, even though delayed."[10]

[7] A South Carolinian, *Atlantic Monthly*, XXXIX (February, 1877), 193.

[8] Columbia *Daily Register*, November 16, 1884; November 26, 1884, quoting
New York Times; Charleston *News and Courier*, November 22, 1884.

[9] Columbia *Daily Register*, November 15, 1884.

[10] *Ibid.*, October 23, 1884; Charleston *News and Courier*, September 26,
1884.

In 1892 a state ticket headed by E. A. Webster was put up, but did not make any showing against Ben Tillman.[11]

The plight of the party is clearly indicated in the reasons put forward in Beaufort by S. J. Bampfield, Negro clerk of court, for not naming a Republican state ticket in 1890. They were: (1) not one leading Republican favored it; (2) the party had not fought a state campaign since the "Hayes treachery" of 1876; (3) the Republican party did not have enough qualified men to make up a ticket; (4) such a ticket would unify the white vote; (5) the Afro-Americans did not have the legally qualified voters to elect it; and (6) such a ticket would engender race friction. "Safety and success for the Negroes of South Carolina," said Bampfield, "lie in conciliation and not in antagonism in their dealing with the whites on State issues. Fourteen years' experience has clearly shown it."[12]

The post-Reconstruction tradition that Republicans were incurably corrupt and the fact that party gatherings usually included a high percentage of federal officeholders were effectively used against the Republicans. A Democratic reporter at the 1880 convention counted among eighty-two Negro and thirty-six white delegates, seventeen officeholders in the revenue, customs, and post-office departments. Of the Negroes he estimated that one-third appeared in the report of the committee that had investigated Reconstruction frauds "and the white delegates, with scarcely an exception, either are, or have been (and hope to be) Federal officeholders."[13]

The view that the only white Republicans were office seekers was somewhat exaggerated. However, it is true that there was in South Carolina no homogeneous white mountain element, as in North Carolina and Tennessee, to ally itself with the Negroes in the Low Country, and consequently the Republican party was always more clearly the "Negro party" in South Carolina than in those neighboring states. Because the line between parties was for the most part the color line, the Democratic reaction to the Republicans was extremely bitter and frequently violent.

The almost exclusive concern with federal patronage and internal politics led to bitter and extended factional struggles which brought

[11] Charleston *News and Courier*, October 1, 1892.
[12] New York *Age*, September 20, 1890, quoting Beaufort *New South*.
[13] Abbeville *Press and Banner*, May 5, 1880.

deep and lasting disarrangements in the Republican party machinery in the face of the disciplined unity displayed by the Democrats. These struggles were almost altogether personal in nature, revolving around jobs rather than policies, and waxed extremely bitter at times. They consisted chiefly of efforts to jostle into position nearer the patronage trough, for the group which controlled the state party naturally controlled the patronage. The process was not out of line with the general practice of American politics, but in South Carolina it was a luxury that Republicans could scarcely afford.

Disunity within the Republican ranks was an important factor in the impotence of the party, and disorderly party gatherings not only weakened the party internally but left it open to ridicule by its opponents.[14]

One can easily see in the Democratic reports, though they were obviously exaggerated, that the conventions were characterized by a disorder that was absent from the Democratic gatherings until Ben Tillman introduced factional controversy equally as bitter as that among the Republicans. A native observer noted that Negroes, who when first enfranchised were on public occasions "sheepish, quiet, awkward, and docile," began after several years of freedom to show "delight in attending, either to mingle in or to look on at, all sorts of assemblages. . . ." Generalizing on their activities, he said:

> At their gatherings all have something to say, and all are up at once. They have a free flow of language, and their older men exhibit a practical, get-at-the-facts disposition (narrow-minded of necessity, yet intense from that very circumstance) which is a near approach to that sterling English quality, hard common sense. They are to the last degree good-humored unless persistently opposed, when they become excited, demonstrative, and violent, in both demeanor and language. While they are speaking, their orators are subjected to all kinds of interruptions,—questions, impertinences, points of order, etc. Consequently much disorder prevails at their meetings.[15]

---

[14] James Welch Patton, "The Republican Party in South Carolina, 1876-1895," in Fletcher Melvin Green (ed.), *Essays in Southern History* (Chapel Hill, 1949), pp. 91-111, is an excellent survey of the Republican party in South Carolina during this period.

[15] A South Carolinian, *Atlantic Monthly*, XXXIX (February, 1877), 192-93.

Less sympathetic white observers gave such descriptions of Republican meetings as the following report on the 1884 state convention:

> From Tuesday at midday until eight o'clock Thursday morning, the Republican Convention, or rather the wrangling, howling mob called a Republican Convention, has been in session in this city . . . and the dusky orator who, towards the small hours of the morning yesterday, expressed his regrets that the reporters were there to take down all the dirty and disgraceful scenes of the night, certainly had cause enough for the utterance of such a wish.[16]

The meeting had been marked by the exchange of such epithets as "dirty, lowlife puppy," "slaves of the lowest kind," and "sandhill coons." During the night two Negro delegates had engaged in a physical encounter as the result of personal insults. In 1892 the convention of the regular Republicans was described as "a terrible rattling of the bones of the Republican party," which bones, unable to get together, "lay scattered in inanimate heaps about the tiled floor of the House of Representatives." This account continued, "The convention was a wrangle from beginning to end, and the fun was ten stories high. There were some humorous scenes, and while there were a good many instances of Cuffee playing at politics, some of the veterans showed remarkable skill and ability in handling their sides of the questions."[17] Another factor contributing to the weakness of the Republican party was the absence of any state program of broad appeal. The biennial platforms of the party showed a singular lack of imagination and a decided sense of futility and self-pity, being confined chiefly to endorsements of national Republican policies and complaints of Democratic "violence and intimidation which has suppressed the Republican vote."[18]

No serious effort was made until the nineties to appeal to the white voters on issues national or local. Edmund William McGregor Mackey, a white Republican, despairing of the success of any such appeal, wrote in 1881:

---

[16] Columbia *Daily Register*, September 26, 1884.

[17] Columbia *State*, September 20, 1892. For examples of how schisms within the party even produced dual candidacies where the party had a fighting chance to seat its congressional candidates, see Charleston *News and Courier*, September 13, October 15, 1888, and July 20, October 15, 19, 1894.

[18] *Appleton's Annual Cyclopaedia*, XIII (1888), 743-44.

Thousands of white voters in South Carolina, who can read and write, as well as those who can't, are too ignorant to have a single political idea save what they imbibe from some crossroad politician, who, in turn, generally gets his information from some fourth or fifth-rate country newspaper, edited by some Democrat, who, ten chances to one, never travelled beyond the limits of the town in which he was born. The ignorance of such voters makes them intolerant, and to them free thought and free speech are crimes. They neither speak nor think for themselves, and they think it a crime for any of their number to speak or think for himself. In this condition has the Democratic party of South Carolina kept the white voters of the State for the past sixty or seventy years; and hence, except at intervals, there never has been but one political party in this State. This is a disgraceful fact, to be attributed only to the death and extinction of free thought and free speech.[19]

The only methods he could suggest for breaking this influence were of such a nature that they would have to be carried out by the national party. Orators of national reputation should be sent into the state; a first class Republican newspaper should be established; a national system of public schools should be established; and white Republicans should migrate into the state.

Such a program would have been rendered difficult by the presence of racial animosity within the Republican party itself. Suggestions that hinted of white predominance in the party were always regarded by Negro Republicans with suspicion. In the convention of 1880, June Mobley, a Negro delegate, declared that the race line had already been drawn within the party, and opposed sending any white delegates to the national convention because, he said, when the time should come to nominate a state ticket there would not be ten white Republicans in the whole state. "They will say it is no use to run a State ticket, because the Democrats will rob you of your votes. I am ashamed of myself for ever supporting such men. . . . When they meet you on the street and nobody is looking they 'damn the Democrats,' but the next thing you know you see them walking arm in arm with a Democrat and

---

[19] Edmund William McGregor Mackey, letter dated February 14, 1881, to Philadelphia *American*, quoted in Columbia *Daily Register*, March 6, 1881.

saying, 'these d--n niggers want to put on too many airs, they want to rise up'."[20]

William Holloway of Charleston, weary of white Republicans, complained in 1882: "Theoretically they are for the colored man all the time, practically they wish him a safe and speedy exit to a more congenial clime, which they . . . never expect to be transported to—but we know mistakes will occur."[21] And Daniel Augustus Straker, complained in 1883 of white Republican leaders as

> . . . these political Iagos who have infested the South and who while they pour into the ear of the colored citizen strife, hatred and ill-will, cajole his enemies and say "you fellows . . . don't understand us white Republicans, we have no more use for the 'nigger' save his vote."[22]

Straker listed a number of other reasons why Negroes should object to the Republican party: the betrayal of Southern Republicans in 1877; failure of the party "to show its power or capability, we know not which, to protect the colored citizen at the ballot-box"; the fostering of caste distinction and the exclusion of Negroes from officeholding, despite the notable exceptions of Douglass, Langston, and Bruce; the winking at and fostering of separate schools; the presence within the Republican party of these who shut the doors of industry to Negroes; failure of the Republican party to enforce the Constitution for fear of Negro equality; and the prevalence of bossism in the Republican party.[23] In spite of all these objections, however, there was no place else to go, and Straker as Republican candidate for lieutenant governor the following year was the only state candidate who remained in the race to the bitter end.

Thomas E. Miller, a constant champion of the Negro cause, had to face the color issue in an unusual way. So light as to be almost indistinguishable from white, reputed to be only one-sixty-fourth Negro, he was given by the white press the sobriquet of "Canary Bird," and frequently found himself on the defensive in the presence of black voters.[24] The white press for political reasons overem-

---

20 Abbeville *Press and Banner,* May 5, 1880.
21 Charleston *New Era,* August 5, 1882.
22 D. A. Straker in New York *Age,* February 16, 1883.
23 New York *Age,* September 1, 1883.
24 Columbia *Daily Register,* October 11, 1890, quoting Atlanta *Journal.*

phasized the caste schism between "the Blacks and the Browns, the latter including the mulatto or educated and high social element, the former being the black Helot caste who do the voting, and who now want the offices as they hold the numerical majority"; but on more than one occasion Miller found it necessary to "exculpate himself from the odium" of his light skin.[25] It was in part on this issue, with the support of the "Helot caste," that George W. Murray rose to displace Miller in 1892 in the black district.

Movements for reform of the party generally met with failure not only because of the jealousy of officeholders, but also because of the overtones of "lily white" sentiment that such movements usually carried. In the spring of 1892 an effort was made to reorganize the Republican party under the leadership of the Reverend R. W. Memminger, an Episcopal minister in Charleston and son of the Confederate Secretary of the Treasury. A state convention of seventy-seven whites and seventy-four Negroes assembled in Columbia in April of that year and heard Memminger put in nomination for Chairman by W. D. Chappelle, a rising figure in the African Methodist Episcopal Church. Chappelle indicated his willingness to accept white leadership by remarking that "When we array race against race there will be on one side education and wealth and on the other ignorance and poverty." Under these circumstances there was nothing for Negroes to do but demonstrate that they were "willing to be led by any hand which is sufficiently strong to insure us the rights and immunities guaranteed us by the Constitution of this country."[26] Memminger then announced that the "Reform Republican party" was organized by people who were "Republicans by conviction, because to us that party represents the principles, policies and measures required by modern civilization, and which are suited to the advancement of the welfare of the whole nation." James Wigg, a Negro member of the legislature from Beaufort, was chairman of the committee that drew up the convention's platform, which clearly appealed to conservative whites for support in opposition to Ben Tillman, decrying "ring or factional influences," and calling for "two well managed opposing parties, each appealing to the people's best judgment for support and supremacy." Arguing that "corruption and race antagonism in our

[25] Charleston *News and Courier*, September 5, 1890; October 25, 1886.
[26] *Ibid.*, April 13, 1892; Columbia *State*, April 13, 1892. The account of the convention is based on these two sources.

politics are not only harmful to our well-being, but should be re-garded as a high crime . . . ," the platform declared that "no man should be a Republican or Democrat because of his color. . . ."[27]

Thomas E. Miller was quick to denounce Memminger in the regular party convention as a person who had said in 1888 that even baptism "can never regenerate a black baby."[28] The test of the two factions came with the selection of a nominee for post-master of Charleston. Memminger, the candidate of his faction, was passed over for William Demosthenes Crum, a Negro physician supported by the regular group.[29]

Several futile efforts were made by the Republican party for statewide fusion with whites who had become disillusioned with the regular Democrats. The first such effort came in 1882 when the Republican party endorsed the state candidates of the Greenback party. The Greenbackers had first appeared in 1880 when a state convention of forty-one whites and four Negroes met in Chester to put out a ticket headed by L. W. R. Blair of Kershaw.[30] But in the election the party displayed a miserable weakness at every level.

During 1882, however, the Greenback party showed some acces-sions of strength. In addition to the complaints that were common to farmers over the nation there was a great deal of dissatisfaction with the state's stock fencing law. E. H. Fishburne, Democratic state senator from Colleton County, dissatisfied with the stock law and the eight ballot box law that was in the process of adoption, broke with his party early in 1882 and in a convention at Summer-ville met with a small group of white and colored citizens of Charleston and Colleton counties to found the "People's Party." The People's party declared that "it needs nothing but the organi-zation of the working class of white men and the colored men, as they would largely be in the majority, to defeat any party or parties who desire to oppress either the one or the other."[31] But

[27] Charleston *News and Courier,* April 13, 1892.

[28] *Ibid.,* April 20, 1892.

[29] *Ibid.,* April 20, July 1, 1892. Because of protests by white businessmen in Charleston and by Senator Matthew Calbraith Butler, Crum's name was later withdrawn. *Ibid.,* July 15, 1892; Columbia *State,* July 3, 1892.

[30] Charleston *News and Courier,* September 29, 1880.

[31] Charleston *New Era,* January 14, 1882; Charleston *News and Courier,* January 4, 1882.

NEGRO LEADERSHIP

From Charleston came ARCHIBALD H. GRIMKÉ, WHITEFIELD J. McKINLAY,
REV. FRANCIS J. GRIMKÉ (front row); A. C. McCLELLAN, REV. J. L. DART,
and WILLIAM D. CRUM (back row). *McClellan founded the Charleston
Training School for Colored Nurses, pictured above.*

PUBLIC SERVICE

The Neptune Volunteer Fire Co., of Greenville, about 1894

Fishburne's party, tarred with the brush of Republicanism, failed to win more than a meagre support. Fishburne was later a delegate to the state Greenback convention.

In January, 1882, a meeting was quietly held in Columbia between Thomas E. Miller and a number of white Greenbackers, including J. Hendrix McLane and W. W. Russell, a prominent leader of the Grange from Pendleton.[32] The decisions reached at this meeting are unknown, but after the Greenbackers nominated McLane for governor in September, the Republican party endorsed his candidacy, though not his platform.[33] A week later McLane appeared with Robert Smalls and Miller to address a Republican mass meeting in Beaufort;[34] in November McLane carried the county of Beaufort and made a considerable showing in the state race, polling 17,719 votes to 67,158 for Hugh S. Thompson, the Democratic candidate.[35]

In the course of the campaign the Greenbackers seem to have thrown a scare into the Democrats. Wade Hampton entered the campaign with a letter to the press in which he warned that ". . . an Independent is, if possible, worse than a Radical, for he is an enemy who steals the livery of Heaven to serve the Devil in."[36] The campaign was marred by serious violence. L. W. R. Blair, the Greenback candidate of 1880, was killed in an argument provoked by the charge and his denial that he had been organizing and attending political meetings of Radical Negroes.[37] At a rally held by the Negroes of Lancaster to hear E. B. C. Cash, Greenback candidate for Congress, the editor of the Lancaster Ledger appeared to speak for the Democrats. He was howled down and dragged from the stand by the Negro audience of about seven hundred. He suffered superficial injuries. Later in the day a Negro procession in the town was fired upon, and four or five Negroes were killed, and several wounded.[38]

In 1890 when Ben Tillman seized control of the Democratic party, Alexander Cheves Haskell, conservative chairman of the

---

[32] Charleston News and Courier, January 23, 1882.
[33] Ibid., September 6, 14, 1882.
[34] Port Royal Palmetto Post, September 21, 1882.
[35] Reports and Resolutions (1882), p. 1719.
[36] Charleston News and Courier, October 5, 1882.
[37] Patton, in Green (ed.), Essays in Southern History, p. 93.
[38] Charleston News and Courier, September 29, 1882.

Democratic party during the campaign of 1876, announced his belief that an independent ticket should be put up to oppose Tillman. In a letter submitted to the papers of the state Haskell professed to see "no assurance that the Tillman government, an unrestrained, powerful minority, will be other than reckless and oppressive in its execution as it has been in its incipiency." Haskell placed great emphasis on his fear that the tendency of the Tillman movement would be to remove such protection of the Negro race as had been provided under Hampton and his successors. Calling for an independent Democratic ticket, he said:

> With this Democratic ticket in the field we should ask the support and maintain the rights of colored voters as we did in 1876. I would not mistake the colored people. The white man controls the property and will control the government, but when the white race divides it is a question with the colored race which party will best govern the State. . . . I wish that the race could be disfranchised if we could have a guarantee of their protection. Their right of suffrage is their nominal protection; the class of white people they support is their real protection.[39]

Extremely conservative Democrats, more fearful of Tillman than concerned over the rights of the Negroes, rallied to the support of Haskell in a state convention on October 9. Prominently displaying the red shirt, symbol of 1876, they nominated Haskell for governor.[40] During the campaign, Haskell continued to appeal for the Negro vote on the rather dubious basis that "the white man controls the property and will control the government. . . ."

In the end, the Haskell appeal to the Negro vote proved abortive. A conference of Negroes, called independently of the Republican party "to counsel together upon their moral, intellectual and political interest," met in Columbia on October 15, with sixty-five persons present, most of whom were ministers and educators. A committee presented a series of four resolutions advising against a Republican ticket; they left the question of support for Haskell up to the Republican state committee; expressed the belief that Negroes "do not desire social equality, nor demand political supremacy," but "do demand an impartial administration of the

---

[39] *Ibid.*, September 30, 1890; Columbia *Daily Register*, November 1, 1890.
[40] Columbia *Daily Register*, October 10, 1890.

government under which we live, and a just and fair share in the administration"; and condemned "bitter partisan feeling and rashness which tend to engender and stir up strife among the races. . . ." These resolutions were adopted. Later in the meeting, however, a motion, recommending that Negroes "for the betterment of their condition . . . vote the Haskell ticket," was put, and carried by a large majority.[41] The endorsement of Haskell, however, was anything but enthusiastic and did not represent the approval of a group that was able to deliver the Negro vote *en bloc.*[42]

The Republican leaders did not show any enthusiasm for delivering the Negro vote to Haskell, but their state committee did endorse his candidacy, pointing to his desire for "a free and fair vote," and Tillman's desire for complete Negro disfranchisement.[43] Although their endorsement enabled Haskell to carry the Low Country counties of Berkeley and Beaufort, Thomas E. Miller said later that the Republican committee had failed to give active support to Haskell because of his equivocal stand on the race issue and his long-time association with a party which in many counties proscribed Negroes. "If Hampton's advice had been taken," Miller wrote a white Conservative, "Tillman never would have dethroned men like you, Haskell and Hampton, because Negroes of Myers type, including myself, would have come to the rescue of the men who made and saved South Carolina."[44] The election, in the end, was a white man's battle, and was easily carried by Tillman.[45]

So the Republican party failed in the last effort at statewide fusion with an organized group of disaffected whites. Tarred with the stigma of corruption, divided against itself, and identified almost altogether with a subordinate caste, the Republican party found itself blocked at every turn by Democratic measures to disfranchise the Negro majority. Disfranchisement measures were more important than all the other factors in Republican weakness, but consideration of them must be postponed temporarily for a glimpse of some of the Negro leaders in post-Reconstruction politics.

----

[41] *Ibid.*, October 16, 1890.

[42] Charleston *News and Courier*, October 16, 1890.

[43] *Ibid.*, October 26, 1890.

[44] Thomas Ezekiel Miller to Theodore D. Jervey, December 19, 1927, Carter G. Woodson Papers.

[45] The vote was Tillman 59,159; Haskell 14,828. *Reports and Resolutions* (1890), I, 604.

4

NEGROES IN POLITICS

DESPITE the weakness of their party, faithful Negro Republicans were rewarded in some Low Country counties with local and legislative positions and in greater numbers with appointive federal offices throughout the state. The most important position occupied by any Negro politician after 1876 was that of United States Representative. Three Negroes were elected to this position from the "black district," which contained a preponderant majority of Negro voters in the Low Country. The black district, first created in the reapportionment of 1882, was conceded by the Democrats until the election of 1886 when they nominated and counted in William Elliott, thereafter a perennial candidate. Ironically, the first Republican elected from the district, E. W. M. Mackey, was white, but he was replaced upon his death in 1884 by Robert Smalls. After 1886, with one exception, Republican Representatives were seated only after prolonged contest before the house, and were usually seated late in the terms for which they had been elected. The three Negroes elected to Congress after Reconstruction were Robert Smalls and Thomas Ezekiel Miller of Beaufort and George Washington Murray of Sumter.

Robert Smalls, "the Gullah Statesman," was the most colorful figure in Republican politics during the period. He retained throughout his career a high degree of popularity among the colored voters and a certain amount of grudging respect from the whites. With the exception of Joseph Hayne Rainey, he served longer in Congress than any other Negro, the greater part of his service coming after 1876. Short and portly and quite dark, although his father was white, Smalls presented the appearance of a powerful physique and spoke forcefully in the Gullah patois of his native region. This, as much as anything, inspired the confidence of his black constituents. Sir George Campbell visited him in Beaufort and wrote that Smalls was ". . . a thoroughly representative man among the people and seems to have their unlimited confidence."[1]

Born in Beaufort in 1839, the son of a Jewish slave owner and a Negro slave woman, Smalls was trained by his father as a sail-maker and afterward became an expert at the wheel. His ability brought him into sudden prominence when early in the Civil War, he took a Confederate transport, the *Planter*, out of Charleston harbor and delivered it to the federal fleet. The *Planter* was taken over by the federal navy and Smalls was thereafter in command, taking part in several minor engagements along the South Carolina coast. Eventually he was ordered to Philadelphia where he remained nine months, and under the tutelage of two white teachers learned the rudiments of the three R's.[2]

Returning to Beaufort after the war, he was elected to the consti-tutional convention of 1868 and later to both houses of the legislature. In 1874 and 1876 he was elected to Congress. Defeated in 1878, he returned when a Republican House seated him after the 1880 election. Displaced by the white Republican, E. W. M. Mackey, in 1882, he returned after Mackey's death in 1884 for a short term and was reelected later in 1884 to his last full term. In 1886 he was defeated by William Elliott, and in 1888 was persuaded to retire from the race in favor of Thomas E. Miller, a younger candidate. After the election of Benjamin Harrison he was appointed collector of the port of Beaufort and retained that position, except for a period during the second Cleveland admin-istration, until his retirement in 1913. He died at Beaufort in 1915.[3]

Although not intimidated, neither was Smalls embittered, and he maintained cordial relations with white as well as colored citizens of his native Beaufort. When his old master died and his former mistress became destitute, Smalls provided her with a home in his

---

[1] Campbell, *White and Black,* p. 361.

[2] Thomas Ezekiel Miller, "Address of Thomas E. Miller, February 10, 1930, in Washington, D. C. on the Occasion of Doing Honor to Congressman Oscar DePriest and the three Former Negro Members of Congress then Living," typescript in Carter G. Woodson Papers.

[3] Samuel Denny Smith, *The Negro in Congress, 1870-1901* (Chapel Hill, 1940), pp. 94-101; *Biographical Directory of the American Congress, 1774-1927* (Washington, 1928), pp. 1532-33.

own house where his wife waited upon her and his horses and carriage were put at her service. This act of kindness deeply impressed the whites.[4]

Smalls' major accomplishments in Congress were to secure appropriations for the improvement of Georgetown harbor and Winyah Bay, to locate a naval station at Parris Island in Beaufort County, and to get appropriations for storehouses and docks. Although he constantly sought appointment to the navy retired list as a captain in recognition of his services during the Civil War, he was never successful.[5]

The man who succeeded Smalls was an individual of distinctly different background and personal qualities. Born in Ferebeeville of free parents in 1849, Thomas Ezekiel Miller began his education in the free Negro schools of Charleston and after the war attended Lincoln University in Pennsylvania. In 1874 he returned to Beaufort County to be elected school commissioner for the county. In 1876 and 1878, he was elected to the lower house of the state legislature; in 1880 to the state senate, and in 1886 to the lower house again. In 1882 he became state chairman of the Republican party and played an important part in the effort of that year to secure a fusion with the Greenbackers. In 1888 he became the Republican nominee for Congress from the Seventh District, and successfully contested that election and the election of 1890. Afterward he was once again, in 1894, elected to a term in the lower house of the state legislature, from which he resigned in 1896 to become the first president of the state Negro college in Orangeburg, where he served for fifteen years until ousted by Governor Cole Blease in 1911. He was a delegate to the constitutional convention of 1895. Miller died in Charleston in 1938.[6]

George Washington Murray, "the Republican Black Eagle," won the Republican nomination in 1892 over Smalls, Miller, and Ellery M. Brayton, a white Republican. Born a slave at Rembert, Sumter County, in 1853, he had no white antecedents. "Judging by his face," an Associated Press report ran, "there is not a drop of white

---

[4] Smith, *The Negro in Congress*, p. 101; Columbia *Daily Register*, April 6, 1884.

[5] Smith, *The Negro in Congress*, pp. 94-101; Charleston *News and Courier*, June 23, 1894.

[6] Smith, *The Negro in Congress*, pp. 101-6; Columbia *Daily Register*, October 11, 1890; *Biographical Directory of the American Congress*, p. 1315.

blood running in his veins, but his voice did not show his African origin." With a "cannon-ball head," and a complexion "of the ace of spades," he was described by his interviewer as "by no means a bad-looking colored man."[7] Left an orphan after the war, he managed to pick up enough education to become a school teacher, attending South Carolina University from 1874 to 1876. Not appearing as a prominent figure in Republican politics until the nineties, he ran for the lower house of the legislature in 1884;[8] in 1888 he became Sumter County chairman of the party, and was appointed in 1889 Inspector of Customs at the port of Charleston. Closely associated with the Colored Farmers Alliance, Murray performed the remarkable feat of rising from the ranks of the party to defeat three of its seasoned leaders for the congressional nomination in 1892, and then surprised everyone by securing a certificate of election from the state board of canvassers. A deviationist from the Republican sound money policy, he favored free silver, and a Tillmanite board refused to count him out because his opponent was a Cleveland Democrat and a proponent of sound money.[9]

In Congress Murray did not disappoint the Tillmanites. In a lengthy speech, his only major effort on the floor during the one full term he served, he presented a shrewd defense of free silver. In this speech he classified Americans into three groups on the currency issue: first, the capitalists who wanted to keep money dear; second, those who owned silver mines and were using their influence to establish free coinage; and a third class "composed of the toiling and producing millions, who are neither gold bugs nor silver bugs," but who found themselves less and less able to meet their obligations because of the stringency of currency. "To the last named class," he said, "nearly all of my constituents, and the whole race of which I am the sole representative, belong."[10] He promised to "vote for the free and unlimited coinage of silver, because I am for the betterment of the miserable condition of my countrymen.

---

[7] Robert Wilson Shufeldt, *The Negro: A Menace to American Civilization* (Boston, 1907), p. 189, quoting Washington *Evening Star,* October 28, 1893.

[8] Columbia *Daily Register,* November 27, 1884.

[9] Smith, *The Negro in Congress,* pp. 106-9; Columbia *State,* November 28, 1892. It was reported during the canvass of 1892 that Tillmanites in the black district had been instructed not to vote in the congressional election, in order to permit Murray to win. Columbia *State,* November 6, 1892.

[10] *Congressional Record,* XXV (53rd Congress, 1st Session), 858.

. . . ."[11] This stand sets Murray apart as unique among South Carolina Republicans.

In 1894 Murray had to do battle in a campaign that developed into a color line fight between blacks and mulattoes as well as a struggle of progressive and conservative viewpoints.[12] Although Murray carried the nominating convention, he found that "Smalls and Miller who seem more desirous of accomplishing my defeat than even Elliott, are doing everything in their power foul or fair, to accomplish their object."[13] Murray contested the election before the state board of canvassers, with "sufficient data to make even democrats ashamed of themselves if that be possible,"[14] but this time was counted out. However, Murray was seated once again in 1896 as the last Negro to represent South Carolina in Congress. He carried on an energetic speaking campaign over the state against the disfranchisement movement in 1895 and was again a candidate for Congress in 1896 and 1898, but was defeated. He returned to Sumter and successfully engaged in farming and was later attracted by the real estate business. In 1904 he was convicted of forgery in Sumter, after which he fled to Chicago where he died in 1926.[15]

Negro Republicans were constantly returned to the General Assembly from the Low Country counties of Beaufort and Georgetown, and on two occasions from Berkeley, after the overthrow of the Radical government.[16] Although most of these men were obscure individuals lost to history as were most of their white colleagues, some were men of ability. They were almost without influence in legislatures dominated by white Democrats, and they sponsored no major legislation, but they went about their business unmolested and were allowed the usual privileges of a minority, including service on minor committees. Frequently, in local legislation dealing with their own counties, they were able to put through measures without interference from the white members. The Negro members

---

[11] *Ibid.,* p. 861.

[12] Charleston *News and Courier,* May 11, 1894.

[13] *Ibid.,* May 3, 1894; George W. Murray to Whitefield J. McKinlay, October 9, 1894, Carter G. Woodson Papers. William Elliott was the Democratic candidate.

[14] George W. Murray to Whitefield J. McKinlay, November, n. d., 1894, *ibid.*

[15] Smith, *The Negro in Congress, 1870-1901,* pp. 106-9; *Biographical Directory of the American Congress,* p. 1347; Columbia *State,* May 21, 22, 1904, and October 12, 20, 1905.

[16] See Appendix.

were generally silent except on matters that vitally concerned the race, such as legislation against miscegenation, the registration and election laws, and laws dealing with liens, labor contracts, and education.

Among the prominent legislators was Bruce H. Williams, born a slave, who represented his native county of Georgetown for twelve years in the state senate, from 1876 to 1888. Shortly after the Civil War he attended high school in Raleigh, North Carolina, and was then ordained to preach in the African Methodist Episcopal Church. He returned to South Carolina and was eventually assigned to Georgetown. He was reputed to be immensely popular with his party in Georgetown, and his "dignified and self-respecting demeanor" during his long term of service won him the respect of members of the legislature.[17]

Another Negro state senator of the period was Robert Simmons, elected from Berkeley County for a single term in 1882. A native of Colleton County, he had attended school on St. Helena Island and afterwards moved to Wadmalaw Island, where, by going into debt for supplies, he was able to build up a successful farming enterprise. Serving as a trustee of the public schools from 1872 until the time of his election to the senate, he never held any other public office, although he ran as an independent candidate for Congress in 1888.[18]

Thomas J. Reynolds of Beaufort was a native of his county. He attended school on St. Helena Island, in Beaufort, at Atlanta University, and at South Carolina University. In the intervals between his attendance at the various schools he taught in Beaufort County and in Georgia, and after the closing of South Carolina University in 1877 returned to Beaufort where he bought a small vessel and entered the coasting trade between Beaufort and Savannah, in which he built up a successful business. His only political experience was a single term in the state senate.[19]

Negro Republicans were more numerous in the lower house, reaching a peak number of nine after the election of 1882 and declining to one after 1896. In 1884 and thereafter, the Charleston *News and Courier* regularly published a biographical survey of the

[17] Charleston *News and Courier*, December 1, 1884.
[18] *Ibid.*, December 11, 1884.
[19] *Ibid.*, December 5, 1884.

members of each legislature, and through these it is possible to trace the Negro members. Several of them are deserving of attention.

Jonathan A. Baxter, elected with Bruce H. Williams in 1884, had been born a free man in Charleston before the war and had learned the shoemaker's trade from his father and pursued it for several years. Educated in the public schools of Georgetown, he became a teacher, and in 1878 served as a commissioner of election in Georgetown.[20] The three members chosen from Beaufort in that year were not distinguished by any especial qualifications. Joseph H. Robinson was "a mechanic and politician by trade," whose chief distinction in the house was his opposition to the liquor trade.[21]

Julius I. Washington, elected from Beaufort in 1886, had attended the public schools and South Carolina University. He then taught school for several years and served as deputy clerk for the collector of customs on Ladies Island, and in 1884 was appointed inspector of customs. In 1886 he was elected to the legislature for the first of two terms. Meanwhile he had read law under W. J. Whipper and was admitted to the bar in 1887. Resigning from the legislature in 1890, he moved to Charleston to accept an appointment as clerk in the Customs House, where he served until 1893. After that he practiced law in Beaufort until 1902, when he became special deputy collector for the port of Beaufort, a position which he held until 1913. He then returned to the practice of law until forced by bad health to retire shortly before his death in 1938.[22]

James Wigg, who made his first appearance in the election of 1890, was a well-to-do farmer of St. Helena township. Born in Beaufort County, during the war Wigg attracted the attention of General David Hunter, upon whom he waited at Hilton Head. After the war, Hunter took him to Washington and placed him at Whalen Institute, where he was said to have become well-versed in theology and "an earnest follower of Swedenborg."[23] Possessed

---

[20] Charleston *News and Courier*, December 1, 1884.

[21] *Ibid.*, December 5, 1884; Columbia *Daily Register*, December 23, 1884.

[22] Charleston *News and Courier*, November 23, 1886, and December 2, 1888; Arthur Bunyan Caldwell (ed.), *History of the American Negro: South Carolina Edition* (Atlanta, 1919), pp. 511-14; Education Division, Works Progress Administration of South Carolina, *70 Years of Progress, 1866-1936* (mimeographed, n.p., n.d.) pp. 13-14.

[23] Theodore Dehon Jervey, *The Slave Trade: Slavery and Color* (Columbia, 1925), pp. 192-93; Charleston *News and Courier*, November 25, 1890.

of an extremely sharp tongue, he frequently put his opponents on
the defensive. Robert B. Anderson of Georgetown was born and
reared in the county. Educated in the public schools, he had become a school-teacher, and served for a time as town warden in
Georgetown.[24] He served four consecutive terms in the legislature
and was a delegate to the constitutional convention of 1895. He
later became postmaster at Georgetown, and "avoided any friction
with the white employees and the public generally. He served out
his term of office and retained the respect of the community."[25]

The last Negro to serve was John W. Bolts, elected in 1898 and
1900 on a fusion ticket from Georgetown, an obscure figure who,
it was said by his colleague, "did nothing during his term of office
to cause any friction between the whites and blacks."[26]

In two counties of the state, Beaufort and Georgetown, Negro
voters in the last two decades of the century exercised a significant
influence. In Beaufort the control was so overwhelming that Ben
Tillman at one time referred contemptuously to the county as a
"niggerdom".[27] An important factor in Republican control of the
county, however, was the presence of a number of whites who had
come South during the Civil War to purchase confiscated lands.
In one of his last statements in the Senate, Wade Hampton proudly
cited Beaufort and Georgetown as evidence that Northern charges
about the suppression of the Negro vote in the South were exaggerated. He pointed out that ". . . two of the counties in my
State, having large negro majorities, have colored Republican representatives in our Legislature, and in one of these counties the
sheriff and the clerk of the court are both colored. They are excel-

---

[24] *Ibid.*

[25] Maham W. Pyatt to the Author, November 21, 1949. Pyatt, a white Democrat elected on a fusion ticket with Anderson, reports that he was told by
Altamont Moses, once chairman of the house ways and means committee, that
Anderson had once saved South Carolina College. "About 1892 or 1893 some
action was proposed in the General Assembly to cut off the appropriation for
the College and Anderson voted in favor of it. Moses went to Anderson and
insisted that he had voted wrong on the question. Anderson told Moses that
he had intended to vote as he did. The appropriation for Claflin College
(Negro) had been cut off and, therefore, he voted against the S. C. College.
Moses told Anderson, 'You change your vote and we will take care of Claflin.'
Anderson did so and the vote being close, this change of vote killed the
motion. Anderson was always a perfectly reliable man. If he made you any
promise, you could be sure that it would be kept."

[26] *Ibid.*

[27] Francis Butler Simkins, *Pitchfork Ben Tillman: South Carolinian* (Baton
Rouge, 1944), p. 153, quoting Charleston *World*, May 12, 1890.

lent officials, and they received the support of white as well as of colored citizens when they were elected."[28]

Sir George Campbell, an Englishman visiting Beaufort, heard that it "had the reputation of being a sort of black paradise, and *per contra,* I rather expected a sort of white hell." He found to his great surprise that it was not.

> At no place that I have seen are the relations of the two races better and more peaceable. . . . The town of Beaufort is a favourite summer resort for white families from the interior. . . . White girls go about as freely and pleasantly as if no black had ever been in power. Here the blacks still control the elections and send their representatives to the State Assembly; but though they elect to the county and municipal offices they by no means elect blacks only. Many whites hold office, and I heard no complaint of colour difficulties in the local administration. . . . I say emphatically that nowhere are the relations between blacks and whites better, and nowhere does a traveller see fewer signs that political difficulties have been fatal to settlement.[29]

Until the election of 1888 the elective county offices were occupied by Republicans, except when vacancies were filled by the governor.[30] In 1888, when the use of money in the Republican county convention was reported to have caused the selection of a ticket of "Northern negroes" who had been leading "profligate and adulterous lives," a group of Negro Republicans broke away to put out a fusion ticket in cooperation with the Democrats. White Democrats nominated candidates for senator, one representative, probate judge, and one county commissioner. Negro Republicans were nominated for sheriff, clerk of court, two representatives, two county commissioners, school commissioner, and coroner.[31] The most prominent Negroes on the ticket were George A. Reed, candidate for sheriff, and S. J. Bampfield, for clerk of court. These were the two to whom Hampton referred as "excellent officials."

The fusion remained in effect until 1895, when a straight Republican ticket was put in the field for the constitutional convention.

---

[28] Congressional Record, XXII (51st Congress, 1st Session), pp. 1419-20.
[29] Campbell, *White and Black,* pp. 177-78.
[30] Port Royal *Palmetto Post,* March 2, November 9, 16, 1882, and March 15, April 26, 1883.
[31] Charleston *News and Courier,* November 4, 14, 1888.

The Republicans elected five Negroes.[32] In 1896, under the new registration law made possible by that convention, the Republicans and Democrats nominated separate tickets, and the election was carried by the Democrats.[33]

In Georgetown County the Democrats agreed in 1880 to a fusion plan under which it was provided that there would be no contest in the general election.[34] The Democrats were given the right to nominate candidates for sheriff, clerk of court, coroner, two county commissioners, and one representative. The Republicans named the senator, one representative, probate judge, school commissioner, and one county commissioner.[35] All of the latter were Negroes except a white probate judge, who served until replaced by a Negro in 1894.[36] George E. Herriott, a light colored Negro, one of the guiding spirits of the fusion arrangement, was for twenty-two years county school commissioner under the plan and for many years county chairman of the Republican party.[37]

Senator Bruce H. Williams enthusiastically predicted after the first year's trial of the "Georgetown plan" that it would become the program for the state at large, and that a new statewide party might arise to put across a plan that "amounts, in a few words, to a fair and equal distribution of the offices without regard to race or party affiliations." "A similar distribution of the offices in the remaining counties of the State and in the executive department of the government," he said, "will be adopted by the new party as one of the strongest planks in its platform, upon which . . . many of the most influential Democrats will take their stand."[38]

Although the plan was never given trial on a large scale, being adopted by Beaufort County from 1888 to 1896 and on the Berkeley County legislative ticket in 1890, it was recognized by the whites as an effective means of conciliation where they could have exer-

---

[32] Columbia *State*, August 26, 1895.

[33] *Reports and Resolutions* (1897), p. 20.

[34] *Reports and Resolutions* (1878), p. 417; *Ibid.* (1880), pp. 578-79.

[35] Charleston *News and Courier*, January 23, 1882; *Reports and Resolutions* (1880), pp. 578-79. The county fusion followed hard on the adoption of a similar plan for the town of Georgetown. Charleston *News and Courier*, April 10, 1879. As late as 1881 there was no white man on the Georgetown police force. Columbia *Daily Register*, September 10, 1881.

[36] *Ibid.*, November 4, 1886; *Reports and Resolutions* (1894), II, 477.

[37] M. W. Pyatt to the Author, November 21, 1949.

[38] Charleston *News and Courier*, January 23, 1882.

cised only a precarious control at the most. Maham W. Pyatt, a Democrat who served in the legislature under the plan stated years later that "The democrats and republicans got along very comfortably under the fusion plan, and there was no friction."[39]

Specific testimony as to the abilities of the local Negro officeholders is not available but in the absence of any severe attack in the Democratic press, it can be assumed that the Negro officeholders measured up to the average of the local officeholders of the day. According to the testimony of Sir George Campbell, Wade Hampton, and Maham W. Pyatt, they were able to operate successfully without any serious friction with the whites.

In local elections outside of Georgetown and Beaufort Negro voters often exercised a perceptible influence. In a number of communities, Negro citizens were given representation in the local government as a matter of course. In St. Matthews, for example, in 1888 there was one colored candidate for warden on both the regular Democratic ticket and an independent ticket.[40] In Lancaster's municipal election of 1881 there was a single ticket in the field; it was made in a public meeting of citizens without regard to party. The main issue was that of licensing drinking establishments in the town, but the friends of prohibition spiked the guns of their opponents by naming for two of the four warden posts "representative men of the colored . . . both of whom never 'look upon the wine when it is red.' "[41] The town of Summerville in the eighties named a Negro, A. S. Blodgett, chief of police in reward for his services to the Democrats in the municipal election.[42] In 1887 when Frank Springs, a Negro candidate for the town council there, claimed to have been elected over one of the regular Democratic candidates, he was seated by a unanimous vote of the council.[43]

The most fruitful source of public office for Negro Republicans was the federal patronage, and except during the Cleveland administrations, most of the federal officeholders in the state after Reconstruction were Republican, either white or black. The more

---

[39] M. W. Pyatt to the Author, November 21, 1949.
[40] Charleston News and Courier, May 30, 1888.
[41] Columbia Daily Register, April 15, 1881.
[42] Yorkville Enquirer, January 28, 1886.
[43] Columbia Daily Register, June 19, 1887.

important offices were occupied by white Republicans, but in other positions, especially postmasterships, Negroes were numerous. The whites generally expressed dissatisfaction with the appointment of Negro postmasters, and, making due allowance for the bias of the white press, it is evident that men were sometimes named who were most conspicuous for their illiteracy and their penchant toward petty thievery.[44]

On the other hand, Eliza M. Davis, postmistress at Summerville for eleven years, gave general satisfaction.[45] J. H. Holloway, postmaster at Marion for fifteen years, forwarded to Washington in 1884 a "numerously signed" petition of the citizens of Marion against his removal. He was a member of the Marion town council, "to which position he has been elected by the votes of the best citizens and has generally received the highest vote on the ticket."[46] A Negro postmaster at Branchville in 1885 secured several Democratic signatures to a petition asking his retention in office.[47]

The two most notable Negro postmasters were Benjamin A. Boseman of Charleston and Charles McDuffie Wilder of Columbia. Boseman, first appointed by President Grant, was a Northerner, "a dapper, pleasant, well-educated man," who reminded a traveller of some of the educated East Indians in Calcutta.[48] Wilder, the Columbia postmaster, also appointed by Grant, but in office at least as late as 1885, was a native of Sumter; a self-made man, he had taught himself to read and write, and during the war had established himself in Columbia as a carpenter. Upon first taking office he was attacked on all sides, but his "business-like management of the Post Office soon disarmed criticism and opposition, and evoked enthusiastic praise from both parties and both races." After examining his office in 1885 an inspector said: "In its finances everything correct. Its records among the best seen. In its administrative details it surpasses all offices visited upon the Atlantic Coast." Wilder also served briefly as president of the board of regents of the State Orphan Asylum and was elected by white

---

[44] For examples of several such cases, see Yorkville *Enquirer*, March 5, 1885.
[45] Columbia *Daily Register*, September 17, 1884.
[46] "J. H. Holloway a candidate for the Post Office of Charleston, S. C.," a broadside dated June 20, 1902, Carter G. Woodson Papers.
[47] Yorkville *Enquirer*, April 16, 1885.
[48] Campbell, *White and Black*, p. 330.

businessmen of Columbia to a directorship in the Columbia Building and Loan Association.[49]

The Democratic party continued to name Negroes to public office in some of the Low Country counties. Paul Jenkins of Colleton was long a county commissioner and David Strother of Darlington was a county commissioner until his death in 1882.[50] Charleston County Democrats put three Negroes on their ticket in each election from 1876 to 1882, electing in 1880 "quiet, unobtrusive men, men of business in Charleston County, . . . highly respected by the people of that County."[51] After 1882 George M. Mears was the only Negro on the Democratic ticket, but he remained in the legislature, almost a totally silent member, until 1892. He had been born before the war of free parents, had received a common school education before the war, and had since that time worked at the trade of ship carpenter. He was always a Democrat, as were many of those who had been free before the war,[52] and was the last Negro Democrat to sit in the legislature. Marshall Jones, a representative from Orangeburg elected in 1886, had previously served four years as a Democratic member of the county board of commissioners and had "discharged the duties of his office with fidelity and entire satisfaction to all classes." He was a man of some property and popular with both races in the county.[53]

William Watts Ball has listed a number of examples of Negro participation in Democratic politics with which he was familiar. In the Barnwell County Democratic convention of 1882 several white men withdrew in favor of Jack Fleming, Negro, when he was nominated for coroner. In one Barnwell convention, Ball recalled, there were 49 Negroes among a total of 203. "These things have long been forgotten in South Carolina," Ball wrote in 1932, "and the grandsons of the white men who could give offices to negro Democrats in the eighteen-eighties deny them now the small privilege of membership in the party."[54]

---

[49] Sketch of Wilder's career by T. McCants Stewart, in New York Age, May 9, 1885. The report of the inspector is quoted by Stewart.

[50] Ball, The State That Forgot: South Carolina's Surrender to Democracy (Indianapolis, 1932), p. 174.

[51] Columbia Daily Register, November 28, 1880.

[52] Charleston News and Courier, November 26, 1884.

[53] Ibid., November 3, 1886.

[54] Ball, The State That Forgot, p. 174

Negro officeholders of the Democratic party were generally referred to by the white press as "very respectable Negroes," but were frequently regarded by their own race as "the mere servile creatures of their political task-masters."[55] Frequently Negro Democrats were prosperous businessmen and farmers, and their adherence to the Democratic party, despite its growing white supremacy sentiments, did no harm to their economic interests.

Negroes were admitted to Democratic precinct clubs in some parts of the state throughout the period. In Chester County, for example, forty Negroes were enrolled on the club books in 1884 and permitted to vote in the primary.[56] The roll of the Stateburg Democratic Club in 1892 showed eight Negro members in a total of sixty-eight, three of whom were still listed in the rolls as late as 1910.[57] In 1886 a Democratic Congressional Convention at Lancaster passed a rule debarring Negroes from the Democratic primary in the Fifth Congressional District, but was strongly rebuked by the white members of the Rock Hill Club, who declared that the ruling was "unjust to the many colored men who have proven their loyalty to that party by supporting its nominees at every election," and that it was "in violation of the pledges made by the party to the colored voters for the past ten years."[58]

But the action of the Democratic Congressional Convention was indicative of the trend in white thinking toward a complete elimination of Negroes from participation in the party. In the Tillmanite state convention of 1890 a rule was adopted providing that in the Democratic primaries "only white Democrats shall be allowed to vote, except that negroes who voted for Gen. Hampton in 1876, and who have voted the Democratic ticket continuously since, may be permitted to vote."[59] This rule, with the passage of years, rapidly eliminated the Negro members of the party.

---

[55] T. J. Mackey in Yorkville *Enquirer,* June 29, 1882.

[56] Charleston *News and Courier,* August 12, 1884.

[57] Minute Book and Roll of the Stateburg Democratic Club, 1890-1910, pp. 14-18, 71, Borough House Papers, Southern Historical Collection, University of North Carolina.

[58] Columbia *Daily Register,* September 25, 1886.

[59] Charleston *News and Courier,* August 15, 1890.

5

NULLIFICATION OF
THE FIFTEENTH AMENDMENT

D ESPITE the promises of Hampton, both fraud and intimidation, sometimes to the extent of violence, had helped to elect him in 1876. These methods were used again in 1878 and 1880. Dissatisfaction with the deleterious effects of such methods, however, and the possibility that one white faction might use fraud against another, led many white Democrats to cast about for some legalistic method of disfranchisement more thorough than the reshuffling of precincts and separation of state and federal elections that had taken place in 1878.

After the election of 1880, a joint committee of the General Assembly was established to study proposals for a new registration and election law. The committee asked Edward McCrady, attorney, historian, and Democratic legislator for an expression of opinion, which he presented in the form of a pamphlet that proposed the only practicable alternative to fraud and violence—an educational qualification for the vote.

> We complain of the great and cruel injury done to the white race in the South by forcing upon us the ignorant negro vote. This has been our cry, and it begins to be heard. The remedy is in our hands. Raise the standard of citizenship, raise the qualifications of voters. But, raise them equally. If we are the superior race we claim to be, we, surely, need not fear the test.[1]

[1] McCrady, *The Necessity for Raising the Standard of Citizenship and the Right of the General Assembly of the State of South Carolina to Impose Qualifications upon Electors* (Charleston, 1881), p. 38; *see also* McCrady, *The Registration of Electors* (Charleston, 1880), and *The Necessity of Education as the Basis of Our Political System* (Charleston, 1880).

The registration and election laws finally produced by the legislature, however, made evident the intention of the legislators to leave the door open to fraud. The registration law, the first passed under the mandate of the Constitution of 1868, permitted registration throughout May and June of 1882. Those eligible by June, 1882, had to register at that time or find themselves perpetually disfranchised. The only additional registration was for those who became eligible subsequent to June, 1882. In addition, provision was made that a person who moved his residence had to register again, even though the move was made within the precinct. Negro tenants and sharecroppers were frequently caught in this trap. In addition to this, the supervisor of registration and his two assistants were given full discretion in deciding the qualifications of a potential voter, and any appellant from their decision had to give notice within five days and bring court action within fifteen days. The supervisor also was given the power, when he believed that persons had died or moved away, to strike their names from the registration list, and a voter falsely stricken from the list might not discover the "mistake" until he attempted to vote. If he were not on the list his registration certificate was not recognized.[2]

For the election itself, the law of 1882 provided separate boxes for eight different classes of offices, national, state, and local.[3] The intent of the "Eight Box Law" was ostensibly to provide an effective literacy test by requiring the voter to choose by the label the proper box for his ballot. In practice, however, it would be simple for election managers to help those illiterates who would vote "right" and let others void their ballots through ignorance.

Thomas E. Miller, leading the helpless Republican opposition in the state senate, cut through the pretense that the laws were intended to provide a legitimate registration and an honest literacy test. "We are told," he said, "that under this trap to catch the unwary the voters of South Carolina, white and black, who were made ignorant and kept in ignorance by our rulers, are to be protected at the ballot box. Is there a Senator here who believes it? No, Senators, it is a libel on our intelligence." The real purpose of the bill, he continued, was

---

[2] *Statutes at Large,* XVII, 1110-16.
[3] *Ibid.,* 1116-21.

keeping the middle classes and the poor whites, together with the negroes, from having anything to do with the elections. If it is not so, why should the bill require an elector to pay $2 before he can have his certificate renewed, if lost? Why should you require a poor working man to deposit $5 before he can take an appeal from the decision of the Supervisor of Registration? Why should you have eight election boxes when our citizens are so ignorant and require all the simplicity in elections? If this bill means a fair election and an honest count, why should you sever the State from the national election?[4]

Contending that the bill was simply an effort of the upper class whites to provide "an opportunity for rings and fossils to retain power . . . ," he predicted a revolt of lower class whites along the lines of the Mahone movement in Virginia.

But William Holloway, conservative Negro editor, approved the law, saying:

Let those who need education to meet the requirements of the law, seek for it, and if they fail to secure enough for the needs of the hour, it will be their own fault, and not the State's. Let the eight box law, as it is called, stand, better to make it sixteen if eight are not enough, than to risk the remanding of the State to the clutches of ignorance and rascality.[5]

Both Miller's and Holloway's attitudes represented either innocence or wishful thinking, for the law was not administered impartially but was utilized for the sole purpose of disfranchising Negroes.

The uses of the registration law were quickly made manifest as the time established for registration passed. A Republican in Hampton County reported that in his neighborhood Democrats were mailed registration certificates without the necessity of reporting to the polling place as the law required. A good many colored voters were rejected in Hampton, ostensibly because the registrar believed them to be too young, and were told to go before the complete board of registration. The board then quietly met without notice, announced that no one had appeared to protest, and adjourned *sine die*.[6]

---

[4] Columbia *Daily Register*, December 3, 1881.

[5] Charleston *New Era*, December 2, 1882.

[6] New York *Daily Tribune*, July 17, 1882.

John Horsey, supervisor of registration for Charleston County, was hauled into federal court because he had conducted his registration by having separate lines for colored and white voters entering the room where registration was carried on.[7] This was obviously designed to simplify the task of freezing out Negro registrants, but it was impossible to prove the assertion with sufficient assurance to convict him, although many colored citizens of Charleston had been prevented from registering.[8]

At the elections themselves the tested methods of fraud and intimidation were still utilized. A Northern reporter observed that it was a common occurrence for crowds of armed whites to jostle Negroes who appeared at the polls, swearing all the while about "damned niggers" who wanted to vote.[9] At the McAlilley's Mill precinct, Chester County, a large crowd of whites gathered early on the morning of election day, 1882. They said they "heard there was going to be a row, and they came early to keep the peace." Armed with pistols, knives, and clubs, they frequently made "threats of a serious nature" during the day while by procrastination the managers kept about a hundred independents and Negroes from voting, and left them outside when the polling place closed. But more subtle methods were sometimes used. At the Witherspoon precinct, Clarendon County, the same day, a narrow passageway, wide enough for only one person to enter and about fifteen feet long, was built at the entrance to the polling place. It was necessary for voters to pass through this in order to reach the ballot box and many colored voters were naturally reluctant to run the gauntlet. At numerous precincts there were reports of whites voting without registration certificates or at the wrong precinct while qualified Negroes were not permitted to vote, with no explanation given.[10]

---

[7] Columbia *Daily Register*, December 6, 1883.

[8] *Ibid.*, December 20, 1883; Charleston *New Era*, July 1, 1882. For an account of other methods whereby Negroes were prevented from registering, see New York *Age*, January 13, 1883, quoting New York *Sun*.

[9] New York *Age*, January 13, 1883, quoting New York *Sun*.

[10] Report of William P. Snyder, Special Assistant U. S. Attorney, District of South Carolina, of the Investigation and Prosecution of Cases in South Carolina for Violation of the Election Laws of the United States, May 4, 1883, General Records, Department of Justice, Source-Chronological Files, South Carolina, Box 653, National Archives. Although limited to the election of 1882, cases cited in this report serve to illustrate methods of fraud and intimidation that were used throughout the period.

These cases, among others, were brought to trial in 1883 by District Attorney Samuel W. Melton, a native white Republican, who had the assistance of Emory Speer of Georgia, assigned as a special prosecutor. Every case resulted in mistrial, the legislature at the suggestion of Governor Hugh S. Thompson having appropriated $10,000 to pay the expenses of the defendants, witnesses, and counsel.[11] It was practically impossible at the time to draw a jury in South Carolina that would convict any white man of violation of the election laws and Melton moved in the spring of 1884 that all the cases be discontinued, saying "I am now persuaded that in the present condition of public sentiment of a large proportion of the people of this State, convictions in these cases are impossible. . . ." The prosecutions were dropped with the permission of the Attorney-General.[12] After that no serious attempts were made at the prosecution of whites for election frauds, with the exception of another unsuccessful case in 1890 in connection with registration in Charleston County.[13]

Democratic control of the instruments of government made it possible for the whites to utilize numerous other methods of reducing the political influence of Negroes. In areas where the Negro majority made bulldozing difficult, the Democratic election managers frequently adopted the ruse of not appearing at the polls on election day.[14] Sometimes this was deliberate; at other times it resulted from fear of election managers that they would not be safe.[15] At the election of 1886 the number of votes thrown out by county boards in the "black district" clearly made the difference between the election of a Democrat and the election of a Republican. The Greenville *News* complained:

> Our side may, and doubtless will, prove that the county
> boards acted within the law in throwing out many boxes and

---

[11] *Senate Journal* (1883), pp. 22-23; Reports and Resolutions (1884), II, xix. $4,054.20 of the appropriation was spent.

[12] *Appleton's Annual Cyclopaedia,* IX (1884), 739.

[13] Abiel Lathrop to the Attorney General, July 23, 1890, General Records, Department of Justice, Source-Chronological Files, File No. 4092, 1890, National Archives. From the District Attorney in South Carolina.

[14] Thomas E. Miller declared that this was a common practice of Democratic election managers. Columbia *Daily Register,* December 3, 1881.

[15] Chester H. Rowell (ed.), *A Historical and Legal Digest of all the Contested Election Cases in the House of Representatives of the United States from the First to the Fifty-Sixth Congress, 1789-1901,* House Miscellaneous Documents, 56th Congress, 2d Session, No. 510, p. 451.

hundreds of votes for irregularities, but the fact will stand out bald and unquestioned that Smalls has been defeated by the official negligence of Democratic officials, appointed by Democratic authority. The inference that the negligence was a pre-arranged plot to deprive the majority of its weight will be too plain and clear for resistance. The State will be put before the country as being party to a plain, deliberate and wanton fraud.[16]

After the election of 1890 the state board refused to certify the Republican congressional candidate, Thomas E. Miller, because his ballots were found not to have been of the required size and color, being printed not on white paper but on "white paper of a distinctly yellow tinge."[17] Although it was later reported that some of the ballots for the Democratic candidate were also defective, Miller was denied a seat in Congress on this technicality.[18]

Through such methods, the Republican vote was cut from 91,870 in 1876 to 13,740 in 1888.[19] By the end of the eighties the Negro vote had been all but eliminated as a factor in the state's politics. Then it was that Benjamin Ryan Tillman entered the scene to capture the Democratic party with a movement that was a mixture of agrarian discontent and the Negrophobia that had been cultivated in the seventies by Tillman's neighbor, Martin W. Gary. From the beginning of his agitation Tillman had been in favor of a constitutional convention to incorporate into the organic law of the state restrictions on the civil rights and suffrage of Negroes.[20] After the Haskell bolt from the Democratic party in 1890, the demand became more insistent, because it was evident that the Negro vote might conceivably occupy a balance of power between two white factions.

----

[16] Charleston *News and Courier*, November 24, 1886, quoting Greenville *News*.

[17] Charleston *News and Courier*, November 12, 1890.

[18] New York *Age*, January 17, 1891, quoting Orangeburg *Plain Speaker*.

[19] E. Eastman Irvine (ed.), *The World Almanac and Book of Facts for 1949* (New York, 1949), pp. 83-84. The vote for presidential electors.

[20] "The Shell Manifesto," Charleston *News and Courier*, January 23, 1890. For a more detailed discussion of Tillman's campaign for disfranchisement, see George Brown Tindall, "The Campaign for the Disfranchisement of Negroes in South Carolina," *Journal of Southern History*, XV (May, 1949), 212-34, and "The Question of Race in the South Carolina Constitutional Convention of 1895," *Journal of Negro History*, XXXVII (July, 1952), 277-303.

Tillman's influence could not secure the passage of a measure for the calling of a convention during his first term as governor. It was only after the election of 1892 that he had a sufficient stranglehold on the General Assembly to choke out the two-thirds vote necessary for the passage of a joint resolution to provide for a referendum on the calling of a convention.[21] After the resolution was passed in 1892 the issue was dormant until the beginning of the election campaign in 1894, the year in which the popular referendum was scheduled.

The state Democratic executive committee in 1894 played upon emotion and fear by pointing out in a pronouncement to the Democrats that the potential colored voting population of the state was about forty thousand more than the white and that white independents intended to capitalize on it to carry the state in 1896. "Fortunately, the opportunity is offered the white people of the State in the coming election to obviate all future danger, and fortify Anglo-Saxon civilization against every assault from within and without, and that is the calling of a constitutional convention to deal with the all important question of suffrage."[22]

The committee also assured the voters that it was possible to disfranchise the Negroes without denying the vote to any white man and, what was more important, without violating the United States Constitution. It was generally understood that this could best be done by something like the Mississippi Plan, the chief feature of which was a literacy qualification with a property alternative and an "understanding clause."[23]

When Tillman himself was asked what measures were in view for accomplishing a limitation of the suffrage, he replied in a statement remarkable for its dictatorial tone:

> That's my secret. Let the people of the state . . . trust me. Let them vote for the convention. The time to discuss the method for reducing the Negro majority is after the convention has been called. . . . If the plan then suggested does not meet their approval they can elect men pledged not to incorporate it in the new Constitution.[24]

---

[21] *House Journal* (1892), p. 418; *Senate Journal* (1892), p. 326.
[22] Columbia *Daily Register*, October 10, 1894.
[23] *Mississippi Constitution* (1890), Art. XII.
[24] Columbia *Daily Register*, October 30, 1894.

At the same time he reviewed the horrors of Reconstruction and expressed alarm at the continued tendency of white men, in spite of this memory, to split into factions and appeal to the Negro vote. Not since Reconstruction, he said, had the issue of the Negro vote come so much to the fore, because not since then had the white people been so dangerously divided.

The white opposition to the convention represented no positive movement to protect Negroes in their political rights. But the Republicans quietly permitted the brunt of opposition to be borne by the Conservatives within the Democratic party. The opposition from this group came from a fear of what the Tillman-controlled convention might do, and to some extent a feeling that the suffrage issue was a sleeping dog that might better be let alone.[25]

As the campaign progressed the pressure became so strong that it was obvious to all that the vote on the convention would be extremely close, although the Tillmanites were assured of winning the gubernatorial and senatorial races by comfortable margins. the final official vote in the referendum was 31,402 for and 29,523 against the convention, a slim majority of 1,879.[26] The general picture was one of Low Country opposition and Up Country support, with exceptions in scattered counties.

The leading Conservative papers of the state claimed fraud, the Charleston *News and Courier* headlining the election news, "A Machine Election—White Men Cheat White Men in South Carolina."[27] Four days after the election the same paper carried accounts of fraud charges in Greenville, Darlington, Aiken, Fairfield, Florence, Orangeburg, and other counties.[28] Samson Pope, independent candidate for governor, issued a statement calling upon the people to "remember that a Constitutional Convention has been called through fraud of the blackest character."[29] The Columbia *State* likewise flatly charged fraud and carried reports from many parts of the state to back up its accusations.[30]

---

[25] Charleston *News and Courier,* October 20, 1894, quoting editorial from Charleston *Sun.*

[26] *Reports and Resolutions* (1894), II, 472.

[27] Charleston *News and Courier,* November 7, 1894.

[28] *Ibid.,* November 10, 1894; *see also ibid.,* November 11-16, 1894.

[29] *Ibid.,* November 12, 1894.

[30] Columbia *State,* November 9, 1894.

The nearest thing to a formal investigation of the charges can be found in testimony on three contested congressional elections held at the same time as the vote on the convention. This approach is unfortunately indirect, but damaging evidence was presented.[31] On the basis of one of these investigations the second district seat was declared vacant on June 1, 1896.[32]

While the Democrats were organizing for the election of convention delegates in August, 1895, there was an unusual degree of political stirring among Negroes and Republicans, greater than had been seen since the stormy days of 1876. On January 4 a call went out for the Republicans to meet in a state convention on February 6, warning that "the very life of suffrage in this State is at stake and other cherished rights and interests are imperiled."[33]

About one hundred delegates, among them twenty-five whites, assembled in Columbia on the day set. Ellery M. Brayton, the party chairman, called upon colored ministers to explain the intricacies of registration to the voters and to encourage them to vote. At the same time he made a direct appeal for fusion with the Conservatives.[34]

The convention stated in its platform that the party was not seeking a return to power but merely the preservation of the citizenship rights of its members. It adopted four planks for the constitution: (1) the document should be submitted to the people; (2) it should make no discrimination against any class of people; (3) it should not reduce taxes for school purposes; and (4) the two major parties should participate in election management. The platform also rehearsed the broken promises of the Democrats in 1876, and the quiet submission of the Republicans to their rule "with docility and faithfulness and hope which must challenge the admiration . . . of the world." It quoted Tillman's charge that white governments up to 1890 had been characterized by "corruption, bribery, political leprosy and imbecility," as well as similar countercharges against the Tillman administrations. "The cries of

---

[31] "Joshua E. Wilson v. John McLaurin," *House Reports,* 54th Congress, 1st Session, No. 1566; "George W. Murray v. William Elliott," *ibid.,* No. 1567; "Thomas B. Johnston v. J. William Stokes," *ibid.,* No. 1229.

[32] *Journal of the House of Representatives of the United States of America* (54th Congress, 1st Session), p. 558.

[33] Columbia *Daily Register,* January 5, 1895.

[34] Columbia *State,* February 7, 1895.

white supremacy and negro rule," said the platform, "are simply exhausted bugaboos which will frighten no man who thinks, and are used by shallow partisans for purposes of deceit."[35]

Negro ministers at the same time were active on their own initiative. In January a call was issued by twelve Negro ministers for a convention to meet February 14 in Columbia with the objective of securing unhampered citizenship rights at least to the "intelligent" of both races, as well as good government and good schools, but above all "for the purpose of getting the Negroes registered to a man and standing ready to vote for any set of men, regardless of their party name, who are in favor of an honestly managed government and opposed to racial, class or impracticable measures being encouched in the new constitution." The call asserted that the ministers who preach "thou shalt not steal" should see to it that the Negro be not robbed of his right to the franchise. The Democrats were likened to an embezzler who started with small sums and gradually became bolder and bolder. The "sugar-coated pledges made by Hampton" in 1876 had by now been broken and the constitutional convention was to be the climax in the process of robbing the Negro of suffrage.[36]

On January 31, a different group of fifteen to twenty Negroes issued a cleverly designed statement after a meeting in Columbia. They called first for the cooperation of "that class of white men whom we know to be too proud, broad and humane to take advantage of the weak." They admitted that disfranchisement might have been justifiable twenty years before, but held that colored taxpayers now paid five times as much property tax as then and that Negro teachers and professional men compared favorably with the whites. The cry of Negro domination, not the Negro, they said, had brought the state to its bad condition.[37]

Fifty preachers appeared for their scheduled meeting on February 14 at Calvary Baptist Church in Columbia. A state executive committee was chosen and it was proposed to organize Negroes all the way down to ward and precinct levels. In addition, the meeting urged colored citizens to put forth every effort to register and

---

[35] Columbia *Daily Register*, February 7, 1895.
[36] *Ibid.*, January 20, 1895; *see also* Yorkville *Enquirer*, January 23, 1895.
[37] Columbia *State*, February 1, 1895.

to secure accurate information about the requirements for registration and about the candidates.[38]

Later the Negro Ministerial Union, formed at this meeting, issued an even stronger statement calling upon the national government to intervene and keep a small desperate minority from trampling constitutional rights underfoot.[39]

Meanwhile, the Beaufort *New South*, edited by S. J. Bampfield, son-in-law of Robert Smalls, reminded readers that "unless some prompt action is taken these white supremacy howlers . . . will succeed in fastening upon the people an oligarchy of fraud that will keep the machine in power and the honest people of the State under their heels for the next half century." "There is clearly a conspiracy against the purity of the ballot box," it warned, "and a determination to continue the system of fraudulent elections that have disgraced South Carolina for so many years and brought reproach upon the people of the State. Indeed there is no longer even an attempt to disguise it. . . ."[40]

During March the Negro Congressman, George W. Murray, set forth on a tour "to canvass the state and educate and arouse our people up to a realization of the situation and what they can do to help themselves."[41] There is evidence that he was well received, being heard by mixed audiences of whites and Negroes in some towns.[42] Murray himself reported "splendid success" and asked a friend in Washington to secure contributions to help in the campaign "to break the chains which are forged and are being forged for all colored Carolinians" by bringing suit against the registration act.[43]

An anomaly in the campaign was the one substantial white citizen, Colonel John J. Dargan, editor of the Sumter *Freeman* and a Red Shirt leader in 1876, who raised his voice in support of the political

<hr/>

[38] Columbia *Daily Register*, February 15, 1895.

[39] Columbia *State*, July 11, 1895.

[40] Beaufort *New South*, March 7, 1895.

[41] George W. Murray to W. McKinlay, March 21, 1895, Carter G. Woodson Papers.

[42] Columbia *State*, March 20, 1895; Charleston *News and Courier*, May 3, 1895.

[43] George W. Murray to W. McKinlay, March 21, 1895, Carter G. Woodson Papers. The suit against the registration law proved unsuccessful. See 67 *Federal Reporter*, pp. 822-32; 69 *Federal Reporter*, pp. 865-67; and Columbia *Daily Register*, November 26, 1895.

rights of Negroes. He ran in Sumter as an independent candidate for the convention and in a speech in the courthouse at Columbia proclaimed that he was "not fighting for white supremacy, but for the supremacy of right and justice, first, last, and all the time." He pointed to Georgetown as the most encouraging example of interracial cooperation in the state, where the offices were divided between whites and Negroes. "If we try this in South Carolina," he said, "it will cure the disease of the State."[44]

Later in the campaign, Dargan, with more courage than caution, invaded the bailiwick of Tillman. A committee, led by the county sheriff, informed him that he would not be permitted to speak in Edgefield, and in the streets he was surrounded by an angry mob that attempted to provoke him by insults into striking the first blow. Dargan managed to make the first train out of town before any violence occurred.[45] The following week, admitting that he had been wrong in stirring up Edgefield unnecessarily, he wrote the Charleston *News and Courier* that he was nevertheless

> more than ever . . . impelled to go forward with my missionary work, proclaiming; Prepare ye the way for a higher and better civilization; a civilization of liberty, equality, and justice for all; justice and equality under the law, and freedom of thought and speech.[46]

That was the last heard from Dargan in the campaign.

During the brief period of registration for the election of delegates a statement was presented to Governor John Gary Evans by a committee with George W. Murray as chairman in which it was complained that "not more than 10,000 electors were registered within the entire state and . . . many more than 100,000 after unparalleled exposure, suffering, and sacrifices remain unregistered and disfranchised." A special session of the legislature was proposed to provide additional periods for registration. Evans naturally was not disposed to lend an ear to any plea for more registration.[47]

In May the Democratic state committee ordered that a primary be held in each county to select party candidates for delegates.

---

[44] Columbia *State*, March 16, 1895.

[45] *Ibid.*, June 28, 1895.

[46] Charleston *News and Courier*, July 5, 1895.

[47] Columbia *Daily Register*, March 15, 1895. Registration still was only for those who had become eligible to vote since 1882.

Candidates were required to file at least ten days in advance a pledge to honor the results of the primary.[48] The possibility of independent revolt was effectively squelched by this means, although a number of Conservatives, including Wade Hampton, advised their followers to stay out of the primary.

Hampton's statement came in a letter from Washington to the editor of the Spartanburg *Herald*. It would carry little weight in all probability, he admitted in a tone of injured pride, but added,

> . . . I have no fear of Negro domination—a cry used only to arouse race prejudice and to put the incoming convention under control of the Ring which now dominates our State.
>
> The negroes have acted of late with rare moderation and liberality, and if we meet them in the same spirit they have shown, they will aid in selecting good representatives for the convention.
>
> I for one am willing to trust them, and they ask only the rights guaranteed to them by the constitution of the United States and that of our own State. "Corruption wins not more than honesty," and I advocate perfect honesty, for defeat on that line is better than victory by fraud.[49]

A meeting of Conservatives in Columbia also advised the people to stay out of the primary and perfect an independent organization. The group included Edward McCrady, A. B. Williams, and N. G. Gonzales.[50] Its influence in the end was nil, not one county outside Charleston sending a solidly Conservative delegation and that group elected on the Democratic ticket.

The primary on July 30, as had been expected, resulted in a sizable victory for the Tillman forces. Membership was settled finally in the general election which left the count of delegates 112 Tillmanites, 42 Conservatives, 6 Republicans.[51] All of the Republicans were Negroes, one coming from Georgetown on a fusion ticket and the other five from Beaufort on a straight Republican ticket.

---

[48] Columbia *Daily Register*, May 16, 1895.

[49] Yorkville *Enquirer*, May 29, 1895, quoting Spartanburg *Herald*.

[50] Columbia *Daily Register*, June 24, 1895.

[51] George Brown Tindall, "The South Carolina Constitutional Convention of 1895" (unpublished Master's thesis, Department of History, University of North Carolina, 1948), pp. 53, 172-73.

The dominant figure of the convention was Ben Tillman, who more than any other one person was responsible for the calling of the convention and for the form which the new constitution took.[52] Other important white delegates were John Gary Evans, John Laurens Manning Irby, George Dionysius Tillman, and John Pendleton Kennedy Bryan.[53]

The six Negro delegates were Robert Smalls, Thomas E. Miller, William J. Whipper, James Wigg, and Isaiah R. Reed, from Beaufort; and Robert B. Anderson, from Georgetown. Some attention has already been given to the activities of all but Whipper and Reed. William J. Whipper, whom Ben Tillman described at one time as the "ablest colored man I ever met," was reared in Michigan and at the outbreak of the Civil War was employed as a clerk in a lawyer's office. During the war he joined a regiment of volunteers and ultimately reached South Carolina. At the end of the war he became a lawyer in Charleston, and later went to Beaufort where he was elected a delegate to the constitutional convention of 1868. In 1868 and 1870 he was elected to the legislature. Elected in 1875 as circuit judge of the first circuit, he was not commissioned by Governor Chamberlain. From 1882 to 1888 he was Probate Judge of Beaufort County, but since 1888 had not held office.[54] Isaiah R. Reed was an attorney in Beaufort and was associated with S. J. Bampfield and G. W. Anderson in the management of the Beaufort *New South*.[55]

Since the major objective of the convention was disfranchisement, the most important standing committee of the convention was the Committee on the Rights of Suffrage, which was appointed on the second day with eight Tillmanite and three Conservative members. Ben Tillman was appointed chairman.[56]

---

[52] For Tillman's part in the convention, see Francis Butler Simkins, *Pitchfork Ben Tillman* pp. 285-309.

[53] The latter was chiefly responsible for the form of the suffrage article in the new constitution, Wallace, *History of South Carolina*, III, 369.

[54] Solomon Breibart, "The South Carolina Constitutional Convention of 1868" (unpublished Master's thesis, Department of History, University of North Carolina, 1932), pp. 71-72; Taylor, *The Negro in South Carolina During the Reconstruction,* pp. 127, 141-42, 228, 233-35, 294.

[55] *Journal of the Constitutional Convention of the State of South Carolina* (Columbia, 1895), p. 736, hereinafter cited as *Convention Journal;* Irvine Garland Penn, *The Afro-American Press and Its Editors* (Springfield, Massachusetts, 1871), pp. 205-6.

[56] *Convention Journal,* p. 22. For various proposals to the Committee, see pp. 42-43, 54, 69-70, 77, 101-2, 111-12, 121-22, 127-28, 151, 152.

The suffrage article proposed by this committee forced each voter to run the gauntlet of numerous suffrage restrictions. First, it provided suffrage for male citizens who could meet the qualifications of age, residence in the state two years, county one year, precinct four months, and payment of the poll tax at least six months before the elections.[57] These were calculated to eliminate many Negroes because of their migratory habits and to disfranchise them in November for not paying their poll taxes in May, a time when ready cash was least available to farmers. But the chief trap was the literacy test, a requirement that each registrant prove to the satisfaction of the board that he could read and write any section of the Constitution. There were two alternatives to the literacy requirement: ownership of taxable property assessed at $300 or more, or ability to "understand" the constitution when it was read aloud.[58] The latter provision was the only permanent registration, but voters were required to qualify under it before January 1, 1898. The other registrants had to renew their registration every ten years.[59] The final obstacle between the prospective voter and the ballot box was to be the local election manager, who was to require of every elector proof of the payment of all taxes assessed against him the previous year.[60]

Additional measures against the Negro vote were provided by a list of disfranchising crimes, including those supposed by the whites to be most frequently committed by Negroes and also those of the most heinous nature. Others disfranchised were idiots, the insane, paupers supported at public expense, and persons in prison.[61]

Two provisions of the committee report did not find their way into the final draft despite Tillman's plea for them. One granted a right of appeal to "any court" when one was denied registration. This was changed to a right of appeal to the Circuit Court of

---

[57] *Constitution of 1895*, Art. II, Sec. 3, 4a.

[58] *Ibid.*, Sec. 4c, 4d.

[59] *Ibid.*, Sec. 4b.

[60] *Ibid.*, Sec. 4a.

[61] *Ibid.*, Sec. 6. Disfranchising crimes included burglary, arson, obtaining goods or money under false pretenses, perjury, forgery, robbery, bribery, adultery, bigamy, wife-beating, house-breaking, receiving stolen goods, breach of trust with fraudulent intent, fornication, sodomy, incest, assault with intent to ravish, miscegenation, larceny, and crimes against the election laws. Murder was not included in the list.

PUBLIC SAFETY

The Capital City Guards, Columbia, a reserve company in the National Guard

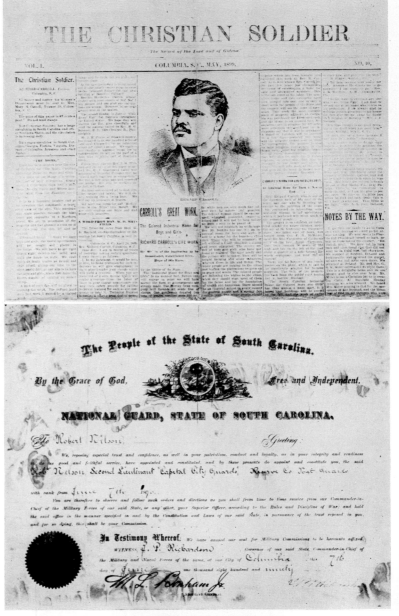

AN EDITOR AND A SOLDIER

The newspaper shows RICHARD CARROLL, *the editor. The commission in the Capital City Guards is dated 1890.*

Appeals only.[62] The other defeated proviso was for minority representation on registration and election boards. Tillman tried to re-incorporate the proviso, making an earnest plea that the nation was watching South Carolina to see if she were willing to make adequate safeguards against fraud. The suffrage committee, he said, unanimously favored the principle of minority representation, but the convention voted it down by 74 to 51.[63]

Discussion of the suffrage provisions for the new constitution brought eloquent speeches from the Negroes for the preservation of unrestricted suffrage. Miller, who made the first speech, reviewed the history of Negroes in America, citing the martyrdom of Crispus Attucks and favorable comments by Charles Pinckney and Henry Laurens as character evidence for the race. Negroes were not aliens, he reminded the delegates, any more than Caucasians. "A residence of our foreparents of near 300 years; birth and rearage here; our adaptation to the wants of the country; our labor and forebearance; our loyalty to the government—are all these elements indices of an alien race?" He made an adroit appeal to those who feared the disfranchisement of the poor whites, quoting remarks by J. L. M. Irby that the $300 property qualification would not be a sufficient alternative for those who were poor as well as illiterate. This point he illustrated with a story about a boy, exploring the banks of the Salkahatchie River, who chanced upon a moccasin and catfish trying to swallow each other. The moccasin was successful in getting the catfish down, but his fins cut the moccasin's throat. The moccasin personified the Tillmanites, he said, and the catfish represented the Conservatives who were achieving their objective of disfranchising the poor whites. Twitting the votaries of the Lost Cause tradition he said:

> The majority of you blame the poor Negro for the humility inflicted upon you during that conflict, but he had nothing to do with it. It was your love of power and your supreme arrogance that brought it upon yourselves. You are too feeble to settle up with government for that grudge. This hatred has been centered on the Negro and he is the innocent sufferer of your spleen.[64]

---

[62] *Ibid.*, Sec. 5; *Convention Journal*, p. 298.

[63] Columbia *State*, November 6, 9, 1895; Columbia *Daily Register*, November 9, 1895.

[64] Mary J. Miller (ed.), *Suffrage Speeches by Negroes in the Constitutional Convention* (n. p., n. d.), pp. 5-13.

Wigg renewed the appeal for a straight literacy qualification, indicating that an additional or alternative property qualification would be acceptable.

> You charge that the Negro is too ignorant to be entrusted with the suffrage. I answer that you have not, nor dare you, make a purely educational test of the right to vote.
>
> You say that he is a figurehead and an encumbrance to the State, that he pays little or no taxes. I answer that you have not and you dare not make a purely property test of the right to vote.[65]

He bluntly attacked the doctrine of white supremacy with the argument that it was sheer fallacy. Every white delegate, he said, had been pledged to the false doctrine of white supremacy, to the securing of it by either honest or dishonest methods. "Beneath this yoke, humiliating as it is, each one of you had to pass; to this pledge each one of you had to subscribe before you could have the privilege of being counted as a delegate to this convention."[66]

The following day Smalls and Whipper were heard. Smalls charged fraud in the committee's suffrage article. The suffrage plan, he said, might fool "the crackers" but no one else as to its essentially fraudulent nature. He dared Tillman to accept a straight literacy qualification which would leave a white majority of fourteen thousand in the electorate. Appealing to the white desire for cheap farm labor, he warned that the Negroes might leave the state if things became too hard for them.[67]

Whipper devoted the first part of his remarks to the denial that Negro government had ever existed in South Carolina, pointing out that Beaufort County offered an example of Negro willingness to accept white officeholders even where they outnumbered the whites by twenty to one. He charged bodies like the convention with inciting the crime of lynching and derided white supremacists for trying to show their superiority by defrauding old slaves.[68]

Pleas by the lesser known and less experienced Reed and Anderson were presented on October 29. Reed deplored the unfair administration of justice to the Negroes, but held that Negroes

---

[65] Columbia *State*, October 26, 1895.
[66] M. J. Miller, *Suffrage Speeches*, pp. 16-21.
[67] Columbia *State*, October 27, 1895.
[68] *Ibid.*

were perfectly willing to let the "intelligent" rule, many having in fact voted for Wade Hampton, Johnson Hagood, and even B. R. Tillman for governor. In conciliatory tone he reminded the whites that they trusted Negroes in many vocations. "You have suffered the negroes to harness . . . your costly steeds; you have suffered them to serve the delicacies of your festal boards; in short, you have suffered them to attend many other vocations of life which come nearer to your honor, nearer to your person and nearer to your property than casting a ballot."[69]

Anderson, the school teacher, pointed with pride to the great strides of progress made by Negroes in the past thirty years and pleaded that he was asking for the suffrage on behalf of 100,000 patriotic citizens. ". . . I am constrained to raise my voice in protest against the passage by this convention of the political scheme . . . proposed by the committee on suffrage. A scheme that will forever rivet the chain of disfranchisement upon the colored people of South Carolina. A scheme that was conceived in equity [iniquity?] and born in sin."[70]

Senator J. L. M. Irby, "the poor man's friend," followed the Negroes two days later with a presentation of his objections to the suffrage scheme. Formerly an ardent Tillmanite and still chairman of the Democratic state committee, he predicted bloodshed if illiterate whites were disfranchised while educated Negroes were permitted to vote. The suffrage article, he said, "builds bombproofs and fortifications for the educated and property owning class . . . while it leaves the poor white man to risk and endure the tests of a hostile court." The understanding clause in his opinion was unconstitutional and would give the ballot to the illiterates only until it came to a test in the federal courts.[71]

Such telling blows had been landed by the Negroes that Tillman felt the necessity for delivering a full dress reply with his one eye cocked to the national audience. He was prepared on October 31 and delivered his speech immediately after Irby's. Most of the speech was concerned with the swindles of Reconstruction days and especially with the taint of fraud that hung about the reputations of Smalls and Whipper. His objective was to answer Whipper's

---

[69] M. J. Miller, *Suffrage Speeches*, pp. 21-22.
[70] Columbia *Daily Register*, October 29, 1895.
[71] *Ibid.*, November 1, 1895.

contention that there had never been "Negro government" by proving the responsibility of the Negro race for corruption under radical administrations. The radical constitution, made by the "ring streaked and striped carpetbagger convention," had been ratified by Negroes and Negroes had "put the little pieces of paper in the box that gave the commission to white scoundrels who were their leaders and the men who debauched them. . . ."

The difficulty of his task Tillman recognized and confessed, when the question of the poor whites arose, "If there was any way under high heaven by which we could do more than we have done, in God's name I would glory and honor the man, and bow down and submit to his leadership if he could show us."

As for the methods to be used by registration boards, he said in reply to a query by Irby:

> I said last night that the chalice was poisoned. Some have said there is fraud in this understanding clause. Some poisons in small doses are very salutary and valuable medicines. If you put it here that a man must understand, and you vest the right to judge whether he understands in an officer, it is a constitutional act. That officer is responsible to his conscience and his God, he is responsible to nobody else. There is no particle of fraud or illegality in it. It is just showing partiality, perhaps, (laughter) or discriminating. . . .[72]

After the Tillman speech Smalls made a denial of his connection with any of the frauds charged against him. The whole matter had been dragged into the debate "to inflame the passions of delegates against Republicans and force them to vote for this most infamous Suffrage Bill, which seeks to take away the right to vote from two-thirds of the qualified voters of the State." Concluding passionately, he proclaimed that his race needed no special defense.

> All they need is an equal chance in the battle of life. I am proud of them, and by their acts toward me, I know that they are not ashamed of me, for they have at all times honored me with their vote.
>
> I stand here the equal of any man. I started out in the war with the Confederates; they threatened to punish me and I left them. I went to the Union army. I fought in seventeen

---

[72] *Convention Journal*, pp. 443-72.

battles to make glorious and perpetuate the flag that some of you trampled under your feet.[73]

Thomas E. Miller, against whom no fraud was intimated, made the point in reply to Sheppard and Tillman that the corruption of one Negro could not be the valid basis for generalization against the race any more than Boss Tweed or T. J. Mackey could be for the entire white race. Tillman's emphasis was laid on fraud in the period 1869-1873 when the Negro was still innocent and incompetent, he claimed. The Negroes began to clean out the corruption in the period of 1873-1876 after they had become more experienced. They had started the investigations and repudiations of bonds that had been continued by the Democratic administrations.[74]

William Henderson of Berkeley, exasperated at the talk by the Negroes and Conservatives of the need for fair elections and perhaps confused by Tillman's irony about "showing partiality," declared frankly:

> We don't propose to have any fair elections. We will get left at that every time. (Laughter) Who will be the managers? Won't they be Democrats and Republicans, and don't you see that will be a bar to the Democrats? I tell you, gentlemen, if we have fair elections in Berkeley we can't carry it. (Laughter) There's no use to talk about it. The black man is learning to read faster than the white man. And if he comes up and can read you have got to let him vote. Now are you going to throw it out (Laughter). . . . We are perfectly disgusted with hearing so much about fair elections. Talk all around, but make it fair and you'll see what'll happen. (Laughter)[75]

Late on November first the suffrage article passed the second reading by 69-37 with only eight Conservatives voting against it.[76] After the elimination of the provisions for minority representation on the boards of registration and for appeal to any court, the measure passed the third reading by 77-41.[77]

The final vote on ratification of the constitution as a whole came on the afternoon of December 4. The convention, with thirty-four

---

[73] *Ibid.*, pp. 473-76.
[74] M. J. Miller, *Suffrage Speeches,* pp. 13-15.
[75] Columbia *Daily Register,* November 2, 1895.
[76] *Convention Journal,* p. 483; Columbia *State,* November 2, 1895.
[77] *Convention Journal,* p. 517.

delegates absent, voted 116 to 7 for the new constitution. Only two white conservatives joined the five Negroes present in voting against it.[78] Despite two motions by Thomas E. Miller to have the constitution submitted to the people for ratification, the document was promulgated to become effective on January 1, 1896.[79]

The most important factors in the disfranchising arrangements were the restrictions hedging registration. These were utilized quite freely by registration officials and were not put to any serious test by Negro citizens, more impressed than ever with the futility of attempting to vote. In October, 1896, it was reported that 50,000 whites and only 5,500 Negroes had registered in the state.[80] Only Georgetown County had a majority of Negroes registered, and there it was only a majority of 861-814, which was wiped out in subsequent years.[81] A resident of Beaufort County reported in 1903 that although literate male Negroes in that county outnumbered the white voters by 3,434 to 927, ". . . registration officials do not allow registered Negro voters to outnumber the whites."[82]

Tillman stated on the floor of the Senate in 1900 that there were about 114,000 registered voters, of whom 14,000 were Negro.[83] Later he told the Senate, "We of the South have never recognized the right of the negro to govern white men, and we never will."[84] James H. Tillman, Ben's nephew, stated in his 1900 campaign for lieutenant-governor, "It is no crime for a supervisor of registration to deny a negro a certificate. . . ."[85]

Some doubt has been expressed by students of the state's history as to the importance of the Constitution of 1895 in disfranchising Negroes.[86] Figures on the decline of the Republican vote would indicate that disfranchisement already had been substantially accomplished. The psychological impact of the convention and the provision for a new registration may have been important in

---

[78] *Ibid.,* p. 725.

[79] *Ibid.,* pp. 89, 284; *Constitution* (1895), Art. XVII, Sec. 11.

[80] Yorkville *Enquirer,* October 7, 1896.

[81] Charleston *News and Courier,* October 8, 1896.

[82] Neils Christensen, Jr., "The Negroes of Beaufort County, South Carolina," *Southern Workman,* XXXII (October, 1903), 481-86.

[83] Yorkville *Enquirer,* February 28, 1900.

[84] *Congressional Record,* XXXIII (56th Congress, 1st Session), 3224.

[85] Charleston *News and Courier,* June 23, 1900.

[86] Simkins and Woody, *South Carolina During Reconstruction,* p. 551.

accelerating the existing trend, but the chief instruments of disfranchisement were still what they had been before the convention—
intimidation, violence and fraud. In the face of the Fifteenth
Amendment this was the only means of securing white majorities
in those few areas where literate Negroes outnumbered literate
whites. Fraud was still practiced in the count, too. Nearly a decade
after the turn of the century a Charlestonian told a traveller of an
election in which he and other Negroes cast Republican ballots,
but the result as announced showed not a single Republican vote.[87]

The Democratic primary, which was first held on a direct statewide basis in 1896, soon became the real election.[88] It has already
been indicated that the Tillmanites had inaugurated in 1890 a rule
that no Negro should vote in the Democratic primaries unless he
had voted Democratic in 1876 and ever since. The quiet establishment of the statewide white primary served to bulwark more
strongly than the Constitution of 1895 the achievement of disfranchisement. Already eliminated from any prospect of influencing
general elections, Negroes were thus eliminated completely from
the only election that had any real meaning.

Meanwhile, one more futile effort was made to revitalize the
Republican party. Early in 1896 a movement was started under the
direction of Lawson D. Melton for the organization of white
Republican clubs in the state. Although this organization came to
be called "lily-white," it was soon learned that George W. Murray
and other Negroes were associated with Melton. When the state
convention of the "Reorganized Republicans" was held in Columbia,
it was found that there were only 54 white delegates among a total
of 250.

The leadership, however, was impressive. In addition to such old
line white Republicans as Melton and Ellery M. Brayton, the group
included W. W. Russell, formerly a Grange and Greenback leader,
and Clarence S. Nettles of Darlington, previously a Conservative.
Negro delegates included such familiar figures as Murray, James
Wigg, W. J. Whipper, S. E. Smith, and George Herriot. But most

---

[87] William Archer, *Through Afro-America, An English Reading of the Race
Problem* (London, 1910), pp. 172-73.

[88] In accordance with a change in the party constitution in 1894. Yorkville
Enquirer, September 26, 1894. For laws establishing the primary, see *Acts and
Joint Resolutions* (1888), pp. 11-12; (1896), p. 56. For registration and
election laws under the new constitution, see *ibid.* (1896), pp. 29-48.

conspicuous of all was the former Tillmanite, Samson Pope of Newberry, who had been independent candidate for governor in 1894, and who was now elected chairman of the "Reorganized Republicans." In addition to supporting generally Republican principles, the party pledged itself to set aside a state constitution" . . . tainted with fraud in its origin; . . . fraudulent in its character, and fraudulent in that it was foisted upon the State without ratification by a popular vote."[89]

In the national convention, however, the regular faction, led by E. A. Webster, Robert Smalls, and Thomas E. Miller, was seated.[90] Attempts at merger were unsuccessful, and both groups put out state tickets.[91] Neither faction, however, was able to put out a state ticket in 1898, although the division of South Carolina Republicans continued, with the "regulars" subsisting on the patronage.

In 1897 George W. Murray, in accordance with the promise of the "Reorganized Republicans," presented to Congress a memorial signed by 355 citizens of South Carolina against counting the electoral vote of the state. The memorial declared that a vast majority of the legally qualified voters of the state were prevented from voting, and that the election was held under the "so-called Constitution of 1895" which was "illegal both in its conception and execution" because of the registration law under which it was called and under which its members were chosen, because the delegates refused to take an oath to support the constitution and laws of the United States, because the constitution was not submitted to the people for ratification, and because its suffrage clause was designed to disfranchise voters in violation of the act of Congress which had readmitted the state to the union in 1868. The petitioners prayed Congress to "take such action as may be necessary to restore a constitutional government to this State and repair the breaches in the Constitution of our country."[92]

Murray, however, apparently still hopeful for the new Republican movement to attract white voters into the party and conscious of

---

[89] Columbia *State,* April 15, 1896; Charleston *News and Courier,* April 15, 1896.

[90] Charleston *News and Courier,* June 14, 1896.

[91] Columbia *State,* September 18, October 8, 1896. The vote for governor in 1896 was W. H. Ellerbe, Democrat, 59,424; Samson Pope, Reorganized Republican, 4,432; R. M. Wallace, Regular Republican, 2,780. *Reports and Resolutions* (1897), p. 15; *see also ibid.* (1899), p. 258.

[92] Columbia *State,* February 9, 1897.

the futility of any effort to overthrow the new constitution by action of Congress, quietly let it be known that he would not push action on the memorial, and it was buried in committee. For this inaction he was branded by Thomas E. Miller "a heartless traitor" to the race. "Nothing can justify his bragging about what he intended to do in securing the franchise of the negroes of the south," said Miller, "and cowardly deserting them before the battle was on. The negroes of the nation will never forgive him."[93]

But the Negro vote, even during the period that it was "legally" proscribed, continued to be the bogey that prevented whites from dividing into two parties or from breaking out of the restrictions imposed by the Democratic primary.[94] With the fading of the Tillman Movement, essentially reactionary in its ultimate results, the state began to relapse into its wonted conservatism. Observers who witnessed the process could well speculate on the prophetic nature of the story Thomas E. Miller told the convention of 1895 about the Tillmanite snake that swallowed the Conservative catfish only to get its throat cut by the fins. The great fear of the Negro vote palsied those who had liberal or progressive tendencies and white Democrats were frequently elected by direct appeals to racial prejudice. The conservative leaders of the state followed a policy of moving very gently or not at all, lest the Negro vote be brought back to life.

---

[93] *Ibid.*, February 12, 1897.

[94] Negroes were declared eligible to vote in the Democratic primary by Judge J. Waties Waring in the case of *Elmore v. Rice* (1947) on the principle that the primary, as an integral part of the election, comes under the Fifteenth Amendment. 72 Federal Supplement 516.

6

NEGROES IN AGRICULTURE

IMPORTANT and dramatic as was the story of disfranchisement, it is to the farms and the fields that one must look for an understanding of the individual lives of a vast majority of the Negro people.

During the period of Reconstruction the productivity of South Carolina agriculture had been built back slowly and painfully toward the level it had reached under the slave regime. The production of cotton by the end of Reconstruction nearly reached the level it had attained before the war, and by 1880 far surpassed the ante-bellum production. After 1880 cotton dominated the agriculture of the state more completely than it had in 1860, so that South Carolina was the leading cotton producing state.[1]

In the production of rice South Carolina also held the lead most of the remainder of the century, although in the over-all picture rice was only one of several minor crops. The growing of this ante-bellum staple continued in the tidewater counties of Beaufort, Colleton, Charleston, Berkeley, and Georgetown until the severe hurricanes of 1893, 1910, and 1911 damaged the plantations so seriously that they could not recover in the face of increasing competition from Louisiana, Arkansas, and Texas. The lowlands where it had been grown were not suited to the production of other crops, and those areas saw a gradual exodus of the Negro laborers.[2]

---

[1] Cotton production was, in bales: 1860—353, 412; 1870—224, 500; 1880—522, 548; 1890—747, 190; 1900—881, 422. Bureau of the Census, *Eleventh Census of the United States: 1890* (Washington, 1892), V, 96; *ibid.* (1900), VI, 425.

[2] *Census* (1890), V, 98; *ibid.* (1900), VI, 94; Duncan Clinch Heyward, *Seed from Madagascar* (Chapel Hill, 1937), gives an account of the rice

Other agricultural products of the state were incidental to the production of cotton and were grown largely for local consumption. Grains, particularly wheat, Indian corn, and oats, were grown widely, as were potatoes. To a lesser extent Irish potatoes were important, along with hogs and cattle, but none of these represented a major economic activity.[3] During the last three decades of the century truck farming became an important activity along the coast, particularly in the area of Charleston, from which fresh vegetables could be transported to the Northern market in forty hours. Between 1879 and 1899, the value of market garden products sold grew from $84,363 to $1,213,759.[4]

By the end of the Reconstruction period the slave labor system for the cultivation of cotton by organized gangs of laborers had been replaced by systems of tenancy, sharecropping, and wage labor the major features of which had become stabilized in the decade following the war. With variations depending upon locale, the landowners, and the personal qualities of individual Negroes themselves, many Negro farm laborers had acquired a degree of independence unlike anything known under the old regime. Yet, for the basic necessities of land, supplies and tools most of the rural Negroes continued to be as completely dependent upon the whites as they had been in the days of slavery.

To a superficial observer, the most striking feature of the new dispensation was the greater dispersal of the rural Negro population together with a tendency of rural Negroes to gather in new settlements near the outskirts of towns and villages. Formerly kept in slave cabins clustered near the residence of the owner or overseer, free Negroes showed a tendency to desert these "relics of their former subjection." The slave quarters on isolated plantations continued to be inhabited, but for the most part they were by the mid-seventies "tenantless and going to ruin."[5]

---

industry in South Carolina from beginning to end with particular emphasis on the part played by the Heyward family, rice planters for many years. For a paternalistic white viewpoint of Negro life on a Georgetown County rice plantation at the turn of the century, see Patience Pennington [Elizabeth Waties Allston Pringle], A Woman Rice Planter (New York, 1913).

[3] Census (1890), V, 93-99; ibid. (1900), VI, 78, 82, 90, 318, 320, 325, 330.

[4] Ibid. (1890), V, 10; ibid. (1900), VI, 322; Philip Alexander Bruce, The Rise of the New South (Philadelphia, 1905), pp. 63-67.

[5] A South Carolinian, "South Carolina Society," Atlantic Monthly, XXXIX (June, 1877), 678.

The Negro cabins in a typical rural district were "dotted here and there at considerable intervals about one of the old plantations," many of them hidden in the low growth of scrub oak or palmetto, with "only a blue line of smoke rising from the low chimney" to indicate their locations. Most of them had no window glasses and the chimneys were frequently made of crossed sticks stuck together with a mixture of moss and clay.[6] The dwellings were frequently of one room, although by the nineties they were usually of two and, infrequently, three rooms. The average home for Negro tenants on a plantation near Jamison, "wearing a disconsolate, tumble-down air," was described as

> . . . a square frame building, unsealed, with a door opening out of a little porch or piazza, and another door or a window opening exactly opposite the first, making a current of air through the house. The chimney is built on one end, and opposite the wide chimney place a partition extending to the ceiling is invariably run across just beyond the door and window described, making almost half the house into another room, which also contains one or two windows, the door opening out into the larger or living room. There is no glass in the windows, which are furnished only with heavy, awkward wooden shutters.[7]

A cultivated Negro, visiting his native state as reporter for a Northern paper, found these hovels "horrible to behold," "uninviting without . . . cheerless within."[8]

A Negro girl born on an Up Country farm in the eighties later recalled her home as a "two-room, frame dwelling which stood at the edge of a sloping field not far from the red clay road," with nearby "an old well, an apple orchard, and an abandoned sawmill." In a garden patch near the house her "mother tended the tomatoes, okra, onions, mustard and turnip plants; in the fields below, father drove his plow through long rows of corn, cotton, and molasses cane." Flower seeds were too extravagant for this tenant family,

---

[6] Isaac Dubose Seabrook, "Before and After, or, The Relation of the Races in the South" (unpublished manuscript in South Caroliniana Library, University of South Carolina, 1895), Chapter III, p. 13.

[7] Charleston *News and Courier,* November 25, 1894, quoting correspondence dated October 29, 1894, from Olive F. Gundby, Jamison, South Carolina, to New York *Evening Post.*

[8] T. McCants Stewart in New York *Age,* May 16, 1885.

but the mother surrounded the cabin with "house leaks" which she had dug up in the woods and planted under the roof drip, and "Four o'clocks bordered the yard, dreamily fragrant in the late afternoon, and between the house and the barn was a row of sunflowers."[9]

The basic diet for the rural family was the ubiquitous "hog and hominy," with occasional delicacies like wheat bread and brown sugar for the coffee. Families that were able to take root in a single location had gardens and poultry; those in more favorable circumstances had pigs and cows.[10] The basic diet in most parts of the state could be supplemented by hunting and fishing, but it was considered desirable by the whites that a Negro should not waste his time in such frivolous pursuits.[11]

Rural Negroes were described by a white contemporary as "ambitious to increase the comforts of life, as well as to give leisure to their females and education to their children."[12] But the exigencies of economic necessity usually forced Negro women to work in the fields. The children, as soon as they were of sufficient size, were also required to help. Infants were taken by their mothers into the fields or left in the cabins with children only slightly larger than themselves. Newspapers frequently reported the death of Negro children in cabins that burned while their parents were away working in the fields.[13]

The desire of rural Negroes for independence can be seen in the observation of a contemporary who found them afflicted with "the fatal disposition that has been the curse of Ireland: the desire, if I may so put it, to burrow in a hole. They will buy an acre or two, build a cottage, move in, and live in sloth and filthiness on what they can raise on their half-cultivated lot."[14] In many parts of the state, there was a willingness on the part of white landowners to have Negroes become owners of small plots, because they

---

[9] Jane Edna Hunter, *A Nickle and a Prayer* (Cleveland, 1940), p. 13.

[10] A South Carolinian, *Atlantic Monthly,* XXXIX (June, 1877), 678-79.

[11] The Greenville *Enterprise and Mountaineer,* February 21, 1883, said in praise of Robert C. Williman of Reedy River Factory, "an exception among the colored race," that "He is a thorough worker, and keeps away from whiskey, neither does he lose his time fishing or hunting."

[12] A South Carolinian, *Atlantic Monthly,* XXXIX (June, 1887), 679.

[13] Charleston *News and Courier,* November 25, 1894, quoting O. F. Gundby in New York *Evening Post.*

[14] A South Carolinian, *Atlantic Monthly,* XXXIX (June, 1877), 679.

thereby became more or less fixed to the soil and provided a ready and ample supply of labor whenever it was needed.[15] On the other hand, some Negro families lived a migratory existence, moving from one farm to another in search of better locations. William Pickens, born on an Up Country farm in 1881, recalled that his family moved "over the river" to Price's place when he was two years old. A year or so later the family moved from Price's to "Clark's place," and after another year moved to Pendleton. From that time until he was eighteen, he could recall "no less than twenty removals of our family."[16]

Despite frequent complaint by whites of the sloth and general worthlessness of the "proverbially ignorant fieldhands of the interior and upland sections" and the "hopelessly ignorant and debased" Negroes living in "the miasmas of the rice and island cotton plantation . . . ,"[17] the whites generally by the end of Reconstruction had come to accept Negroes as the best available labor. Said the Charleston *News and Courier:*

> The colored man, from his habits of life, familiarity with our system of farming, tractability and the cheaper rate at which he is content to live, is believed by most people to be the best laborer that can be had for this country. . . . The Negro with all his failings is the best and the only available successful laborer we have. He is accustomed to the ways of our people, is capable of enduring all kinds of drudgery, and above all the almost torrid heat of our summers. [T]he white laborer no sooner begins to prosper than he rises above his keeping, becomes insolent and will not brook command. Not so with the negro. He may *'laugh, grow fat and prosper,'* but still he is the same polite respectful Sambo.[18]

The precedent established in ante-bellum experimentation with white tenant farming was rapidly spread after the Civil War both among the freedmen and the poor whites, owing its rapid spread, though not its origin, to the necessity for other systems of tenure and labor after the abolition of slavery. Negro farm laborers, desirous of independence from the ante-bellum gang system and

---

[15] Campbell, *White and Black*, p. 329.

[16] William Pickens, *Bursting Bonds* (Boston, 1923), pp. 9, 11.

[17] Alexander Kelley McClure, *The South: Its Industrial, Financial and Political Condition* (Philadelphia, 1886), p. 47.

[18] Charleston *News and Courier,* January 21, 1881.

unable to secure the ownership of land, found in various forms of tenancy and sharecropping the most satisfactory available compromise between their wishes and the desire of the whites to maintain close supervision over the labor force.[19]

By 1880 the system had been widely accepted by both whites and Negroes in the Piedmont region as the proper solution to their problems. At first, the freedmen formed an agricultural proletariat, having nothing to offer but their labor. The landlord furnished the land, shelter, rations, seed, tools, stock, and stock-feed, and took one-half of the crop. This system prevailed widely in 1880, although in some sections of the Piedmont, notably Greenville, Fairfield, and Spartanburg counties, the landlord took two-thirds of the crop, leaving only one-third to the laborer. A more favorable arrangement was sometimes reached under which laborers rented the land for a share of the crop, for a specified amount of the crop, or even for cash, and furnished their own supplies. Where the arrangement was for a share of the crop the landlord's portion usually amounted to one-third or one-fourth.[20] Cash rental, of course, varied from place to place, depending upon the value of the land, but in 1880 it generally ranged between $3 and $5 per acre.[21]

In the lower portions of the state a somewhat different plan prevailed, involving a sharing of the land rather than of the crop. Here the compromise of Negro laborers with white landlords brought about a system that more nearly resembled the ante-bellum gang system. Under an early version of this plan the laborer worked under supervision and in return received a house, rations, three acres of land separate from the plantation, and a mule and plow every other Saturday to work it, with $16 in cash at the end of the year. But in 1867 a number of laborers proposed to work only four days, feed themselves, and take double the land and mule work.[22] In 1879 it was reported in Kershaw County that most of the labor contracts took this form.[23] With the passage of years variations on the system required laborers to work from two to five

---

[19] For a discussion of ante-bellum tenancy, see Marjorie Mendenhall, "The Rise of Southern Tenancy," *Yale Review,* XXVII (September, 1937), 110-29.

[20] *Handbook of 1883,* pp. 155-56.

[21] *Ibid.,* pp. 156-57.

[22] *Ibid.,* p. 83.

[23] Columbia *Daily Register,* January 28, 1879.

days a week with various amounts of land and other perquisites in return.[24]

On the sea islands south of Charleston the "two day" variant became widely established.[25] Under this system on Edisto Island the Negro laborer was furnished with five to seven acres of land, a house, and the privilege of using the wood on his place. In return he promised to give two days of work each week, usually performed Monday and Tuesday, and the rest of the week he had to work his own crop. In a survey made during 1880 it was reported that the laborer was expected to work two "tasks," or half an acre a day (in some places an acre a day), so that during the week he cultivated one or two acres for the landlord.[26] A reporter for the Charleston *News and Courier* said that he "should think the negroes would be very well satisfied, as I have seen them returning from the fields having accomplished their day's work by 9 o'clock in the morning. The head of the family puts his wife and children to work, and accomplishes in three hours what it would take him all day to do."[27]

Wage labor was the least popular system with Negro workers because of the lack of independence that it entailed, but it was widely lauded by the white planters because it permitted them to exercise a close control not only over the laborer but over methods of cultivation. Wages for this type of labor fluctuated between forty and seventy-five cents a day. This was in addition to shelter, fuel, and board, which usually consisted of a ration of three pounds of bacon and one peck of grits a week.[28] But in particularly bad times

---

[24] *Handbook of 1883*, pp. 83-84.

[25] For an example of a "two day" contract, see contract dated January 10, 1880, in James B. and R. B. Heyward Papers, Southern Historical Collection, University of North Carolina.

[26] The Charleston *News and Courier*, April 22, 1880, carries a lengthy survey by J. K. Blackman of conditions on John's, James, Wadmalaw, and Edisto islands, the major sea islands to the south of Charleston; *see also* Harry Hammond, "Cotton Production," *Census* (1880), VI, 60-61.

[27] Charleston *News and Courier*, April 22, 1880.

[28] *Ibid.; Handbook of 1883*, pp. 29, 65, 83, 98, 164. The state commissioner of agriculture reported in 1885 an average wage for male farm laborers of $0.45 per day, $8.72 per month, and $90.75 per year with board. "Annual Report of the Commissioner of Agriculture of the State of South Carolina, 1885," *Reports and Resolutions* (1885), II, 105; *see also* William C. and E. T. Coker, "Day Labor Account Book for 1880," South Caroliniana Library, University of South Carolina, which shows daily wages of forty to seventy-five cents for various jobs.

wages sank to lower levels. Around Jamison in 1894 they were generally thirty cents a day.[29]

During the cotton-picking season, when great numbers of rural Negroes hired out, wages were paid to pickers on the basis of weight, generally ranging from thirty to fifty cents per hundred pounds. In one week of September, 1879, Albert Grant of Darlington County and four members of his family received wages of $8.54 for 2,138 pounds of cotton—payment at the rate of forty cents a hundred pounds. Duncan Dixon, with Kate and Peg (apparently his wife and daughter), working Monday through Wednesday (Kate and Peg working only Wednesday), was credited with wages of $4.16. One dollar of this he received in cash, together with corn, flour, tobacco, coffee, molasses, and bacon from the landlords' store to the amount of $4.10, thereby going into debt to the landlords for ninety-four cents.[30]

Wages for cotton picking in this region apparently remained constant, for it was reported twelve years later that forty cents per hundred pounds was being paid.[31] On the Fantz Plantation near Pendleton in the late eighties, the rate was thirty cents,[32] while in the neighborhood of Orangeburg the rate in 1891 was forty cents.[33] The father of Jane Edna Hunter, an Up Country Negro farmer, after giving up his livestock and farm equipment to move into the town of Pendleton in 1890, found that he could get work digging ditches on nearby farms for seventy-five cents a rod. On some days he was able to dig as much as one and a half rods, and found wage labor more profitable than tenant farming had been.[34]

Wages, however, were sometimes better on paper than in reality. Despite state legislation passed in 1872 to force employers to pay plantation laborers in currency, the laborer frequently received payment in scrip redeemable at some definite or indefinite future date or valid only in the plantation stores. A loophole in the law permitted payment in scrip where there was specific provision for

---

[29] Charleston *News and Courier*, November 25, 1894, quoting O. F. Gundby in New York *Evening Post*.

[30] William C. and E. T. Coker, "Cotton Account Book, 1879-1884," South Caroliniana Library, University of South Carolina, pp. 2-3.

[31] Charleston *News and Courier*, September 12, 1891.

[32] Hunter, *A Nickle and a Prayer*, p. 26.

[33] Charleston *News and Courier*, September 13, 1891.

[34] Hunter, *A Nickle and a Prayer*, pp. 23-24.

it in the labor contract,[35] but it seems unlikely that it was always necessary to utilize this loophole in order to evade the intent of the law. Sometimes payment took the form of credits in the books of the plantation store. Thus the family of Duncan Dixon (mentioned above) took its week's wages for cotton picking in the form of merchandise. The system of payment in scrip was especially prevalent on rice plantations.

The state's one Negro congressman, Thomas E. Miller, in 1891 presented a number of plantation checks for publication in the *Congressional Record*. One read "Due the bearer 25 CENTS For plantation work, Payable March 1, 1889. A. M. MANIGAULT. Jan. 1, 1885." Another check was good for "$2 TWO DOLLARS $2 For labor under contract," with no specified date of payment. Other checks were inscribed "Good for 25 TWENTY-FIVE CENTS 25 In trade," "Eldorado Plantation, 25 CENTS In merchandise," and "PALO ALTO STORE. Due the bearer in trade 25 CTS. J. & S. C. DOSS."[36] "No one knows but God," said Miller, "how many heartaches and disappointments these promises to pay have caused the innocent holders, for in many cases the employers failed long before the time of their redemption, and left the laborer poor indeed, with no possession other than the remembrance of how he toiled and how magnificently his master entertained upon the fruit of his labor."[37]

The general desire of Negro farmers to become independent landowners has already been noted. However, after the early days of Reconstruction there was little active attention given in government policy to the possibility of establishing the freedmen as landowners. During the Civil War, in the area of Port Royal and St. Helena Islands, a quantity of land had been confiscated in default of a special direct tax levied by Congress and sold to Northerners and Negroes. The number of purchasers was 2,300 and the amount sold was 23,844 acres.[38] Much of this land remained in the hands of Negroes after the war, and was tenaciously held by them, so that as late as the 1930's St. Helena Island constituted a unique

---

[35] *Statutes at Large*, XV, 216.

[36] *Congressional Record*, XXII (51st Congress, 2d Session), pp. 2695-96.

[37] *Ibid.*, p. 2694.

[38] *Handbook of 1883*, p. 431; Charleston *News and Courier*, December 26, 1888, quoting Thomas D. Howard, "The Freedman's Paradise," *Unitarian Review*, n. d.

society of "black yeomanry" that attracted the special attention and study of sociologists.[39]

In January, 1865, General William T. Sherman issued his famous Field Order No. 15, setting aside the sea islands from Charleston south and the rice plantations for thirty miles inland for the exclusive use of Negroes, but this measure was undone four months later by President Johnson.[40] Lengthy discussion of the land question in the Radical constitutional convention of 1868 culminated in the authorization of a land commission, which was later established by the legislature with authority to issue bonds to the amount of $900,000 to purchase lands for sale in small plots to settlers.[41] This, however, was of scant significance in view of the fact that the total agricultural property in the state was valued at $59,535,219 in 1870,[42] and much of the money available to the land commission was reported to have been frittered away by corruption.[43]

The landholdings of the black yeomanry created in Beaufort County during the Civil War were generally small, ranging from one to twenty-five acres. Cotton was seldom cultivated on more than fifteen acres under one management. In 1880 Harry Hammond described the area thus:

> Much of the land is uncultivated, and the remainder, in small patches, varying from one-eighth of an acre and less to three acres in size, is planted in corn, cotton, and sweet potatoes, curiously intermingled. Nowhere in the State, not even among the gardens on Charleston Neck, is the system of small culture so strikingly illustrated. The farmers usually own a cow, a mule or horse, and the work stock is sufficiently numerous, though of a very inferior quality. Farm fixtures are of the simplest and cheapest description. There is seldom any shelter for the stock, the cabin of the proprietor being generally the only house on the premises. The stock is fed on marsh grass, with a little corn, and is, in a large measure, sub-

---

[39] Thomas Jackson Woofter, *Black Yeomanry* (New York, 1930); Guion Griffis Johnson, *A Social History of the Sea Islands, with Special Reference to St. Helena Island, South Carolina* (Chapel Hill, 1930); Guy Benton Johnson, *Folk Culture on St. Helena Island, South Carolina* (Chapel Hill, 1930).

[40] Simkins and Woody, *South Carolina During Reconstruction*, pp. 28-32.

[41] Taylor, *The Negro in South Carolina During the Reconstruction*, pp. 133-34, 164-65.

[42] *Census* (1890), V, 94.

[43] Taylor, *The Negro in South Carolina During the Reconstruction*, pp. 54-55.

sisted by being picketed out, when not at work, to graze on such weeds as the fallow spontaneously furnishes. Plows are numerous enough, but the chief reliance is upon the hoe, which, for several generations, was the only implement known to agriculturists on this coast.[44]

In the late sixties the phosphate mining industry had its beginnings, and in the eighties grew to enormous proportions in Beaufort County. Phosphates and related industries provided numerous jobs for the men of the area.[45] During Reconstruction the Port Royal and Augusta Railroad was completed and many of the men found jobs on the road or in the harbor of Port Royal loading and unloading vessels.[46] Not the least of the advantages enjoyed by the workers of this region was the political influence, no doubt built upon economic independence as well as preponderance of population, that Negroes had under the leadership of men like Robert Smalls, W. J. Whipper, and Thomas E. Miller.

The St. Helena area, despite the fact that it, too, had its share of white merchants and the lien system, was generally regarded as something of an idyllic racial island. Sir George Campbell, after a visit with Robert Smalls to the island, was favorably impressed. "These country people", he said, "seem to have many carts and nice ponies. Their houses are tolerable, and altogether seem to be comfortable. The farms seem fairly cultivated, especially the cotton crop. The houses have all been built since the war, and some of them show signs of decided improvement."[47] A Northern visitor who had been in the area during the war found a decade later continued improvement, which he attributed largely to the work of the Penn Normal and Industrial School at Frogmore. He found newly built houses with second stories or half stories added, and glazed windows in the place of the board shutters. Occasionally Venetian blinds appeared, and he found to his surprise that internal furnishings sometimes included sewing machines and cabinet organs.[48]

---

[44] *Handbook of 1883*, p. 31.
[45] See Chapter VII.
[46] The Port Royal Railroad was opened March 1, 1873. Reorganized as Port Royal and Augusta Railroad in 1878. Henry V. Poor, *Manual of the Railroads of the United States for 1883* (New York, 1883), p. 451; Hammond, in *Census* (1880), VI, 61.
[47] Campbell, *White and Black*, p. 343.
[48] Charleston *News and Courier*, December 26, 1888, quoting Howard, "The Freedman's Paradise," *Unitarian Review*, n. d.

However, it was noted that the small landholdings resulted in a thriftless use of the land. There was reputed to be a constantly diminishing area of arable land "resulting from the very imperfect system of culture their lack of means forces them to adopt." A survey in 1913 showed that in the four "blackest townships" the area owned by Negroes had diminished from 62,195½ acres in 1876 to 50,913 acres in 1912 while at the same time the number of owners had increased almost threefold so that the average size of the Negro landholding had decreased from 25.9 acres to 7 acres. Much of this decrease resulted from subdivision of the land among heirs.[49]

A devastating blow, from which the area was long in recovering, was struck in 1893 by the severe hurricane of August 27, which completely inundated the low-lying sea islands. It was estimated that 1,000 lives were lost on the islands near Beaufort, and the growing crops were ruined by the salt water. The phosphate industry also was paralyzed by the blow, and never recovered in that area.[50]

A comparison of the amount of land sold under the provisions of the wartime confiscation with the statistics of Negro land ownership in the area of Beaufort in 1876 shows that the greater amount of acreage was obtained by Negroes through their own efforts. In the remainder of the state this was universally the means whereby Negro farmers came into possession of the land. Faced by an economic situation in which the whites were dominant, many of them nevertheless succeeded remarkably in realizing the goal of home ownership set by editor William Holloway of Charleston, who advised his Negro readers: "Nothing can be accomplished, by waiting for somebody to do something for you, or for some political change to effect a benefit in your behalf. The wiser plan is to get to work yourself, and see that your affairs are put in shape for any circumstance that may arise. . . . Nothing is more important than getting a home. . . ."[51]

By 1880 a small minority of Negro farmers were reported as owning their homes or farms. In Greenville County sixteen per cent

[49] Christensen, "Fifty Years of Freedom: Conditions in the Sea Coast Regions," *Annals of the American Academy of Political and Social Science,* XLIX (September, 1913), 63.

[50] *Appleton's Annual Cyclopaedia.* XVIII (1893), 691.

[51] Charleston *New Era,* April 7, 1883.

owned either house or land. In Spartanburg, Fairfield, Chester, and Laurens the proportion was estimated as five per cent. In Newberry, York, and Abbeville, the number was negligible.[52] In the Upper Pine Belt, about five per cent were reported as owners in Aiken County, and from three to five per cent in Marlboro and Marion.[53] In the Lower Pine Belt county of Colleton, only about two per cent owned land or houses.[54]

Wherever Negro farmers achieved noticeable success the white press was quick to point with pride. The *News and Courier*, in connection with a report on successful Negro farmers stated that ". . . there is nothing in his [the Negro's] present condition to excite the commiseration of 'the great Christian North,' or warrant the untempered conclusions of many eminent would-be political philosophers of that section."[55] One of the well-to-do Negroes was Joseph Alexander Owens, described as "the largest property holder and most successful colored man in Barnwell County." At the close of the war he had owned no property. By 1881 he owned two stores, had a productive plantation, and a credit of $5,000 in Savannah. He was a Democratic representative in the state legislature.

Ben Garrett of the Blue House section of Colleton County owned nothing at the end of the war. By 1881 he had 105 acres of land, was out of debt, and had money to lend.[56] Sea Island Negroes, on John's, James, Wadmalaw, and Edisto Islands were estimated to own more than ten thousand acres of land, valued at $300,000.[57] The Orangeburg *Democrat* reported in 1881 an unusual number of land conveyances in the county, about one-third of them for land purchased by Negroes. "Our Northern friends," said the *Democrat*, "who charge the South with a desire to keep the negroes from becoming landowners may stick a pin here."[58]

Within a few miles of Newberry, in the Piedmont, Lewis Duckett was the owner of a plantation of 796 acres, 9 head of stock, 10 milk cows, 4 yearlings, and 25 hogs. He reported his crop, on the

---

[52] *Handbook of 1883*, p. 155.
[53] *Ibid.*, pp. 84-85.
[54] *Ibid.*, p. 59.
[55] Charleston *News and Courier*, January 5, 1881.
[56] *Ibid.*
[57] *Ibid.*, April 22, 1880.
[58] Columbia *Daily Register*, February 25, 1881, quoting Orangeburg *Democrat*, February 24, 1881.

portion of the farm he managed himself, as 61 bales of cotton, 1,200 bushels of corn, and 800 bushels of red rust proof oats. His renters made 57 bales of cotton, 700 bushels of oats, and 150 bushels of wheat. He estimated that his farm would bring $7,000 at auction.[59] On Edisto Island in 1880 John Thorne owned 250 acres of land, a large store and storehouse, a gin-house with six gins, and was reputed to be worth between $15,000 and $20,000 [60] The holdings of these individuals are impressive when compared to the average size of 143 acres for all farms in the state.[61]

Independent merchants who frequently doubled as planters and landlords were the sources of supplies and rations for the rural populace. Plantation stores were prevalent especially where the gang system was established. Through the plantation stores the landlords supplied laborers who had been promised rations under sharecropping or land sharing contracts, and sold to those who had cash or had been credited with wages on the books or in scrip. The plantation Negroes sometimes bought supplies for a week at one time, but enjoyed livening up their uneventful lives by crowding into the stores each night to buy daily supplies.[62]

Country stores independent of plantations were more numerous, supplying Negroes who owned their farms or who had tenant contracts under which they furnished their own supplies and rations, and providing the supplies for landlords who had agreed to "stand for" the tenants. Almost invariably the merchants were forced to advance their merchandise on a promise of future payment, and always in such cases they assumed a lien on the crop to be produced by the person receiving the merchandise. Because of the great risk involved, the lack of competition, and the complete dependence of the farmers on them, the merchants charged from twenty-five to a hundred per cent markup or interest on supplies furnished on promise of future payment.[63]

It was reported in 1880 that in the Piedmont region, "The system of credits and advances prevails to a large extent, consuming from one-third to three-fifths of the crop before it is harvested." In eleven counties of the Piedmont that year the number of liens

---

[59] Columbia *Daily Register*, February 27, 1881.
[60] Charleston *News and Courier*, April 22, 1880.
[61] *Census* (1890), V, 92.
[62] Heyward, *Seed from Madagascar*, p. 183.
[63] Columbia *Daily Register*, December 9, 1881.

nearly equalled the number of farms.[64] An anonymous letter in the Columbia *Daily Register* in 1881 indicated the severe incidence of markups and interest by suggesting that the usury law be amended to permit loans at twelve per cent instead of seven, a limit which made cash credit unavailable. Farmers could then supply their needs more cheaply with cash and landlords could supply their tenants at the relatively low rate of twenty-five per cent in order to lessen their burden![65]

The lien system also served to ensnare the farmers and croppers into growing a continuous round of cotton. The merchant who took a lien demanded a cash crop on which he could realize quickly if he had to foreclose.

Despite the evils and frequent denunciations of the system, Negro tenants and owners who were able to supply themselves through it sometimes found kind words for a scheme that freed them to a degree from control by landlords. "Their consolation," said a white editor, "and it is fallacious, is that they are perfectly free from control by any one, and while the lien law will give them credit, they will continue to live under this foolish delusion."[66]

Robert Simmons, a Negro farmer of Berkeley County, remarked in the state senate that "He had been poor and had been forced to mortgage his crops to get supplies, but by good management had accumulated property and become so well off that at present he could afford to make advances himself to his poorer neighbors."[67] Without the lien system, said Simmons, he would have been forced to give up farming. Mat Garrett, a Negro farmer of Greenville County, also demonstrated the way in which good use might be made of the lien system. In 1879 he rented a small farm and went into debt for both guano and supplies. The first year he made enough surplus to buy a mule and to pay all of his expenses for the following year, except for guano. By late summer of 1882 he estimated his prospective crop as thirteen bales of cotton, two hundred and fifty bushels of corn, one hundred pounds of tobacco, and forty or fifty bushels of peas. In the spring he had harvested twenty-five bushels of wheat. He and his wife alone had accomplished this without going into debt after the first two years. They

---

[64] *Handbook of 1883*, p. 154.
[65] Columbia *Daily Register*, December 9, 1881.
[66] Columbia *Daily Register*, December 5, 1877, quoting the *Keowee Courier*.
[67] Columbia *Daily Register*, December 16, 1884.

still had on hand enough corn and bacon to supply them for the remainder of the year and enough hogs to supply the next year's bacon.[68]

But for the less able and less fortunate contemporaries of Robert Simmons and Mat Garrett the picture was not so bright. Under the furnishing system the Negro tenants generally turned their crops over at the end of the year to the party advancing to them, and after paying their debts, received the balance, if any. The family of William Pickens, living at the foothills of the mountains, found that "It always took the whole of what was earned to pay for the scant 'rations' that were advanced to the family, and at settlement time there would be a margin of debt to keep the family perennially bound to a virtual owner." This family managed to escape virtual serfdom because a man in Pendleton who ran a bar and hotel was willing to pay off the margin of debt and move the family to town in order to have the father become a man of all work and the mother a cook. "They went," said Pickens, "as one instinctively moves from a greater toward a lesser pain."[69]

But the greater pain of perennial indebtedness was inescapable for most, and the whole system was an invitation to the practice of deceit and fraud by sharp-dealing merchants. A white observer said: "The entire earnings of these people, pass through the hands of local white traders, and are greatly reduced in the process. To these traders they look for every class of goods for use or adornment which they need or do not need, from a pin to coffin; from a pound of bacon to the decision of a personal quarrel. . . . The goods which they purchase are usually of coarse quality and low grade, but they do not buy them at correspondingly low prices. The profits charged on goods are far higher than they ought to be in a healthy business. . . ." He concluded that "the worst foe of the struggling negro race is the cunning white man of low tone, be he trader or politician. He is the vampire who sucks and never sates. . . . Thus there is possible a species of free slavery, this slavery of free ignorance to designing wit, cunning and greed."[70]

Of 4,645 stores in the state in 1880 Negroes owned only 49. They operated 25 in the coastal region, 5 in the Lower Pine Belt, 16 in

---

[68] Greenville *Enterprise and Mountaineer,* August 30, 1882.

[69] P ckens, *Bursting Bonds,* p. 13.

[70] S abrook, "Before and After," Chapter III, p. 16.

the Upper Pine Belt, and 3 in the Piedmont.[71] At the end of the century only 457 Negroes listed themselves with census enumerators as merchants and dealers, some of whom were probably clerks and many of whom were located in the towns.[72] Here and there affluent Negroes like Robert Simmons of Berkeley County and John Thorne of Edisto Island, were in a position to make advances to their colored neighbors, but on the whole the rural Negroes were dependent upon the economically dominant whites. "As the negro establishes no supply stores of his own," a white commented in 1895, "and waives all competition he is compelled to accept the salesman's dictum."[73]

The lien system had grown up without plan and probably with little realization that it was to become a permanent system of agricultural credit. In the first years after the war the planters found it impossible to offer any other security for advances than anticipated crops, for land was too cheap to be acceptable security. The General Assembly in 1866 gave legal recognition to this system. Persons making advances became entitled to a lien on the crop in preference of all other liens, provided a contract were made in writing by the parties to the agreement and duly registered in the county courthouse.[74]

The lien law of 1866 was retained on the statute books by the Radical Republicans, with the addition of a clause that gave the laborer, whether working on shares or for wages, a prior lien on the crop.[75] While that addition was left on the statute books by the Democrats, it was obviously difficult for impoverished laborers to enforce their rights, and this legislation was rendered less and less meaningful by changes enacted in subsequent Democratic legislatures.

Bourbon legislators shifted the emphasis toward the expansion of the legal privileges of the landlord. Grievances of landlords against merchants found frequent expression in the press and in the legislature long before Ben Tillman organized his movement

---

[71] *Handbook of 1883*, p. 661.

[72] Bureau of the Census, *Negroes in the United States* (Washington, 1904), pp. 184-87.

[73] Seabrook, "Before and After," Chapter III, p. 16.

[74] *Statutes at Large*, XIII, 366$_{12}$-366$_{13}$.

[75] *Revised Statutes of the State of South Carolina* (Columbia, 1873), pp. 557-58. Hereinafter cited as *Revised Statutes* (1873).

of agrarian protest. One objection was that the lien system encouraged the small time poor white and Negro tenant "to squat on poor ridges and set themselves up as farmers, with a bull yearling and a scooter plow, a side of bacon and a few sacks of guano as supplies."[76] In short, advances by merchants made it more difficult for landlords to secure labor on their own terms.

However, no one seemed able to offer a workable substitute for the lien system. The first Democratic legislature, in its special session of 1877, boldly resolved the issue by repealing the legislation guaranteeing merchants' liens, effective January 1, 1878.[77] This move was supported by Negro Republican Hastings Gantt of Beaufort County, who was happy to find the legislature "now disposed to protect the farmers and make them stand on their own responsibility, and learn how to make and to keep what they make. It is our duty to make such laws as to bring our people up to a sense that they must take care of themselves, and not take what they make to the stores and sacrifice it there. The sooner they understand how to get along without this lien law the better." His colleague, Thomas Hamilton, a Negro from the same county, protested. The farmers, he recognized, would require credit in some form, and the proposal to throw them on their own resources was no adequate solution to their needs, for their resources were entirely too scant. Nevertheless, most of the Negro representatives followed Gantt's lead and voted for the repeal proposition.[78]

By the following March, three months after the effectiveness of the repeal, the spring credit situation had become so stringent that the General Assembly reenacted the merchants' lien legislation in precisely the same language. This was intended to be only a temporary expedient, but in December, 1878, the legislation was once again made permanent.[79] Repeal was an inadequate solution in the absence of other sources of agricultural credit, but it was again and again to find advocates among exasperated farmers.[80]

---

[76] Columbia *Daily Register*, December 5, 1877, quoting *Keowee Courier;* *ibid.*, December 14, 1881, quoting letter dated October 5, 1881, from J. B. Humbert, Tumbling Shoals, to Charleston *News and Courier; ibid.*, December 24, 1881, letter dated December 19, 1881, from James R. Magill, Russell Place, Kershaw County.

[77] *Statutes at Large*, XVI, 265.

[78] Columbia *Daily Register*, May 13, 1877; *House Journal* (1877, special session), p. 98.

[79] *Statutes at Large*, XVI, 410-11, 713-14.

[80] See debates in the legislature as reported in Columbia *Daily Register*, December 9, 10, 1881, and December 16, 1884.

Liens for the landlord on the crops raised on his rented lands had been added to the merchants' and laborers' liens by the Republican legislature in 1874. Under that legislation it was provided that the land, whether rented for cash or on shares ". . . shall be deemed and taken to be an advance for agricultural purposes." Upon reducing the condition of this "advance" of land to writing and properly recording it, the landowner was entitled to a lien "in preference to all other liens existing or otherwise, to an amount not exceeding one-third of the entire crop. . . ."[81]

The Democrats, in connection with their reenactment of the merchants' lien law in 1878, strengthened the landlords' liens so that they should be valid over one-third of the crops grown on his land without recording or filing. A lien over more than one-third of the crop, forbidden under Republican legislation, now became permissible if it were reduced to writing and properly filed in the court house.[82] In December, 1878, after the Democrats had secured nearly complete domination of the legislature, the legislation was further strengthened by a clause providing that "the landlord shall have a lien on all the crops raised by the tenant for all advances made by the landlord during the year."[83]

With these changes, strengthening the hold of the landlord over crops grown on his lands, the lien laws assumed permanent shape. In all their essentials the laws had been enacted before the overthrow of the Radical Republicans, and what had started as a temporary expedient to meet the lack of capital immediately after the war, had become the permanent credit system of agriculture. Sporadic opposition to a system that upheld "the thriftless, idle, worthless class,"[84] the merchants, continued to be voiced by the landlord class, which was influential in the Democratic party, and efforts were made again in 1881 and 1884 to repeal the merchants' liens, but they were unsuccessful. In the only available record vote, the three Negro members of the state senate in 1884 all voted with the majority against the repeal of merchants' liens.[85]

The only major legislation with regard to agricultural liens after 1878 was passed in 1884 and 1885. The legislation of 1884 provided

---

[81] *Statutes at Large*, XV, 788, 844.
[82] *Ibid.*, XVI, 410-11.
[83] *Ibid.*, pp. 743-44.
[84] Columbia *Daily Register*, December 9, 1881.
[85] *Senate Journal* (1884), p. 212.

for the enforcement of landlords' and merchants' liens less than
$100 by constables or sheriffs, who were authorized to seize crops
upon the issuance of warrants from trial justices.[86] The act of
1885 clarified earlier legislation by giving priority to the liens in
inverse order to the time of their enactment; first priority to the
landlord's lien for rent, second priority to the laborer's, and third
priority to all other liens. This act also reaffirmed the validity of
the landlord's contract "whether the same be in writing or verbal."[87]

Labor contract laws were a related field of legislation pertinent
to the status of Negro agricultural laborers. In this field, too, it is
significant to find that the Reconstruction legislation was essentially
conservative in nature. All labor contracts, under the Republican
law, had to be witnessed by one or more disinterested persons,
and upon the request of either party, had to be executed before
a trial justice, whose duty it was to read the contract and explain
its contents to the interested parties. Such contracts, it was provided,
"shall clearly set forth the conditions upon which the laborer or
laborers engaged to work, embracing the length of time, the amount
of money to be paid, and when; if it be on shares of crops, what
portion of the crop or crops." Wherever labor was performed on
shares, the division should be made by a mutually acceptable third
party or by the trial justice nearest resident. Punishment was provided for either party's attempting to practice fraud or to remove
the crop surreptitiously. It is significant, however, that if the landlord, his agent, or the "disinterested party" were guilty of fraud,
the punishment was specifically limited, whereas for the laborer
it was not defined. The landlord or his agent was liable to a fine
of from $50 to $500; the disinterested party to a similar fine, or
imprisonment of one month to a year; the laborer was "liable to
fine and imprisonment, according to the gravity of the offence, upon
proof to conviction before a Trial Justice, or a Court of competent
jurisdiction."[88]

One of the most oppressive features of labor contract legislation
was that which permitted verbal contracts. Agreements between
landowner and tenant for periods of less than one year could be
made orally under legislation in effect before the end of the Reconstruction period, and this legislation was preserved jealously as

---

[86] *Statutes at Large*, XVIII, 751-52.
[87] *Ibid.*, XIX, 146.
[88] *Revised Statutes* (1873), pp. 490-92.

an excellent means of labor control.[89] After 1878 it was possible for the landlord to secure a lien over the entire crop by an oral contract.

Among the landlords an attempt to entice away laborers to work on another farm or in another state was a cardinal sin. In addition to extensive use of the power of social pressure to maintain the adherence of laborers to their masters, increasingly stringent legislation was employed. In 1880 it was made a misdemeanor for any person to "entice or persuade, by any means whatsoever, any tenant or tenants, servant or servants, laborer or laborers under contract with another . . . to violate such contract," or even to hire such a person, knowing him to be under contract to another.[90]

In 1889, after the state Supreme Court had invalidated the old Republican legislation providing unequal punishments for persons guilty of fraud in violation of contracts, the Democratic legislature passed a new act which lessened considerably the punishment of landlords and their agents, and provided specifically the same punishment for laborers—a fine of $5 to $100 or imprisonment for ten to thirty days.[91]

The incidence of such laws, of course, fell heavily on the Negro laborer with the instruments of enforcement altogether under the control of the whites. In 1891 Thomas E. Miller complained that his people had ". . . struggled in a land where they receive little assistance from the courts and where the juries are systematically formed to oppress them; where they work often on the promise to pay; where they receive no protection from the labor law. . . ."[92] The use to which the verbal contract was put by white masters is indicated in his complaint that

> In my State, if the employer states verbally that the unpaid laborer of his plantation contracted to work for the year no other farmer dares employ the man if he attempts to break the contract rather than work for nothing: for down there it is a misdemeanor so to do, the penalty is heavy, and the farmer who employs the unpaid, starving laborer of his neighbor is the victim of the court.[93]

---

[89] *Ibid.*, p. 433.
[90] *Statutes at Large*, XVII, 423.
[91] *Ibid.*, XX, 381-82.
[92] *Congressional Record*, XXII (51st Congress, 2d Session), 2693.
[93] *Ibid.*

But in 1897, still not satisfied with its farm labor legislation, the General Assembly enacted a law to provide punishment for the laborer who had received advances in money or supplies and afterward failed to perform "the reasonable service required of him by the terms of the said contract." Such persons were liable to imprisonment of twenty to thirty days or fines of $25 to $100.[94]

Actual enforcement of the 1889 and 1897 legislation against the violation of contract by laborers, however, was seldom necessary, and the mere threat of its use or mere knowledge of its existence was sufficient to keep Negro laborers in virtual bondage. This legislation, together with the permissible verbal contract, made it possible for an unscrupulous landlord to utilize the laws to keep his laborers in a state of perpetual peonage. When a group of Negro laborers at the Loudon Place in Marlboro County struck in 1898, the white owner simply had six of the "ring-leaders" arrested and placed in jail. At the trial, all of them "realized their condition, expressed a willingness to resume work and behave themselves," and were allowed to do so after paying all costs. A few days later it was reported that "Everything on 'Loudon' is quiet and everybody is at work."[95]

The legislature had, however, overreached itself in the headlong rush toward reaction and this legislation was declared void when a *habeas corpus* case was brought by Jack Hollman in the state Supreme Court in 1907. Justice C. A. Woods in a unanimous decision held the law to be unconstitutional and void on the ground that it required involuntary servitude. "It is nothing in support of the statute," said Justice Woods, ". . . that it enforces involuntary servitude on account of a debt by the compulsion of a statute providing for indictment and imprisonment for quitting such service, rather than allowing the employer to compel it under a guard. In contemplation of the law the compulsion to such service by the fear of punishment under a criminal statute is more powerful than any guard which the employer could station."[96]

But such legislation, even though declared unconstitutional, reveals the drift of white attitudes and the climate of opinion in which Negro laborers had to work. The trial justices, or magistrates,

---

[94] *Statutes at Large*, XXII, 457.
[95] Charleston *News and Courier*, October 5, 1898.
[96] *Ex Parte Hollman*, 79 S. C. Reports 22.

with whom the laborer was more apt to deal than with the courts, did not always demonstrate the judicial temper shown by the Supreme Court in 1907. One Negro spoke of trial justices as men "whose judgment and decisions the 'Boss' influences as I would the movements of a devoted dog."[97]

In view of the notorious difficulty of organizing a scattered rural population for mutual benefit and in view of the subordinate social and economic status of Negro laborers it is not surprising that efforts to organize them were generally sporadic and ineffectual. Here and there local efforts were made to organize and bargain for or dictate the terms of labor in the late seventies and through the eighties. In Abbeville and Edgefield counties a number of Negro agricultural wage laborers were reported early in 1879 to have made a combination to demand for their services $110 a year, or in case of failure to get that price, to refuse to work.[98] The ineffectiveness of the combination is indicated by the fact that the prevailing wage in Edgefield County the following year was $75.[99] In Barnwell County a group of "colored land leaguers" were reported in 1881 to be pledging themselves "to work for no white man after the present year for love, money or an interest in crops." They preferred renting land and getting advances.[100] However, there was no further report of the "land leaguers" after the white press had apprised its readers of their existence.

Efforts at more widespread organization were scarcely more successful in the hostile atmosphere of Bourbon and Tillmanite South Carolina, for white landlords viewed with a jaundiced eye any effort to organize their workers. The first suggestion of widespread organization that received serious attention was a proposal made in the Richmond convention of the Knights of Labor in 1886 for a campaign to organize colored agricultural labor in the South. The suggestion quickly brought the introduction of a bill in the legislature to make it a misdemeanor for any organization to interfere in agricultural labor contracts. State Senator Marion Moise expressed concern that "without some such law a half-dozen secret emissaries of the Knights of Labor could pass from place to place and stop work on one hundred plantations." The public mind, he

---

[97] New York *Age*, May 16, 1885.
[98] Columbia *Daily Register*, January 16, 1879.
[99] *Handbook of 1883*, p. 155.
[100] Charleston *News and Courier*, April 8, 1881, quoting the Barnwell *People*.

felt, should be satisfied "that those who attempted to bring about wholesale plantation strikes at the most critical period to the farmer and thus plunge the country into appalling disaster ought to be and would be punished." The bill, however, was postponed because it seemed apparent that concern over the issue was not justified, and was never passed.[101]

However, in the winter of 1886-1887, a member of the Knights of Labor, Hiram A. Hoover, came south to organize Negro laborers into a group that was called "The Co-operative Workers of America." Hoover felt that in order to evade intimidation he would have to resort to clandestine organization. Therefore, he inaugurated oaths of secrecy and meetings held under cover of darkness, usually in Negro churches, with sentries posted at the doors. The primary objective seems to have been the formation of cooperative stores to eliminate dependence upon the rural merchant; in his enthusiasm Hoover assured the members of the organization that through cooperative stores they would be able to purchase their necessities at half price. If the plan were adopted, "We will own everything in a short time," he said.[102]

Organization apparently began in Georgia, and soon spread into South Carolina, but the secret nature of the organization quickly cast suspicion upon it wherever whites got rumors of the nocturnal meetings. During May, 1887, when local organizers started several small clubs in the Fairview township of Greenville County the whites sent a squad of mounted men to investigate. The secretary of the nearest "Hoover club" was found and asked to surrender his list of membership, and a squad was sent for each of the seventeen members. An informal court was then held and the society "put on trial." A correspondent from Greenville described the proceedings as follows:

> The negroes were examined separately and coincided in the statement that they had been induced to join by the promise of the organizer that after July rations would be issued to all members at half the present prices. Some of them had ideas of a strike some time in the future for a dollar a day for farm

---

[101] *Senate Journal* (1886), p. 240; Charleston *News and Courier*, December 17, 1886; Columbia *Daily Register*, December 18, 1886.

[102] Charleston *News and Courier*, July 6, 1887, quoting New York *Herald*, July 3, 1887. Report of interview with Walter Vrooman of the Socialist Labor Party, a friend of Hoover.

laborers but they had no definite time or plans. All denied solemnly that there was a word or thought of action against the landlords or white people. . . . The folly of the whole business was pointed out to them and they were notified that the white people would not allow any such organization to exist in secret.[103]

The same procedure was followed at Hopewell Church, near Fountain Inn, where twenty-one "Hooverites" were "arrested," questioned with similar results, warned and released.[104]

When the movement spread into adjoining Laurens County the press began to be filled with alarums about Negroes "who have been made to believe that this county belongs to them." A Laurens correspondent reported that, despite its secrecy, the aims of the organization had become known. "They think they will obtain their rights quickest," he wrote, "by exterminating the older whites and enslaving the young men. The young women they will take for their wives. The whites in the neighborhood are alarmed but they are determined as brave men to defend their hearthstones and the women with their blood, if need be."[105]

The *News and Courier*, after mature consideration and further investigation, determined that the movement aimed at no uprising or threat of violence. Furthermore, it concluded that a strike was unlikely because so many of the Negroes worked for a share of the crop and would only lose by going on strike.[106] The hue and cry continued to mount so that a Negro newspaper in North Carolina expressed the fear that the "chivalry of South Carolina" were planning another Hamburg massacre or "some such diabolism."[107] Lee Minor, a member of the Neptune Fire Company of Greenville and head of the Cooperative organization in that area found it inadvisable to leave Greenville for a meeting at nearby Dacusville. He "grinned expressively and said he didn't believe it would be best for him to go outside of Greenville city until the excitement had died out."[108] He insisted that the excitement was groundless,

---

[103] Charleston *News and Courier*, July 1, 1887.
[104] *Ibid.*
[105] *Ibid.*, June 20, 1887.
[106] *Ibid.*, June 23, 1887.
[107] Washington (D. C.) *Bee*, July 23, 1887, quoting the Enfield (N. C.) *Progress*.
[108] Columbia *Daily Register*, July 1, 1887.

that the Cooperative Workers did not advocate or encourage violation of the law or damage to person or property. But the secret
nature of the organization played upon the trepidation of apprehen-
sive whites and rendered it completely ineffective. It is doubtful,
however, that any such organization could have succeeded, as the
experience of the Colored Farmers Alliance in the following years
indicated.

The Colored Farmers' National Alliance and Co-operative Union,
which had its origin in Texas in 1886,[109] began to spread into South
Carolina in 1888 under the direction of T. E. Pratt of Cheraw. There
was a Colored Farmers Alliance in the Cedar Creek community
of Lancaster County as early as September, 1888, which was reputed to be interested in raising the wages of cotton pickers to a
minimum of fifty cents per hundred pounds, and other groups in
Chester County before the end of the year.[110] During the winter
of 1888-1889 the movement spread rapidly through the Piedmont
and into the rest of the state.[111] The organizers of Alliance groups
do not seem to have faced any intimidation of the sort faced by
the Cooperative Workers, and proceeded without molestation and
with neutral and occasionally sympathetic reaction from the white
farmers who had been drawn into the white Alliance movement.

By April, 1889, twelve sub-Alliances were in existence in Union
County, where they held a meeting in the county courthouse at
which John D. Norris, a school teacher and organizer, described
the purposes of the organization.

> The object . . . is to elevate the colored people of America
> by teaching them to love their country and their homes, to
> care more for their helpless and destitute and to labor more
> earnestly for the education of themselves and their children.
> Especially to improve themselves in agricultural pursuits, to
> become better farmers and laborers and less wasteful in their
> methods of living, to be more obedient to the civil and criminal
> law and withdraw their attention from political partisanship,
> to become better citizens and truer husbands and wives.[112]

---

[109] John Donald Hicks, *The Populist Revolt* (Minneapolis, 1931), pp. 114-15.
[110] Yorkville *Enquirer*, September 26, 1888; Columbia *Daily Register*,
December 13, 1888.
[111] Columbia *Daily Register*, March 17, 23, 29, 1889.
[112] Charleston *News and Courier*, April 25, 1889.

Information about the activities of the Colored Alliance is elusive, but it is clear that by August, 1889, a statewide organization had been perfected under the leadership of T. E. Pratt. Among the objectives of the Alliance were the establishment of cooperative stores, the organization of support for the sub-treasury plan of the white Alliance, the use of cotton bagging instead of jute bagging, and a minimum wage for cotton pickers of fifty cents per hundred pounds.[113] By November of 1889 the Colored Alliance had 112 clubs and in February, 1890, the state organization reported 237 clubs fully organized. State lecturer Thomas Powers reported in August, 1890, a membership of 30,000. In 1890 a Colored Alliance State Exchange was established with a capital stock of $2,500. A state paper, the *Alliance Aid of South Carolina* was established in Sumter.[114]

During 1890 efforts were made to convert the Alliance into a political organization to support Republican candidates,[115] and at least one leader of the South Carolina Colored Alliance attended the conference at Ocala, Florida, in 1890 which drew up a political program that presaged the entrance of the Alliances into Populist politics.[116] A local group in Marlboro County even passed a resolution of support for Ben Tillman, then the white farmers' candidate for his first term as governor,[117] but the leadership successfully fought the commitment of the state organization to any partisan political activity.

During 1890, a schism, the origins of which are not clear, occurred in the State Alliance, and an independent group was organized under the leadership of W. J. Grant of Charleston.[118] The organization began to founder in the fall of 1891 with an abortive effort by R. M. Humphrey to organize a Southwide strike of Negro cotton pickers for higher wages. Some Negro cotton pickers in the neigh-

---

[113] Columbia *Daily Register*, August 14, 1889 and August 23, 1890.

[114] Charleston *News and Courier*, February 28, and August 3, 1890. R. M. Humphrey of Houston, Texas, the national leader of the Colored Alliance, reported in December, 1890, that the Alliance had 90,000 members in South Carolina. Charleston *News and Courier*, September 10, 1891. His figure was probably exaggerated. *Statutes at Large*, XX, 1008; Columbia *Daily Register*, August 23, 1890.

[115] Charleston *News and Courier*, August 3, 1890; Columbia *Daily Register*, August 6, 1890.

[116] Charleston *News and Courier*, July 2, 1891.

[117] Columbia *Daily Register*, June 28, 1890.

[118] Charleston *News and Courier*, January 12, September 10, 1891.

borhood of Orangeburg and Florence, joined the strike,[119] but it
was unsuccessful, and after that the decline of the colored Alliance
was rapid. At the meeting of the state Alliance in 1892 a membership of only 25,000 was claimed, a drastic decrease from the 40,000
members of 1891. After that meeting all mention of the Alliance
disappeared from the state press.[120]

The practical accomplishments of the Cooperative and Alliance
movements were small, but they undoubtedly had some influence in
acquainting Negro farmers with the principles of the cooperative
movement and the value of mutual effort in meeting their problems.
The Alliance spread the knowledge of improved methods of agriculture during its brief career and whetted the appetite for more.
In the late nineties the state Negro college in Orangeburg began
sending its professor of agriculture, J. W. Hoffman, throughout the
state to organize and address local Colored Farmers Institutes in
which he urged more intensive and more diversified farming, looking toward the development of truck farming and dairying, and
lectured on the care of fruit trees and equipment, the terracing of
hillsides, utilization of waste lands, and the production of fertilizers
on the farm.[121]

Another happy form of organized activity were the county and
state fairs organized by and for Negro farmers. In 1889 the Colored
Agricultural and Mechanical Association of South Carolina was
organized under the leadership of A. E. Hampton of Columbia with
a capital stock of $2,000 for the purpose of conducting an annual
fair.[122] The first colored state fair was held in Columbia beginning
January 1, 1890, with about 600 exhibits of poultry, field crops,
manufactures, stock, and household and fancy articles.[123] Thereafter
an annual state fair was held in Columbia. The idea of holding
county fairs was also taken up in many places, Abbeville holding

[119] *Ibid.,* September 10, 13, 15, 1891.

[120] Columbia *State,* July 16, 1892. Alliance groups, however, were scheduled
to participate in the Columbia Emancipation Day celebration of 1893. Columbia *State,* December 26, 1892.

[121] Charleston *News and Courier,* August 12, 1898, and May 26, 1899;
"Annual Report of the Board of Trustees of the Colored Normal, Industrial,
Agricultural and Mechanical College of South Carolina: 1898," *Reports and
Resolutions* (1899), II, 275.

[122] *Statutes at Large,* XX, 1008.

[123] Charleston *News and Courier,* January 2, 1890.

one as early as 1879.[124] At the York County Colored Industrial Fair, held in October, 1897, the exhibits were reported to be quite numerous and creditable, especially in the department of household products such as bread, cakes, preserves, jellies, wines, and pickles. Among the agricultural exhibits nearly all crops were represented, including corn, cotton, wheat, oats, pumpkins, and other items. The social aspect of the fairs was perhaps their chief *raison d'etre,* and entertainments at this fair included sack races, bean bag races, bicycle races, and a contest between two bands, after a procession through town, in which they were judged on the basis of "attack, time, dynamics, finesse, force and tone."[125]

By the end of Reconstruction the continued subordinate and dependent status of the Negro agricultural laborer had been clearly defined under the labor and tenancy arrangements set up by the Radical Republicans. During the next two and a half decades he remained in a clearly subordinate and insecure position. Although a special report to the United States Attorney General on peonage in 1907 indicated an encouraging trend in the recent decision of the state Supreme Court invalidating the state agricultural labor law, and although it was stated that no reports of peonage had been received "recently" from South Carolina,[126] yet it is clear that virtual peonage had existed under the prevailing lien system for the great numbers who were unable to get ahead of the game and who remained in perennial debt to the lien merchants and landlords. In the state laws of 1880 and 1889 a form of serfdom, binding the worker to the soil under verbal and written labor contracts, was elevated to the status of statute law; and under the law of 1897, which remained in effect for a decade, outright peonage was given the active cooperation of the law.

Disfranchised and practically without political influence Negro laborers had by the end of the century no hope for a political redress of grievances. More and more their leaders advised them to abjure the dead-end path of politics for the path of escape that led toward property ownership. "Go to the farm," said the Reverend Richard Carroll to a group celebrating Emancipation Day, 1898,

---

124 Columbia *Daily Register,* December 12, 1879, quoting Abbeville *Medium,* December 10, 1879.

125 Yorkville *Enquirer,* October 9, 1897.

126 Charles W. Russell, *Report on Peonage* (Washington, 1907), p. 35.

in Sumter. "Let the white folks have the cities, factories and offices, let us hold to the country. We need money; money and property."[127] Even Thomas E. Miller, a politician most of his life, was by 1898 advising Negroes to look elsewhere than to politics for their economic welfare. Addressing a Colored Farmers' Institute in Laurens he advised farmers to seek long-term leases and then set to work making improvements and increasing soil fertility. Political activities, he warned, must under no circumstances be permitted to interfere with the relations of landlord and tenant.[128] "Show me a people that is frugal," he said three years later, "and I shall show you a people that is strong, virtuous, wealthy, and happy."[129]

Unfortunately for this study, census statistics on agriculture did not classify farm operatives according to race until 1900, but a clear picture of the position of Negro farmers at the end of the century is possible. A continued predominance of agriculture over all other occupations is indicated by the fact that out of a total of 363,121 Negroes gainfully employed in the state, 267,326 were engaged in agriculture. Of this number 95,352 males and 85,002 females were listed merely as "agricultural laborers," but the definition of the term is too inexact to admit of any interpretation.[130] However, wage laborers are left entirely out of the statistics of tenure, and farms operated by Negro wage earners under the supervision of white landowners or overseers were probably returned as farms operated by whites. The following table illustrates the status of farms reported to be operated by Negroes in 1900:[131]

| | No. of Farms | | Acreage: June 1, 1900 | | |
	Total	With Buildings	Total	Improved	Pct. Improved
S. C.	85,401	82,098	3,792,076	2,273,824	60.0
Owners	15,503	15,237	792,704	369,177	46.6
Part owners	3,376	3,322	162,800	97,060	59.6
Tenants and owners	91	89	7,163	3,085	43.1
Managers	180	170	46,170	13,215	28.6
Cash tenants	42,434	40,547	1,768,497	1,080,297	61.1
Share tenants	23,817	22,733	1,014,742	710,990	70.1

[127] Charleston *News and Courier*, January 4, 1898; *see also* Columbia *State*, January 4, 1898.

[128] Charleston *News and Courier*, August 4, 1898.

[129] T. E. Miller, *Address on Negro Day in the South Carolina Interstate and West Indian Exposition, January 1, 1902.* (Orangeburg, 1901), p. 9.

[130] Bureau of the Census, *Negroes in the United States*, pp. 184-87.

[131] *Ibid.*, pp. 310-11.

	Total Value of Farm Property: June 1, 1900	Value of Products: 1899	Expenditures: 1899 Labor	Fertilizers
S. C.	$44,001,272	$26,590,042	$1,210,370	$1,504,550
Owners	9,068,210	4,751,682	243,110	207,090
Part owners	1,826,183	974,600	60,690	53,320
Tenants and owners	64,619	31,170	2,230	2,060
Managers	433,551	144,450	38,020	9,330
Cash tenants	19,177,515	12,322,130	526,590	657,360
share tenants	13,431,194	8,366,010	339,730	575,390

The position of the Negro farmer relative to the white farmer is indicated by the following table, showing the percentage of the total statistics for all farms which applied to farms operated by Negroes:[132]

Number of farms 55.0

Acreage 27.1

Improved acreage 39.4

Total value 28.6

Land and improvements 30.2

Buildings 21.3

Implements and machinery 24.0

Livestock 32.0

Value of products: 1899 .... 38.9

Value of products not fed to livestock 39.4

Expenditure for labor: 1899 .... 19.8

Expenditure for fertilizers: 1899 .... 33.5

A comparison of the statistics of land and home ownership with the estimates for 1880 reveals a great degree of progress in the two decades. Whereas the proportion of rural Negroes owning their land or homes in 1880 was estimated as from two to five per cent in various counties, with a high estimate of sixteen per cent in Greenville, by 1890 Negroes owned 13,075, or approximately 20.5 per cent of all Negro farm homes and 12,048 of these were unencumbered.[133] In 1900 they owned 18,874, or approximately 22.1 per cent of all Negro farm homes, and of these it was estimated on the basis of incomplete statistics that about 78.9 per cent were owned without encumbrance.[134]

Thus it is clear that despite the hindrances of an impoverished agriculture, hostile labor laws, and general economic subordination,

---

[132] *Ibid.*, p. 90.

[133] *Handbook of 1883*, pp. 59, 84-85, 155; Bureau of the Census, *Negro Population*, 1790-1915 (Washington, 1915), p. 469.

[134] Bureau of the Census, *Negroes in the United States*, pp. 188-89.

many Negroes had, as Thomas E. Miller told Congress, ". . . achieved a success founded upon material prosperity and accumulated wealth the equal of which has never been accomplished by pauperized serfs or peasants in any part of the universe."[135] A path of escape from complete economic subordination was open, and over fifteen thousand Negroes, in the spirit of Horatio Alger, travelled the difficult path from wage labor to share tenancy, from share to cash tenancy, and from there to part ownership and full ownership of their farms and homes.

---

[135] *Congressional Record,* XXII (51st Congress, 2d Session), 2693.

7

NONAGRICULTURAL PURSUITS

ALTHOUGH an overwhelming majority of the gainfully employed Negroes in South Carolina were engaged in agriculture during the last decades of the century, a significant minority were engaged in other pursuits. In 1890 out of a total of 289,550 Negroes over the age of ten who were employed, 223,496 worked in agriculture, fisheries, and mining. A majority of the remaining 66,054 were engaged in domestic and personal services, but others had by that time gone into trade and transportation, manufacturing and mechanical industries, and into various professional services.[1] These small groups, however, were important, especially the professional group of slightly over two thousand, for among them were found the most enterprising workers and the most articulate leaders—those who had struck out into fields formerly closed to Negroes. In the decade after 1890 these various groups grew slowly but steadily, as the following table will illustrate:[2]

Negroes, Ten Years of Age and Over, Gainfully Employed in 1900

	Male	Female	Total
All occupations	224,561	138,560	363,121
Agriculture	173,278	94,048	267,326
Nonagricultural occupations	51,283	44,512	95,795
Professional service	1,627	1,019	2,646
Domestic and personal service	27,611	41,037	68,648
Trade and transport	8,238	219	8,457
Manufacturing and mechanical pursuits	13,807	2,237	16,044

[1] *Compendium of the United States Census* (1890), III, 440-51.
[2] Bureau of the Census, *Negroes in the United States*, pp. 184-87.

Even the nonagricultural pursuits did not tend in every case, however, to alter the predominantly rural nature of Negro activities, for some of the most important industries in which Negroes worked were rural. The newest of these was the phosphate mining industry, which had developed only since the war and was important in rebuilding the prosperity of Charleston, Beaufort, and Port Royal. The presence of deposits of phosphatic rock in the neighborhood of Charleston and Beaufort was known at least as early as 1797 and was mentioned by Robert Mills in 1826, by Edward Ruffin in 1844, and by various other authorities. Not until after the Civil War was it recognized that the rock was a valuable source of phosphoric acid, used in all the commercial fertilizers of the United States. In 1866 Dr. St. Julien Ravenel organized an association for the manufacture of fertilizer, and in 1867 a factory was established. During the same year the Charleston Mining and Manufacturing Company was organized with a paid-in capital of $1,000,000, to work the Ashley River beds. Meanwhile, Dr. Ravenel organized another company to work deposits along the Wando River, and after that numerous other concerns devoted to the mining and processing of phosphate rock were organized in the Low Country.[3] Shipments of crude phosphate from the port of Charleston from 1867 to 1889 totalled 2,997,245 long tons and from Beaufort in the same period, 2,180,506 long tons. The total value of these shipments from both ports was $33,000,000.[4] The industry therefore provided employment for larger numbers of longshoremen and other shipping workers, both white and black, in addition to workers directly connected with the mining and processing of phosphates. In 1878 the state Inspector of Phosphates reported on seventeen companies engaged in river mining alone.[5] Companies that mined navigable streams paid to the state a royalty of $1.00 a ton, which provided a sizable portion of the state government's income.[6]

The principal deposits were along the Stono, Ashley, Cooper, and Wando rivers in the neighborhood of Charleston; in the Beaufort River and its branches; along the Coosaw River and Chisolms

---

[3] Simkins and Woody, *South Carolina During Reconstruction*, pp. 305-6; Edward Willis, "Phosphate Rock," *Census* (1890), VII, 681.

[4] Willis, in *Census* (1890), VII, 686.

[5] "Report of Inspector of Phosphates on the River Mining Companies of South Carolina," *Reports and Resolutions* (1878), pp. 283-85.

[6] *Reports and Resolutions* (1877-1878), p. 520.

Island; and in the area of the Edisto River and Horse Shoe Creek.[7] Mining of the rock involved crude and rough work, and unskilled Negroes of the Low Country provided an abundant supply of labor. The rock was found both on dry land and in the river beds. Land mining was a simple process, since the rock was usually at or near the surface, and involved the digging of long trenches to remove overlying dirt, after which the rock was loosened by pick and shovel and thrown on scows or flatboats within reach in shoal water. In some places expert divers operated in deep water and were able to bring to the surface by hand sizable rocks that would require several men to handle out of the water. In many places Negro farmers operated independently as rock pickers and sold their rock to nearby mining and fertilizer companies.[8]

Negro labor was employed almost exclusively in the phosphate mines, and although mining provided wage laborers a comparatively remunerative occupation, it was extremely difficult and, in the case of river mining, unhealthful. In the fall of 1881 the mines tried the experiment of employing Italian laborers, who worked on railroads during the summer and were attracted to the South during the winter. After trying these for three winters, the foreman at one mine observed that they worked hard, never left the labor camp, had "not a woman or a piece of music among them," lived altogether on bread, water, tea, and macaroni, and most important of all, "Their coming . . . improved the character of negro labor. . . ." Another foreman observed, "They have a capital effect on the negroes, and show them, in a practical way, that the miners are not alone dependent upon them for their labor."[9] But an observer noted in 1890 that the Italians, after several years' trial, "were soon replaced by Negroes, who for climatic and other reasons are better adapted to the work."[10] For the most part the mines were operated by Negro wage labor, but to some extent by Negro convict labor.

---

[7] Willis, in *Census* (1890), VII, 682.

[8] *Ibid.*, pp. 682-83; Woofter, *Black Yeomanry*, pp. 86-87.

[9] Charleston *News and Courier*, March 1, 1884.

[10] Willis, in *Census* (1890), VII, 682. The practice of seeking immigrant laborers from the Northern market was continued on a minor scale at least as late as 1893. By this time, however, Italians were not looked upon as an altogether reliable source of labor. "It is not long after they get here before there is a row, and complaint is made to the foreign consuls. Year after year the Italians are arrested and sent to jail for violating their contracts." Columbia *State*, January 22, 1893.

The labor paid comparatively well. In 1889, 4,608 laborers in phosphate mining, working an average of 225 days, received an average daily wage of ninety-seven cents,[11] which was substantially above the thirty to seventy-five cent wage paid to day laborers by the farmers. It is little wonder, then, that many Negro men went to mine phosphate rock, and left the women and children to work their farms.

The phosphate industry rapidly declined at the turn of the century. After the hurricane of 1893, it never recovered in the Beaufort area and commercial phosphate mining in that region was over by 1894. One by one other companies reduced their operations and went out of business in the face of competition from Florida rock, which had a higher content of phosphoric acid. The Coosaw Mining Company, one of the largest, went out of business in 1904.[12]

Lumbering was an important operation in some parts of the state. The principal centers of lumbering were Charleston and Georgetown counties, but lumbering operations were scattered about the state, chiefly along the coast, the Pee Dee River, and along the various railroad lines. Hampton and Barnwell counties, connected to the coast by the Port Royal and Augusta Railroad, were important inland centers of lumbering operations. The manufacture of rough red and white oak split staves and headings for the European and West Indian trade was important, rice tierces and rosin barrels were made from pine, and at Plantersville in Georgetown County and other points along the coast quantities of handmade cypress shingles were manufactured in the swamps.[13] The Atlantic Coast Lumber Company moved into the area of Georgetown around the turn of the century, and numbers of Negroes, left without work by the decline of rice planting, went to Georgetown to work in the lumber mill while others stayed in the country to cut timber for the company or for sale to the company.[14] In 1900, 4,585 white and Negro wage earners were employed in the lumber and timber products industry.[15]

Important in the eighties and nineties, though in decline, was the production of naval stores. Employing 4,619 operatives with total

---

[11] Willis, in *Census* (1890), VII, 685.
[12] Woofter, *Black Yeomanry*, pp. 86-87.
[13] *Census* (1880), IX, 518-19.
[14] M. W. Pyatt to the Author, November 21, 1949.
[15] *Census* (1900), VIII, Part II, 833-34.

wages of $555,460 in 1880, the industry dropped to 2,116 operatives in 1890 and to 886, with wages of $135,575, in 1900.[16] However, it was in this industry that Randall D. George, reputed at his death in 1891 to be the wealthiest Negro in South Carolina, made his fortune. Born in Whiteville, North Carolina, about 1849, he moved to Williamsburg County, South Carolina, when quite young— whether as a slave or a free man is uncertain. By 1883 he was said to be the largest landowner in Colleton County and in that year paid $20,500 cash for a large tract of land in that county.[17] Most of his time was devoted to the naval stores business, and he was one of the largest shippers of rosins and turpentines into Charleston, operating stills in Colleton, Williamsburg, and Orangeburg counties. At his death in 1891, his estate was estimated at from $100,000 to $150,000, including not only pine lands and stills in three counties, but also real estate valued at $27,000 in Washington and $15,000 worth of real estate in Charleston.[18] Although he did not enter politics as a candidate, he was a political Warwick who frequently financed Republican candidates and especially favored Negro candidates against the "carpetbag" wing of the party. Thomas E. Miller's two campaigns for Congress were in large part financed by George, and, as a result of Miller's influence, George was appointed supervisor of the 1890 census for the Charleston district.[19]

The general national growth in railroad mileage had a lesser counterpart in South Carolina in the last half of the nineteenth century. In the period from 1870 to 1899 the total mileage more than doubled from 1,139 to 2,791.59 miles.[20] Although some of the labor in railroad building, as in phosphate mining, was convict, this building offered an opportunity for a number of Negroes to escape the vicious circle of agricultural labor and the lien system. By 1900 railroads in the state employed 2,941 Negroes in one capacity or another.[21]

Despite the growth of a considerable white artisan group in the towns, Negro workers continued to be an important factor in the

---

[16] *Ibid.* (1880), II, 175-76; *ibid.* (1900), VIII, Part II, 833-34; *Compendium of the U. S. Census* (1890), III, 834-37.

[17] Charleston *News and Courier*, April 12, 1883.

[18] *Ibid.*, June 3, 6, 1891.

[19] *Ibid.*, January 15, 1889; February 6, 8, 1890.

[20] *Poor's Manual of Railroads* (New York, 1900), p. vi.

[21] Bureau of the Census, *Negroes in the United States*, p. 184-87.

skilled labor supply. In the barbering profession, traditionally a Negro monopoly, colored barbers were gradually being relegated to serving only Negro customers, but the tradition persisted and scattered Negro barbers still serve white customers in the state. Thirty-nine of them gathered in Greenville in 1888 to organize a State Barber's Union for "mutual benefit and regulation of prices and the elevation of the trade."[22] The census of 1900 listed 545 Negro barbers and hairdressers in the state.[23]

In trades which involved less personal contact Negro workmen gave white artisans competition almost as severe as that given whites by skilled slaves and free Negroes before the Civil War. A white editor lamented in 1889:

> . . . As soon as the negro acquires some "knowledge of books" he deserts his cotton patch and seeks some other means of making a livelihood. As yet but little is seen of him in the mercantile or professional world, but as a mechanic he is making himself felt all over the South. In some communities he has actually driven the white mechanic to the wall and is making a comfortable living at prices 25 to 50 percent less than the white man can afford to work for. (Cheaper cost of living for the negro.) And while he may do inferior work, it is nevertheless a fact he is gradually elbowing the white mechanic out of the way, in many places at least, accepting work at prices at which it is literally impossible for the white mechanic to live.[24]

For the capable skilled worker, however, wages were better by contemporary standards than this complaint might indicate. In 1894 Negro carpenters in Charleston received $8.00 or more per week, and stone masons, plasterers, and bricklayers asked $9.00 to $12.00 per week. "Accustomed to obey the white race, they are as workmen admirably competent and entirely pliable in the hands of a just and stern white boss," a Northern reporter observed. "Like that faithful animal the dog the more you chastise them the better they work. . . . Certainly large gangs of negro carpenters or masons

---

[22] Yorkville *Enquirer*, October 31, 1888.

[23] Bureau of the Census, *Negroes in the United States*, pp. 184-87.

[24] Columbia *Daily Register*, October 1, 1889, quoting Lancaster *Review*.

work rapidly and admirably under white direction, and particularly if the overseer be of Northern citizenship."[25]

In Charleston, where at the turn of the century there were seventy-five to eighty union masons and twelve to twenty-five non-union, and several hundred carpenters, plus a number of black-smiths, painters, wheelwrights, and plumbers, a survey indicated that the masons got $3.00 for a nine hour day and carpenters $1.75 to $2.50 for the same. In Columbia the same survey showed 386 skilled workmen, probably a gross underestimate. In the Up Country town of Greenville the small Negro population showed a high ratio of skilled workers, with forty carpenters, fifty masons and plasterers, fifteen blacksmiths, fifteen shoemakers, and fourteen painters, besides an indefinite number of tinners, plumbers, harness makers, and other artisans. Other Up Country towns, Anderson, Aiken, and Chester reported similar high ratios of skilled workers.[26] Sundry minor urban industries, such as a Bent Wood factory in Columbia, gave employment to a limited number of Negroes.[27]

Negro women in the towns were occupied for the most part in unskilled domestic work. The Negro laundress was a familiar figure until well into the twentieth century.[28] The only skilled occupation into which Negro women went in any number was that of dress-making and sewing. Negro colleges offered courses in these skills, and it is likely that some Negro women who had attended them went home to establish small sewing schools.[29] In all, more than half the adult women were employed in one occupation or another.

The largest industry in the state, textiles, largely a growth of the post-Reconstruction period, avoided Negro laborers almost alto-gether, except in menial unskilled pursuits. Although slaves had been used successfully in the fifties in at least one mill, the Saluda Factory near Columbia, it was generally assumed in later efforts that the trial of Negro labor was experimental and had dubious

---

[25] Charleston News and Courier, March 22, 1894, quoting M. M. S. in Philadelphia Times.

[26] William Edmund Burghardt DuBois (ed.), The Negro Artisan (Atlanta, 1902), p. 141.

[27] Columbia Daily Register, January 23, 1886.

[28] There were 12,558 in 1900. Bureau of the Census, Negroes in the United States, p. 186.

[29] Ida Bozeman Gladden, wife of a Greenville minister and a former student at Tuskegee, did so. Ida Bozeman Gladden to Booker Taliaferro Washington, n. d., Booker Taliaferro Washington Papers, Manuscripts Division, Library of Congress.

prospects for success. In addition, efforts to employ Negro labor in factories that had employed whites brought on clashes or threats of clashes between the blacks and the displaced white workers. In Charleston during 1890, an effort to substitute gradually Negro labor for white in a cotton mill resulted in several minor rows and finally a pitched battle in which the whites ran the Negroes away. The few who returned were quietly discharged.[30]

During the nineties the white press produced many columns of speculation on the value of Negro workers in textile mills, but in almost every case the comment was based on theory rather than experience. A mill superintendent in Spartanburg, who had no experience with colored operatives, saw no reason why they were not "physically and morally competent to do mill work if properly trained," while another at Piedmont, who had worked with Negro slaves in a cotton mill, remembered that "they were very hard to manage even then," and believed that they could not be made into first-class workmen.[31] The Greenville *News* in 1896 brought on a spate of editorial comment when, in an editorial on a small mill in Bamberg manned by colored labor, it commented that "negro labor in some of the factories is not very distant in the future, unless white factory workers can be brought here from New England." [32]

The Columbia *State*, taking issue with the *News*, argued that the South was capable of operating "ten times its present number of spindles" with white labor, and looked on the cotton mills "not merely as agencies to make money for their stockholders, but as contributors to the improvement of the very large class of white peoples who . . . should have the gate of advancement opened to them." Offering better wages than the farms, the mills provided places where people could be brought together near convenient schooling places. Two major objections to the employment of Negroes would be the clustering of Negro population around the towns and the lowering of wages for the whites.[33] The Charleston *Evening Post*, however, felt that sentiment would not enter the question. "The laws of industry are merciless. They do not draw

[30] Columbia *Daily Register*, September 17, 1890.
[31] Charleston *News and Courier*, September 26, 1893.
[32] Columbia *State*, April 24, 1896, quoting Greenville *News*.
[33] Columbia *State*, April 24, 1896.

the color line. If it is demonstrated that colored labor can be utilized in mills and at a lower cost than white, a demand for it will at once arise." [34] But the *Evening Post* saw no cause for alarm, for if the use of Negro labor did develop, it would be a step toward skills, a higher standard of living and higher wages for Negroes, which would lead to better citizenship. On only one point was the white press unanimous, and that was that white and black labor should not be mixed in the same factory.

Toward the end of the nineties several new experiments with Negro factory labor were made. An established knitting mill in Charleston, "bowing before the imperative demand for cheap labor," discharged its white employees in October, 1896, to hire Negro labor.[35] By the following summer, there were eighty-five Negroes employed on sixty-five machines, turning out three hundred pairs of socks per day. The factory was reported to be "running along smoothly and without the least trouble." [36] The Beaufort Knitting Mills, established in 1897, began operations with twenty young colored women, and were ready to take on twenty more operatives in a short time.[37] In October, 1897, when wages for fifteen women in the Charleston Shoe Factory were changed from a weekly to a piecework basis, forty-five whites walked out, and Negro labor was called in to break the strike. The shoe factory was the third mill in Charleston to turn to Negro labor, for the Charleston Cotton Mill, after a protracted period of unprofitable operation, had begun to try Negro labor.[38] The *News and Courier* saw in this

> an important, maybe a dangerous experiment; but the reward would be so great should success follow that the hazard she [Charleston] takes is justified. Negro labor is the cheapest labor this country has ever known. Commercial progress and prosperity in these days demand cheap labor. Should Charleston discover that she can set a million spindles to humming in her midst by putting her colored population to work she will not only rid herself of an incubus, which has handicapped her

---

[34] Quoted *ibid.*, April 20, 1896.
[35] Charleston *News and Courier*, October 13, 1897.
[36] *Ibid.*, July 22, 1897.
[37] *Ibid.*, May 24, 1897.
[38] *Ibid.*, October 13, 14, 1897.

hopelessly in the race for prosperity, but she will have blazed a way which her sister cities will not be slow to follow.[39]

When former white operatives issued "threatening posters" and intimated that they might resort to violence, the unsympathetic *News and Courier* reminded them that the mill community "is too remote from other mills to hope for assistance. It is greatly outnumbered by negro laborers in Charleston, and in a 'race war' with the negroes it would stand in need of protection."[40] The operation of the Charleston Cotton Mill, however, continued to be unprofitable, and it was sold in 1899 to John H. Montgomery, a capitalist of Spartanburg.[41]

Renamed the Vesta Cotton Mill, it was outfitted with new machinery and recommenced operations in 1899. The management appealed to colored ministers and other leaders of the Negro community to encourage Negro laborers to work in the mill, and it was operated through 1900 almost exclusively with Negro labor.[42] The Colored Ministers' Union passed a resolution expressing appreciation of the opportunity presented their race;[43] and Negro leaders in Charleston, recognizing the significance of the experiment, did what they could to encourage Negroes to work efficiently in the mill.[44] Girls employed were offered $7.80 a month while learning, after which they made from $12 to $15 per month. Tenements were offered at twenty-five cents per room per week.[45]

Yet, by the end of 1900 the mill had once again failed. Various reasons were offered by those associated with the mill, but for the most part it was blamed on the inefficiency of Negro labor. George W. Williams, a prominent stockholder, noted that Negro leaders in the community helped all they could, "but they could not make efficiency where it wasn't"; Williams estimated that where a white worker could get ninety-two per cent out of a machine a Negro could only get seventy-six. "The negroes, shunning 'the opportunity of their lives,' would go for oysters in the oyster season,

---

[39] *Ibid.*, October 13, 1897.

[40] *Ibid.*, June 28, 1897.

[41] *Ibid.*, March 7, 1899.

[42] *Ibid.*, March 25, 1899; Columbia *State*, March 7, 18, 1899.

[43] Charleston *News and Courier*, December 12, 1899.

[44] Broadus Mitchell, *The Rise of Cotton Mills in the South* (Baltimore, 1921), p. 217.

[45] Columbia *State*, June 16, 1900.

and then for strawberries in the strawberry season."[46] Another stockholder thought that the mill had failed because it was expected
to pay dividends on a capitalization enlarged by the installation
of new machinery, and because of the malign influence of the mill's
selling agents, who "took every means to show the colored labor
unprofitable."[47] H. E. C. Bryant, a reporter sent by the Charlotte
(N. C.) *Observer* to investigate the failure, noted that the mill had
failed twice with white labor and twice with Negro labor since its
establishment in 1882. Bryant was told by the managers that among
the Negro workers, "We had as good lappers, speeders, spindle
attendants, and weavers as you could find anywhere."[48] Thomas
E. Miller attributed labor irregularities to cheap wages, "because
the girls and boys can make more money by picking strawberries,
Irish potatoes, carrots and other garden produce on the truck farms
adjacent to the city in five hours, than they can in ten hours working in the factories"; he insisted that "conditions for making money
in cotton factories with Negro labor in lower Carolina, are superior
to those in upper Carolina where white labor is employed."[49]

Negro labor was never seriously tried on a large scale in any
other factory in the state, and the Charleston mill, with its record
of failures in the past, scarcely offered a fair trial. But industrialists,
already willing to believe in Negro inferiority, took its experience
as conclusive.

In Columbia during 1897 and 1898 an abortive effort was made to
organize a cotton mill owned and operated by Negroes. After pur-
chasing a building with 24,000 feet of floor space and enlarging it to
32,000, the Elmwood Manufacturing Company installed 250 looms
and 10,000 spindles which it had bought from a mill in New England. An experienced textile man was brought down from Maine to
be superintendent,[50] but before the end of the summer, after an op-
timistic start in March, the mill was closed while the Negro workers
were still in training. The *News and Courier* commented that the

---

[46] Mitchell, *The Rise of Cotton Mills in the South*, pp. 217-18.

[47] *Ibid.*, p. 218. Mitchell gives on pp. 216-19 an account of interviews with
several persons connected with the ownership and management of the mill.

[48] "The Negro Cotton Mill Failure," *Outlook*, LXVII (March 2, 1901),
468a-69, quoting Charlotte (N. C.) *Observer*.

[49] T. E. Miller, *Address Delivered on Negro Day in the South Carolina
Interstate and West Indian Exposition, January 1, 1902*, p. 11.

[50] Columbia *State*, February 18, March 24, 1898.

effort had "absolutely afforded no chance of ascertaining whether colored labor could or would not be used to advantage."[51]

Very few Negroes, perhaps only one, had the opportunity of the anonymous individual who worked for the Abbeville *Press and Banner* as a compositor. When the story got abroad in the state during 1887 that the *Press and Banner* employed a Negro, the comments of other white newspapers were revealing of the white attitudes that faced skilled Negroes who attempted to rise in competition with whites. The Newberry *Observer* asked pointedly what should be thought of "this move in the direction of cheap labor and of crowding young white men out of a field of industry peculiarly suited to them?" It answered its question with a protest against "what we regard as a lowering of a profession that needs above all things to be kept on a high plane."[52] But other editors, including E. B. Ragsdale of the Winnsboro *News and Herald*, thought that success depended upon intellect rather than race. "The Color line," said Ragsdale, "may be drawn at the door of the drawing room. It cannot be drawn at the door of the workshop."[53]

The Greenville *News* observed that the Newberry editor had missed "the cream of the joke," because the paper under attack was the one most violently opposed to the free school system for Negroes and most violently abusive of the Episcopal bishop of the diocese because he insisted upon the right of a Negro who had been duly ordained to sit in the Episcopal convention, and yet the same paper worked a Negro printer alongside white employees. "It is no business of ours," said the *News*, "and we do not question the right of any man to manage his own business as he likes; but the admirable consistency of public precept and private practice extorts our wonder."[54]

Sporadic efforts at the organization of Negro industrial workers, like similar efforts among agricultural workers, produced more smoke than fire. Isolated and in great part unaware of the benefits to be gained from unionization, Negro laborers found it difficult,

---

[51] Charleston *News and Courier*, August 16, 1898.

[52] Thomas Dionysius Clark, *The Southern Country Editor* (Indianapolis, 1948), p. 204.

[53] *Ibid.*

[54] Port Royal *Palmetto Post*, July 14, 1887, quoting Greenville *News*.

whenever they asserted themselves, to maintain any degree of solidarity because of employers' and official hostility and the ready supply of cheap labor that could be employed to break strikes. Negro workers frequently had such poor self-discipline as to be unable to prevent outbreaks of violence. The absence of any general organization caused a lack of solidarity among the workers, and the general practice in the case of sporadic strikes was for employers to hire replacements for striking workers. This practice of course created situations in which it was difficult to prevent violence.

Negroes employed by the Pacific Guano Company in dredging and hauling phosphate rock in Beaufort County struck in 1877 when it was reported that "some changes would take place in the manner of employing and remunerating the laborers." When new hands were brought in on the conditions rejected by the strikers, a mob of old hands collected, armed with guns and other weapons, attacked the camp of the new workers, and brought on a general melee in which seven or eight were wounded, none very seriously. Sheriff Wilson, a white Republican, proceeded to the scene with a constable and arrested the "ring leaders."[55] In 1885, when a gang of workers were brought into Port Royal to work on the railroad, they were attacked and driven away and fled up the tracks. Citizens who were called to the scene pursued them and persuaded nine of the fourteen to come back. The town council voted six extra policemen to protect the workers. Ten men were arrested and charged with being in the mob that attacked the workers.[56]

When Asbury C. Latimer of the Cooperative Cotton Seed Oil Mill in Belton reduced the wages of Negro workers from seventy-five to sixty cents a day, they went out on strike and were charged with threatening to flog another man who refused to leave his work and join them. Arrest of two "ringleaders" checked the "uprising" and the company sought other laborers to fill the places of those who struck.[57] After the hurricane of 1893 when Charleston Neck was crowded with thousands of idle "cyclone refugees" from the sea islands, the fertilizer works of the area reduced wages from a dollar to seventy-five cents a day. Workers went out on

---

[55] Charleston *News and Courier*, May 24, 1877.
[56] Port Royal *Palmetto Post*, October 29, 1885.
[57] Charleston *News and Courier*, December 1, 1890.

strike in protest, but the refugees were eager to get work. When a number of them were hired, strikers sought to prevent them from working and mounted police were sent to the scene for their protection.[58]

Occasionally, however, moderate successes were secured. At Florence in 1898 about seventy-five tobacco stemmers at the Gordon-Wright Company went out, and because of the immense amount of tobacco on hand, the company agreed to a raise of five cents per hundred pounds. "Those who took part in the strike were very orderly and behaved in such a way that the Messrs. Gorman [sic] did not object to their returning to work."[59]

Charleston, the metropolitan center of the state, was naturally the center of whatever successful trade union organization the Negro workers had in the state. The outstanding example was the Longshoremen's Protective Union Association, originally chartered in 1869 for a term of twelve years, and rechartered in 1880 for twenty-one years largely as a result of the work of C. H. Simonton, a white Democratic member of the legislature and legal representative of the union.[60] The union had a long record of successful operation and was for a long period able to keep longshoremen's wages in Charleston above the rates for similar work in other South Atlantic ports. Longshoremen in Port Royal imitated the Charleston example and organized in 1874 the Longshoremen's Protective Union Association of Port Royal which was active at least as late as 1885.[61] In that year the members went on strike to force a wage of fifteen cents per hour for general work and twenty cents an hour for loading timber and lumber. But a number of bolters slipped away to the docks where with some outside help they loaded and discharged steamships bound to and from New York. When loyal union members appeared to hurl epithets at the bolters they engaged in such "boisterous and noisy language" that eight of them were arrested for riot. Lumber stevedores and longshoremen, however, finally came to an understanding under which the union wage was paid.[62]

---

[58] Columbia *State*, January 23, 1894.
[59] Charleston *News and Courier*, October 8, 1898.
[60] Simkins and Woody, *South Carolina During Reconstruction*, pp. 370-71; *Acts and Joint Resolutions* (1868-1869), p. 231 and (1880), p. 345; *House Journal* (1880), p. 367.
[61] *Acts and Joint Resolutions* (1873-1874), p. 586.
[62] Port Royal *Palmetto Post*, October 22, 1895.

In 1877 when a British vessel bound from Charleston to LeHavre was being loaded by workers under a stevedore who did not recognize the union or its rules, a crowd of Negro union members gathered in East Bay Street. A melee followed, and Mayor George I. Cunningham, Republican, attempted to settle the affair by persuasion, but eventually ordered police with Winchesters and fixed bayonets to move up East Bay from the corner of Broad and disperse the rioters. Only one arrest was made, and the *News and Courier* reported with obvious distaste that the prisoner was "unconditionally released" by the mayor.[63] The affair brought on a presentment of the grand jury requesting the legislature to revoke the union's charter, but the presentment was referred to a legislative committee and no action was taken, possibly because of the Republican majority that still existed in the upper house.[64]

Thereafter the longshoremen's union continued to operate quietly and successfully, but was weakened in 1890 by the intrusion of the race issue. Over sixty white members of the longshoremen's association, complaining that "where any evils were to be remedied they were always adjusted in favor of the colored men," withdrew to form the Workingmen's United Labor Benevolent Association. The secretary of the group explained that it did not intend to interfere in any way with wages or hours.[65] Four years later the white group was reported to have a membership of over two hundred and claimed its purposes to be purely benevolent.[66]

In 1898 C. H. Betts, an agent of the Johnson Blue Cross Line, imported twenty-four men from Port Royal in an effort to break the power of the Longshoremen's Protective Union Association. On November eleventh union members working for the Johnson Line were told to pack their tools and leave work at about ten a. m. When the men from Port Royal arrived at about one o'clock a riot occurred. Only one man was injured, but the men from Port Royal decided to return home despite a promise of protection from the chief of police. Meanwhile several officers and members of the union, including its president, were arrested.[67] The agent who had

---

[63] Charleston *News and Courier*, February 11, 1877.

[64] Charleston *News and Courier*, July 3, 1877; *Senate Journal* (1877-1878), p. 8.

[65] Charleston *News and Courier*, February 6, 1890.

[66] *Ibid.*, February 8, 1894.

[67] *Ibid.*, November 12, 13, 1898.

imported workers from Port Royal argued that the port of Charleston was in danger of losing business because of the high wage rates required by the union. Longshoremen in Charleston were paid $23 a day for a crew of five, a foreman and four men, whereas those in Savannah, Wilmington, Port Royal, and Brunswick were paid only $13 for a similar crew.[68] The union, faced by determination of shippers to reduce the pay rates and with several of its officers and members under arrest, decided to lower its rate for a crew from $23 to $20.50 and to increase the hours from eight to nine.[69]

Betts, however, determined to press his advantage, brought in thirty longshoremen from Savannah two days after this reduction [70] and on the following day appeared before the Chamber of Commerce, which resolved that the wages of labor should be brought down to the level of Savannah and other Atlantic ports.[71] The longshoremen countered with a statement that they would agree to lower wages provided other rates at the port, such as those for the storing of cotton, were also brought in line with those of competing ports. The union appointed a committee of five to join with the commercial bodies of the city to investigate the possibility of cutting all charges not in line with those of other ports.[72] This counter-proposal apparently did not meet with the approval of the commercial bodies, for all mention of the issue disappeared from the press immediately afterwards.

Skilled carpenters and bricklayers in Charleston also maintained effective unions. The Bricklayers Union Number One of South Carolina was organized in 1881 and affiliated with the International Bricklayers Union. In 1886 it demanded a raise in the pay of bricklayers from $3 to $5 a day.[73] The union included both white and Negro members, and the editor of a Negro paper in Charleston noted that a parade of the union members in 1886 presented

> quite a curiosity, especially when we take into consideration the mixture of the Union, being white and black. It is a fact that black and white men can dwell together in peace, even in

---

[68] *Ibid.*, November 12, 1898.
[69] *Ibid.*, November 15, 1898.
[70] *Ibid.*, November 17, 1898.
[71] *Ibid.*, November 18, 1898.
[72] *Ibid.*, November 23, 1898.
[73] *Ibid.*, September 17, 1886.

South Carolina. The order presented a very fine appearance, and the sight will not be soon forgotten.[74]

Negro carpenters of Charleston were organized, so they claimed, to establish suitable rules and regulations as to the qualifications of members, and to eliminate the difficulty of "the large number of 'saw and hatchet' jacklegs who were constantly coming into competition with them." Their chairman claimed "that there was not a boss in the city who was opposed to the movement."[75] In 1883 they were invited by the international brotherhood to affiliate and received the invitation sympathetically,[76] but there is no information to indicate whether or not they acted upon it. Indication of the continued vitality of the union movement in Charleston was given by the presence in the Labor Day parade of 1900 of nearly a thousand men, a majority of whom were colored.[77]

The Knights of Labor entered South Carolina during 1886, the peak year of their operation, and organized assemblies of colored workers in at least three communities, Greenville, Florence, and Charleston, but the only widespread attention that they attracted was in the organization of Negro agricultural workers through the Cooperative Workers of America.[78] The decline of the movement set in shortly after it entered the state, and Ellery M. Brayton complained in the Republican convention of 1888 that representatives of the Knights who came to the state "to organize the colored labor, or to tell them of better conditions elsewhere, had been driven from the State."[79] The Knights secured no positive accomplishment in South Carolina.

Negro leaders consistently urged upon their people the establishment and patronage of enterprises owned by Negroes. William Holloway of the Charleston New Era urged his readers to "get homes; engage in business of a commercial character, and deal with each other. The patronage of a single ward will support a store;

---

[74] Charleston Recorder, November 6, 1886.

[75] Charleston News and Courier, September 5, 1883.

[76] Ibid; Charleston New Era, September 8, 1883.

[77] Charleston News and Courier, September 4, 1900.

[78] Yorkville Enquirer, April 29, November 17, 1886. One local of the Knights of Labor, location not specified, was reported in South Carolina as early as 1883. There were eighteen in 1888. Frederick Meyers, "The Knights of Labor in the South," Southern Economic Journal, VI (April, 1940), 483.

[79] Columbia Daily Register, May 2, 1888.

that store will need a clerk, and maybe other assistants; these needs will give employment and put money in pockets. Don't wait to make a big beginning; start in a small way, and develop your enterprise."[80] The wealthiest men in the world, he continued, had started in small undertakings and risen to control corporations and even communities. Another editor in Charleston was lamenting as late as 1898 that "The white man is not against negro enterprises and negro prosperity. . . . It is the negro who hates to see another negro get up in the world."[81] In Columbia another Negro editor complained that the inconsistency of colored buyers would be obvious to anyone who strolled through the business part of the city and visited both colored and white merchants. "Why will we say 'Negro stores ought to succeed'?" he asked, "and yet so many of us are doing nothing to bring success. Rank inconsistency is not a strong enough term for the actions of such people."[82]

Yet the Reverend J. L. Dart of Charleston stated at the founding meeting of the National Negro Business Men's League in 1900 that there were about sixty Negroes engaged in legitimate and profitable business in his city with a capital of about $250,000, and "the whites are disposed to extend the hand of help to every black man who is struggling to make his way up in business."[83] A survey of the Negro businessmen of the state listed in 1899 all Negro enterprises with stocks of goods for sale or with $500 or more capital invested. On this basis 123 Negro businessmen were reported in the state, almost half of whom were located in Charleston.[84] Among these there can be identified Charles C. Leslie, wholesale and retail commission dealer in fish, oysters, game, and poultry, who operated two stalls in the fish market and

---

[80] Charleston *New Era*, April 14, 1883.

[81] Columbia *State*, November 8, 1898, quoting Charleston *Messenger*.

[82] Columbia *State*, February 15, 1898, quoting Columbia *Recorder*.

[83] Charleston *News and Courier*, August 28, 1900. The meeting was in Boston.

[84] William Edmund Burghardt DuBois (ed.), *The Negro in Business* (Atlanta, 1899), pp. 34-35. The 53 enterprises credited to Negroes in Charleston included undertakers, grocers, dealers in fish, oysters, and game, livery stable operators, wagon makers and wheelwrights, printers, druggists, shoe store operators, tailors, barbers, contractors, and one each fan maker, upholsterer, photographer, stone cutter, truck farmer, tinner, and paint store operator. Where reported, the capital invested ranged from $300.00 to $100,000.00, the latter being in a truck farm. One livery stable reported a capital of $20,000.00, one dealer in fish, oysters, and game, $30,000.00.

maintained offices at numbers 18 and 20 Market Street.[85] During the eighties the Cation brothers operated a restaurant that was patronized by whites, but it was not included in the report of enterprises operating at the end of the century.[86]

During 1886 a total of 1037 Negro depositors in Charleston banks were reported to have to their credit $124,936.35. This indicated, said the *News and Courier*, that the colored people were "rapidly regaining the ground they lost by the failure of the Freedmen's Bank, and . . . putting their money where it will do the most good."[87] William Demosthenes Crum, colored physician and politi-

Bank	Colored Depositors	Amount Deposited	Largest Deposit
Germania Savings Bank	642	$ 73,344.57	$1,870.24
South Carolina Loan and Trust Co.	275	28,000.00	2,000.00
Carolina Savings Bank	33	12,099.78	366.66 (avg.)
Charleston Savings Institution	91	10,492.00	. . . .
Hibernian Savings Bank	16	11,000.00	. . . .
TOTALS	1,057	$124,936.35	$ . . . . . .

ical leader, estimated in 1903 that colored citizens of Charleston owned in the aggregate over one million dollars worth of real and personal property and that there was "hardly a street in the city that they do not possess and pay taxes on from one to thirty thousand dollars worth of real estate."[88] Negro leaders told a visitor in 1910 that citizens of their race owned real estate assessed at $1,500,000, the assessment representing about sixty per cent of actual value.[89]

---

[85] Charles C. Leslie to W. J. McKinlay, February 5, 1897, Carter G. Woodson Papers.

[86] Charleston *New Era*, March 17, 1883.

[87] Charleston *News and Courier*, May 7, 1886. Deposits were distributed as follows:

[88] William Demosthenes Crum to W. J. McKinlay, January 26, 1903, Carter G. Woodson Papers. In the letter presenting these figures, Crum was refuting smaller figures presented by Mayor James A. Smythe in his argument before the Senate Committee on Commerce against Crum's confirmation as Collector of the Port of Charleston. Said Crum: "When the Gridiron Club was in Charleston, Mayor Smythe was dubbed the 'Ananias of the South,' which was very appropriate and the distinguished gentleman from So. Ca. certainly capped the climax and took the honors belonging to that title when he appeared before the Committee on Commerce and prostituted the statistics of the financial standing of the colored citizens of Charleston." It is possible that Crum exaggerated in the opposite direction.

[89] Archer, *Through Afro-America, an English Reading of the Race Problem* p. 169.

In Columbia at the end of the century Negroes operated about twenty-five grocery, dry goods, and clothing stores varying from suburban shops to I. J. Miller's well-stocked clothing store in the business center of town. Having started on a shoestring in the mid-eighties, Miller had by 1898 a stock estimated at $10,000, and employed three clerks. R. J. Palmer, a merchant tailor with a stock valued at several thousand dollars, also operated in the main business section of town and occupied a building valued at eight thousand dollars. J. P. Evans, grocer, and Mrs. Carolina Alston, in dry goods, had a number of white customers as well as colored. Other Negro enterprises included one drug store, two harness and saddlery shops, five confectioners, seventeen boot and shoe repair shops, six blacksmith and wheelwright shops, two butchers, three newspapers with two job printing offices, twenty barber shops, two undertakers, two mattress manufacturers, and three tailoring establishments. Among the carpenters and brickmasons, ninety per cent of whom were colored, there were at least a half dozen contractors.[90]

Beaufort, long the center of Negro political influence, showed a meager business development among Negroes in comparison with that of the remainder of the state. In 1878 there was said to be only one small store in the town kept by a Negro and even in the surrounding countryside the stores were kept by "German Jews and suchlike people."[91] A visitor, when told that there was a kind of black aristocracy, found it to consist of officials and several colored lawyers in criminal practice. There were one or two tailor shops and a small harnessmaker and several carpenters and tradesmen, some of whom undertook small contracts.[92] In 1892, 539 Negroes in the town of Beaufort owned taxable real property assessed at $195,945 and personal property at $4,315, while 174 whites owned real property of $443,900 and personal property of $149,-320.[93] Among the Negro property owners was Joe McKnight, a bricklayer, who owned nearly three blocks of buildings on Lawrence Street in 1886. He had been for sixty-five years a resident of Beaufort.[94]

---

[90] H. E. Lindsay, "Negro Business Men of Columbia, S. C.," in W. E. B. DuBois (ed.), *The Negro in Business*, pp. 62-63.
[91] Campbell, *White and Black* p. 339.
[92] *Ibid.*
[93] Port Royal *Palmetto Post*, August 11, 1892.
[94] *Ibid.*, January 28, 1886.

Negro home ownership is another criterion of the economic progress of the urban Negro. While fewer Negroes in the towns than on the farms owned the houses they occupied by 1900, it is probable that their houses were on the whole more substantial than the cabins occupied by farmers. Of a total of 74,507 non-farm homes occupied by Negroes in 1900 only 7,996, or 12.8 per cent, were owned by the occupants.[95]

Negroes controlled practically no banking and credit facilities. The South Carolina Banking Association, organized at Florence in 1891, had a capital stock of $12,500 divided into five hundred shares and was the largest endeavor, if not the only one, of this type undertaken.[96] Out of thirteen Negro building and loan associations reported in the nation in 1899, there was one in South Carolina, at Anderson.[97] At least two Negroes, however, were associated with whites in building and loan associations. An association organized by leading white businessmen of Charleston elected Richard Birnie, Negro, a director in 1883,[98] and Charles McDuffie Wilder, postmaster of Columbia, served as a director of the Columbia Building and Loan Association, which was also controlled by whites.[99]

Negro professional people, like Negro businessmen, served chiefly their own race; they were occupied mainly as teachers, clergymen, lawyers, doctors, and newspapermen. In 1900 the census reported 1,365 Negroes who classified themselves as teachers.[100] There were 3,270 Negro teachers in the public schools, but most of these probably were classified in other lines of work because of the extremely short school terms.[101] Clergymen numbered 1,042; government officials, 31; lawyers, 29; and physicians, 43. There were also four dentists.[102]

The training of Negro lawyers, as that of white lawyers during the period, usually came through reading law under some person

---

[95] Bureau of the Census, *Negroes in the United States*, pp. 188-90.

[96] Columbia *Daily Register*, October 5, 1890; Charleston *News and Courier*, January 2, 1891.

[97] DuBois (ed.), *The Negro in Business*, p. 13.

[98] Charleston *New Era*, April 28, 1883.

[99] New York *Age*, May 9, 1885.

[100] Bureau of the Census, *Negroes in the United States*, pp. 184-87.

[101] *Reports and Resolutions* (1901), I, 212-13.

[102] Bureau of the Census, *Negroes in the United States*, pp. 184-87.

already a member of the bar. Julius I. Washington, of Beaufort, for example, read law under W. J. Whipper, probate judge of the county, before his admission to the bar in 1887.[103] However, some legal training was carried on by Claflin College and Allen University. Claflin College in 1881 appointed to its chair of law Jonathan Jasper Wright, former justice of the state Supreme Court, who conducted his classes in Queen Street, Charleston, until his death in 1885.[104]

Allen University in Columbia had on its staff during the eighties Daniel Augustus Straker, one of the ablest colored lawyers in the state. Straker, a native of Barbados, where he was born in the 1840's, had come to the United States in 1868 and taught school for a short time in Louisville, Kentucky. He then attended Howard University Law School in Washington, and finally came to Charleston in 1875 as an inspector in the custom house. Shortly afterward, he moved to Orangeburg where he set up a law practice. Appointed in 1880 as a special inspector to act with R. B. Elliott, special agent of the Treasury Department in Charleston, he moved to Columbia in 1882 to teach at Allen and practice law in the local courts.[105]

The first two classes graduated by Straker showed so high a standard in examination before the state Supreme Court "as to elicit special commendation from the Judges."[106] However, in 1887 Straker found his teaching and law practice so unremunerative that he removed to Detroit, Michigan. The Columbia press reported that while "The personal and property rights of his colored clients have been faithfully and in most cases successfully represented, their poverty as a class has left his labor in their behalf unremunerative and compels him to seek another field for the exercise of legal talents which will win renown and money under other conditions than those which interpose an insuperable barrier here." Straker took with him to the North letters of commendation from Governor J. P. Richardson, Senator Wade Hampton, all three justices of the Supreme Court, and from Joseph D. Pope, law pro-

---

[103] Caldwell, *History of the American Negro: South Carolina Edition*, p. 511.

[104] Fitchett, "The Role of Claflin College in Negro Life in South Carolina," *Journal of Negro Education*, XII (Winter, 1943), 49; Robert Hilliard Woody, "Jonathan Jasper Wright, Associate Justice of the Supreme Court of South Carolina, 1870-1877," *Journal of Negro History*, XVIII (April, 1933), 131.

[105] New York *Age*, September 22, 1883.

[106] Columbia *Daily Register*, June 12, 1885.

fessor of South Carolina College. In recounting his departure the Columbia *Daily Register* said that "he was among the very few leading Republicans who could safely undertake to challenge the respect of the whites or his own race, on the ground of his character and record."[107]

Negro lawyers naturally were centered in the Low Country areas of largest Negro population, particularly in Beaufort County, where such political figures as Thomas E. Miller, Julius I. Washington, and W. J. Whipper practiced. Whipper, Probate Judge of Beaufort County for several terms during the eighties, had been the center of attention as one of the supposedly corrupt judges elected by the legislature in 1875, but a white townsman in 1882 found him to be "rather profligate than vicious," a man who "combined with his extravagant and spendthrift habits . . . a good many qualities of generosity and goodness of heart." He had been very favorably impressed with Whipper upon hearing him defend before a colored jury a white youth charged with the murder of a colored youth, and at another time observed him interpose his body to protect two white men threatened by a Negro mob, "a position requiring pluck and courage that have blanched even white men under opposite conditions."[108] Legal papers connected with Whipper's practice indicate that it was considerable.[109]

Samuel J. Lee, born on the plantation of Samuel McGowan in Abbeville County in 1844, served after the Civil War as circuit solicitor and as a special federal land agent in Alabama for the detection of fraudulent entries of public lands. Moving to Charleston in 1882, he had a considerable practice until his death in 1895. "His knowledge of criminal law was excellent and his acute and clear perception, his facility for grasping points and making the most of every slip in his opponent's argument made him a reputation of which any man would be proud."[110]

---

[107] *Ibid.*, July 24, 1887. In Detroit, Straker established himself as something of an authority on the South and published two volumes: *The New South Investigated* (Detroit, 1888), which naturally concerns itself largely with South Carolina, and *Negro Suffrage in the South* (Detroit, 1906).

[108] Charleston *News and Courier*, January 12, 1882.

[109] William J. Whipper Papers, Moorland Foundation, Howard University Library.

[110] Charleston *News and Courier*, April 2, 1895, obituary; *see also* Columbia *Daily Register*, April 10, 1883.

Not all Negro attorneys were as conspicuous in Republican politics as these. While F. D. J. Lawrence of Beaufort, a Democrat,[111] seems to have been unique in his politics, such lawyers as A. E. Hampton and T. A. Saxon of Richland County,[112] W. W. Still of Beaufort,[113] John B. Edwards and T. St. Mark Sasportas of Charleston,[114] and J. C. Whittaker [115] of Sumter operated quietly without conspicuous forays into politics. As in the case of D. A. Straker, most Negro lawyers found that a clientele of the impoverished members of their race scarcely provided sufficient income, and were forced to go into numerous sidelines. For example, W. T. Andrews of Sumter, in addition to being a lawyer, was a notary public, school teacher, life insurance, real estate, and loan agent, and editor of the *Defender*.[116]

Negro doctors did not appear in any number until the nineties. George Campbell was told in Beaufort that one Northern colored man had tried to practice there during the Reconstruction period, but was "very extortionate" and distrusted by his own race, and finally went away.[117] T. Thomas Fortune, Negro editor of the New York *Age*, found on a trip to Charleston in 1890 three colored physicians: William Demosthenes Crum, A. C. McClellan, and William Henry Johnson. Crum, a pioneer physician, had graduated from Howard University in 1880, and shortly afterward located in his home town of Charleston. In addition to a lucrative practice, he was occupied in the Negro political and social life of the city.[118] Crum enjoyed the respect of white citizens because of his deference to their race convictions. When the daughter of William

---

[111] Yorkville *Enquirer*, May 16, 1888.

[112] Port Royal *Palmetto Post*, May 19, 1887.

[113] *Ibid.*

[114] See John B. Edwards to W. J. McKinlay, May 24, 1899, Carter G. Woodson Papers.

[115] Columbia *Daily Register*, February 11, 1887. At the February, 1887, term of court in Sumter the Negro law firm of Edwards and Whittaker monopolized nearly all the business. In about two-thirds of the cases they appeared for the defendants. *Ibid.*, February 24, 1887.

[116] W. T. Andrews to W. J. McKinlay, n. d., Carter G. Woodson Papers.

[117] Campbell, *White and Black*, p. 339.

[118] Fitchett, "The Status of the Free Negro in Charleston, South Carolina, and His Descendants in Modern Society," *Journal of Negro History*, XXXII (October, 1947), 444; New York *Age*, May 24, 1890.

Wilberforce, the English abolitionist, visited him, he permitted her to ride in the carriage while he walked alongside it.[119]

A. C. McClellan, like Crum, was reported in 1890 to have established an independent position in Charleston. He had graduated from Howard Medical College in the eighties, after having been a midshipman at Annapolis one year, and set up his practice in Charleston about 1884.[120] In 1897 he founded the Charleston Training School for Colored Nurses, which still exists.[121] The branch of obstetrical nursing in the school was under L. Hughes Brown, a graduate of the Women's Medical College of Philadelphia, and wife of a colored Presbyterian minister.[122] William Henry Johnson, born in Charleston in 1865, was awarded his M. D. by Howard University in 1887 and began practice immediately thereafter in Charleston.[123] Joseph A. Robinson, a native of Charleston with free Negro background, graduated in 1893 from the Medical School of Howard University as an honor student, and returned to his native city to set up practice.[124]

Columbia had at the end of the century three Negro physicians: C. C. Johnson, C. L. Walton, and Matilda Arabelle Evans.[125] Dr. Evans, born in Aiken County in the seventies, had attended Schofield Industrial School, worked her way through Oberlin College, taught at Schofield and then attended the Women's Medical College in Philadelphia, where she won her M. D. degree in 1897. After locating in Columbia the same year, she became "an apostle of

---

[119] Simkins, *Pitchfork Ben Tillman,* p. 416. Crum enjoyed the favor of white citizens, being put in charge of the Negro department of Charleston's South Carolina Interstate and West Indian Exposition of 1901-1902, and President Theodore Roosevelt was assured by leading citizens while he was at the Exposition "that Crum was one of the best citizens of Charleston, an admirable man in every way. . . ." When Roosevelt nominated him at the end of 1902, however, "the very Charlestonians who had praised Crum now went into hysterics," and mobilized against his confirmation. The long battle that Roosevelt waged for confirmation, 1902-1909, is described briefly in *ibid.*, pp. 416-18. *See also* on the subject the voluminous correspondence of Crum and others with W. J. McKinlay, Carter G. Woodson Papers.

[120] Charleston *News and Courier,* January 16, 1897.

[121] *Ibid.*

[122] *Ibid.*

[123] Fitchett, *Journal of Negro History,* XXXII (October, 1947), 444; Caldwell, *History of the American Negro: South Carolina Edition,* pp. 647-49.

[124] Fitchett, *Journal of Negro History,* XXXII (October, 1947), 444.

[125] Lindsay, "Negro Business Men of Columbia, S. C.," in DuBois (ed.), *The Negro in Business,* pp. 62-63.

sanitation and better living conditions" as well as a doctor, and soon organized a nurse's training school which grew into St. Luke Hospital and had in 1918 fourteen rooms and twenty beds.[126]

In 1899 the Negro physicians of the state organized a state association in a meeting at Spartanburg. Principal movers of the organization were Doctors Harry and Rhodes of Spartanburg who were reputed to "have made money and gained the respect of the people at large.[127]

Negro newspapers of the post-Reconstruction period were generally short-lived publications of poor quality. Handicapped by a lack of advertisers, lack of money, and the scarcity of literate readers to which they could address themselves, they might with some reason be classified under other headings than economic activity. But inspired by a desire for uplift and sometimes over-sanguine as to their prospects, Negro editors brought forth a quantity of weekly, semi-monthly, and monthly journals which flourished briefly and died quietly. The *Journal of Enterprise,* published by the Reverend S. H. Jefferson in Abbeville, brought commendation from the whites in 1883 by its stand that "the improvement and education of the colored people must be brought about by their own efforts, and not by political action or additional Federal legislation."[128] Samuel J. Lee published briefly a Radical organ, the *Vindicator,* in Sumter.[129] Charleston occasionally had more than one Negro weekly competing for public favor. In 1883 the *Palmetto Press,*[130] edited by R. L. Smith, competed with the more conservative *New Era,* edited by William Holloway. In the mid-eighties they were replaced by the Charleston *Recorder,*[131] published by the Reverend J. E. Hayne, Baptist minister, and in 1888 the Reverend C. W. McCall moved his *Monitor* from Cheraw to Charleston.[132] Hayne, after the turn of the century, published a weekly titled

---

[126] Caldwell, *History of the American Negro: South Carolina Edition,* pp. 393-95.

[127] Columbia *State,* April 28, 1899.

[128] Charleston *News and Courier,* October 11, 1883.

[129] Columbia *Daily Register,* February 5, 1882.

[130] *Ibid.,* July 19, 1883.

[131] Two issues of this paper have been preserved in the Duke University Library. Charleston *Recorder,* November 6, 1886, and August 27, 1887.

[132] One issue, May 26, 1888, has been examined through the courtesy of Mesdames Mae Holloway Purcell and Susan Dart Butler of the Dart Hall Branch of the Charleston Free Library.

the *Hamitic Palladium,* which, its editor said, "discusses the live questions of the times, and will from time to time give valuable articles on 'Ham's Place in History,' etc."[133] S. H. Jefferson, who had edited the *Journal of Enterprise* in Abbeville was in 1890 associated with C. Pierce Nelson in the publication of the Columbia *Palmetto Gleaner,* "devoted to the moral, religious, and intellectual progress of the colored race."[134] In 1895 a survey reported Negro editors as operating ten papers, as follows:

Aiken Court House	*Little Observer*	Semi-Monthly
Beaufort	*New South*	Weekly
Bennettsville	*Pee Dee Educator*	Semi-Monthly
Brunson	*Hampton County Elevator*	Weekly
Charleston	*Enquirer*	Weekly
Chester	*South Carolina Herald*	Weekly
Columbia	*People's Recorder*	Weekly
Florence	*Baptist Herald*	Semi-Monthly
Vaucluse	*South Carolina Tribune*	Weekly [135]

This survey missed the Charleston *Messenger,* a weekly published in 1895 by Francis P. Crum.[136] A survey in 1899 revealed only six papers, and of those published in 1895 only the *Pee Dee Educator* and *People's Recorder* had survived. Four new papers were the Columbia *Christian Soldier,* the Spartanburg *Piedmont Indicator,* the Columbia *South Carolina Standard,* and the Charleston *Observer.*[137]

Of the numerous Negro weeklies published in the eighties and nineties only four demonstrated the quality and tenacity to survive for more than a year or two. The Bennettsville *Pee Dee Educator,* founded in 1879 by Edward James Sawyer, was still publishing twenty years later. Sawyer, a native of Fayetteville, North Carolina, had come to South Carolina while the South Carolina University was open to Negroes. After it was closed he completed his college

---

[133] This paper is advertised inside the back cover of Joseph E. Hayne, *Are the White People of the South the Negro's Best Friends? or The Only Just Human Methods of Solving Race Problems* (Philadelphia, 1903).

[134] Columbia *Daily Register,* August 20, 1890.

[135] James T. Haley (ed.), *Afro-American Encyclopedia* (Nashville, 1895), p. 134.

[136] Francis P. Crum to Booker T. Washington, September 12, 1895, Booker T. Washington Papers.

[137] DuBois (ed.), *The Negro in Business,* p. 74.

course at Allen University in 1882. In addition to his newspaper work he was engaged in a number of other activities which, perhaps, supported the paper. In 1878 he became principal of the Bennettsville Graded School, a position which he retained fifteen years and relinquished because of the pressure of other duties. Meanwhile he had opened a store which he still operated in 1918 as the oldest merchant in the city. In 1883 he was admitted to the bar and had an occasional law practice. Under Presidents Hayes and Harrison he was postmaster of Bennettsville.[138] Unfortunately, no copy of the paper is today available.

The Beaufort *Sea Island News,* founded in 1879, was apparently the direct successor to the Beaufort *Tribune,* which had been established in 1874 as an independent Republican paper by a white named W. M. French.[139] Because of the demise of the major Republican journals with the collapse of the Chamberlain government, the *Sea Island News* was for many years the leading Republican newspaper in the state. Its editor, P. B. Morris, made it a "bright and spicy journal . . ., the best colored newspaper published in the South." When Morris died in 1891 his obituary recorded that, "A Republican in politics, he was never an offensive partisan. Tenacious of his own opinions he was tolerant of the opinions of those who differed from him, and so he made friends of all."[140] The newspaper apparently died with him.

Its place was taken immediately by the *New South,* edited by S. J. Bampfield, clerk of court of the county, who was associated in the enterprise with G. W. Anderson, a teacher at the Beaufort Normal and Industrial Academy, and I. Randall Reid, an attorney and a deputy sheriff of Beaufort.[141] A seven column weekly of four pages, the paper carried national dispatches from the Southern Associated Press and a respectable amount of national advertising.[142] It compared favorably with small town white weeklies of similar circulation.

---

[138] Caldwell, *History of the American Negro: South Carolina Edition,* pp. 265-67; J. A. W. Thomas, *A History of Marlboro County with Traditions and Sketches of Numerous Families* (Atlanta, 1897), p. 281.

[139] Woody, *Republican Newspapers of South Carolina* (Charlottesville, Virginia, 1936), pp. 24-25.

[140] Charleston *News and Courier,* November 20, 1891; *American Newspaper Directory* (New York, 1884), p. 440.

[141] Penn, *The Afro-American Press and Its Editors,* pp. 205-10.

[142] The author has examined the issue of March 7, 1897, in the South Caroliniana Library, University of South Carolina.

The Charleston *New Era,* though published only from 1880 to 1885, is of particular interest because a considerable file of scattered issues running from 1880 to 1884 has been preserved.[143] Published by William Holloway, it began as the official organ of the Charleston County Republican party,[144] but quickly shifted to an independent line which stamped Holloway as a fellow traveller of the Democratic party, and brought him from his contemporary, the Savannah (Ga.) *Echo,* the appellation of "the *Uncle Remus* of South Carolina."[145]

Supporting the Eight-Box Law and consistently backing Democratic candidates, Holloway insisted that he was following an independent line, and did, in fact, urge upon the Democrats the nomination on their state ticket in 1882 of a Negro, or of some white men who had been enlisted in the Confederate Army instead of the persistent parade of brigadiers.[146] He illustrated the political dilemma of the Negro when he complained of the "Coxcomb, who has been brought to quod, in the drag-net of events, who prates of how *he* and the Country, eventuated our liberty." For such Republicans he had only "laughter, sneers and jeers. We have seen too much of hand shaking with the 'Negro,' to his face, so to speak, and plotting his degradation behind his back, that we know pretty well, what estimate to put upon our political dogmatists, that cross our path now-a-days."[147] Not in politics, but in commercial and economic organization Holloway saw the way to Negro development. "It is wisdom, then," he said, "to strive to that end, and to cut loose from 'entangling alliances,' that boot us no good. To inculcate such sentiment, is the essence of independent journalism."[148] It is clear that, whatever the merits of his approach, Holloway showed prophetic vision of the drift that Negro opinion was to take before the end of the century.

---

[143] In the Duke University Library.
[144] Charleston *News and Courier,* September 1, 1880.
[145] Quoted in Charleston *New Era,* April 28, 1883.
[146] *Ibid.,* July 29, 1882.
[147] *Ibid.,* April 7, 1883.
[148] *Ibid.*

8

THE LIBERIAN EXODUS

THE Negro penchant for migration which became notorious after the Civil War was the outgrowth of unsettled conditions and the novelty of freedom, but was kept alive by the poverty that Negroes experienced as the mudsills of a depressed agriculture. Without worldly goods, Negroes could easily pull up stakes and move off in search of better conditons and better employers. The mobility of the Negro sharecropper has been a constant factor in the South since the Civil War. In addition to the mobility brought about by the search for improved economic conditions, railway excursions became an important part of Negro social life. The Negroes, said a white observer, "are literally crazy about travelling. The railroad officials are continually importuned by them to run extra trains, excursion trains, and so on, on all sorts of occasions: holidays, picnics, Sunday-school celebrations, church dedications, funerals of their prominent men, circuses, public executions. . . . They attract whole counties of negroes, and it is delightful to witness their childish wonder and enjoyment and behavior on the cars."[1]

So common had these practices become that by the end of Reconstruction it was axiomatic among whites that delight in travel was a racial characteristic of the Negroes. "The Negro rarely possesses any home attachments," said one. "He is continually on the wing . . .; and as he can with facility ingratiate himself among strangers of his own color, he would not be disconcerted were he as quickly transported from one State to another as Aladdin's wife or as Noureddin in the Thousand and One Nights."[2]

---

[1] A South Carolinian, *Atlantic Monthly*, XXXIX (February, 1877), 682.
[2] *Ibid.*, p. 677.

[153]

The violent political campaign of 1876 and its aftermath brought widespread uncertainty among the Negroes of the state and interest in the possibility of emigration. The great interest in emigration was not confined to South Carolina but was a Southwide phenomenon that had as its causes not only the political weakness of the Negroes and the general restriction of civil rights but also their economic subordination and the general difficulty of getting ahead in agriculture, their chief source of livelihood. It culminated in 1879 in the wholesale removal of great numbers of Negroes from the lower Mississippi Valley to the West, particularly Kansas.[3] In South Carolina, on the other hand, interest was at first centered almost altogether on Liberia, both because of its greater accessibility from the east coast and because of the work already undertaken by the American Colonization Society in transporting small numbers of Negroes to Africa.[4]

Congressman Richard H. Cain, Negro minister and newspaper publisher of Charleston, noted in January, 1877, a "deep and growing interest taken by the Colored people . . . in the subject of Emigration," and wrote to the secretary of the Colonization Society for information on arrangements for passage to Liberia. "The Colored people of the South," he said, "are tired of the constant struggle for life and liberty with such results as the 'Missippi [sic] Plan' and prefer going where no such obstacles are in their way of enjoying their Liberty."[5] During the first four months of 1877, while the rival Chamberlain and Hampton governments were struggling for ascendancy, Cain reported interest in the possibility of emigration to be spreading daily.[6] In his *Missionary Record* he reported "communications from various persons and from all sections of the country on the subject of emigration to Africa. Thousands of colored people in South Carolina would leave if the means of transportation were furnished them."[7] Movements to

---

[3] Woodson, *A Century of Negro Migration* (Washington, 1918), pp. 134-43; Vernon Lane Wharton, *The Negro in Mississippi, 1865-1890* (Chapel Hill, 1947), pp. 106-17.

[4] Simkins and Woody, *South Carolina During Reconstruction*, 234; *African Repository*, LIII (January, 1877), 26-27.

[5] Richard Harvey Cain to William Coppinger, January 25, 1877, American Colonization Society Papers, Vol. 196, Library of Congress.

[6] R. H. Cain to W. Coppinger, February 12, 1877, *ibid.*

[7] *African Repository*, LIII (April, 1877), 39, quoting Charleston *Missionary Record.*

organize for removal to Liberia were reported in the counties of Abbeville, Laurens, Oconee, Pickens, Newberry, Lexington, Marlboro, Georgetown, Colleton, Barnwell, Aiken, Edgefield, Beaufort, and Charleston.[8]

Negroes were particularly eager to leave Edgefield County, center of the "Straightout" white supremacy Democrats. H. N. Bouey, Republican probate judge, retired by the election of 1876, said that if a ship could be started for Liberia from Charleston or Beaufort in January it would not be able to carry the fifth man who was ready to go. "Of course, this upheaval is caused by their political and general mistreatment in this County—But I advise them to take it all quietly and christianly, for I believe God is in the move."[9] Bouey himself was ready to return to school teaching, "and in Liberia at that," and expressed sincere hope that some way would be made available to carry "the best men and women of this county" who wished to go in January after their crops had been gathered.[10]

Bouey was to be an important figure in the organization of the effort to carry out a mass exodus. In the spring of 1877 he was selected as a juror in the United States District Court in Charleston, and there met George Curtis, another juror, native of British Guiana and resident of Beaufort, who was also full of the spirit of emigration. The two men sought out the Reverend B. F. Porter, pastor of Morris Brown A. M. E. Church, who was very enthusiastic about the idea. By chance, Professor J. C. Hazeley, a native African, was in Charleston at the same time to deliver lectures on the advantages of emigration. On the fourth of July a celebration was held at the Morris Brown Church at which a number of addresses were delivered on behalf of emigration.[11] On July 26 a mass meeting was called to celebrate the thirtieth anniversary of the Liberian Declaration of Independence. A parade culminated at the Mall where four thousand Negroes gathered to hear George Curtis read the Liberian Declaration of Independence and the Reverend B. F. Porter deliver a twenty minute address in favor

---

[8] *Ibid.*

[9] Harrison N. Bouey to W. Coppinger, May 23, 1877, American Colonization Society Papers, Vol. 197.

[10] H. N. Bouey to W. Coppinger, May 31, 1877, *ibid.*

[11] J. C. Hazeley to W. Coppinger, July 4, 10, 14, 1877, *ibid.*, Vol. 198; Charleston *News and Courier*, April 16, 1878.

of the exodus. A proposition made by Porter for the formation of a stock company with thirty thousand shares of stock at $10 a share "met with much evident favor,"[12] and the Liberian Exodus Joint Stock Steamship Company with B. F. Porter as president and H. N. Bouey as secretary was soon thereafter organized.[13]

Obvious enthusiasm for the project all over the state caused immediate white reaction against the prospect of losing cheap colored labor. A rumor went about that J. C. Hazeley was being paid $200 a month by the American Colonization Society to get the Negroes to leave and that Senators Blaine, Conkling, and Morton were getting up subscriptions of $2,000,000 in the North to send Negroes to Liberia in order to ruin the whites in the South.[14] Prominent white lawyers and businessmen in Charleston were accused of trying to bribe Hazeley to lecture against the emigration scheme.[15] In Edgefield the whites charged the leaders of the emigration movement "with seeking revenge against them on account of their political ascension in this state and county," and sought to dissuade colored laborers by paying them only in drafts on merchants, which would be good only in Edgefield, and would therefore keep them from leaving.[16] In addition, John Mardenborough, a Negro attorney of Edgefield, wrote to William Coppinger, "Sir, you cannot imagine the deplorable condition of the colored people here," and reported white planters to be spreading a rumor that the emigration scheme was really an effort to entice the Negroes away to Cuba, where they would be sold in slavery.[17]

But white opposition and efforts at obstruction served only to fan the flames. R. H. Cain kept in his *Missionary Record* a standing editorial headed "Ho for Africa! One million men wanted for Africa."[18] Martin R. Delany, recently appointed trial justice in Charleston, was quickly brought into the movement. He had travelled extensively in Africa before the Civil War and had been in the fifties active on behalf of a scheme to colonize the Niger

[12] Charleston *News and Courier*, July 27, 1877.

[13] H. N. Bouey to W. Coppinger, November 27, 1877, American Colonization Society Papers, Vol. 199.

[14] J. C. Hazeley to W. Coppinger, July 10, 1877, *ibid.*, Vol. 198.

[15] J. C. Hazeley to W. Coppinger, July 14, 1877, *ibid.*

[16] H. N. Bouey to W. Coppinger, July 10, 1877, *ibid.*

[17] John Mardenborough to W. Coppinger, June 6, 1877, *ibid.*, Vol. 197.

[18] Charleston *News and Courier*, April 16, 1878.

Valley with Negroes from the United States.[19] B. F. Porter appeared in Columbia in August to speak on behalf of the colonization scheme, and in the northern tier of counties June Mobley, a colored citizen of Union County, travelled about making speeches in favor of Liberian emigration to all who would listen. He argued that it would be impossible for whites and blacks to live together in South Carolina as citizens. The black man would always "take his place in the kitchen," to use the speaker's words. He saw no way in which Negroes could prosper, for in order to prosper they must become landowners. That would be extremely difficult, he argued, because of the repeal of the lien law. Mobley, however, warned against precipitate action, and asked for contributions so that he could make a trip to Africa and bring back a report on conditions.[20]

Rumors of the fertility of the Liberian soil and the salubrity of the Liberian climate reached fantastic proportions. One laborer told a reporter he understood potatoes grew to such proportions in Liberia that one would more than supply a large family for a whole day, that it was necessary when one wanted sugar or syrup only to bore a gimlet hole in a tree, that certain trees produced bacon, and that fires were almost unknown, the heat of the sun being enough for cooking purposes.[21] Jasper Smith of Union, having heard that Congress had appropriated $100,000 for emigration, sent a petition for aid signed by a number of his neighbors, to be presented to the Congress.[22]

The Negro churches were at first opposed to the movement for fear of losing some of their best members, but as time went by they fell in line with the general hue and cry, applying their zeal to "their appointed work" of carrying the religion of Christ into the jungles of Africa. In addition, colored ministers advanced the argument that the discontented should be encouraged to emigrate because their presence would be a general detriment to the communities in which they lived if they were unable to get away.[23]

---

[19] Frank A. Rollin, *Life and Public Services of Martin R. Delany* (Boston, 1883), pp. 84-85, 96; Charleston *News and Courier*, April 16, 1878.

[20] Columbia *Daily Register*, August 21, 1877; Yorkville *Enquirer*, September 27, October 1, 1877.

[21] Charleston *News and Courier*, August 21, 1877.

[22] Jasper Smith to W. Coppinger, January 3, 1878, American Colonization Society Papers, Vol. 200.

[23] Charleston *News and Courier*, April 16, 1878.

The responsive chord that emigration propaganda struck among Negroes all over the state is indicated by the volume of mail that was received from various points in the state by William Coppinger, Secretary of the American Colonization Society. Although Coppinger's group was not organically connected with the company formed in Charleston during 1877, it was to him that many, including the officers of the Charleston group, turned for information. William G. White of Claflin University wrote to get information because, he said, "Many are desirous of emigrating. . . ."[24] William Martin of Columbia reported that he had received more than fifty requests for information from different parts of the state.[25] I. H. Rivers reported from Blackville that Negroes in his neighborhood were making up clubs to aid the emigration movement and that his club wanted five hundred copies of the latest issue of the *African Repository*.[26] Samuel J. Lee wrote from Aiken that he had had numerous inquiries about conditions in Liberia and wanted reliable information.[27] James G. G. A. Talley of Mount Jory, Union County, planned to make up a company in his neighborhood, and E. J. Furby of Society Hill estimated that two hundred families from Marlboro County would go, one hundred having already signed to go if they could get help.[28] From a farm near Guthriesville in York County, George Black wrote that he had heard much talk among the colored people of his neighborhood about Liberia and had heard June Mobley say "the colonization society out nort have send sum of our people to liberia." He wrote for "sum of papers that would give me a better understanding about going to liberia as I am won among the menny that am in favor of going." He had a wife and three children and was willing to sacrifice everything he had "to give them there liberty which I consider very sacraid."[29]

George W. West, leader of a group that had collected in Charleston, wrote that if they could not get away, "the poor people Will Die with grief from the treatments they have to incout [sic] with. We have to keep our mouths shut for Everything they say to us

---

24 William G. White to W. Coppinger, March 14, 1877, American Colonization Society Papers, Vol. 196.

25 William Martin to W. Coppinger, May 3, 1877, *ibid.*, Vol. 197.

26 I. H. Rivers to W. Coppinger, August 8, 1877, *ibid.*, Vol. 198.

27 Samuel J. Lee to W. Coppinger, September 19, 1877, *ibid.*

28 James G. G. A. Talley to W. Coppinger, October 1, 1877, *ibid.*, Vol. 199.

29 George Black to W. Coppinger, October 16, 1877, *ibid.*

We are no more then dogs here in S. C. and i am going to Lookout a place for them on the St. Paul's River and try through the Lords help to get them out."[30] Nelson Davies of Yorkville, however, reported in February, 1878, that a party he had collected to emigrate had been dissuaded by people who had been to Liberia and returned, having become dissatisfied.[31] There was a large group of these in York County, apparently some of those who had been sent by the Colonization Society during the Reconstruction period.

In Chester the Negroes of the county were reported during August, 1877, to be "afflicted with the Liberia fever. . . . Their feelings have been so wrought upon . . . that there is no doubt that a large number of them, if not a majority, would take their departure with little or no preparation. . . . At some places in the county the desire to shake off the dust of their feet against this Democratic State is so great, that they are talking of selling out their crops and their personal effects, save what they would need in their new home."[32] But the reporter who made this observation concluded that the emigration excitement would end in talk, for the very simple reason that those who wanted to go were destitute of the means to go. The white press attempted to dissuade those who wanted to emigrate by warning that the entire scheme was fraudulent. The Columbia *Daily Register* headed its account of a meeting addressed by B. F. Porter, "The Liberian Fraud,"[33] and warned the Negroes that the "whole scheme is gotten up by a few sharpers of your own race and a lot of white rascals, who would delude you by first robbing you of your little hard earnings and then leave you to die in the jungles of the native wilds of your ancestors. . . ."[34] From Ellenton it was reported that the Negroes took no stock whatever in the "Liberian humbug," although numbers of them were migrating from Barnwell to Beaufort, "a sort of negro paradise."[35] The Orangeburg *Taxpayer* expressed fear "that many an honest darkey has been deluded into this trap by designing and dishonest men."[36] In January, 1878, when parties of Negroes began to arrive

---

[30] George West to W. Coppinger, November 19, 1878, American Colonization Society Papers, Vol. 203.
[31] Nelson Davies to W. Coppinger, February 5, 12, *ibid.*, Vol. 200.
[32] Yorkville *Enquirer*, August 30, 1877.
[33] Columbia *Daily Register*, August 21, 1877.
[34] *Ibid.*, August 19, 1877.
[35] Charleston *News and Courier*, January 22, 1878.
[36] Charleston *News and Courier*, March 26, 1878, quoting Orangeburg *Taxpayer*.

in Charleston, having heard that a ship was available to take them to Liberia, they found none available, and the officers of the exodus association offered to get them jobs in the nearby phosphate works. The *News and Courier* bemoaned the fact that whipping had been abolished as a punishment in South Carolina, but suggested that "if the deluded colored people, from Georgia and South Carolina, were to vigorously apply forty lashes save one, to the fat backs of the sharpers who have swindled them, public opinion would not condemn the deed very severely!"[37]

Meanwhile, however, the exodus association had acquired a fund of $6,000 from the sale of stock and its president, B. F. Porter, under pressure from the emigrants who had arrived prematurely in Charleston, left in January to select a ship.[38] On March 18 the bark *Azor* arrived in the port of Charleston, "gaily decorated with flags which fluttered in the brisk breeze." It was of clipper build, of 411 and 97-100ths tons burden, with "a rakish look, indicative of fast sailing." Having come from Boston in fourteen days, the captain estimated that he could make Monrovia in twenty-five. The vessel had 19 berths for cabin passengers, and 140 berths for steerage passengers.[39]

On the twenty-first of March the bark was consecrated at a special religious service at White Point Garden, in the presence of five thousand Negroes. The ladies of St. Joseph's Union presented to Martin R. Delany the flag of Liberia and several addresses were made, all breathing missionary zeal. B. F. Porter remarked that the consecration of a ship was a little unusual, "but the colored race was one that eminently believed in God, and was learning to believe in the evangelization of the millions of their people who now sat in darkness." The Reverend Henry M. Turner told the crowd that the vessel "was not only to bear a load of humanity, but to take back the culture, education, and religion acquired here. The work inaugurated then would never stop until the blaze of Gospel truth should glitter over the whole broad African continent."[40]

---

[37] Charleston *News and Courier*, January 3, 1878.

[38] *Ibid.; For Africa! Special Voyage to Monrovia, Liberia,* broadside dated January 16, 1879, in American Colonization Society Papers, Vol. 204.

[39] Charleston *News and Courier*, March 19, 1878.

[40] *Ibid.,* March 22, 1878; *see also African Repository,* LIV (July, 1878), 77-78.

During the following month arrangements were made for the departure of the vessel, and exactly one month after the consecration the *Azor* sailed out of Charleston with 206 emigrants aboard, 175 having been left ashore when it was discovered that the emigrants, in their enthusiasm, had overloaded the ship. The association purchased a plantation on the Wando River for them to occupy until it returned.[41] Two churches were organized among the emigrants, the African Methodist Episcopal Church under the Reverend S. Flegler, and the Shiloh Baptist Church, with a clerk and seven deacons.[42] The *News and Courier,* still doubtful of the wisdom of the emigration, said the friends of the race wished the emigrants, "most sincerely, complete success in their undertaking, and bid them with one voice, Godspeed!"[43]

A. B. Williams, then a young reporter for the *News and Courier* accompanied the emigrants on their voyage to Monrovia and wrote a comprehensive account of the trip. On the way over he found that various motives had animated them. Some were going because they thought they would have a better chance to "rise in the world" with easily procured land and social equality with their neighbors, while others were tired of renting or working out and wanted to be their own masters. An emigrant from Georgia said that farm laborers had no security for their earnings and therefore no reason to work. Others "ground the 'Outrage Mill' " freely, and complained of "Ku-Klux," "Night Hawks," and "political persecutions." "By constant repetition of and additions to these tales of horror they get to put implicit confidence in them, and such groundless fears have probably really something to do with this movement. It seems though that in the main various and widely differing opinions and views brought the emigrants to Charleston. Once there, they were soon rallied under the general watchwords of 'Political persecution' and 'Social equality.' "[44]

The management of the association was guilty of several serious blunders which caused a frightful mortality from fever; 23 of the 206 emigrants died before reaching Africa.[45] The water supply was

---

[41] Charleston *News and Courier,* April 23, 1878.
[42] *African Repository,* LIV (July, 1878), 78.
[43] Charleston *News and Courier,* April 18, 1878.
[44] Williams, *The Liberian Exodus* (Charleston, 1878), p. 11.
[45] Charleston *News and Courier,* June 17, 1878.

insufficient and gave out shortly before the arrival at Sierra Leone. The flour was coarse and black, the meal poor, being stigmatized as "kiln-dried stuff, only fit for hogs to eat," the rice was broken and dirty, and the meat was only enough to last when carefully doled out; although all of it except five barrels belonged to the "six months' stores," intended for the support of the emigrants after their arrival in Liberia, all of it was used on the voyage.[46]

In addition, despite the law requiring the presence of a doctor on board, there was no doctor on the vessel. Arrangements had been made by B. F. Porter for Dr. J. W. Watts of Washington to accompany the *Azor,* but when he failed to arrive George Curtis volunteered to be the physician and was so presented to the Custom-House officials. Although he had never practiced, he claimed to have a knowledge of medicine, and since his wife was a regular nurse it was thought that the passengers could get along.[47] Williams observed that Curtis knew about as much of medicine "as a street car mule." During the voyage he prowled about the decks with a small book called *The Mariner's Medical Guide* in one hand and compounds extracted from the medicine chest in the other. "It is horrible," said Williams, "to think of a blundering ignoramus like this man having charge of the health of some three hundred people, a large majority of whom were women and children. It is only Heaven's mercy that there are not even more deaths to record."[48]

---

[46] Williams, *The Liberian Exodus,* p. 2.

[47] Report of interview with B. F. Porter in Baltimore, July 9, 1878, in dispatch to New York *Herald,* n.d. See unidentified clipping in volume titled *Azor* in Edward Willis Pamphlets, South Carolina Historical Society.

[48] Williams, *The Liberian Exodus,* p. 6. The ebullient and irresponsible George Curtis was a constant source of difficulty to the movement. When the Liberian Exodus Company was barely under way he had had illusions of getting the Charleston Chamber of Commerce to join with the Liberian government in raising a loan of $2,000,000 with which to establish a line of steamers between the two countries "on a grand scale." Later, an appeal through the *News and Courier* for help for the emigrants had to be disavowed by Martin R. Delany, who wrote, "Mr. Curtis of his own volition has not attended, except casually, the meetings of the board of directors for several months, and consequently could know but little of what was going on. His article and call for help was gratuitous, entirely unauthorized, and no such aid . . . is needed." Meanwhile it was disclosed he had deserted his wife, two of his own children, and three of hers by a previous marriage when he moved to Charleston. His only defense was, that "If every *liaison* is to be deemed a marriage, then we have a sufficient number of Utahs without going to the particular Territory of that name." It was later reported by a returning emigrant that he had deserted in Liberia the wife who had migrated there with him and had "a sweetheart"

The vessel arrived at Sierra Leone on May 19, where additional debts were incurred by the captain for supplies, pilotage, and, when the vessel became becalmed, for towage. The passengers were finally delivered in Monrovia on June 3.[49] After a forty-two days' journey, with the replenishing of supplies at Sierra Leone, there were still barely three weeks' supplies for the emigrants, including the ship's stores, which were turned over to them by the captain. Mitchell Williams, an emigrant who died on the voyage, had receipts for $558.20 for provisions, a share in a grist mill, dry goods, a due bill, and stock. His widow found in Monrovia that she had only the stock, dry goods, about fifteen dollars' worth of provisions, and the papers. There was no sign of any grist mill.[50]

The additional expenses incurred at Sierra Leone proved to be the burden that broke the back of the Liberian Exodus Joint Stock Steamship Company. Late in May, 1878, bills for $1,680 reached the company, $1,050 of which was for towage charged by the British steamer, *Senegal*.[51] Appeals for help were sent out to the American Colonization Society, and offers were made to transport its emigrants on the *Azor* more cheaply than Yates and Porterfield, the company with which the society had been dealing.[52] Captain Holmes, who had been trying to buy the *Azor* at the time it was purchased by Porter for the Company, was hired on the understanding that he was familiar with the coast of Africa and would open a profitable trade to the profit of the company and himself. Holmes, however, returned to Charleston without any freight, "but breathing death and slaughter to all concerned." He then obtained a full freight for London, worth $3,000 or more, but the income was all squandered on expenses. From London he wrote that he would sail to Africa for a home freight, but was next heard from late in 1878 off the Charleston bar, without freight or revenue. He was naturally suspected of engineering a swindle in order to get possession of the vessel.[53]

in Liberia. Charleston *News and Courier*, August 6, 17, 1877; *ibid.*, April 5, 6, 17, 1878; *ibid.*, May 13, 1879; George Curtis to William Coppinger, July 27, 1877, American Colonization Society Papers, Vol. 198.

[49] Charleston *News and Courier*, June 17, 24, 1878.

[50] Williams, *The Liberian Exodus*, p. 33.

[51] Martin R. Delany to Eli K. Price, July 12, 1878, American Colonization Society Papers, Vol. 202.

[52] *Ibid.*, H. N. Bouey to W. Coppinger, January 16, 1879, *ibid.*, Vol. 204.

[53] Unidentified clipping from a Negro newspaper, *Azor*, Edward Willis Pamphlets, South Carolina Historical Society.

In January, 1879, the Company announced another trip to Liberia, with the object of clearing the vessel of the heavy debt against her. This time the voyage was not for the stockholders of the company, but a regular fare of $40 for steerage passengers and $65 for cabin passengers was charged. The officers of the company admitted that they had bought the vessel when they had but $6,000 on hand, because emigrants were already pouring into Charleston, and that more than three hundred had been left in the city who were unable to make the trip, but they promised that "No such blunders will be permitted to occur again."[54] The departure date was set at February 20, but the ship never left.

Meanwhile, a libel against the *Azor* had been filed in the United States Admiralty Court in Charleston by Captain W. E. Holmes and Mate Sidney E. Horne for back wages and money loaned to the company, by the firm of Fuller and Chase for the cost of the anchor, and by Anna M. Gaillard, wife of a former state senator from Charleston who had gone on the first trip of the *Azor*, for $1,021 advanced for the purpose of fitting out the bark.[55] Late in March the company announced a mass meeting at Gibbs Farm near Charleston to raise not less than $5,000, "which must be raised at once or our property will go into the hands of Northern sharpers. . . ."[56] It was apparently unsuccessful, however, for Major Edward Willis, a white legal representative of the company, wrote to John H. B. Latrobe of the American Colonization Society in October that the company would require a loan to save the *Azor*.[57]

In November the vessel was sold at auction by order of the court, and was purchased for $2,950 by Edward Willis, representative of the company, acting for F. S. Rodgers, a wealthy white merchant.[58] This transaction was undertaken on the understanding that the Liberian Exodus Joint Stock Steamship Company would repurchase the vessel from Rodgers. At the time of Rodgers' purchase

---

[54] *For Africa! Voyage to Monrovia, Liberia*, in *Azor*, Edward Willis Pamphlets.

[55] Charleston *News and Courier*, February 1, March 12, July 7, 1879; Edward Willis to John H. B. Latrobe, October 2, 1879, American Colonization Society Papers, Vol. 207.

[56] *Save Our Ship the Azor!*, broadside dated March 31, 1879, in *Azor*, Edward Willis Pamphlets.

[57] E. Willis to J. H. B. Latrobe, October 2, 1879, American Colonization Society Papers, Vol. 207.

[58] Charleston *News and Courier*, November 9, 1879.

the company furnished $450 of the purchase price and made a contract authorizing it to repurchase the vessel for the remainder of the price Rodgers had paid plus $175, or a total of $2,675, provided the amount was in Rodgers' hands by November 11, 1880.[59] Rodgers, however, sold the vessel to parties in Boston five months before the expiration of the contract, and when the company presented him the $2,675 on the due date, the vessel had long since been out of his hands. "The transaction has surprised everybody," wrote Martin R. Delany, "as this merchant is very wealthy, was commended as being very reliable, and generally reputed to be a gentleman of unswerving integrity."[60] A suit which was entered by the company to recover $7,325 on the contract from Rodgers dragged on through the courts until 1884. A circuit court ruled in 1883 that the company was not a legal corporation because it was incorporated under a law that gave no authority to incorporate navigation companies, but this decision was reversed in 1884 by the state Supreme Court, which ruled that the defendant had contracted with the Liberian Exodus Company, and therefore had no right to question its legal existence later; the Court also ruled that the charter could be taken away from the company only by suit commenced by the attorney general of the state. It then remanded the case to the lower court.[61] There is, however, no evidence that the company was ever able to recover, since Rodgers had ample resources and the company did not have enough to continue the litigation.

Liberia was not made more attractive by the reports which were spread far and wide of mismanagement and fatalities on the first *Azor* voyage nor by the subsequent reports of emigrants who returned to the United States. In May, 1879, Spencer Reeves of Milledgeville, Georgia, an *Azor* emigrant, returned to his home, complaining that Liberia had been misrepresented to him. He had lost his wife and youngest child.[62] But the *Monrovia*, on which Reeves had returned to New York, was reported to be

[59] *Liberian Exodus Joint-Stock Steamship Company v. Rodgers*, 21 S. C. Reports, p. 27.

[60] M. R. Delany to W. Coppinger, December 18, 1880, American Colonization Society Papers, Vol. 211.

[61] *Liberian Exodus Joint-Stock Steamship Company v. Rodgers*, 21 S. C. Reports, p. 27.

[62] Charleston *News and Courier*, May 9, 13, 1879.

preparing a return voyage to Liberia with about eighty Negroes, many of them from the northern counties of South Carolina.[63] In December, 1879, the *Monrovia* brought back to New York eighteen more *Azor* emigrants who reported that not one in the *Azor* party would remain if he had the means to return. Most of them, because of their poverty and the dissipation of their supplies during the voyage, were said to have been thrown on the charity of the Liberians.[64]

Success in Liberia was achieved, but the reports of successful emigrants did not arrive until years after the assumption of general failure had been widely accepted. One emigrant wrote in 1880: "Almost every week I see some of the *Azor* people living at Poor Bar, and they report themselves as doing well. Those at Bonneville are greatly elated at their success. I don't think that there is one of them that could be induced to return to America on any account—things remaining in that country as they are now." The same correspondent reported 173 of the *Azor* emigrants, to his own knowledge, to be still in Liberia, and others perhaps in the interior, contrary to stories that the majority had died or returned to America.[65]

Saul Hill, a native of York, reported four years later that he had established a successful coffee farm of seven hundred acres, the entire crop of which he sold to a Philadelphia firm, and was planning to send for his father. His success, however, was attributed by the Columbia *Daily Register* to the fact that he had been in good financial circumstances when he left. "A number of other colored men went to Liberia at the same time, but some of them returned in a year or so afterward as poor as church mice and thoroughly disgusted with the new country."[66]

---

[63] *Ibid.*, May 9, 1879.

[64] Yorkville *Enquirer*, December 11, 1879, quoting New York *Herald*. A comical aspect of the difficulties experienced in Liberia was presented when the Charleston *News and Courier* reported that the United States minister in Liberia had sent the State Department an account of the secession of a number of native tribes in the interior in which he attributed the secession fever to the *Azor* emigrants who had brought to Liberia the heresy of state rights. Charleston *News and Courier*, August 18, 1879. It later appeared that the trouble was engineered by British imperialists looking toward a seizure of Liberia. *Ibid.*, August 26, 1879.

[65] D. B. Warner to W. Coppinger, January 5, 1880, letter published in Philadelphia *Christian Recorder* and quoted in Charleston *News and Courier*, March 13, 1880.

[66] Columbia *Daily Register*, December 17, 1884.

In 1890 it was reported that Charleston had furnished to Liberia some of its most prominent citizens. C. L. Parsons, Chief Justice of the Liberian Supreme Court, was a native of Charleston. Clement Irons, another native of Charleston, had built the first steamship constructed in Liberia. It had been launched on the St. Paul's River in December, 1888.[67] In 1891 the Reverend David Frazier, an emigrant from South Carolina, was elected to the Liberian Senate. He had opened a coffee farm with twenty thousand trees and was hoping to have thirty thousand the following year.[68]

But despite the success of these individuals, the Liberian Exodus Joint Stock Steamship Company must be put down as a failure. The causes of failure are numerous, but they cannot all be attributed to the officers of the company. The difficulties experienced on the voyage from want of supplies were the natural error of inexperienced persons. Porter claimed that the depletion of the water supply had resulted from extravagant waste.[69] The additional heavy expenses incurred at Sierra Leone were entirely unforeseen, but the company could be blamed for operating on such a close margin that unforeseen expenses could not be handled. The officers of the company sought to explain this away as having resulted from the enthusiasm of the emigrants who had gathered in Charleston in great numbers early in 1878 and had practically forced the company to purchase the *Azor* before it had sufficient funds on hand.[70] The plan of B. F. Porter to organize a regular trade between Charleston and Monrovia was not altogether impractical, but was undone by either the swindling, or the incompetency, of the white captain of the vessel. The final loss of the *Azor* was due to a man who took advantage of the financial stringency of the company to make a contract which he later violated, perhaps on the assumption that the company could not raise the money to reclaim the ship.

The whole project was destroyed by the accumulation of unforeseen debts, the remorseless pressure of creditors, the pitiless

---

[67] *African Repository*, LXVI (January, 1890), 28-29.
[68] Columbia *Daily Register*, July 24, 1891, quoting Winnsboro *News*.
[69] Report of interview with B. F. Porter in Baltimore, July 9, 1878, in a dispatch to New York *Herald*, n.d. See unidentified clipping in *Azor*, Edward Willis Pamphlets.
[70] *For Africa! Voyage to Monrovia, Liberia*, in *Azor*, Edward Willis Pamphlets.

propaganda by the white press that "Curtis & Co. are humbugs,"[71] and, finally, by lengthy and devious litigation. Although the idea of emigration to Africa was an unrealistic solution for the problems of Southern Negroes, there was sufficient interest in South Carolina to have made the Liberian Exodus Company a minor success had it not been destroyed by the concatenation of unfortunate circumstances.

---

[71] Charleston *News and Courier*, June 19, 1878.

9

THE MIGRATORY URGE

FROM unsuccessful returnees and from newspaper stories about their miserable condition Negroes generally learned to be wary of Liberian exodus schemes.[1] The apparently complete failure of the *Azor* project caused potential emigrants to turn their attention elsewhere. The most logical and easily accessible area was the West. As early as September, 1877, in the midst of the Liberian fever, a meeting to discuss the possibilities of migration to Texas attracted a throng of Negroes in the town of Rock Hill. A committee was selected for the purpose of viewing the country and reporting back.[2] In January, 1878, about forty Negroes departed from nearby Chester for Kansas. "They were not pleased with Democratic rule."[3]

The Southwide movement that reached major proportions in 1879 attracted the attention of Negro leaders who assembled in convention at Nashville on May 7 of that year with delegates from fourteen states, including South Carolina. Under the chairmanship of Congressman John R. Lynch of Mississippi, the body passed a resolution that "the colored people should emigrate to those States and Territories where they can enjoy all the rights which are guaranteed

---

[1] However, as late as 1886 there was sufficient interest that a man calling himself "Rev. J. C. Davidson," an alleged Baptist minister, swindled a number of Negroes in the area of Fort Mill by promising to furnish a train which would take them to New York, whence they would be taken to Liberia. Although a number of would-be emigrants had paid their passage money, neither the train nor "Davidson" appeared at the scheduled time for departure. Columbia *Daily Register*, December 24, 1886.

[2] Yorkville *Enquirer*, September 20, 1877.

[3] Charleston *News and Courier*, January 31, 1878.

by the laws and Constitution of the United States. . . ," and asked an appropriation of $500,000 from Congress to help the cause.[4]

The interest in migration to the West did not quickly abate, and in 1879, 1880, and 1881 various numbers of Negroes were reported to have migrated from South Carolina to Kansas.[5] During 1878 and 1879 there was also a sizable migration of Negroes, estimated at 1,500, from the counties of Barnwell, Hampton, and Colleton, into the Republican county of Beaufort.[6] Immigrants to Beaufort complained that they had been driven away from their homes by political persecution, and that when they returned for their friends some of them were shot at by white farmers who accused them of coming back to entice away the laborers.[7] A white reporter in Beaufort found the Negro Republican leaders in that area, many of them landholders, to be opposed to the idea of emigration. In fact, he suspected them of favoring Negro immigration into the state so that they could once again hold the reins of power.[8]

The largest single exodus movement came from "bloody Edgefield" in the last week of 1881. Between December 24 and 31 an estimated five thousand Negroes left their homes with Arkansas as the goal.[9] There had been in the area the usual complaints of political oppression which was more severe in Edgefield than in most parts of the state, Negroes complaining "that they cannot vote at the elections and if they do vote that their ballots are not counted; that they have no representation in the government, and that their rights are in the keeping of a hostile political party."[10] But it is probable that in most cases the economic push was stronger than the fear of personal danger and political persecution. The complaints of the laborers in the area were summarized as follows by Narciso G. Gonzales, then a young reporter for the Charleston *News and Courier*:

> "For ten years," as they express it, "we have tried to make money and have not been able to do so. We are poorer now

---

[4] *Appleton's Annual Cyclopaedia*, IV (1879), 358.
[5] Columbia *Daily Register*, December 14, 1879; January 8, 1880; December 23, 1881.
[6] *Appleton's Annual Cyclopaedia*, IV (1879), 813.
[7] Columbia *Daily Register*, January 28, 1879.
[8] Charleston *News and Courier*, May 3, 1879.
[9] *Ibid.*, January 2, 1882; *Appleton's Annual Cyclopaedia*, VI (1881), 813.
[10] Charleston *News and Courier*, January 2, 1882.

than when we began, we have less, in fact we have nothing. We have not lived extravagantly, we have exercised all the economy we knew how to use and we are going further down hill every day. There is no help for us here, there's no use in trying to get along under the old conditions any longer, and so we have just determined to go somewhere else and take a new start."[11]

The labor system in the exodus area was generally a tenancy system that involved the payment of a stipulated amount of cotton for every acre under cultivation. On the average the rent amounted to one bale of 450 pounds for from six to ten acres of land, the tenant being required to furnish his own fertilizer, stock, and farming implements. "The result of the system was that, after the guano and supplies had been paid for, there was nothing left at the end of the year for the laborers. . . . The soil is very thin, and without heavy fertilizing will produce nothing like a fair crop." In nearby areas not affected by the exodus movement the prevailing labor system was a sharecropping arrangement under which the owners furnished the stock and implements and the laborers received one-third of the crop. Another factor of which the Negroes in the exodus area complained was the law requiring the fencing of livestock, which was too expensive for their means. They were, therefore, dependent on "the flesh of a few ill-favored hogs" for meat.

In the fall of 1881 the movement took shape with the organization of a number of emigration societies. The largest was formed near Trenton by William H. Lawson, a former Republican school commissioner of Aiken County who had been teaching near Trenton for several years, and John Hammond, a black Baptist preacher with no education but with a powerful influence over his people. The society held meetings two nights a week through the fall at a church five miles from Trenton, and the meetings were large and enthusiastic; they were so open (whites frequently attended) that most whites did not take the movement seriously until emigration actually began. Dues were $1.00. About the middle of November Lawson, Hammond, and Spencer Dearing, another member of the society, went to spy out the territory 150 miles beyond Little Rock. They brought back a story of wages of $12 to $20 a month and

---

[11] *Ibid.* Except where otherwise indicated, the account of the Edgefield exodus is based on this source.

government lands to be secured by the payment of 12½ cents per acre.

When a majority of the members of the society decided to go, another assessment was levied, and Hammond left to arrange for the trains. On December 20 Spencer Dearing left Trenton with a party of 150 bound for Augusta, and two days later a general exodus began, groups of tens and fifties,. many whole families, moving toward Augusta. From the twenty-second until noon of Christmas Day columns of emigrants, consisting of members of the Hammond society, another society from near Johnston's, and a few persons from Lexington County moved through Trenton in the direction of Augusta. Men and women walked, "children and sick were hauled on wagons, upon which were also transported the movable property and household treasures of the marching column, packed in paper-covered trunks and boxes of curious construction. The wagons either belonged to the more thrifty of the emigrants or were furnished by the white farmers of the neighborhood, to whom the negroes transferred their cattle and hogs and the little remnants of their crops as payment for their services."

The train scheduled for departure from Augusta was not available as expected on the day after Christmas, and crowds gathered in the depot to await the arrival of Hammond and his chartered train for "Rockansas." The crowd became so large and disorderly that authorities in Augusta forced them to leave the Union Depot to hunt some other place to bivouac. "Many of them recrossed the river and camped upon the commons in historic Hamburg. The party presented a most pitiful spectacle as they lay encamped on the high bluff of the Savannah, exposed to the first chilling blasts of winter, without preparations for outdoor living, sorrowing over their misfortunes and no doubt longing for the fleshpots of Edgefield." The train, however, arrived during the night of the twenty-sixth and several hundred left via Atlanta, and on the following day several hundred more left. During the last few days of the year many more wagons passed through Trenton—"bound for the promised land." Some of them, instead of going to Augusta, headed toward the coastal counties of Beaufort, Colleton, Charleston, and Hampton.

By the end of the year it was said that some of the most extensive plantations in the area were left without a single colored laborer, and a number of whites were beginning to talk of leaving the county because of the stock fencing law and the acute shortage of labor. The New York *Tribune* chortled that, "The planters of Edgefield County, South Carolina, who have been conspicuous for years for their zeal in maintaining red-shirted rifle-clubs to terrify the blacks in political campaigns, find at last that there in a Nemesis in human affairs."[12]

In the state senate Thomas E. Miller, Negro Republican, introduced a resolution for the appointment of a committee of three senators "to investigate and report to this Chamber forthwith, what are the grievances under which our people are laboring, to the extent that they are compelled to leave their homes and native State at a time when South Carolina needs an increase of labor to develop her eminent resources."[13] The resolution, however, was indefinitely postponed by a vote of twenty-two to six, despite Miller's argument that if the stories were left uncontradicted about poor crops, poor lands, and the stock law, the immigration bureau (interested in importing whites) would find it impossible to entice a single person into South Carolina.[14] It is interesting to note that the Democratic senator from Edgefield voted with the three Republicans against postponing Miller's resolution, as well as the two Democratic senators from Charleston, who were probably worried about the effect on that port of the emigration from the hinterland.

Although the Edgefield exodus was the last that threatened to depopulate a sizable area of the state, the movement for emigration was not dissipated during the following two decades. Depressed agriculture and economic and political oppression served as a persistent push for emigration. A white man of Greenville County reported in 1882 that he was constantly approached by his black neighbors who asked him to get assistance from the government in Washington so that they could emigrate.[15] While the old Reconstruction rumor of "forty acres and a mule" had died a hard death by the end of the seventies, there persisted a feeling that

---

[12] Charleston *New Era*, January 14, 1882, quoting New York *Tribune*.

[13] *Senate Journal* (1881-1882), p. 361.

[14] *Ibid.*, p. 371; Charleston *News and Courier*, January 3, 1882.

[15] Lardner Gibbon to Benjamin Harris Brewster, May 18, 1882. General Records, Department of Justice, Source-Chronological File, South Carolina, Box 652, National Archives.

the government in Washington would yet do something toward helping the Negroes obtain lands in the West, a sentiment encouraged by the Nashville convention's request in 1879 for a federal appropriation to aid emigration and by vague notions of public lands available at low cost in the West.

Large farmers in the West and the major railroads maintained regular agents whose job it was to entice emigrants from the Southeast, and the railroads had special emigrant rates. Since federal aid was not forthcoming, Negro emigrants, like the latter-day Joads of Oklahoma, were at the mercy of labor and railroad agents and their propaganda of better conditions and higher wages in the West. At the end of 1881 the emigrant rate from Greenville to Little Rock was $22.50, and during the months of October and November of that year fifty-six adults and twenty-two children, mostly colored, left Greenville for western points, most of them going to Arkansas, although some of them went to Memphis and others to Texas.[16]

The methods that were adopted by emigrant agents were later recalled by William Pickens, who went as a child with his family from Pendleton to Arkansas. An agent representing a planter in the Mississippi River valley of Arkansas persuaded the elder Pickens to sign a contract to move his entire family to that state.

> In order to appreciate the persuasions which the agent used, the ignorance and superstition of such families would have to be understood. Ignorant people are too quick to believe tales of other places and other times. . . .
>
> To such a group reports from the outside world come with a feeling of other worldliness. The agent said that Arkansas was a tropical country of soft and balmy air, where cocoanuts, oranges, lemons and bananas grew. Ordinary things like corn and cotton, with little cultivation, grew an enormous yield.
>
> On the 15th of January, 1888, the agent made all the arrangements, purchased tickets, and we boarded the train in Seneca, S. C., bound toward Atlanta, Ga. Our route lay through Birmingham and Memphis and at each change of trains there seemed to be some representative of the scheme to see us properly forwarded, like so much freight billed for we knew not where. It was midwinter, but with all the unquestioning

---

[16] Columbia *Daily Register*, November 24, 1881.

faith and good cheer of our race we expected to land at the other end of our journey in bright sunshine and spring weather.

And a comical looking lot we must have been. We had no travelling cases, but each one bore some curious burden—sacks of clothes, quilts, bags, bundles and baskets. When we left our home the weather was comparatively mild, but as fate would have it, the nearer we got to Arkansas, the colder it became. In Memphis the snow was deep and the wind biting. The faith and enthusiasm of the party grew less; perhaps the older heads were waking up to a suspicion. The further we got from our South Carolina home, the dearer it seemed, as is true of most things in their first abandonment.[17]

In 1882 an emigrant who had gone to Arkansas from Greenville and returned for his family and friends described the procedure at the other end of the line, where

> . . . they were met by a land agent, who took charge of them at the depot where they disembarked and provided for them by accomodating them in large buildings which have been erected for the purpose near the principal points at which the final stop is made, until some arrangement is made for the purchase of a small lot of ground by the emigrants. In cases where they are without means, they are housed until they can obtain work, which is said to be very plentiful and remunerative on the farms in that section, the wages for hands being from twelve to twenty dollars per month, board included.[18]

The press continued to report sporadically through the eighties and nineties the departure of groups of emigrants. In November, 1883, fourteen families passed through Greenville on the way from Laurens to Arkansas. A year later 125 persons left Laurens for Little Rock. The Chattanooga *Times* reported not less than two hundred colored emigrants from South Carolina to have passed through that town during one week of November, 1884. During January, 1884, several large parties, one of them numbering 150, left Newberry, bound for Texas. From Florence a party of one hundred left at one time for Arkansas in 1885. In 1886 fifty-one left Barnwell County, and the people around Beldock, near Barnwell, were reported to "have the Arkansas fever badly. They are selling

---

[17] Pickens, *Bursting Bonds,* pp. 21-23.
[18] Charleston *News and Courier,* January 24, 1882.

their corn at forty cents a bushel, so anxious are they to go to
'the Rock.' "

Around Lancaster in 1886 the "exodus fever" was serious because
of the scarcity of grain and meat, which was said to be greater
than at any time since 1865. Continuous heavy rains during the
spring and summer and the cutting off of the last crop of oats in
the previous winter had left the white farmers without "the means
to assist or quiet the minds of the negroes." In 1890 sixty Negro
emigrants from Newberry passed through Anderson on the way to
Arkansas, and during one week at the beginning of 1890 between
3,500 and 4,000 Negroes from North and South Carolina passed
through Charleston on the way to Florida, Alabama, and Georgia.
In 1898 and 1899 accounts of emigrations from the state were still
found in the papers.[19]

Another feature of the Negro migration, meanwhile, was in
the gradual urbanization of South Carolina. Attracted by the
gregarious nature of community life and the growing economic
opportunity for domestics and laborers in minor industries Negroes
drifted into the towns. In 1880 when there were only three towns
of more than four thousand population (Greenville, Columbia, and
Charleston) there were 35,765 Negroes, constituting 54.0 per cent
of the population. By 1890 there were in towns of more than 2,500
population 64,146 Negroes, still constituting 54.0 per cent of the
population. During the nineties the Negro population in towns
of this size grew by more than 20,000, so that in 1900 there were
84,358 Negroes residing in towns. But the white urban population
had meanwhile increased so rapidly, because of the growth of
the textile industry, that Negroes in 1900 constituted only 49.3
per cent of the urban population.[20] Of the total Negro population,
only 10.8 per cent were residing in the towns, and many of these
towns were so small and so closely allied to the agricultural
economy as to be semi-rural in nature. They were, in fact, re-

---

[19] *Ibid.*, January 9, 1882, November 20, 1883, January 19, 1884, November
15, 1886, January 4, 1890; Yorkville *Enquirer,* January 15, 1885, November
10, 1886, March 18, 1899; Columbia *State,* December 21, 1898, January 10,
1899.

[20] Bureau of the Census, *Negroes in the United States,* pp. 241-46. It should
be noted that the figures for 1880 apply only to towns of 4,000 or more population, whereas those for 1890 and 1900 apply to towns of 2,500 or more.

garded by the farmers as pools of Negro labor to be tapped when the need for labor was at its peak.[21]

The whites of the state viewed the emigration of Negroes with mixed emotions and contradictory attitudes. Their dilemma was indicated by Narciso G. Gonzales when he said, "Politically speaking there are far too many negroes in South Carolina, but from an industrial standpoint there is room for many more."[22] The white press reported with obvious relish the story of Negro emigrants such as Horace Gilsey, who passed through Augusta on his way home from Arkansas to Newberry in 1887. In Augusta he was reported to have said to a white editor, "I declar, boss, dem 'Kansas folks am de biggest story tellers. Dey done fooled me outa everything I work hard fur dis ten year. I'se goin' back to Caroliny—and I'se gwine to stay dar, too. Any nigger dreaming 'bout happy homes in de West better wake up quick and stay in Caroliny."[23] It was reported that Gilsey had been compelled to walk all the way back from Arkansas. A large group that had gone to Mississippi in 1887 appealed to a white friend near St. Matthews who put up $500 to pay for the return of about twenty families.[24] Jess Jackson, an 'exoduster' from Laurens, wrote an imploring letter to a white friend begging for money with which to pay his way back. He described the emigrants to Arkansas as being out of work and out of money, and the weather as alternating torrents of rain and freezing cold.[25]

The circulation of such stories was not altogether without the ulterior motive of dissuading other potential emigrants from leaving, but the white editors also employed direct language in warning Negro residents of the state against "cunning thieves" who "go about the country distracting the minds of the negroes, who are frequently found in comfortable circumstances, rob them of their money, and entice them off, to desert their homes, accumulations and friends."[26] The Laurens Herald warned:

> It will not do to shut our eyes to the fact that if the present
> emigration fever among the negroes is not abated by some

[21] Hammond, in *Report of the Industrial Commission on Agricultural Labor*, House Document 179, 57th Congress, 1st Session, p. 819.

[22] Charleston *News and Courier*, January 2, 1882.

[23] *Ibid.*, January 1, 1887.

[24] *Ibid.*, February 10, 1887.

[25] *Ibid.*, January 29, 1885.

[26] Charleston *News and Courier*, January 9, 1882, quoting Barnwell *Sentinel*.

means, the agricultural interests of the country must suffer severely. And if these interests suffer, commerce and manufactures and every other interest must suffer in a corresponding degree. It will not do to treat the matter lightly, and say, "Let the 'nigger' slide." We need his services and it is too late now to look elsewhere for a substitute. . . .[27]

On the other hand there was strong sentiment, particularly among Democratic politicians, in favor of the emigration. Senator Butler expressed to a press reporter in 1879 the belief that "the departure of 100,000 darkies from the South would prove beneficial to our industries."[28] In 1883 he was still advocating emigration, but had raised his figures, recommending that 200,000 should leave South Carolina alone. The Charleston *New Era,* a Negro journal, thrown into a dudgeon by the Senator's extravagant proposition, informed its readers, "Well, now, they 'aint' going, having determined that they have birthrights here as well as the erudite Senator. 'Them's facts, and don't you forget it!' "[29]

Among the Negro leaders there was a division of sentiment similar to that among the whites. Joseph H. Rainey, a former Congressman, was interviewed in New York where he recounted to a reporter the story of several outrages against Negroes in the South and argued that "For the sake of humanity the movement ought to be encouraged."[30] Bishop Benjamin William Arnett of the African Methodist Episcopal Church, in a commencement address at Claflin College in 1889 told the students that Negroes should emigrate for several reasons: first, the former relation of master and slave was not forgotten in the South; second, the settlement of new areas brought prosperity, as had been demonstrated by the history of western settlement; and third, a man's class status was so fixed in his home community that it required "an extra amount of individuality to rise above ones-self." In a Greeley-like peroration the Bishop urged the graduates,

> Get up and Go! Go, take your family with you. Go as one of the pioneers, and you will have a pioneer's reward. It will

---

[27] Quoted in Charleston *News and Courier,* January 9, 1882.

[28] *Ibid.,* June 9, 1879.

[29] Charleston *New Era,* August 4, 1883.

[30] Unidentified clipping in J. C. Galloway Scrapbook, Moorland Foundation, Howard University, Washington.

PEDDLERS AND PROPRIETOR

The street venders (1879) called their wares, and PETER LINDAU *sold shoes made in his own shop, in Charleston.*

ORGANIZED RELIGION AND ORGANIZED LABOR

The Board of Stewards of the Centenary Methodist Church, Charleston (above), and S. C. Chapter No. 1 of the International Bricklayers, Masons, and Plasterers Union, Charleston (below).

not affect the farming interest of the State to have some of the labor to go out. It will give those that remain more work and better wages. It will help those that remain to take better care of their families, to save money, and to be more comfortable while living.[31]

Most of the Negro politicians, however, as Robert Smalls and Sam Lee, were for obvious reasons opposed to the emigration movement.[32]

The movement out of the state depended upon factors other than gratuitous advice from the leaders of either race, and the efforts of white landlords to halt the movement naturally took more forceful forms than mere good advice. On the whole, in such action as was taken, the attitude of white landlords who wanted a cheap and plentiful source of labor prevailed. In the migration to the Republican county of Beaufort in 1879, at least, white planters resorted to the shotgun method of retaining their laborers. It was inevitable, too, that with the reins of government in their hands the whites who opposed emigration should attempt to use their political power to prevent it. Legal measures designed to stop the flow of emigration were of two types: (1) labor contract legislation prohibiting under heavy fines the breaking of written or verbal contracts by the laborer under conditions that were finally described by the state Supreme Court as peonage;[33] and (2) measures prohibiting the activities of emigrant agents.

There were two measures in the latter category passed during the period under consideration. In a law of 1880 any person who enticed away a laborer under contract, whether verbal or in writing, was made liable to a fine of $25 to $100, or imprisonment from ten to thirty days.[34] Not only emigrant agents, but neighboring farmers within the state fell under its prohibition. Further effort was made in 1891 to limit the activities of emigrant agents by

---

[31] Benjamin William Arnett, *The Annual Address Delivered Before the Faculty, Students and Friends of Claflin University and the Claflin College of Agriculture and Mechanical Institute, May 22nd, 1889, Orangeburg, S. C.* (Columbia, 1889), p. 32.

[32] Campbell, *White and Black*, p. 342; Columbia *Daily Register*, January 10, 1882.

[33] For labor contract legislation, see *Revised Statutes* (1873), pp. 433, 490; *Statutes at Large*, XVII, 423; XX, 381-82; XXII, 457; *Ex parte Hollman*, 79 S. C. Reports 22. *See also* Chapter VI.

[34] *Acts and Joint Resolutions*, p. 423.

a law requiring an agent to pay a license fee of $500 for each county in which he hired laborers to work outside the state.[35] James Wigg of Beaufort, an adroit needler of white delegates in the constitutional convention of 1895, pointed to this act when Ben Tillman, remarking on the "negro difficulty," said that he would put no hindrance in the way of the Negro's leaving the state. Tillman had, of course, signed the bill, but stated that after the fashion of most governors, he had signed without question bills in which he had no particular interest, and that he wished to apologize to the state for having done so. To the merriment of the convention, white delegate W. D. Evans, in ironic tones, apologized to the people of the state for having introduced the bill in the General Assembly.[36] In 1897, however, when R. B. Anderson, the only Negro member of the legislature, introduced a bill to repeal the emigrant agent act, it was postponed indefinitely by a vote of eighty to thirty-four. When Anderson protested this as out of order, the bill was recommitted.[37] In 1907 the act was further strengthened by requiring an additional $2,000 license fee per year in each county where the agent operated. With this modification it was still on the books in 1942.[38]

United States Senator Matthew Calbraith Butler meanwhile continued his support for the idea of emigration and early in 1890 introduced into the United States Senate a bill to provide federal aid to all Negroes who wanted to emigrate to Africa. The bill attracted a great deal of attention, and when Carlyle McKinley, sometime poet and editorialist for the *News and Courier,* published in the same year a thin volume entitled *An Appeal to Pharaoh,* also advocating the idea of complete geographical separation of the races, discussion of the idea became widespread.[39] But once again the whites viewed the idea with mixed emotions. For one, like M. L. Donaldson, chief manager of the Farmer's State Alliance, who opposed the bill upon consulting his own interests, but favored it "from a patriotic point of view,"[40] there were many like ex-

[35] *Code of Laws of South Carolina* (Clinton, 1942), p. 1377.
[36] Columbia *Daily Register,* October 25, 26, 1895.
[37] *House Journal* (1897), pp. 76, 138, 139.
[38] *Code of Laws of South Carolina* (1942), pp. 1377, 1378.
[39] Carlyle McKinley, *An Appeal to Pharaoh: The Negro Problem and Its Radical Solution* (New York, 1890. Second edition: Columbia, 1907).
[40] Charleston *News and Courier,* January 22, 1890.

Governor Thompson who argued that "The removal of large numbers of negroes, if it could be successfully accomplished—which is open to serious question—would retard temporarily, if it did not arrest permanently, the progress of the South. I believe that the negroes are here to stay. With all their faults and short-comings there is at least no Anarchist-making material in them."[41] In the Senate, however, Wade Hampton came to the defense of his colleague, pointing out that the bill did not propose forcible emigration but only assistance to those who wished to emigrate.

> Mr. President, it is not hostility to the negro which prompts the desire for his removal from amongst us; it is a deep-seated, ineradicable race antagonism, and it is idle for us to shut our eyes to this fact and to endeavor to conceal it. . . . Philanthropists may deplore it and fanatics deny it, but it has existed from time immemorial, and will undoubtedly continue to do so until the last millenium, or perhaps to "the last syllable of recorded time."[42]

Negro leaders were by this time almost unanimously opposed to emigration, a conservative attitude naturally characterizing those who had carved out social and economic positions for themselves. Professor William Lewis Bulkley of Claflin College favored the Butler plan to help those who desired to emigrate but opposed the idea of emigration itself.[43] J. H. M. Pollard, rector of St. Mark's Episcopal Church in Charleston, said:

> This country is indebted to me and my children for two hundred years' labor of my African forefathers. Let them settle that account first and then, but not till then, will we listen to any proposition to leave our homes and firesides for the satisfaction of others, who have no more right here than ourselves. . . .
>
> But this scheme did not orginate to benefit the black man. It is simply a method to get him out of the white man's way. The white man has been exterminating all the races with which he has come in contact, but the patience and endurance of the negro have overturned his fondest speculations and set at defiance his most potential weapon, and now he comes be-

---

[41] *Ibid.*, January 23, 1890.
[42] *Congressional Record*, XXI (51st Congress, 1st Session), 972.
[43] Charleston *News and Courier*, February 2, 1890.

seeching the negro to redeem the land of his forefathers and throwing out some inducements by way of free transportation to get rid of him. . . .

If something could be done to send all of the political demagogues out of the country and our respectable newspapers would put a stop to this constant agitation, everything would end in an amicable and satisfactory manner to all concerned. Let us all, both white and black, do our duty in that state of life to which it has pleased God to call us, and adjust ourselves as quickly as possible to our present surroundings, and then peace and prosperity shall attend us. All this talk of the superiority of the one race and the inferiority of another, and of the impossibility of two different races occupying the same territory and living amicably together, is the merest bosh, intended only to satisfy the vain machinations of unjust men. We are friends, and we are going to live together and die together, all the agitation to the contrary notwithstanding.[44]

Robert Smalls argued that "All the negro wants is to be let alone. . . ." He invited those in counties where life and property were not protected to migrate to Beaufort County, "where I hardly think it probable that any prisoner will ever be taken from jail by a mob and lynched, let his color or offence be what it may." He favored emigration only from communities where it was absolutely impossible for whites and Negroes to live together in peace, and then not out of the United States.[45]

With opposition from those who considered the idea impracticable, including Zebulon Baird Vance of North Carolina, and those who, like John James Ingalls of Kansas, suspected Southern whites of a design to exterminate the Negroes, the Butler bill was permitted to die.[46]

The idea of white immigration into the state attracted a great deal of attention contemporaneously with Negro emigration, but far smaller results were achieved. While the idea of white immigration was not altogether inconsistent with the desire of great num-

---

[44] *Ibid.*

[45] *Ibid.*

[46] *Congressional Record,* XXI (51st Congress, 1st Session), 970, 971; *Journal of the Senate of the United States of America* (51st Congress, 1st Session), pp. 39, 67, 81, 92, 101, 104.

bers of the whites to keep numerous and cheap Negro laborers, the efforts to get white immigrants were hindered by the low wages generally prevailing and the great amount of competition from Negro labor that was inevitable. Immediately after the Civil War the conservative state government had established an office of commissioner of immigration, which functioned under John A. Wagener with meagre results for three years. It was abolished by the Radical government in 1868.[47]

In the Democratic state convention of 1878 D. Wyatt Aiken, a leader of the Grange, introduced a resolution for the establishment of a state "bureau of immigration, statistics, mining and agriculture," the chief purpose of which would be to secure immigrants.[48] In 1880 the office of state Commissioner of Agriculture was established, with immigration as one of the matters coming under its jurisdiction, and in 1881 the office of Superintendent of Immigration was established under the commissioner and Dr. E. M. Boykin chosen to fill it.[49]

During the first year of its activity interest in immigration reached its peak; newspapers, ignoring the presence of numerous poor whites already in the state, sought the introduction of immigrant labor.[50] During his first year in office Boykin was very active, travelling to Castle Garden to make arrangements for immigrants to be sent to South Carolina. "He seems to be intent chiefly upon getting laborers who are able to take the place of the negroes," said the Charleston *Deutsche Zeitung*.[51] His efforts, however, brought only 534 immigrants, most of whom were settled on farms, and by November the Abbeville *Press and Banner* was calling for the abolition of the office, declaring it "a worse than useless expense."[52] In the following two years it was found that the accomplishment of Boykin would not justify the outlay, and economy-

---

[47] *Statutes at Large*, XIII 380-81; Simkins and Woody, *South Carolina During Reconstruction*, pp. 244-46.

[48] Columbia *Daily Register*, August 2, 1878.

[49] *Reports and Resolutions* (1880), p. 477; (1881-1882), pp. 187-88.

[50] "We want white immigrants. Bring the mills here and they will come. Colored labor will raise the cotton, and white immigrants will convert it into yarn." Mitchell, *The Rise of Cotton Mills in the South*, p. 205, quoting Charleston *News and Courier*, February 8, 1881, quoting Winnsboro *News*.

[51] *Ibid.*, quoting Charleston *Deutsche Zeitung*, April 25, 1881.

[52] *Ibid.*, quoting Charleston *News and Courier*, November 25, 1881, quoting Abbeville *Press and Banner*.

minded legislators abolished the office in 1882 and devolved its
duties upon the Commissioner of Agriculture.[53] After that, although
there was sporadic talk of immigration little was actually accomplished. "It was largely a matter of politics," one white commented.[54]

While it is not possible to draw specific conclusions from the
census data on nativity, since they do not indicate the date of
migration from the place of birth, it is none the less clear that
the widespread concern with the issue of Negro emigration during
the eighties and nineties was not altogether unjustified. In 1900
there were 113,897 Negroes native to South Carolina living in other
parts of the United States as compared to 93,498 in 1880.[55] Sub-
tract from the first figure 14,269 Negroes who had migrated into
the state before 1900 and there is found to have been a net loss of
99,628.[56] Most of the emigrants had gone to the states of the Lower
South, but the lure of the West is indicated by the departure of
more than 18,000 to the Southwestern states of Arkansas, Texas,
and Louisiana, although larger numbers of 32,640 and 17,905 had
gone to the nearby states of Georgia and Florida respectively.
Kansas, the mecca of 1879, had in 1900 only 389 Negroes of South
Carolina birth.[57] At the same time 40,249 whites born outside the
state had become residents of South Carolina in addition to 5,528
foreign born.[58] Meanwhile, lest the emphasis here upon the Negro
should obscure contemporaneous white emigration there were 119,-
395 whites who had departed the state of their birth.[59] Comparison
of the figures demonstrates that there had been a net loss of
73,618 whites.

The net results of the emigration of both races was to change
the racial composition of the state's population but little and to
retard but little the increase in the state's population, both Negro

---

[53] *Reports and Resolutions* (1882), pp. 61-62.

[54] Milledge L. Bonham, quoted in Mitchell, *The Rise of Cotton Mills in the
South*, p. 206.

[55] *Census* (1900), Vol. I, Part I, clxiii; (1880), I, 488.

[56] *Census* (1900), Vol. I, Part I, clxiii.

[57] *Ibid.*, clxiii, p. 705. 84,429 of the 113,897 were living in the lower Southern States, 19,989 in other states of the upper South, 4,707 in Northeastern
States, 564 in Western States, and 225 in upper Central States.

[58] *Ibid.*, clxxiv, clxxxviii.

[59] *Compendium of the Twelfth Census*, p. 53.

and white.[60] But the prevalence of Negro interest in emigration
and of ambivalent white concern with the problem is one measure
of the economic and racial discontent that plagued South Carolina.

[60] The population increase is best indicated by a table:

	Total	Negro	White
1870	705,606	415,814	289,667
1880	995,577	604,332	391,105
1890	1,151,149	688,934	462,008
1900	1,340,316	782,321	557,807

See Bureau of the Census, *Negro Population, 1790-1915,* pp. 43-44; *Compendium of the Ninth Census,* pp. 8, 10, 12. Minor discrepancies are apparent in totals because of omission of Indian and Mongolian population.

10

THE NEGRO CHURCH

ONE of the most significant and permanent social changes wrought during Reconstruction was the establishment of separate Negro churches and the growth of independent Negro denominational organizations. Even before the Civil War there had been a few Negro churches in Charleston,[1] and "pray's houses"[2] had been scattered over the countryside where ministers, white and black, exhorted the slaves. But the most common practice had been for Negroes to worship in the churches of the whites, where they were admitted into membership although not to a share in the control of church affairs.

Immediately after the war there was some evidence of a desire among white church leaders to retain their Negro membership, but most of the Negroes flocked into new organizations which sprang up spontaneously or were sponsored by Northern missionaries of various faiths and of both races. By the end of Recon-

---

[1] There were in Charleston the African Methodist Episcopal Church which flourished under the ministry of Morris Brown, 1817-1822, and the Zion Presbyterian Church, recognized by the Charleston Presbytery in 1855, and perhaps others. Woodson, *History of the Negro Church*, p. 67; Septima Chappell Smith, "The Development and History of Some Negro Churches in South Carolina" (unpublished Master's thesis, Department of Education, University of South Carolina, 1942), pp. 7-8. The earliest known Negro Baptist Church in the United States was founded on the plantation of George Galphin at Silver Bluff, across the Savannah River from Augusta, Georgia, sometime between 1773 and 1775. Woodson, *History of the Negro Church*, p. 67; Lewis Garnett Jordan, *Negro Baptist History, U. S. A.* (Nashville, 1930), p. 58.

[2] Samuel Miller Lawton, "Abstract of the Religious Life of South Carolina Coastal and Sea Island Negroes" in *Contributions to Education*, No. 242 (Nashville, 1939), pp. 2-3. Although in most works the term is printed "praise house," Lawton reached the conclusion that this was the proper spelling because "de Pray's house" is "way oner go fur pray."

struction the church organizations and worship services of the two races were entirely separate, although there were small vestigial evidences of the old unity, particularly in the Episcopal and Presbyterian Churches.

The most important denominations with Negro membership were the Baptist, African Methodist Episcopal, African Methodist Episcopal Zion, Colored Methodist Episcopal, Reformed Episcopal, Presbyterian, and Protestant Episcopal.

By the end of the century the Baptists outnumbered all other Negro denominations combined.[3] There were two major reasons for this. First, the early Baptists were a comparatively radical sect with widespread appeal to the lower classes and worked with evangelical fervor that readily appealed to the unlettered. Second, their congregational form of organization made it possible after the Civil War for individual churches to be organized without the approval of any episcopal body. They could then affiliate or divide as they saw fit.

Some of the Negro Baptist churches grew directly out of the white churches. The Mount Moriah Church of Camden was an example. It was formed when, on January 22, 1866, some sixty-six Negroes withdrew from the First Baptist Church of Camden to organize a separate congregation. Monroe Boykin, a former slave, was ordained minister by two missionaries from the North. He served the church thirty-four years, and his son, J. W. Boykin, who succeeded him, was still minister of the church in 1950.[4]

The experience of Monroe Boykin in organizing and preaching to five churches other than the Mount Moriah Church is typical, but does not compare to the mighty deeds of the Reverend Alexander Bettis, also a former slave, who organized more than forty Baptist churches, and two associations (the Storm Branch and Mount Canaan Baptist associations), and an industrial school be-

---

[3] Bureau of the Census, *Religious Bodies: 1906* (Washington, 1910), I, 264-67.

[4] Columbia *Record*, February 10, 1950; Albert Weitherspoon Pegues, *Our Baptist Ministers and Schools* (Springfield, Massachusetts, 1892), pp. 75-78. For the story of the organization of a new congregation by the Negro members of Trinity Methodist Church, Charleston, see W. H. Lawrence, *The Centenary Souvenir, Containing a History of Centenary Church, Charleston, and An Account of the Life and Labors of Rev. R. V. Lawrence, Father of the Pastor of Centenary Church, Charleston, 1885* (Philadelphia, 1885), p. 9.

tween the end of the Civil War and his death in 1895. He was at
one time the pastor of ten churches and continuously of four.[5]

The mushroom growth of Negro Baptist churches out of the
white churches and out of the "pray's houses" only slowly coalesced
into the larger organizations and conventions. The Morris Street
Baptist Church of Charleston, the leading church of its denomination in the state, was instrumental in forming an association in
1867.[6] Alexander Bettis later organized two in the upper part of the
state,[7] and others apparently were formed, but there was no statewide organization until 1876. This was largely the work of E. M.
Brawley and of the Morris Street Baptist Church, under the leadership of Jacob Legare, its pastor.

Brawley, who had been born in Charleston of free parents in
1851, attended school in Charleston as a child, but at the age of
ten had gone to Philadelphia where he attended the Institution for
Colored Youth. Returning to Charleston after the war, he became
an apprentice shoemaker. Later he attended Howard University
for three months during 1870, but transferred to the college at
Lewisburg, Pennsylvania (now Bucknell), where, aided by friends,
he worked his way by giving voice lessons and by preaching during vacations. He joined the Baptist church in Lewisburg and was
licensed to preach during his sophomore year. When he was
graduated in 1875 he was ordained by the Lewisburg church and
was immediately given a commission by the American Baptist
Publication Society as missionary for South Carolina.

When he arrived in the state he found numerous churches but
scant organization. There were few Sunday schools and the associations were crudely organized, large, and unwieldy. Brawley was
at first regarded with suspicion by his conservative brethren, who
did not comprehend his proposed innovations. Gradually, however,
he gained their confidence, organized Sunday schools, helped the
associations to put their organizations in order, and finally formed
the Colored Baptist Educational, Missionary, and Sunday School
Convention at Sumter in 1876. Brawley became corresponding

---

[5] Pegues, *Our Baptist Ministers and Schools*, pp. 75-78; Alfred W. Nicholson, *Brief Sketch of the Life and Labors of Rev. Alexander Bettis* (Trenton,
South Carolina, 1913), pp. 25-33, 52.

[6] Pegues, *Our Baptist Ministers and Schools*, p. 149.

[7] Nicholson, *Brief Sketch of the Life and Labors of Rev. Alexander Bettis*,
pp. 33-34.

secretary and financial agent of the convention and directed its work until 1883, when he resigned to accept the presidency of a Baptist college in Alabama.

During the period of his leadership the Baptist convention carried on state mission work, and through Harrison N. Bouey and the congregation that went to Liberia on the *Azor*, opened a mission field in Africa. At the time of Brawley's resignation, the convention had 550 affiliated churches, 350 ordained preachers, and a membership of approximately 100,000.[8] In 1892 the secretary of the state convention reported an organization including 28 associations, 781 churches, 507 ordained ministers, and 123,375 members. Church property was valued at $476,128 and contributions during the year 1891-1892 had been $223,437 in addition to Sunday school contributions of $747.46.[9]

In accordance with their particularist tradition, the Baptists had a rival state convention in addition to independent groups and churches. This convention had been organized just prior to the Sumter Convention by Alexander Bettis, who gathered together the two associations that he had formed with some other smaller groups into the Baptist Home Mission State Convention of South Carolina under the presidency of the Reverend J. Watts.[10] The reason for the failure of the two groups to merge is uncertain, the biographer of Bettis saying that "he was not in sympathy with the manner in which the Sumter Convention was organized, and . . . he always considered that organization to be too prodigal in the use of money. . . ."[11] The Bettis group, with its strength concentrated in Aiken and Edgefield counties, continued an independent existence at least as late as 1913.[12] No figures are available on the size of the Bettis group, but the census of 1890 showed 860 Negro Baptist churches in the state with a total membership only slightly above the comparable figures presented by the Colored Baptist Educational, Missionary, and Sunday School Convention in 1892, so that it is clear that nearly all the Negro Baptist churches were by the nineties affiliated with the latter group, and through

---

[8] Pegues, *Our Baptist Ministers and Schools*, pp. 78-82, 149-50.

[9] Charleston *News and Courier*, May 6, 1892.

[10] Nicholson, *Brief Sketch of the Life and Labors of Rev. Alexander Bettis*, pp. 35-36.

[11] *Ibid.*, p. 36.

[12] *Ibid.*

it with the National Baptist Convention organized at Montgomery, Alabama, in 1880.[13]

The African Methodist Episcopal Church, dormant in South Carolina from 1822 until 1865 because of white hostility, was reorganized in the latter year by a group under the leadership of Bishop Daniel Alexander Payne, who had been exiled from his native Charleston for thirty years.[14] Under the leadership of energetic ministers, the most successful of whom was Richard Harvey Cain, the African Methodists had by the end of Reconstruction established themselves as the second largest Negro denomination in the state. The Emanuel Church in Charleston, organized by Cain, was the leading church of this denomination, with a membership in 1883 of 3,878.[15] So rapidly did the growth of the African Methodists proceed that it was found necessary at the 1878 meeting of the South Carolina Conference to divide the state into two conferences, the upper part of the state taking the name of the Columbia Annual Conference. At the first meeting of this conference there were reported to be in the upper part of the state 181 churches, 298 local preachers, 21,331 members, and 7,381 probationers. Further expansion brought the formation of the South Carolina (North East) Conference at Marion in 1892, with a membership of 11,756. Further elaboration of the church organization in the early twentieth century brought the formation of the Piedmont Conference in 1909 and the Palmetto Conference, embracing Georgetown, Williamsburg, Berkeley, and part of Charleston counties, in 1911.[16]

When the original South Carolina Conference held its Quarto-Centennial celebration in 1890 it was found to have more members than before the subdivision in 1878, and was sponsoring the Reverend Samuel J. Campbell as its missionary to Liberia, where it had sent the Reverend S. F. Flegler on the *Azor* in 1878.[17] The

---

[13] Jordan, *Negro Baptist History, U. S. A.,* pp. 114-15.

[14] Richard Robert Wright, Jr. (ed.), *The Encyclopaedia of the African Methodist Episcopal Church* (Philadelphia, 1947), p. 509.

[15] Unindentified clipping, July, 1883, *Pamphlets, 1878-84,* Edward Willis Pamphlets, Charleston Library Society.

[16] Wright (ed.), *The Encyclopaedia of the African Methodist Episcopal Church,* pp. 509-10.

[17] Arnett (ed.), *Proceedings of the Quarto-Centennial Conference of the African M. E. Church, of South Carolina, at Charleston, S. C., May 15, 16, and 17, 1889* (Xenia, Ohio, 1890), pp. 155, 251.

membership of the African Methodist Church was greater in South
Carolina than in any other single state. Its members were scattered
over the entire state, but concentrated their greatest numbers in
the Low Country, especially in the neighborhood of Charleston.[18]
It exercised a healthful influence because of the emphasis laid upon
the training of its clergy by Bishop Daniel A. Payne. The African
Methodists of South Carolina established Allen University in
Columbia in 1881 to serve chiefly as a training school for their
ministers.[19]

The African Methodist Episcopal Zion Church was strong in the
Northern counties where its predominant strength in North Carolina spilled across the border. Organized at Chester in 1867, the
South Carolina Conference in 1890 had 130 churches with 45,880
members located in seventeen counties, but was strongest in Spartanburg, Lancaster, York, Chester, Union, Newberry, and Fairfield.[20] The South Carolina Conference had by 1895 established
the Lancaster High School.[21] It never attempted to enter the field
of higher education, as did some of the other denominations, probably because of the location nearby of Livingstone College, in
Salisbury, North Carolina, which was supported by the Zion
Church.

The Northern Methodist Episcopal Church re-established its
organization throughout the South after the Civil War, but the
Southern conferences were composed almost altogether of Negro
members. The South Carolina Conference was organized in 1865
by two Northern missionaries, T. Willard Lewis and Alonzo Webster, the father of the Republican politician.[22] Because of the Northern leadership this group early became an influential force and
in 1869 founded Claflin College in Orangeburg.[23]

This group, however, because of the conspicuous presence of
Northern whites immediately after the Civil War, long labored

---

[18] *Census* (1890), IX, 549.

[19] *Handbook of 1883*, p. 327.

[20] James Walker Hood, *One Hundred Years of the African Methodist Episcopal Zion Church* (New York, 1895), pp. 359-60; Yorkville *Enquirer*, November 25, 29, 1899; *Census* (1890), IX, 563.

[21] Hood, *One Hundred Years of the African Methodist Episcopal Zion
Church*, p. 360.

[22] Lawrence, *Centenary Souvenir*, pp. 7-11.

[23] *Ibid.*, p. 17

under the handicap of white suspicion that it was a Radical political machine. A report adopted by the Conference at Greenville in 1879 was described by the local white paper as "entirely devoted to politics, prepared in the kind of language to reach and have effect with the colored race, and calculated to do more mischief among the negroes than the speeches of a score of Radical politicians." The paper further declared that the Northern Methodists "have held on to the great mass of the colored Methodists, and have thoroughly trained and drilled them in hatred of and opposition to the whites."[24] Sentiment against Northern influence also made itself felt among the Negro members of the church and E. H. Coit, pastor of the Wesley Methodist Episcopal Church in Charleston, severed his connection with the church in 1892 because of his feeling that race prejudice was put ahead of principle by Northern whites in the promotion of the clergymen of the church.[25]

With the passage of time, and with a dwindling number of Northern white ministers in the denomination, white suspicions were allayed. By 1894 the South Carolina Conference was entirely under the direction of a Negro ministry, except for the Reverend A. C. Dutton, presiding elder of the Orangeburg District.[26]

Under good leadership the Methodist Episcopal Church prospered and in 1890 had more separate organizations than any other Negro Methodist body, and ranked second in the value of church property, although in membership it lagged behind both the African Methodists and the Zionists.[27]

The colored Methodists who had remained in the Methodist Episcopal Church, South, after the Civil War were in 1870 organized by that group into the Colored Methodist Episcopal Church, of which Richard H. Vanderhorst of South Carolina was named one of the two bishops.[28] The group had identical articles of religion, a similar form of government, and the same discipline as the parent body. The body long suffered from the suspicions of Negroes because of this close relationship, but by 1890 the feeling was reported to be disappearing because the Colored Methodist Church had es-

---

[24] Yorkville *Enquirer*, February 6, 1879, quoting Greenville *News*.

[25] Charleston *News and Courier*, December 2, 1892.

[26] *Ibid.*, January 8, 1894.

[27] *Census* (1890), IX, 516-17.

[28] Charles Henry Phillips, *History of the Colored Methodist Episcopal Church in America* (Jackson, Tennessee, 1898), pp. 26, 41-42.

tablished its independence.[29] In 1886 irreconcilable differences of the Sydney Park African Methodist Church in Columbia with the parent body caused it to transfer its allegiance to the Colored Methodists. The congregation of over six hundred brought the Colored Methodists a membership and leadership which gave them a prestige they had formerly lacked.[30] In 1890, however, they had only 34 churches in the state with a membership of 3,468.[31]

A fifth Negro Methodist group was organized as a result of a schism in the African Methodist Church in 1884. At a meeting of the South Carolina Conference of the African Methodists at Georgetown in 1884, the Reverend William E. Johnson, a former state senator from Sumter, was suspended for insubordination in a dispute over the method of electing ministerial delegates to the General Conference.[32] He immediately became the leader of a group of malcontents who were unhappy over what they thought was the excessive influence of Northern elements in the church.

Johnson's activities brought on several incidents. When he invaded the Graham's Chapel Church near Charleston to convince its members that they should withdraw from the parent body he was hauled into court by the pastor of the church on the charge of perpetrating a malicious disturbance of the meeting.[33]

The Morris Brown Church, meanwhile, was split by the dispute, a group of Johnson's followers seizing the building under the authority of a group of trustees who had been deposed by the Reverend Samuel Washington, the recognized minister of the church. Members of the church, angry at the effort of Washington, an immigrant from Nevis, to maintain control, held possession of the church and carried on services under the leadership of the Reverend J. E. Hayne, a native preacher who had been suspended by the church two years previously.[34] A state jury of ten whites and two Negroes was unable to agree on the legal administrators of the church.[35]

---

[29] *Census* (1890), IX, 604.

[30] Phillips, *History of the Colored Methodist Episcopal Church in America,* pp. 142-43.

[31] *Census,* 1890, IX, 609.

[32] Bureau of the Census, *Religious Bodies: 1906,* II, 492; Charleston *News and Courier,* May 6, 1884.

[33] Charleston *News and Courier,* May 7, 1884.

[34] *Ibid.,* May 6, 7, 8, 1884.

[35] *Ibid.,* June 5, 1884.

Finally a settlement was reached after a visit by Bishop H. M. Turner, who announced that Washington would be restored for twenty-four hours, after which he would be transferred to Louisville. Then the suspension of J. E. Hayne was lifted and he was made pastor of the church. By means of this surrender to the congregation the Bishop kept the Morris Brown Church within the African Methodist denomination.[36]

W. E. Johnson, however, called a convention in January, 1885, with delegates from the lower part of South Carolina and from Savannah. At this meeting the Independent African Methodist Episcopal Church was organized under his presidency.[37] It operated under a nonepiscopal form of organization until 1896 when it was decided to establish an episcopacy in order to achieve a more permanent form. Under the name Reformed Methodist Union Episcopal Church, which was adopted at that time, the group had, in 1906, 55 churches with 4,235 members, but in the next three decades it rapidly declined until in 1936 it had only 23 churches and 1,731 members in the state, and 2 churches with 105 members in Georgia.[38]

The Protestant Episcopal Church maintained longer than any other white denomination in the state the ante-bellum tradition of bi-racial membership. Most of its Negro membership, however, was attracted to other denominations and it had only small numbers of Negroes by the end of the century. An important cause of the decline in Negro membership was the greater attractiveness of other denominations in which the climate was less aristocratic and in which Negroes exercised control over the organization. Another was the controversy brought about by the effort of a Negro congregation in Charleston to receive equal treatment in the diocesan conventions.

The roots of this controversy lie in the early days of Reconstruction, when all the Episcopal churches of Charleston were closed upon the occupation of the city by federal forces. The opening of Grace Church, the only one in operation for a time, did not provide sufficient room to accommodate the Negro members.

---

[36] *Ibid.*, July 1, 2, 3, 1884.

[37] *Ibid.*, June 5, October 9, 1884; January 23, 1885.

[38] *Ibid.*; Bureau of the Census, *Religious Bodies: 1906*, II, 492; *Religious Bodies: 1936* (Washington, 1941), II, 1229.

A group of leading colored men then founded an independent congregation which grew into St. Mark's Church. Like the white congregations, St. Mark's was largely made up of those persons who had some claim to gentility, consisting chiefly of those who had been free Negroes under the old regime. They called a white minister, the Reverend J. B. Seabrook, to be their rector. He served until 1877 when, upon his death, the Reverend A. Toomer Porter, another white minister, assumed charge until 1887; since then it has had a Negro rector.[39] As early as 1866 the congregation sought advice on admission to the Diocesan Convention, but was advised to wait until St. Mark's had proved its permanency. Finally, in 1875 application was made.[40] By this time the church had put up a building costing $18,000. With a congregation of 187 communicants the church made contributions of $2,220, making it in 1875 the ninth congregation in the Diocese in money contributions.[41]

The application of the congregation was referred to a commission of clergymen and laymen for recommendation to the convention of 1876. Three members brought in a majority report opposing the admission of St. Mark's. Their first major objection to the congregation was the fact that it was chiefly made up of ante-bellum free Negroes, who were largely of mixed blood. "It is this class in which miscegenation is seen, and which tempts to miscegenation," said the report. "If miscegenation should be encouraged amongst us, then this class should be cherished and advanced." The report then proceeded to comment on the danger of the withdrawal of white congregations if the Negroes were admitted, the right of the convention to grant or to refuse admission to congregations, and its feeling that "St. Mark's congregation cannot send competent delegates."[42]

A minority report by the Reverend James H. Elliott advised admission of St. Mark's, arguing that the separation of the congregation had arisen from a want of accommodations in the white

[39] Charleston News and Courier, May 17, 1876, October 2, 1886; George Freeman Bragg, Jr., History of the Afro-American Group of the Episcopal Church (Baltimore, 1922), p. 237.

[40] Charleston News and Courier, October 2, 1886.

[41] Journal of the Annual Convention of the Protestant Episcopal Church in the Diocese of South Carolina (1876), p. 62. Hereinafter cited as Diocesan Journal.

[42] Ibid., pp. 24-43; Charleston News and Courier, May 13, 1876.

churches and that representation in the convention did not involve social intermingling. "To deny them representation," said Elliott, "would be to oppose the drift of events [the political campaign of 1876 was not yet under way], the apparent leadings of Providence, and the sentiment of the civilized world." Colored delegates, he reminded the convention, had been admitted to the conventions in North Carolina, Georgia, and Florida. A second minority report by the Reverend C. C. Pinckney advocated admission as a means of creating a link between the white and Negro population and as a means of extending the conservative influence of the Episcopal Church over the Negroes, and proposed suffragan, or missionary, bishops for the Negroes.[43]

The debate which followed indicated a sharp division of opinion between the leading clergymen and the lay delegates. The Reverend A. Toomer Porter argued that the convention should yield to the inevitable.

> If unhappily you should reject St. Mark's at this Convention, you will not have gotten rid of the question. I venture to predict it will meet you again at the next Convention, and at the next and the next, till finally that is done most ungraciously which could so easily have been done gracefully a year ago, which mistake may even now be retrieved. . . . For that this question is certain, sooner or later, to be decided in the affirmative, is as sure as that in Christ Jesus there is neither barbarian, Scythian, bond or free; but we are all one in Christ, and that the Great God over us is no respecter of persons.[44]

The bishop of the diocese, the Right Reverend William Bell White Howe, spoke in agreement with Porter, arguing that the church should act on principle rather than expediency.

> . . . I ask you not as Carolinians, but as representatives of the Church in Convention assembled—if the two races in this State, under adverse influences, are drifting asunder, one from the other—shall the Church of God catch the evil infection, and instead of trying to put a stay to it, rather add fuel to the flame? I do not argue from expediency, as you will have

---

[43] *Diocesan Journal* (1876), pp. 43-53, 55-56; Charleston *News and Courier,* May 13, 1876.

[44] Charleston *News and Courier,* May 17, 1876.

seen from my remarks, but from sound ecclesiastical principle; but not unfrequently the best results attend upon adherence to well established principle, and if the action of this Convention should be such as to bear witness of our willingness to give all their dues, even in opposition to a very strong social and traditional pressure, I am sure it would do much to make for peace and conciliate confidence. But if it did not have any such result, nevertheless, I know, and am assured, that it would witness for the Church in this Diocese with Him who has pronounced a benediction upon the peace makers. And then, too, though the world outside of us, in the approaching political canvass, should roar loudly and angrily, as small doubt it will do, like a tempestuous sea which cannot rest . . . , yet shall this Convention be a lighthouse upon a rock, whose steady flame of truth and love shall burn without a flicker from the blasts without, shining far and wide throughout our State, because mindful of the words of Him who said, "Ye are the light of the world, a city that is set on a hill cannot be hid. Let your light so shine before men that they may *see* your good works, and glorify your Father who is in Heaven."[45]

A motion to admit representatives of St. Mark's was lost, however, by a nonconcurrence of orders, the clergy voting seventeen to nine in favor and the laity seventeen to twelve in opposition.[46] After that day there was no further application by St. Mark's for admission to the convention, but the status of the congregation continued to stimulate controversy.

In 1875 Thaddeus Saltus, a native Negro, was accepted by the bishop as a postulant, and in 1881 he was ordained a deacon and made the assistant minister of St. Mark's. Thereafter, the question of colored clergymen, rather than that of lay representatives, was the issue. Being placed upon the list of clergy by the bishop, Saltus took his seat in the conventions of 1881 and 1882 without incident. In 1883 he was absent because of sickness.[47] The Reverend H. C. Bishop took his place in 1884 and was seated in the convention of 1885, along with Thomas G. Harper, a deacon, and as-

---

[45] *Diocesan Journal* (1876), pp. 62-63.

[46] Charleston *News and Courier,* May 13, 1876.

[47] *Ibid.,* October 2, 1886; John Kershaw, "The Issue in South Carolina," *Church Review,* L (October, 1887), 388.

sistant minister of St. Luke's, a Negro congregation in Columbia. When these two ministers went to the communion table and partook of the sacrament with the others, an effort was made to exclude them from the convention, but failed to pass because of a nonconcurrence of orders.[48] In 1886 there was no colored minister in the convention, but a great deal of time was taken up by a discussion of the issue, with an obvious intent on the part of the laymen to prevent the seating of any more Negroes.[49]

In response to a public appeal from the congregation of St. Mark's for a Negro minister to replace the overworked Dr. Porter, the Reverend J. H. M. Pollard, was appointed in the following year. Pollard was a native of Virginia who had graduated from a normal school in Petersburg in 1874. He had thereafter passed his examinations for the diaconate, and subsequently studied in a theological school at Petersburg. In 1886 he was ordained to the priesthood, and shortly thereafter went to Charleston. He had attended the diocesan convention of Virginia since 1880, and in 1887 was placed on the list of ministers by the bishop of South Carolina.[50]

In 1887 another effort was made by lay delegates to force the expulsion of the Negro minister, but once again failed because of a nonconcurrence of orders. Since the bishop adamantly refused to remove Pollard, the white delegates from twenty-one parishes withdrew from the convention and issued a statement of the causes which led to their withdrawal. Their paper consisted chiefly of a chronological review of the controversy.[51] They were answered by E. M. Seabrook, a lay member of the church, in a pamphlet in which he contended that to exclude a qualified clergyman would be a violation of the constitution and canons of the church. "To make a *Christian Church a race Church,* is to attempt to put back the hands on the clock of time over two thousand years, and to get back to the period before the birth of Christ—*and this in the Nineteenth Century!* It cannot be done; it is an impossibility."[52]

---

[48] Charleston *News and Courier,* May 13, 1885.

[49] *Ibid.,* October 2, 1886.

[50] *Ibid.;* E. M. Seabrook, *The Law and the Gospel as Applied to the Questions Before the Diocesan Convention of the Episcopal Church of the Diocese of South Carolina, 1887* (Charleston, 1887), p. 5.

[51] *Statement of the Causes Which Led to the Withdrawal of the Deputies From the Late Diocesan Convention of South Carolina, Prepared by the Committee Appointed for That Purpose* (Charleston, 1887).

[52] Seabrook, *The Law and the Gospel,* p. 15.

The pamphlet by Seabrook was but one of the many pamphlets and articles that the controversy brought forth from articulate Episcopalians. John S. Fairly, in one entitled *The Negro In His Relations to the Church,* argued that history proved the incapacity of Negroes because of the fact that both races were descended from Noah who must have "lived and taught among his descendants the negroes, just as he lived and taught among their white brethren, for three hundred years after the flood." But the Negroes forgot Noah's teaching, and when they came from Africa were pagans.[53]

In the 1888 convention Dr. A. Toomer Porter, convinced that the sentiment for the exclusion of Negroes would utterly split the diocese unless conciliated, introduced a resolution calling for a commission of three clergymen and three laymen to consult with the vestries and clergymen of the colored churches as to the complete separation of the colored congregations into another organization under the bishop of the diocese.[54] The proposal was not accepted by the colored congregations; they preferred to continue their independent status under the bishop of the diocese;[55] and in 1889 it was decided to retain in the convention such colored ministers as were already seated, but that no more should be seated.[56] In 1892 the diocese appointed an "Archdeacon for Work Among the Colored People," who began his duties on February 1, 1892, and reported to the convention in that year the existence of twenty-one mission stations aside from St. Mark's that were

[53] John S. Fairly, *The Negro In His Relations to the Church* (Charleston, 1889), p. 4. On this controversy, *see also* E. E. Bellinger, *Counter Statement: A Reply to the "Statement" by the Deputies Who Withdrew From the Late Diocesan Convention of South Carolina* (Charleston, 1888); *Memorial From St. Mark's Church, Charleston, S. C. (Colored Congregation) to the Bishops, Clergy and Laity of the Protestant Episcopal Church in the U. S. Asking the Wisdom and Love of the Church to Devise Some Method of Relief and for Direction as to Their Duty in Their Painful Position* (Charleston, 1886) [Also published in Charleston *News and Courier,* October 2, 1886]; *A Reply to the Statement of Messrs. Memminger, McCrady, and Others, as to the Causes of the Withdrawal of Certain Deputies From the Diocesan Convention of South Carolina, of 1887* (Charleston, 1888); R. S. Trapier *et al.* (compilers), *A Protest Against the Admission of Any Other Than the White Race in the Councils of the Protestant Episcopal Church of the Diocese of South Carolina* (Charleston, 1890).

[54] Charleston *News and Courier,* May 3, 1888.

[55] *Ibid.,* April 16, May 4, 1888.

[56] *Constitution and Canons of the Protestant Episcopal Church in the Diocese of South Carolina* (Charleston, 1897), Art. III, Sec. 2.

carrying on work among the Negroes.[57] This work was expanded until there were thirty-two mission stations in 1899.[58]

Meanwhile, however, Pollard remained in South Carolina, ministering to St. Mark's and carrying on mission work elsewhere, until he moved to North Carolina in 1898.[59] The last Negro minister having been dropped from the list of those eligible to sit in the convention, the parishes that had seceded in 1887, eleven of which still remained out, returned to the fold in the convention of 1898.[60] The controversy over the Negroes' status then became dormant for a long period. However, in 1945, the state having been divided into two dioceses, the Diocese of Upper South Carolina voted to give full representation to Negroes of the diocese. The Diocese of South Carolina, including the lower part of the state, still had not admitted Negroes to representation as late as 1947.[61]

In 1888 attention was called to the fact that the majority of the Negro Episcopalians of the state, because of the bitter opposition to their representation in the Protestant Episcopal Church, had joined the Reformed Episcopal Church. The new Church, which had originated in Kentucky in 1873, entered the state in 1875, and under the direction of P. F. Stevens, a native white missionary, brought most of the rural colored congregations into the new establishment.[62] In 1888 they invited St. Mark's to join "a body which first recognized us as fit to be entrusted with full church privileges." The press, however, reported that St. Mark's would not join because its "congregation is composed of the *creme de la creme* of the Southern light colored aristocracy and are as firmly wedded to the forms of the 'Henglish' aristocratic worship as their white brethren."[63] The Reformed Episcopal Church, however, had in 1906 twice as many colored members as the older group.[64]

---

[57] *Diocesan Journal* (1892), p. 93.

[58] *Ibid.* (1899), p. 97.

[59] *Ibid.* (1898), p. 81.

[60] *Ibid.*, pp. 16, 19.

[61] Frank Loescher, *The Protestant Church and the Negro: A Pattern of Segregation* (New York, 1948), pp. 54-55.

[62] Bureau of the Census, *Religious Bodies: 1906*, II, 597-98; P. F. Stevens in *Centennial Edition of the Charleston News and Courier*, 1903. Stevens, who was Bishop of the Reformed Episcopal Church in 1888, was also School Commissioner for Charleston County. Columbia *Daily Register*, June 24, 1888.

[63] Columbia *Daily Register*, June 24, 1888.

[64] Reformed Episcopal, 2,252; Protestant Episcopal, 1,130. Bureau of the Census, *Religious Bodies: 1906*, I, 558.

The Presbyterian Church, half of whose members in 1860 were Negro slaves, had by the end of the Reconstruction period lost almost its entire colored membership. A few remained as members of the white churches, but others formed separate congregations which affiliated with the Northern Presbyterian Church. Only a small number of Negro congregations retained their affiliation with the Southern Presbyterians. Some Sunday school and mission school teaching was continued by Southern white Presbyterians. A minister in the Rock Hill area was reported in 1894 to be conducting a class of fourteen colored ministers, and a white church in the neighborhood reported a large class of colored people in the Sunday school. However, such secular education as was carried on by Presbyterians was chiefly the work of the Northern group.[65]

In 1879 the colored churches Zion (founded in 1850), Hopewell, Aimwell, and Salem were taken from the roll of the Charleston Presbytery, having connected themselves with the Presbytery of Atlantic.[66] This presbytery was in turn affiliated with the Synod of Atlantic, a division of the Northern Presbyterians which had Negro members in the states of North Carolina, Georgia, and Florida, as well as South Carolina. By 1896 the Synod of Atlantic had 4,885 communicants in the state of South Carolina. There were two presbyteries with 67 churches and 36 ministers.[67]

As late as 1896, however, there were still Negro churches affiliated with the Southern Presbyterians. In the neighborhood of Abbeville in that year a number of colored churches were united in the Independent Presbytery of Abbeville, which received the aid and encouragement of the Athens (white) Presbytery.[68]

The growing sentiment among whites for segregation brought in 1894 a refusal from the Charleston Presbytery to accept the candidacy of Reuben James, a Negro, for the ministry. The presbytery at the same time petitioned the General Assembly to hasten the establishment of an Independent African Presbyterian Church. A minority protested, and the synod declared the action illegal in

---

[65] Frank Dudley Jones and W. H. Mills (eds.), *History of the Presbyterian Church in South Carolina Since 1850* (Columbia, 1926), pp. 277, 371-72.

[66] *Ibid.*, p. 146.

[67] *Minutes of the General Assembly of the Presbyterian Church in the United States of America*, XVII (1894), 402-3, 734-35.

[68] Jones and Mills (eds.), *History of the Presbyterian Church in South Carolina Since 1850*, pp. 270-72.

denying the application of James solely on account of his color
This interpretation was upheld by the General Assembly meeting
at Memphis in 1896. The presbytery, however, took exception to
this, and justified its action in rejecting James, not because he was
colored, but because "the Presbytery was dissatisfied with the policy of the assembly's committee on colored evangelization," and
wished to hasten the establishment of an independent Negro
church.[69] The census of religious bodies taken in 1906, reported no
more Negro churches in the state affiliated with the Southern Presbyterians.[70]

Not attracted by the sedate atmosphere of the Episcopal and
Presbyterian faiths, and repelled by their indecisive efforts to meet
the problem of the color line, Negroes were attracted to the
churches which they could control. Yet their denominational pref-
erences, on the whole, were approximately the same as those of
their white neighbors—large numbers of Baptists and Methodists,
fewer of Episcopalians, Presbyterians, and other faiths. The most
reliable figures on the relative strength of churches at the end of the
century were those gathered by a special religious census in 1906.
They showed Negro church members to be affiliated with the following denominations:

	Negro Organi- zations	Church Edifices	Halls	Communi- cants
National Baptist Convention ..	1,317	1,310	8	219,841
African Methodist Episcopal ..	632	635	3	79,220
Methodist Episcopal	395	406	6	54,097
A f r i c a n Methodist Episcopal Zion	193	186	9	19,058
Presbyterian C h u r c h in the United States of America (Northern)	111	111	1	8,026
Colored Methodist Episcopal ..	72	74	1	4,850
Reformed Methodist U n i o n Episcopal	56	57	..	4,235
Reformed Episcopal	38	42	2	2,252
Protestant Episcopal	21	12	..	1,130
Methodist Protestant	11	8	1	683

---

[69] *Ibid.*, pp. 253-56; Columbia *State*, October 17, 1896.
[70] Bureau of the Census, *Religious Bodies:* 1906, I, 558-59.

	Negro Organi- zations	Church Edifices	Halls	Communi- cants
Congregational	6	6	..	377
Disciples of Christ	6	5	..	202
Roman Catholic	1	1	..	170
Church of God and Saints of Christ	1	1	..	8 [71]

The significant position of the church in the Negro community enhanced the social position and power of the Negro ministers. Forming the largest and most articulate group of professional men in the Negro community they figured prominently for both good and evil in the most important movements of the race. Negro ministers were vocal leaders of the emigration movement and vocal opponents of it. Negro ministers figured prominently in political conventions, others urged their flocks to eschew politics. Some were important agents of conciliation with the whites, while others bitterly denounced them. And in the movement for education, Negro churches and their ministers were extremely important.

Pathetic ignorance was all too often a conspicuous quality of the ministers. A. B. Williams, observing one of them during the voyage of the *Azor,* found him

> . . . a man of really earnest piety, who does his best according to his lights. But the lights are so dim. He lacks entirely the education and training which many colored ministers— especially in the cities—possess. He seems barely able to read and write, mispronouncing the simplest words, and producing painfully ludicrous effects at the most solemn moments. With crude, twisted and half developed ideas and reasonings on subjects, he covered up and hopelessly confused what meaning he had, with a flood of misapplied, miscalled, and confounded words.
>
> . . . Heaven only knows what diverse, tangled and mistaken ideas and theories these poor darkened minds do extract from the shapeless mass of confused words, sentences and metaphors hurled upon them by their teachers.[72]

---

[71] *Ibid.*
[72] A. B. Williams, *The Liberian Exodus,* p. 4.

An observer in Beaufort at the end of the century found the Baptist preachers in the town to be "young, able, well-educated ministers of strong character who exert a very considerable influence for good"; and the Methodists to be "men of character, education and push." But the Baptist preachers in the country areas were "local products," who "appeal to emotion instead of teaching morality. As a rule they are hardly above their surroundings and exert little if any uplifting influence." Methodist ministers, on the other hand, were somewhat better because they were wakened and broadened by being shifted from place to place. The Methodists could be "reached . . . and moulded in bulk by the controlling power of their church." But, "It would seem that there can be no hope for improvement among the Baptist ministers until the people, of whom they are a reflection, improve. . . ."[73] Not all the ministers were guilty of incompetence only; others like the preacher Jacob Wilson, who sold from the pulpit a paper that purported to be a letter from Jesus Christ, were guilty of profiteering on their congregations.[74]

But for men of sincerity and ability, interested in advancing the cause of their people, the ministry offered the most promising field of service and the most effective medium of propaganda. Numbers of them fought their way up from slavery through poverty to become responsible leaders.

One of these was J. J. Durham, born a slave in Spartanburg County, where as a young man, shortly after the war, he followed the blacksmith trade, using his spare moments to teach himself to read and write. He was ordained in 1868 and became the minister of a small Baptist church in Spartanburg County, where he preached for eighteen months, receiving for his services about eighteen dollars. But disturbed by his ignorance, he entered school in Greenville, where he managed to stay for three years, after which he got a tutor in Latin and Greek to prepare him for admission to the senior preparatory class of South Carolina University. He entered the university in 1874 and stayed until the Democrats closed it, after which he attended Atlanta University and was finally graduated from Fisk University in 1880. He returned to Columbia to take charge of a church, but, still restless at his ignorance, went

---

[73] Christensen, *Southern Workman*, XXXII (October, 1903), 481-86.
[74] Clark, *The Southern Country Editor*, p. 189.

back to Nashville to enter the Meharry Medical College, from which he graduated in 1882 as valedictorian of his class. He then moved to Society Hill where he served the community as both minister and doctor until the following year, when he replaced E. M. Brawley as missionary of the American Baptist Publication Society and as secretary of the state Baptist convention, in which position he served for eight years, after which he returned to the active ministry.[75]

John L. Dart was born a free Negro and graduated from Avery Normal Institute in Charleston as the valedictorian of its first graduating class in 1872. He then attended Atlanta University and Newton Theological Seminary in Massachusetts. After teaching and preaching in the North and in Georgia, he returned to Charleston in 1886 to become the pastor of Morris Street Church.[76] In 1895 he founded the Charleston Industrial Institute, a school devoted to the vocational training of Negro youths. The building in which this school was conducted today houses the Dart Hall Branch of the Charleston Free Library.[77]

Richard Carroll was another Baptist minister of ability. Born in Barnwell County during the death-throes of slavery, he benefitted from the fact that his mother was a trusted house-servant on a large plantation. Educated at Benedict College in Columbia he developed unusual gifts of eloquence which he devoted largely to efforts for interracial understanding. A chaplain during the Spanish-American War, he returned to Columbia to establish a home for Negro orphans and juvenile delinquents. Later he became an evangelist to the Negroes of the South under the direction of the white Baptist Home Mission Board of Atlanta. In this position it was said that he exercised an eloquence that made it possible for him "to tell white people the truth about certain significant things in the relation of the two races without giving offense." This he did "with such wonderful tact that his white audiences always want to hear him again."[78]

---

[75] Pegues, *Our Baptist Ministers and Schools,* pp. 183-87.

[76] *Ibid.,* pp. 145-50.

[77] Charleston *News and Courier,* June 1, 1894; November 13, 1897; December 6, 1899.

[78] Clement Richardson (ed.), *National Cyclopedia of the Colored Race* (Montgomery, 1919), p. 449.

William David Chappelle was another native product, born near the end of the war in Fairfield County. He was graduated from Allen University at the age of thirty and went on to a preaching career of a decade, after which he became secretary and treasurer of the African Methodist Sunday School Union, in which position he prepared and edited Sunday school literature for eight years and established the A. M. E. Printing House in Nashville. After serving as president of Allen University, 1898-1899 and 1908-1912, he became a bishop in the church in 1912 and was in 1916 assigned to his home state.[79]

W. H. Heard, "the plucky and energetic pastor" of an African Methodist Church in Charleston, was found in 1887 pushing a case against the Georgia Railroad before the Interstate Commerce Commission to force equal accommodation for colored passengers. Heard was later assigned as the bishop of West Africa.[80]

The ancient appeal of the Christian faith to the meek and poor in spirit had been a powerful force in bringing ante-bellum slaves into the fold, and, with the fading of the extravagant hopes of Reconstruction days, this appeal once again made the church a center of hope for many Negroes. Religion, as he experienced it, provided for the Negro church member a merciful relief from the hopeless monotony of grinding poverty and ignorance in the promise of better days to come.

Furthermore, the Negro church established itself as an important social center during the first decade after the Civil War, and with the decline of Republican politics its importance as a center of social and uplift activity was enhanced. In addition to the ordinary activities of the church there were frequently camp meetings and singing conventions at which the populace gathered from miles around. The Warrenton Circuit of the African Methodist Church sponsored after 1887 an annual singing convention near Abbeville at which choirs gathered from the neighboring churches to engage in cooperative and competitive singing. At the first of these conventions, the choirs of four churches responded to their names with separate singing during the morning. During the after-

---

[79] *Ibid.*, p. 314.

[80] New York *Age*, October 22, 1887; Lewellyn L. Berry, *A Century of Missions of the African Methodist Episcopal Church, 1840-1940* (New York, 1942), pp. 150-51.

noon the audience heard addresses on music interspersed by the chanting and singing of various groups. Once the speakers had exhausted their remarks on "the perfectness of music, the perfectness of education, the perfectness of religion," the remainder of the day was spent in singing. Frequently outside speakers were brought in, most of whom merely belabored platitudes, but some of whom, like an official of the Colored Alliance, came with an eye to the main chance and the objective of educating and proselyting.[81] The St. Paul Camp Meeting Association of the African Methodist Church in Colleton County presented spectacles that outshone the Abbeville Singing Convention. Incorporated by the legislature in 1891 as a body politic, the stewards of this organization were empowered to license or prohibit the sale of merchandise within one mile of the camp ground and to appoint peace officers who should have police powers.[82]

Animated and boisterous ceremonies were characteristic of many Negro religious services. The biographer of Alexander Bettis said that during his lifetime, "Excitement, shouting, hallelujahs, which were then so large a part of negro worship—as even now it is unfortunately too much so—were condemned and discouraged by him. And unmerciful was he in his scathing denunciation of the 'whangdoodle' preacher who, by the cadence of a tuneful voice, strove to produce such demonstrations."[83] A white observer, describing one such service, said: "They sing and shout, and dance the holy dance, and jump over the benches, and have a regular jubilee time."[84] The Charleston earthquake of 1886 was attributed by many of the homeless Negroes, who gathered on Washington and Marion squares in tents and temporary wooden sheds, to the wrath of God; and the noise of excited religious demonstrations kept more sedate citizens from their sleep. Dr. A. Toomer Porter, white pastor of the St. Mark's Church, appealed to the Negro pastors through the press.

----

[81] *Minutes of the First, Second and Third Sessions of the Abbeville Singing Convention of the A. M. E. Church, Held in St. Peter's Church, 1887, 1888, and 1889, to Which is Appended a Sketch of the Life and Work of Rev. James T. Baker* (Abbeville, 1889), pp. 3-7.

[82] *Acts and Joint Resolutions* (1891), pp. 1340-41.

[83] Nicholson, *Brief Sketch of the Life and Labors of Rev. Alexander Bettis,* p. 32.

[84] Charleston *News and Courier,* August 20, 1898.

Do stop these repeated so-called religious scenes, singing and loud praying, and stentorian preaching. God is not deaf, and I don't suppose all the congregations are, and need not be 'hollered' at so. . . . You will never elevate your people thus, and you antagonize the two races. The average white man does not make excuses and allowances for their antecedents and surroundings, and looks on with contempt, and says, What is the use to try to elevate those savages?[85]

The weaknesses of the Negro churches, however, did not prevent their growing in numbers and influence with the passage of time. If the significant influence that they wielded in the community was all too often devoted to the perpetuation of superstition and emotionalism, they provided at the same time spiritual sustenance to a people starved for the things that give human life significance. If they served too often as havens for religious charlatans, they provided a medium through which leadership could be, and was, developed. If they too often perpetuated ignorance, they provided the institutional and propaganda media through which the cause of Negro education was promoted. And through the conduct of independent churches Negroes found training in organization, management, finance, self-government, and self-reliance.

---

[85] *Ibid.*, September 10, 1886.

11

EDUCATION

ON the morning of May 1, 1877, the Republican claimant to the position of State Superintendent of Education found a guard barring the entry to his office in the State House.[1] Thus Hugh Smith Thompson, the first Democratic state superintendent, came into possession of the office and records which normally would have been turned over to him during the month of November, 1876. He found most of the schools closed because of the near-anarchy that had existed for the preceding six months.[2]

Superintendent Thompson inherited a school system six years old, dating from the school act of 1870. In the Constitution of 1868 the state had been required to establish and support a system of public schools open to both races. That document provided, on paper, an ideal toward which the state school system was to be struggling far into the twentieth century. The constitution contemplated a uniform system of free schools with one school to be kept open at least six months in each district, and the General Assembly was enjoined to require at least twenty-four months' attendance of each child, six to sixteen, once the system was established.[3]

Justus K. Jillson, a white Republican from Massachusetts, was elected state superintendent in 1868 and served until 1876. By an act of 1868 Jillson was authorized to conduct a census of the youths from five to eighteen years of age. Beyond that nothing substantial

---

[1] The Republican claimant was John R. Tolbert. Abbeville *Press and Banner,* May 2, 1877.

[2] *Reports and Resolutions* (1877-1878), p. 375.

[3] *Constitution of 1868,* Art. X, Sec. 3-4.

was done until the enactment of the school law of 1870, which provided for boards of county examiners and popularly elected district trustees. The system was to be financed by poll taxes, legislative appropriations, and voluntary local taxation.[4]

Because of defects in the law Jillson's position was little more than that of a clerk distributing funds and gathering such statistics as he could get rather than that of superintendent of a state system. Control was left in the hands of the county commissioners, elected locally.[5] When Jillson left office in 1876 he had been for several years unable to assemble a quorum of the State Board of Education, made up of the county commissioners.[6]

However, in the face of numerous difficulties, the Republican government had by 1876 established a system that included 2,776 schools and 3,068 teachers.[7] In the words of A. D. Mayo, historian of the postwar Southern school systems,

> Whatever may be charged upon the Reconstruction government . . . , there can be no doubt that the best thing effected by it was the introduction of the American system of schools for all people. . . . It was a great thing to commit the old Commonwealth to the American idea of universal education; to secure appropriations from the legislature, even if they were not paid with regularity; to awaken into life a body of 3,000 native teachers, however destitute many of them may have been of high qualifications for this great profession, and make it possible that the people should tax themselves to the extent, in 1876, of $130,000 for the support of district schools.[8]

Professors Simkins and Woody speculated that if the Radical government had not been overthrown "it would have given the state a school system as good as that which took its place."[9]

General public support for the public school system, though by no means unanimous, found expression during the campaign of

----

[4] *Statutes at Large*, XIV, 339-48.

[5] Amory Dwight Mayo, "The Final Establishment of the Common School System in North Carolina, South Carolina, and Georgia, 1863-1900," *Reports of the Commissioner of Education* (1904), I, 1026.

[6] Thompson, *The Establishment of the Public School System of South Carolina* (Columbia, 1927), p. 15.

[7] *Reports and Resolutions* (1876-1877), pp. 339, 341.

[8] Mayo, in *Reports of the Commissioner of Education* (1904), I, 1031.

[9] Simkins and Woody, *South Carolina During Reconstruction*, p. 442.

CHARLESTON NORMAL AND INDUSTRIAL SCHOOL

The old school, laying the cornerstone for the new school, and the new school completed in 1898 (top to bottom).

SOCIAL LIFE

The Unity and Friendship Society, of Charleston, celebrated its forty-fourth anniversary in 1888

1876 in the endorsement by both parties of a constitutional amendment levying a statewide property tax of two mills to be applied to the public schools. Under this provision, submitted by the Republican legislature, approved by the voters, and ratified by the Democratic legislature in 1878, the tax money was to be kept in the counties and distributed to the various school districts on the basis of their enrollment.[10] During the campaign of 1876, Hampton consistently promised Negroes *"greater facilities for education than you have now or ever had before."*[11]

In Jillson's last annual report, for the year ending June 30, 1876, there were 123,085 pupils listed, 70,802 of whom were Negroes. There were 1,931 white and 1,087 Negro teachers.[12] In no case was there mixing of the races in the public schools, except where there were white teachers for Negro schools. There was an unsuccessful attempt in 1873 to eliminate segregation at the State Institution for the Education of the Deaf, Dumb, and the Blind at Cedar Springs, and there was a mixed student body, predominantly Negro, at the state university from 1873 to 1877.[13]

The condition of the schools in 1877, judging from the figures Thompson was able to put together, was somewhat worse than in the preceding year, but much better than might have been expected during the drawn out political battles of 1876-1877. Out of a total of 2,674 teachers there were now 949 Negroes. School enrollment had dropped about 20,000 from the previous year, three-fourths of the decline among Negro pupils. The income of the school fund for the year amounted to $189,332.80 and the expenditures were $226,020.62.[14] Greater financial stability, however, was soon insured by the ratification of the constitutional two mill tax.

One of the difficulties against which Thompson and his successors found it necessary to struggle was the hostility of large elements

---

[10] *Constitution of 1868*, Amendment to Art. X, Sec. 5, approved January 26, 1878. See Francis Newton Thorpe (ed.), *The Federal and State Constitutions, Colonial Charters, and Other Organic Laws* (Washington, 1909), VI, 3306.

[11] Hampton, *Free Men! Free Ballots!! Free Schools!!!*, p. 5.

[12] *Reports and Resolutions* (1876-1877), p. 338.

[13] Simkins and Woody, *South Carolina During Reconstruction*, p. 439. For an account by a former Negro student of the period when Negroes attended the state university, see Columbia *State*, May 8, 1911. This was called to my attention by Professor Albert N. Sanders of Furman University.

[14] *Reports and Resolutions* (1877), pp. 413-14.

of the white population to the public school system. Hostility was aroused in some by the simple fact that the system had been an innovation of the Radical government. Others feared it because they had interpreted as a ban on segregation a constitutional provision requiring that the schools be open to both races, although it was never so interpreted by either Republican or Democratic officials. Another and more serious source of hostility to the system was the sentiment for economy in government.

The apostles of economy by no means confined their attack to the Negro schools, although they naturally concentrated it there. A Gaffney editor said, "No sophistry or false reasoning can ever convince us that the industrious and self-denying citizen should be taxed to educate the children of indolent and immoral parents";[15] and an Abbeville editor was contending as late as 1887 that the arguments for public schools could be used with equal, if not greater, effect for a free public beef market. "Does not the Bible itself command us to feed the hungry, to cloth [sic] the naked, and to give water to the thirsty? But where does it command us to educate little negroes?"[16] This sentiment, where it did not oppose the public school system as a whole, resolved itself into a cry of "White men's money for white men's children,"[17] and the argument that Negro schools should be entitled only to the funds collected from Negro taxpayers. Although such a system was never adopted formally it was actually put into effect by the process of channelling most of the school fund into the white schools.[18]

Another source of opposition to Negro schools was the fear that education of Negroes would destroy whatever barriers might be put in the way of the franchise by literacy qualifications. Edward McCrady, in arguing for a literacy qualification, said, "The friends and advocates of the negro cannot surely object to this. We will only delay his voting until he can read and write, and thus, until he can protect himself from fraud in the use of the ballot."[19] Yet speaking to the students of Erskine College shortly thereafter he

---

[15] Charleston *News and Courier*, May 12, 1884, quoting Gaffney *Carolinian*.

[16] Abbeville *Press and Banner*, June 1, 1887.

[17] Charleston *News and Courier*, May 12, 1884, quoting Greenville *News*.

[18] J. A. Brown of Charleston calculated in 1900 that the Negro schools in Hampton County got little, if any, of the money paid in by white taxpayers. Charleston *News and Courier*, June 23, 1900.

[19] McCrady, *The Registration of Electors*, p. 11.

expressed a fear that must have haunted most men of his convictions:

> But I do tremble at the idea that the time should come when the negroes of the South, forced by outside pressure and sustained by outside aid, should at least for the while, be better educated than the masses of the whites. . . .[20]

Immediately after the Democratic victory in 1877 the air was filled with talk of economy and white supremacy, and the advocates of both could find in the public schools an object of hostility. Thompson went along with the economy drive by requesting an appropriation of only $100,000 in 1877 in contrast to $250,000 in 1876 and recommending that the schools be kept closed until January 1, 1878.[21] These were only temporary measures, however, until he could get his second breath. He was at the same time urging ratification of the two mill tax amendment.[22]

Despite the widespread hostility to state-supported education there was a feeling among the Democratic leaders that they had a moral obligation to continue the development of the public school system for both races. In his inaugural address Wade Hampton repeated his party's pledges to provide an efficient school system for all.[23] Again, in a message to the General Assembly, he reminded the members, "We must not forget that among the pledges of reform made by us there is none to which we are more solemnly committed than the placing within the reach of all classes the means of education."[24]

The campaign of 1878 found Hampton's adjutant general, Johnson Hagood, reminding an audience that

> It is no fault of the negro that citizenship has been thrust upon him; nor is it a crime in him that he lacks the culture of the white man. Educate his children that the next generation may be better qualified for the duties that are before them; teach in kindness the freedman of to-day how to discharge those that

---

[20] McCrady, *The Necessity of Education as the Basis of Our Political System,* p. 15.

[21] *Reports and Resolutions* (1876-1877), pp. 360-61; *ibid.* (1877-1878), p. 375.

[22] *Ibid.* (1877-1878), p. 379.

[23] *House Journal* (1876), pp. 39-42.

[24] *Ibid.* (1877), p. 18.

are upon him, and ere long South Carolina will present an united people.[25]

Hugh S. Thompson proudly stated in 1879 that the Negroes got their full share of the school fund. Increased attendance he cited as evidence that Negroes were not denied the benefits of education. In a statement that in coming years would have sounded strange on the lips of a Democratic politician, he said: "True philanthropy and sound statesmanship alike teach that the best way to elevate the negro and render him secure in his political rights is to educate him."[26] In following this policy the Democratic administrations until 1880, at least, continued to increase total expenditures for both white and Negro schools, as the following table shows: [27]

Expended during	Whites	Per capita	Negroes	Per capita
1876-1877	$ 85,874	$1.85	$103,478	$1.85
1877-1878	147,702	2.73	168,495	2.71
1878-1879	157,788	2.70	173,261	2.70
1879-1880	168,516	2.75	182,899	2.51

The school law of 1878, the plan of which was until recently the basis of the state's school system, was the work of a committee of four educators called together by Superintendent Thompson. The outstanding feature of the new measure was the centralization of direction in a state board of examiners, consisting of the state superintendent and four members appointed by the governor. Although the county commissioner was still elected, the other two members of the county board were chosen by the state board. The county boards, in turn, named the district trustees. A system was established for the appeal of any decision to the state board.[28]

In one respect centralization worked against Negroes, for in Georgetown and Beaufort, where the Republicans still named the

---

[25] Charleston *News and Courier*, August 19, 1878.

[26] *Reports and Resolutions* (1879), pp. 362, 365.

[27] Columbia *Daily Register*, May 24, 1881. These figures are ostensibly quoted from the state superintendent's report for 1880, but apparently came actually from a supplemental report on finances which was promised in the report for 1880 but which does not appear in the regular series of state documents. These are the last figures that differentiate expenditures for white and Negro schools before 1895. See *Reports and Resolutions* (1880), p. 363. The per capita expenditures were computed by the author to the nearest cent on the basis of total enrollment.

[28] *Statutes at Large*, XIV, 571-86.

county commissioner, they were unable to name the board that served with him. In finances, on the other hand, decentralization worked to the disadvantage of Negroes. It was provided that the income from poll taxes should be expended in the district where collected rather than simply in the county. The lack of centralized administration of finances makes it difficult to judge from the available statistics just what treatment was given to the Negro schools. It can be said with certainty only that there were variations depending upon the district trustees and county boards, and that as time passed less attention was paid to the pledges of 1876 by local officials who had had nothing to do with making them. Some light is shed upon this situation by the first report of the State Supervisor of Elementary Rural Schools in 1910, in which he said:

> Frequently the county superintendent does not know where they [the Negro Schools] are located and sometimes the district board cannot tell where the negro school is taught. It is customary for the board of trustees to allot a certain amount of money to the Negroes and allow them to use it as they please. A teacher is employed and no further questions are asked, except concerning enrollment at the end of the session.[29]

One result of the system of allotting income from the two mill tax in proportion to enrollment was that the white schools in black-belt counties were better financed than those elsewhere, for the money brought in on the basis of the large district enrollment was channelled into the white schools which had only a small portion of that enrollment.[30]

The chief accomplishment of Thompson and his immediate successors was the reconciliation of the opponents of the public school system. Lengthy arguments appear in Thompson's report against those who would deny the right of the state to control education at all, those who objected to universal free education, and those with specific objections to the system as established in South Carolina.[31] A successor, Asbury Coward, reported in 1886 that "the largest and most dangerous" class opposed to public education were those who opposed the education of Negroes on the ground that "To educate a Negro is to spoil a laborer and train up a

---

[29] *Annual Report of the State Superintendent of Education* (1910), p. 120.
[30] *Reports and Resolutions* (1912), II, 93-95.
[31] *Reports and Resolutions* (1879), pp. 369-87.

candidate for the Penitentiary." In the same report Coward indicated that the memory of the pledges of 1876 was still alive:

> The faithful fulfillment of the pledges of 1876 in this matter
> of education has already converted a dangerously disturbing
> element into at least a passive one in our political life. Would
> the ruthless violation of those pledges secure to us more of
> peace and genuine prosperity? [32]

In 1887 State Superintendent James H. Rice, after a tour of every
county in the state, drew a somewhat brighter picture of a public
"more than ever aroused to the duty of elementary training for
their children."[33]

But slow development characterized the evolution of the schools
until 1895. In that year $552,637.24 was spent on the state's school
system, only $90,000 more than in the last year of Jillson's adminis-
tration.[34] In intervening years the expenditures had reached a peak
of $563,743.66 in 1893-1894,[35] but on the whole there was little de-
viation in the expenditures from the figure set under Jillson, the
general trend being a slightly perceptible rise, somewhat accelerated
toward the end of the century. The relative financial treatment of
white and Negro schools between the school year ending in 1880
and that ending in 1895 is impossible to ascertain. However, in that
period the school expenditures had risen from $2.75 to $3.11 per
capita for whites, while dropping from $2.51 to $1.05 for Negroes.[36]
Whether this trend set in before the Tillman administration it is
impossible to say. It is clear that although in the first years of the
Democratic government, from 1877 to 1880, per capita expendit-
tures for white and Negro schools were approximately equal, and
although in 1880 the state was still spending more on its Negro
schools than its white schools, by 1895 more than twice as much
was being spent on white schools as on Negro schools and nearly
three times as much per pupil.

The average length of session, which had been three months for
all schools when Hugh S. Thompson came into office, was reported

32 *Ibid.* (1886), p. 7.
33 *Ibid.* (1887), I, 321.
34 *Ibid.* (1876-1877), pp. 360-61; *ibid.* (1897), pp. 274-76.
35 *Ibid.* (1896), I, 439.
36 Columbia *Daily Register*, May 24, 1881; *Reports and Resolutions* (1897),
pp. 274-76. The per capita expenditures were computed by the author on the
basis of total enrollment.

for 1895-1896 as 3.95 months for whites and 3.25 months for Negroes.[37] The enrollment of Negro pupils which had dropped to 55,952 in 1876-1877 had shown a gradual increase to 119,292 in 1894-1895 while total expenditures on their schools had actually declined.[38]

From these figures it can be seen that there was no improvement in the financial condition of the Negro schools during the first two decades of Democratic rule. Despite pious and apparently sincere pronouncements by the Democratic leaders of post-Reconstruction days about their concern for the education of Negroes, the most that can be said for their efforts after the first few years is that they did retain and consolidate the system that had been established by the Republican administrations.

The basic problem of inadequate facilities and inadequate teachers plagued the Negro schools throughout the period. William Pickens' description of the country school that he attended near Pendleton in the eighties gives a distinct impression of the difficulties under which rural schools labored.

> It was a characteristic Negro schoolhouse built of logs, with one door and one window, the latter having no panes and being closed by a board shutter which swung on leather hinges outward. The house was not larger than a comfortable bedroom and had a "fire-place" opposite the door. The children faced the fire-place, so that the scant light fell through the door upon their books. There were no desks; the seats were long board benches with no backs. The teacher insisted that the students sit in statuesque postures, not moving a limb too often. Persuasion to study and good deportment consisted of a hickory switch, a cone-shaped paper "dunce cap" and a stool on which the offender must stand on one foot for an enormous length of time. Although I had readily learned my elements under sympathetic tutelage at home, about all I remember of this first schooling is the menancing words of the teacher, the movements of that switch and the astonishing balancing acts of the dunce cap wearers. The chief fountain of academic knowledge in such schools was the famous ole "blue-back speller." After leaving the nonsense syllables in the beginning

---

[37] *Reports and Resolutions* (1897), p. 75.
[38] *Ibid.* (1877), p. 413; *ibid.* (1896), I, 437.

of that book, the mile-stones of attainment were first the page of dissyllables beginning with "baker" and secondly the page of polysyllables containing "compressibility." A person interested in your advancement might ask first had you "got to 'baker' yet," and secondly could you spell "compressibility."[39]

The sessions of this school lasted "for only a few hot weeks of summer after the 'laying by' of the crops, and for a few cold weeks of winter between the last of harvest and the time for clearing the fields."[40]

On the other hand, some of the Negro schools in urban areas compared favorably with the best public schools of the land. The Howard Free School of Columbia, under the direction of William M. Dart, an 1876 graduate of South Carolina University, had ten teachers in 1880, each of whom held a first grade certificate from the state superintendent. The curriculum included reading, writing, arithmetic, geography, United States history, and English grammar in the lower grades, and expanded in the upper grades to include algebra, ancient history, and natural history.[41] Beaufort, too, was reported to have an "excellent" teaching force and a "fairly adequate" building by the end of the century.[42]

But the brightest spot in an otherwise disheartening situation was the city of Charleston, where C. G. Memminger had labored both before and after the war for the establishment of a system of graded schools. In 1867 the Morris Street School for colored children was opened under the aegis of a school board composed of leading white citizens, and by October, 1879, had an enrollment of over a thousand pupils and a daily average attendance of ninety-three per cent. Mary Street School, another graded school for Negroes, had at the same time thirteen teachers and over six hundred pupils.[43] In all there were 3,586 Negro pupils enrolled in the Charleston city schools in 1878-1879, and the expenditures in that year were nearly one-fifth as much as those for the entire state system.[44] Winnsboro in 1878 was the first town outside of Charles-

---

[39] Pickens, *Bursting Bonds*, pp. 9-11.
[40] *Ibid.*, p. 12.
[41] Columbia *Daily Register*, February 3, 1880.
[42] Christensen, in *Southern Workman*, XXXII (October, 1903), p. 483.
[43] *Reports and Resolutions* (1879), pp. 362-63.
[44] *Ibid.*, pp. 404-7, Charleston expenditures were $65,676.29; the state expenditures were $319,320.43.

ton to adopt the system of voluntary local taxation for city schools, but by 1883 eight other towns had followed. In the Constitution of 1895 the system was provided for under a general law. In towns which adopted the system, schools for both white and black fared better than in rural areas.[45]

The lack of efficient teachers was a constant source of difficulty. Thompson complained that it was frequently necessary to pay teachers in certificates of indebtedness, and that while white Southerners could not be obtained to teach Negroes, few Northerners would come South for the low salaries that were offered.[46] Slowly and painfully a corps of Negro teachers was built up. In this connection a valuable innovation under the administration of Thompson was the beginning of state and county summer teachers' institutes, a poor substitute for thorough training, but quite effective for the situation with which the schools were then faced. In 1880 the first statewide "Normal Institute" for white teachers was held in Spartanburg. The first county teachers' institute for Negroes was held in Charleston the same year under the direction of Bishop P. F. Stevens of the Reformed Episcopal Church, who was also county commissioner of education. In July of 1881 the first state-wide Negro teachers' institute was held in Columbia under the direction of H. P. Montgomery, a Negro of Washington, D. C. The enrollment was 185.[47] After that, state and county institutes were annual events.

But there was no remedy for the low salary scales. As late as 1900 the state superintendent recommended that the average salary for colored teachers should be approximately doubled, to $160.60![48]

The superintendent complained in his 1899 report that county boards found it necessary to accept inferior teachers in order to keep the Negro schools going at all.[49] At the same time the school boards often insisted on giving examinations that tested applicants for knowledge far beyond that required for elementary teachers. In a letter to the state superintendent, Ellen Murray of the Penn School at Frogmore complained that girls trained to be teachers

---

[45] Thompson, *Establishment of the Public School,* p. 26.
[46] G. Campbell, *White and Black,* p. 319.
[47] Thompson, *Establishment of the Public School,* pp. 37-38.
[48] *Reports and Resolutions* (1901), I, 611-12.
[49] *Ibid.* (1900), II, 302.

could scarcely afford to take jobs paying $20 and $30 a month and that, besides, they found questions on their examinations about Shakespeare, Pope, and Thackeray completely beyond their ken. Ellen Murray's description of the training given teachers at the Penn School is an informative commentary on the status of the Negro schools.

> Being taught on Normal lines, they know how to make blackboards out of old boxes and writing books out of wrapping paper, how to teach geography by outlines in the sand, and to teach the alphabet by the headlines of newspapers, to teach temperance by songs, and they know how to keep a school in order without using the whip.
>
> They teach arithmetic by the help of corn kernels and teach their pupils how to keep simple accounts, make change, and reckon interest.[50]

In meeting the problem of teachers, however, there was no concerted program for the improvement of the teaching staff. The state superintendent merely recommended that lower qualifications be demanded of Negro teachers.[51] Indicative of the program was the expenditure of $8,638.72 on summer schools for white teachers in 1899 and $1,154.70 on summer schools for Negro teachers. There was a state school for whites and a county school in every county except Beaufort. The Negroes had no state school that year and it was found "impractical" to have more than eight county schools for Negroes because of the expense and the lack of competent instructors.[52]

Charleston consistently met the problem by employing white teachers for the Negro schools. Walter Hines Page noted that Southern whites who held these positions did not suffer ostracism from the white community, although Northern whites did.[53] However, after 1888 there were constant complaints from Negroes in the city that Negro teachers should be employed, and although there were but two Negro teachers in the whole city school sys-

---

[50] *Ibid.*, pp. 321-23.

[51] *Ibid.*, p. 302.

[52] *Ibid.*, pp. 339-41.

[53] Walter Hines Page to Horace E. Scudder, March 18, 1899, in Burton J. Hendrick, *The Training of an American: The Earlier Life and Letters of Walter H. Page* (Boston and New York, 1928), p. 395.

tem as late as 1896, the situation rapidly changed after the turn of the century.[54]

Throughout the period there was a consciousness of a close tie between education and the suffrage. Education became an important issue in the constitutional convention of 1895, not only in its own right, but because it was so closely bound up with the suffrage. If the whites were to establish an educational qualification for the suffrage in order to disfranchise the Negroes they would need to secure their own position further by providing for an adequate school system for their own people. Ben Tillman early recognized the connection between suffrage and education and the Tillmanite governor John Gary Evans said in his inaugural address of 1894, speaking of education, "We have performed our duty to the negro possibly too liberally, as a study of the reports will show."[55]

Varying attitudes were held by members of the convention. The insecure hold that public education had on some was indicated by one member who could see no need for a full-time county commissioner when the schools were in session only forty or fifty days in the year,[56] and by another who wanted to abolish the offices of state superintendent and county commissioner and devolve their duties, which he apparently thought to be chiefly fiscal in nature, on the comptroller-general and the county commissioners.[57] Others expressed different attitudes. One proposed that only professional teachers be eligible to the state board of education,[58] and R. B. Anderson, Georgetown Negro, introduced a resolution for compulsory attendance of all children seven to twelve, but his proposal ran headlong into the white supremacy sentiment and was lost.[59]

The convention's education committee brought out a plan that provided in detail for the organization of a state school system. It was essentially the same plan as that already prevailing, except that there was provision for popular election of the local trustees.[60]

----

[54] Charleston *News and Courier*, March 23, 30, April 14, 1888; March 3, 1896; May 25, 1899.

[55] *House Journal* (1894), p. 133.

[56] Columbia *Daily Register*, November 14, 1895.

[57] *Convention Journal*, p. 91.

[58] *Ibid.*, pp. 151-52.

[59] *Ibid.*, pp. 127, 308.

[60] *Ibid.*, pp. 308-10.

This, however, was amended over the vociferous objection of Robert Smalls so that the method of electing trustees need not be uniform.[61] The amendment was designed to make it possible for the legislature to prevent the election of Negro trustees in areas where Negroes predominated.

The most significant change enacted by the constitutional convention was in raising the property tax for schools from two to three mills, which was still to be collected in each county and apportioned among the districts in proportion to the number of pupils; and in the provision that any district could levy additional taxes above that amount after November 1, 1898.[62] To taxpayers who might be excited over the possible high cost of the system, the chairman of the education committee pointed out that it was a necessary price for white supremacy. "It is foolish to say any other race can get control of this State if we are educated. Education is the great lever of civilization. It can be gotten only by taxation."[63] Tillman strongly urged the adoption of the program, reminding the delegates that by enacting the three mill tax they could secure education against a future legislature fearful of the wealthy and the ignorant, both of whom might be in an unholy alliance against public education.[64] A movement to increase the poll tax also had the blessing of Tillman, but failed by a vote of 103-20, drawing the condemnation that an increase would be inequitable. A provision for free public school textbooks was likewise lost.[65]

The Constitution of 1895, like that of 1868, was an important milestone in the progress of public education. Although the increase in public school funds had been brought about largely by arguments for white supremacy, it brought some benefits to the Negro schools by a process of trickling down. But as the white school fund grew by leaps and bounds, the expenditures for Negroes increased slowly, so that discrepancies continued to grow. By the end of the century the total expenditures for Negro schools had surpassed the previous recorded high of 1879-1880. In 1919-1920, per capita expenditures for Negro schools finally surpassed those

[61] Columbia *Daily Register*, November 16, 1895.
[62] *Convention Journal*, pp. 308-10.
[63] Columbia *Daily Register*, November 14, 1895.
[64] *Ibid.*, November 15, 1895.
[65] *Convention Journal*, pp. 561-63, 578

reached during the Hampton administration, but by then the white schools were receiving more than eight times as much per capita.[66]

Partly as a result of the white supremacy campaign, interest in industrial and agricultural education for Negroes increased. Gone were the days of Thompson's and Hagood's purpose of making the Negro a good citizen. The new dispensation emphasized the subordination of Negroes, but gradually recognized the value of vocational education to the Negro in his subordinate role.

Whatever the motives of the dominant whites, the Negro schools by the end of the century were beginning to emerge from the financial slough. The decrease of Negro illiteracy from 78.5 per cent in 1880 to 52.8 per cent in 1900[67] indicated that progress had been made despite the deficiencies, but that the road ahead was still long and difficult.

Outside the state-controlled public school system there were a number of private academies offering elementary and secondary training to Negroes. Some of these, founded during the Reconstruction era, had long and useful careers, and the continuing interest of Negroes in education caused their numbers to grow both through efforts of the race and the assistance of whites, North and South.

Most of the academies founded during the Reconstruction period were the products of Northern philanthropy. The oldest of these was the Penn Normal and Industrial School, founded at Frogmore on St. Helena Island in 1862. Laura M. Towne and Ellen Murray carried on the work until 1905, when it was taken over by Rossa B. Cooley and Grace B. House, former teachers at Hampton Institute in Virginia.[68] The Penn School continued its useful independent existence until 1948, when it was absorbed into the state public school system.[69]

The Mather Industrial School near Beaufort was founded during the Reconstruction period by Rachel C. Mather, a white native of

---

[66] In 1919-1920 the per capita expenditures reached $26.08 for whites and $3.04 for Negroes. *Reports and Resolutions* (1921), II, 231. Compare this with the earlier figures, *supra*.

[67] *Census* (1880), I, 920, 924; Bureau of the Census, *Negro Population, 1790-1915*, p. 419.

[68] See Holland (ed.), *Letters and Diary of Laura M. Towne,* and Cooley, *School Acres, an Adventure in Rural Education.*

[69] Columbia *Record*, May 6, 1948.

Boston, Massachusetts, and was still operating in the early nineties with a corps of six teachers in addition to Mrs. Mather. Three of these were supported by the Woman's Baptist Home Mission Society, one by the county authorities, and two from Mrs. Mather's own resources.[70] The Wallingford Academy in Charleston, founded in 1865 by the Presbyterian Board of Missions for Freedmen, had in 1885 a force of six instructors in addition to the principal and an enrollment of 651.[71] The Avery Normal Institute was founded in Charleston in 1865 by Francis L. Cardozo under the auspices of the American Missionary Association. By 1880 the school occupied a building erected at a cost of $25,000 and had a teaching corps of a principal and eight assistants. The school offered, in addition to the "common branches," courses in history, government and economics, languages and literature, mathematics, bookkeeping, school management, methods of teaching, natural philosophy, and physiology.[72]

The Schofield Normal and Industrial School of Aiken was opened in 1868 by Martha Schofield, a Pennsylvania Quaker, under the auspices of the Freedmen's Commission of Germantown, Pennsylvania. It was conducted in a frame building erected by the Freedmen's Bureau in 1870 until the erection in 1882 of a large two story brick structure. Martha Schofield was one of the pioneers of vocational education for Negroes, and by the turn of the century the school was offering, in addition to a regular high school education, training in carpentry, farming, harness-making, blacksmithing, wheelwrighting, shoemaking, sewing, cooking, millinery, housekeeping, and laundry work. It had a plant equipment worth $5,000, an endowment of $37,000, sixteen teachers, and a library of 1,500 volumes.[73]

Brainerd Institute, founded by the Presbyterian Board of Missions for Freedmen at Chester in 1868, became a permanent in-

---

[70] Pegues, *Our Baptist Ministers and Schools,* pp. 620-22.

[71] Charleston *News and Courier,* September 1, 1885; *see also* Charleston *New Era,* April 7, 1883.

[72] City of Charleston, *Year Book* (1880), pp. 125-26.

[73] Charleston *News and Courier,* August 4, 1882; Matilda Arabelle Evans, *Martha Schofield, Pioneer Negro Educator* (Columbia, 1916), p. 13; South Carolina Department of Agriculture, Commerce, and Immigration, *Handbook of South Carolina* (Columbia, 1907), p. 219. Hereinafter cited as *Handbook of 1907.*

stitution of learning on the secondary level. It had by 1894 two hundred pupils and had ambitiously expanded its program to include two years of college work.[74] Brewer Normal, Industrial, and Agricultural Institute, founded by the American Missionary Association at Greenwood in 1872, likewise followed a process of vigorous growth. In 1890 it reported over 230 students, and had refused between 75 and 100 for want of space.[75]

The multiplication of academies continued after the Reconstruction period. Alexander Bettis, Baptist minister of Edgefield County, organized among the numerous churches he founded an educational association whose objective was to foster the training of ministers. On the fourth of July, 1881, a vast crowd assembled on the ground chosen for the erection of an academy to cut trees and make a clearing for its building. This was completed in six months and dedicated on the first of January, 1882. On the same day the school was formally opened. It was for many years under the direction of Bettis, a man who learned to read but never to write, and his pathetic, yet efficient, interest in the cause of education established it on a firm foundation. After his death the direction of the school was taken over by Alfred W. Nicholson, educated by Bettis' association at the Schofield School and Atlanta University.[76]

In 1882, E. W. Williams, a Negro minister of the Northern Presbyterian Church, secured the aid of Northern philanthropy to establish Ferguson Academy in Abbeville. The school, offering instruction on the elementary level, had by 1886 an average daily attendance of about sixty-five students taught by Ferguson and his wife. They were trained in grammar, history, geography, arithmetic, "and other branches usually taught in the common schools."[77] In 1893, Williams, having transferred his allegiance to the Southern Presbyterians, founded another school in Abbeville that was named the Ferguson and Williams Normal and Polytechnic School and

---

[74] Charleston *News and Courier*, June 16, 1894.

[75] Taylor, *The Negro in South Carolina During the Reconstruction*, pp. 95-96.

[76] Nicholson, *Brief Sketch of the Life and Labors of Rev. Alexander Bettis*, pp. 26-29, 70-80.

[77] Washington *Bee*, July 10, 1886, quoting Abbeville *Press and Banner*.

placed under the control of the Southern Presbyterians. It was closed in 1920.[78]

Northern church members as late as the nineties still showed an interest in the development of Negro schools, and the Northern Presbyterian Board of Missions for Freedmen founded in 1894 a school for the Negro youth of Beaufort after having for a number of years assisted Negro education through contributions to the public schools. Under the direction of G. M. Elliott, pastor of the Negro Presbyterian Church in Beaufort, the school had four teachers in 1897 offering instruction in four departments: primary, grammar, normal, and high school. From an enrollment of 21 in 1894 it increased to an enrollment of 189 in 1897.[79]

During the nineties a flowering of interest in vocational education brought the establishment of numerous industrial schools. Among these can be listed the Colored Industrial School and Asylum, founded by T. A. J. Clemons in Spartanburg, 1891;[80] the Charleston Normal and Industrial Institute, established by J. L. Dart, 1894;[81] Sterling Industrial College (now Sterling High School), established in Greenville under D. M. Minus for the "intellectual, industrial, and religious training" of Negro youth, 1896;[82] the Edisto Island Industrial School, founded by J. J. Johnson, 1897;[83] and the Voorhees Normal and Industrial School, founded at Denmark in 1897 by Elizabeth Evelyn Wright through the assistance of the Protestant Episcopal Church.[84] In every case these schools were founded through Negro initiative, although in most cases they were assisted in some measure by whites, North and South.

By the end of the century Negroes also had four colleges. The first of these, Claflin University, was founded in 1869 through the enterprise of a group of Methodist Episcopal clergymen, and was

---

[78] Washington *Bee*, December 5, 1896; Jones and Mills (eds.), *History of the Presbyterian Church in South Carolina Since 1850*, pp. 372-73.

[79] Charleston *News and Courier*, June 26, 1894; May 24, 1897.

[80] Columbia *Daily Register*, March 21, 1891.

[81] Mildred Hone, *The Former Charleston Normal and Industrial Institute, now Dart Hall*, n.p., n.d., p. 1.

[82] *Handbook of 1907*, pp. 219-20.

[83] Charleston *News and Courier*, April 1, 1897.

[84] Clipping from *The Diocese* (official organ of the Protestant Episcopal Diocese of South Carolina), May, 1947, in William Godber Hinson Papers, Charleston Library Society.

chartered by an act of incorporation which provided that no professor be required "to have any particular complexion" and that no student should be refused admission on account of "race, complexion, or religious opinion.[85]

For a short while during Reconstruction, Negroes attended South Carolina University, and some, like William M. Dart, were graduated. The entrance of the first Negro student in October, 1873, resulted in some resignations from the faculty and student body, but the university continued to function until 1877 when the Democrats came into power.[86] In 1877 the university was quickly closed by the new Democratic legislature and its Negro and Northern white faculty members dismissed.[87] This action left the Democratic administration in the anomalous position of supporting an institution for the education of Negroes, but none for whites until 1880, when the South Carolina College of Agriculture and Mechanical Arts was opened on the campus of the old South Carolina College.[88]

The state college for Negroes had been established in Orangeburg in 1872 under the name of South Carolina Agricultural College and Mechanics Institute. The nine-man board of trustees, chosen by the legislature, was entrusted with the money available to the state under the Morrill Land Grant Act of 1862. The college collaborated closely with Claflin University and had a peculiar legal relationship to it. While the board elected by the legislature was a separate group with its own chairman, it constituted at the same time, together with the trustees of Claflin, a single board which could also elect a chairman, a situation which prevailed until 1878.[89] The president of Claflin University was at the same time Secretary of the Agricultural College.[90]

The state was entitled to land scrip for 180,000 acres. The scrip was sold for $191,000 which was invested in state bonds as a permanent fund for the agricultural and mechanical college. A 116 acre tract of land adjoining Claflin University was purchased for use as an experimental farm. Income from the land scrip fund

---

[85] *Statutes at Large*, XIV, 303.

[86] *Reports and Resolutions* (1874-1875), Appendix.

[87] *Acts and Joint Resolutions* (1877, extra session), pp. 314-15.

[88] *Reports and Resolutions* (1880), p. 643.

[89] *Acts and Joint Resolutions* (1871-1872), pp. 172-75.

[90] *Reports and Resolutions* (1877-1878), pp. 829, 832.

was sufficient in the autumn of 1874 for instruction to begin, with the state supplying a professor of mathematics and Claflin University the rest of the teachers.[91]

In the fall of 1877 attendance was 145 and the instruction available through the combined faculty of seven included English grammar and literature, mental and moral science, mathematics, Latin, Greek, physics, agricultural chemistry, modern languages, and music, in addition to the practical instruction available from work on the experimental farm and in a recently built carpentry shop.[92] Some indication is given in the secretary's report for 1877 that the instruction was chiefly on the secondary level:

> The first care has been to have the pupils well drilled in the common English branches, and then advance them to higher grades of English, classical, and scientific studies only as they were found prepared. To this end the school has been thoroughly graded and classified on an English course, extending through a period of four years.[93]

In 1877 the college added a normal department which was by 1879 offering a three year course.[94]

In the general reorganization of the educational system in 1878 the Agricultural College and Mechanics Institute was given the name Claflin College. It retained so close a relationship with Claflin University as to be indistinguishable from it, the white Methodist minister, Edward Cooke, retaining his dual capacity as head of both institutions. Legally, however, Claflin College, together with the South Carolina College, constituted the University of South Carolina under a single board of trustees. In 1879 the land scrip fund was divided so that half of it went to the support of the South Carolina College of Agriculture and Mechanical Arts for whites which was opened in 1880.[95]

The state dealt generously with Claflin. In 1879 Superintendent Thompson reported an annual appropriation of $7,500 from the

---

[91] *Ibid.*, p. 829.
[92] *Ibid.*, 830-31.
[93] *Ibid.*, p. 830.
[94] *Ibid.*, (1879), p. 364.
[95] *Acts and Joint Resolutions* (1877-1878), pp. 532-36; *Statutes at Large*, XVII, 82-83.

state at a time when there was no state college for whites. In the spring of 1879 there was an enrollment of 119 in the three schools: the College of Liberal Arts, the Normal School, and the Grammar School.[96] A machine shop was added in 1883 by means of a grant from the John F. Slater Fund.[97]

By the early nineties the annual appropriation had been lowered to $5,000 and efforts were made in the legislature to eliminate even that,[98] but the state continued to support the college in connection with Claflin University until 1895. By that year the combined faculty had grown from seven to a total of thirty-six.[99] The enrollment was 570 in 1894-1895 as compared to 145 in 1876-1877. In 1890 the university was offering the following courses of study: college classical, college scientific, college philosophical, college preparatory, normal, English, kindergarten, English Bible, music, and art, in addition to agricultural and mechanical training. Among the twenty-seven industrial courses were the following: art needlework, blacksmithing, bricklaying, cabinet-making, domestic economy, engineering (steam), merchandising, and printing.[100] College degrees offered by Claflin in 1892 were Ph. B., A. B., and B. S.[101]

All did not go well with this peculiar collaboration of church and state, however. Among whites there was always a suspicion of the supposed radical tendencies of the Methodist Episcopal Church, and among Negro Baptists a considerable agitation against "giving to one school of distinctive denominational creed, what should either be given to a State school free from all denominational control, or . . . should be divided among the several denominational schools in the State on the basis of their numerical strength."[102]

The six Negro delegates to the constitutional convention of 1895 skillfully exploited this feeling to secure a separate state college for Negroes. R. B. Anderson complained that a great part of the control of the university rested with the Methodist Church, but

---

[96] *Reports and Resolutions* (1879), pp. 363-65.
[97] *Ibid.* (1884), II, 517.
[98] Columbia *Daily Register,* December 18, 20, 1889.
[99] *Reports and Resolutions* (1891), I, 446-47.
[100] *Ibid.; ibid.* (1896), I, 610.
[101] *Ibid.* (1893), I, 319.
[102] Columbia *State,* December 2, 1892.

he declared that the Negroes of the state wanted a school entirely free of sectarian control.[103] Thomas E. Miller proposed that the state establish a school entirely separate from the Methodist controlled university and provide that only "Southern men or women of the Negro race" be on the faculty.[104]

This agitation led Ben Tillman to move for the establishment of a separate school in Orangeburg to be given the unfortunate name of Colored Normal, Industrial, Agricultural, and Mechanical College of South Carolina. Because of the desire of Negroes for additional jobs and the interest of both races in eliminating Northern denominational influences, the motion was quickly accepted.[105]

Thomas E. Miller as a member of the legislature introduced early in 1896 a bill for the severance of Claflin College from Claflin University and its transformation into the Negro college provided for in the new constitution. This bill, amended to provide that "The Principal or President and corps of instructors shall be of the negro race," became law on March 3, 1896. It provided that the college should be established before the end of the year. A board of trustees consisting of six members elected by the legislature with the governor as *ex officio* chairman was instructed to assume control over the property of Claflin College. The bill also called for an annual appropriation of $5,000 for five years and for the furnishing of convict labor by the state penitentiary on request to carry out a building program.[106] On March 7, 1876, Thomas E. Miller resigned from the legislature to assume the presidency.[107]

The new college opened in the fall of 1896 with college, normal, preparatory, model school, music, art, industrial, mechanical, and agricultural departments, and with a faculty including graduates of Howard, Harvard, Colgate, Oberlin, and Lincoln Universities, West Point, Drew Theological Seminary, and Benedict College.[108] By 1903 it possessed two large buildings, six houses for professors, a kitchen and dining hall, a machine shop, dairy stable, barn, and

---

[103] Columbia *Daily Register*, November 17, 1895.

[104] *Convention Journal*, pp. 577, 580.

[105] *Ibid.*, p. 581.

[106] *House Journal* (1896), p. 158; *Acts and Joint Resolutions* (1896), pp. 173-75.

[107] *House Journal* (1896), p. 878.

[108] *Reports and Resolutions* (1897), I, 184.

engine and boiler room in addition to several small buildings. A legislative committee which investigated the school in that year reported, "All this has been done under the management of the President, Thomas E. Miller, who has certainly accomplished wonders with the amount of money he has had to work with. We believe he is striving hard for the upbuilding of his race, and that the college is doing a good work for the negro."[109] In the same year Governor Miles B. McSweeny spoke approvingly of the economical principles on which the college had been operated, with only $62,500 of state appropriations in its entire history up to that time, an average of less than $9,000 per year.[110]

During the period of their collaboration from 1872 to 1896 the church and state developed in Orangeburg the leading center for the education of Negro leaders in the state. A survey of 178 graduates from the normal department between 1879 and 1896 shows that 91 of them went into the teaching profession. Others served as ministers, physicians, farmers, brickmasons, lawyers, merchants, college professors, editors, and government officials.[111] After 1882, when the first class was graduated in the college department, Claflin produced college graduates who served in the leading professions.[112] The leavening effect of this group on the Negro population of the state has been important. Since 1896 Claflin and the Colored Normal, Industrial, Agricultural, and Mechanical College have continued to operate on adjoining campuses.

In Columbia a similar center of higher education grew out of the establishment of two church schools, Benedict College and Allen University, on adjoining campuses. The first of these was founded in 1871 by the American Baptist Home Mission Society through the benefaction of Mrs. Bethesba A. Benedict of Pawtucket, Rhode Island. At first named Benedict Institute, in honor of the donor's deceased husband, Stephen Benedict, the school was intended as a center for the training of Baptist ministers and teachers. The first pupil was a Baptist preacher, sixty-six years old. Through continued gifts from Mrs. Benedict and the work of its second president, the Reverend Lewis Colby, in gathering donations from

---

[109] *House Journal* (1903) p. 209.
[110] *Reports and Resolutions* (1903), II, 288.
[111] Fitchett, *Journal of Negro Education,* XII (Winter, 1943), 53.
[112] *Ibid.,* p. 52.

the Negro Baptists of the state the school rapidly increased its physical plant in the early eighties. Under the direction of a series of competent heads, Timothy S. Dodge, Lewis Colby, E. J. Goodspeed, and C. E. Becker, the Institute grew from its humble beginnings to be chartered in 1894 as Benedict College. By 1907 it had a campus of twenty acres, eleven buildings, among them the only Carnegie Library for Negroes in the state, and an endowment fund of more than $125,000. It had a library of 10,700 volumes and a corps of twenty-one teachers.[113]

Allen University grew out of Payne Institute, established at Cokesbury in 1871 by the Abbeville District of the African Methodist Episcopal Church. In 1880 the Columbia and South Carolina Annual Conferences of the church merged it into Allen University, which was opened in Columbia in the following year. Beginning with a faculty of six, among whom the outstanding members were D. A. Straker, dean of the law department, and Joseph W. Morris, professor of mathematics and ancient languages, the school graduated in its first nine years seventy-five students: twelve from the collegiate department, fifteen from the law department, and forty-eight from the normal department. By 1907 it had two large brick buildings: Arnett Hall, with fifty large rooms used for offices, recitation rooms, and a women's dormitory; and Coppin Hall, "one of the most imposing buildings ever erected and controlled by the Negro race," a four-story brick structure with recitation rooms, chapel, and dormitory space. By that time it had a faculty of thirteen, all Negro, and had graduated 556 students in its twenty-six years of existence.[114]

Allen and Benedict, like Claflin and the state college for Negroes, have continued to this day a service of great value to the Negroes of the state.

---

[113] Pegues, *Our Baptist Ministers and Schools,* pp. 591-95; *Handbook of 1907,* p. 218.

[114] Arnett (ed.), *Proceedings of the Quarto-Centennial Conference of the African M. E. Church of South Carolina* pp. 78-79, 81; *Handbook of 1883,* pp. 527-28; *Handbook of 1907,* p. 219.

12

THE CONTEXT OF VIOLENCE

A STRAIN of violence has always characterized race relations in the South. Force was a basic factor in the creation and maintenance of Negro slavery. Force, sometimes combined with violence and terror, had long been a traditional means of meeting interracial difficulties that whites felt could not be resolved in any other way. After the Civil War the application of force, with the removal of the ameliorating effects of paternalism, came to be characterized more by violence than it had been before. This was not only because of the greater possibilities for violence that were presented by the release of Negroes from the protection of their masters but because of the Northern intervention and fears resulting therefrom of the greater possibility of Negro counteraction and of Negro equality.

Belton O'Neall Townsend observed, however, that the atrocities of the Ku Klux Klan during the Reconstruction period were not a new development. "The Ku-Klux Klan with its night visits and whippings and murders was the legitimate offspring of the patrol. Every Southern gentleman used to serve on the night patrol, the chief duty of which was to whip severely any negro found away from home without a pass from his master."[1] The ancient fear of slave insurrections had its equivalent in the New South, but added to it was the fear of a vague and unknown thing, "social equality." This new terror made the reaction of whites far more violent toward acts of crime by Negroes and toward assertiveness or efforts by Negroes to press their new-found rights.

---

[1] A South Carolinian, *Atlantic Monthly*, XXXIX (April, 1877), 470-71.

The application of violence in such circumstances demonstrated the long-standing practice of applying a double standard of morality to interracial matters. "In all ordinary cases," observed Townsend, "Southerners act morally quite like other people; but whenever the line of conduct to which they are urged by one of their peculiarities comes under the prohibition of a moral law, they are very apt to disregard that law altogether and go ahead, or put such a forced construction on it as will justify their actions."[2] The peculiarities to which Townsend referred were these: (1) white Southerners had "slender regard" for the rights of Negroes; (2) they were unusually intolerant of opposition or difference of opinion, especially in political matters; and (3) dissipation and the doctrines of the code of honor prevailed widely among the whites.

The tradition of violence was by no means confined merely to interracial relations, but also found expression in hostility toward white Republicans and other unorthodox individuals, and in the practice of the *code duello,* either in formal or in Western-style gun battles. These things had their counterpart among Negroes in the hostility toward Negro Democrats and other unorthodox individuals and in a similar proclivity for settling personal arguments by violence.

The doctrine of the code of honor, originating with the planters of the Old South, among whom a "reputation for gallantry and generosity became highly esteemed . . . ," caused many individuals in seeking to attain its standards to degenerate into "bravoes and spendthrifts; the character of the fire-eater became almost as much admired as that of the gentleman. The passing of high words and blows, canings, cowhidings, and so on, all terminated by the drawing of knives or pistols, together with hostile correspondences and duels, became everyday occurrences in the South. . . ." Under these circumstances some sensitive persons were so afraid that politeness would be considered an expression of fear that they became almost professional bullies, "always acting and speaking insultingly to prove they were not afraid to fight. . . ." Many others felt that they had to act aggressively, or even fight a duel on occasion, in order to vindicate their courage.

A disregard for inflicting pain and shedding blood became lamentably common. All, even boys but just in their teens, were

_____
[2] *Ibid.,* p. 467.

in the habit of wearing a pistol, as the slightest provocation would ordinarily reveal. It became well-nigh impossible to get a jury to convict any one (especially an aristocrat) of the most evident murder, provided he had exhibited daring in committing it, or had given his victim a chance to defend himself.[3]

This tradition long prevailed, and as late as 1892, the *News and Courier* found it to be an occasion for wonder when a jury convicted a white man of murder.[4]

The *code duello* was long an accepted, if not an active, tradition. As late as 1878 a pamphlet entitled *The Code of Honor* was published in Charleston. This little booklet explained that "Honor is the sentiment by which a high estimate is placed upon individual rights, social repute and personal self-respect. These are not always adequately protected by the laws and tribunals of the civil organization. There are cases of insults grievous and degrading, for which there is no action at law." Appended to the pamphlet were "Rules for the Government of Principals and Seconds in Personal Difficulties."[5] It took the killing of a prominent white citizen in the celebrated Cash-Shannon duel of 1882 to bring about such a revulsion of popular opinion, abetted by the editorials of Francis Warrington Dawson in the *News and Courier,* that the tradition of dueling soon became unfashionable.[6]

The practice of carrying concealed weapons, however, long persisted and the use of them in perpetrating sudden death to show that one "resented" insults was all too common. To meet the situation the legislature sought in 1878 to punish assault and battery committed with firearms on the streets or in places of public resort.[7] Governor W. D. Simpson noted in his 1879 message to the legislature that one of the greatest evils left in the track of the Civil War was a disregard for human life, a feeling "fed and stimulated by that dangerous practice of carrying concealed and deadly weapons."[8] In 1880 the legislature went further in declaring

[3] *Ibid.,* p. 468.
[4] Charleston *News and Courier,* May 11, 1892.
[5] Robert Barnwell Rhett, *The Code of Honor: Its Rationale and Uses, by the Tests of Common Sense and Good Morals, With the Effects of Its Preventive Remedies* (Charleston, 1878), pp. 3, 35-44.
[6] Wallace, *History of South Carolina,* III, 330-32.
[7] *Acts and Joint Resolutions* (1878), p. 687.
[8] *Senate Journal* (1879-1880), p. 12.

even the carrying of a concealed weapon to be a misdemeanor, punishable by a fine of not more than $200, or imprisonment for not more than twelve months. In the case of assault or of manslaughter committed with such concealed weapon, the judge was empowered to provide punishment in addition to the regular sentence of three to twelve months in the state penitentiary or a fine of not more than $200.[9] Edward McCrady urged passage of the law to rescue the good name of the state. Capital and immigration shunned the state, he said, "because we are called a bloodthirsty people."[10]

The ineffectiveness of this act, however, is indicated by the passage in 1897 of an amendment lowering the penalty for carrying a concealed weapon to forfeiture of the weapon and a fine of $20 to $100, or imprisonment for ten to thirty days, and the elimination of the additional punishment in the cases of assault or other misuse of the weapon. A provision was substituted merely calling for a separate count in the indictment for the carrying of a concealed weapon.[11] Anything more, it was apparently felt, could not be enforced. As late as 1900 a state judge, in his charge to a grand jury, attributed the high homicide rate of the state to "the deplorable custom of carrying pistols, a custom carried to such an extent, that our State may be regarded as an armed camp in times of peace. Our young men and boys, black and white, rich and poor, seem to think that their outfit is not complete without a pistol. . . ."[12]

In a situation of this sort there is little wonder that Negroes accused of crimes against whites were sometimes punished summarily by a mob violence which had at least the passive support of a large portion of the white community. Early justification for the practice of lynch law was found in the argument that the Republican governments of the Reconstruction period did not furnish suf-ficient protection to the white populace. The editor of the Columbia *Daily Register,* in expressing approval of the lynching of four Negroes for the murder of an aged white couple in Edgefield in 1876, put it thus:

> In determining whether on any given occasion, (as the one, for instance, which is now present to all minds,) in a nominally

---

[9] *Acts and Joint Resolutions* (1880), pp. 447-48.
[10] Columbia *Daily Register,* December 14, 1880.
[11] *Acts and Joint Resolutions* (1897), pp. 423-24.
[12] Charleston *News and Courier,* April 3, 1900.

more advanced and civilized state of things, lynch law is ever justifiable or excusable, we must be careful to be just and not to be deceived by words. It is easy to talk about civilization, the sanctity of the law and the efficiency of its machinery to secure justice, but apply the probe and see whether these reputed blessings really exist, and whether these safe-guards are or can be made effective. We once had a civilization in South Carolina, and we may be said to have one still. But, like learning, virtue, integrity, and honor, it is in banishment. It is a thing apart, cowering in a corner. It exerts but a negative and feeble influence upon what we call the government. . . . After all, Judge Lynch is an abler judge and a more humane man and a truer discerner of equity than many who have figured as justices in our reconstructed and semibarbarous era.[13]

A paper in Edgefield, "no advocate or apologist for lynch law," expressed a feeling that the time had come "for the people to save themselves. In this last and crowning outrage, at least, summary vengeance—justice!—was the only course left us."[14]

A Charleston editor, disturbed by the prevalence of violence in the state in 1877, found the situation

. . . hardly to be wondered at when we recollect that, for nearly ten years, the law has been so administered in South Carolina that, virtually, the white man has had no rights which the negro was bound to respect. A black villain might burn his employer's barn or his dwelling-house, or waylay and murder him, with but slight chance of ever being caught. If caught, it was next to impossible to convict him, and if convicted, there was nothing for him to fear but a few months, or at most a few years, in the Penitentiary, where he lived better than he did at home, and where he would be contented to remain for the rest of his days were it not for his ineffable laziness, which made the work there, light as it was, something of a punishment. The result of all this has been that the law has lost its terrors for our criminal classes, and that in many sections of the State the people, like those in frontier countries, have been, and are still, obliged to depend for safety on their individual vigilance and courage.[15]

---

[13] Columbia *Daily Register*, May 28, 1876.
[14] *Ibid.*, June 2, 1876, quoting Edgefield *Advertiser*.
[15] Charleston *News and Courier*, May 12, 1877.

For years after this there was a tendency in the white press to approve, or to deprecate only mildly, the application of lynch law to victims guilty, or suspected, of murder or rape. After the lynching in Hampton of a Negro murderer in 1880 the *News and Courier* argued that "Lynch-law as applied to Louis Kinder, is not mob-law. The brute put himself outside the pale of the law, and was dealt with accordingly. . . . It will be a woeful day for South Carolina when crimes of a particular class are only punished, if punished at all, after long imprisonment, a tedious trial and the procrastination which lawyers practice on behalf of their clients."[16] In the case of the lynching of two Negroes accused of rape and murder at Prosperity in 1881 the same paper noted in an editorial that the members of the mob "represented society at large, and were the exponents of a law that is older than governments, and more venerable than the constitutions of States."[17]

Once the Democratic regime had become solidly established, however, there was a perceptible change in the outlook of the white press, which showed less and less tendency to condone lynching for any cause other than the rape of a white woman. Condemning the lynching in 1883 of a Negro charged with theft and assault, the *News and Courier* argued that appeal by whites to "higher law" should be tolerated "only when such resort is necessary to protect their women and their homes." But in cases of rape only "the swift and certain reprisal of the quick bullet and the hasty noose, suffices, in a community like South Carolina, where such villanies are of race against race, to menace sternly and repress effectually an ever ready wave of kindred crime."[18]

Statistics on lynchings in the state have been gathered for 1882 and for every year since. In the period from 1882 to the end of the century there was not a year in which South Carolina did not experience at least one lynching. The figures as given by two different sources are as follows:[19]

---

[16] *Ibid.*, March 5, 1880.

[17] *Ibid.*, January 20, 1881.

[18] *Ibid.*, January 3, 1883.

[19] James Elbert Cutler, *Lynch-Law: An Investigation Into the History of Lynching in the United States* (New York, 1905), p. 183; *Thirty Years of Lynching in the United States: 1889-1918* (New York: National Association for the Advancement of Colored People, 1919), 88-91. Cutler's figures were gathered from the files of the Chicago *Tribune* and the N. A. A. C. P. figures list only such lynchings "as were authenticated by such evidence as was given

Year	James Elbert Cutler	National Association for the Advancement of Colored People
1882	6	..
1883	3	..
1884	1	..
1885	1	..
1886	4	..
1887	2	..
1888	2	..
1889	5	12
1890	4	3
1891	1	1
1892	5	5
1893	11	6
1894	5	5
1895	5	8
1896	4	4
1897	6	6
1898	5	14
1899	1	1
1900	2	2

It would be profitless to examine in detail the gruesome circumstances of all the lynchings that took place during this period. But the significance of lynching was broader than its ghastly effects upon the mob and its victim. Lynching became, willy-nilly, a factor in the establishment of a white terror that transformed the fluid situation created by the Reconstruction back into a rigid caste system of white supremacy. And to understand the effects of this terror it is necessary to examine a few specific instances of mob violence.

The indiscriminate incidence of mob violence is illustrated by a mass lynching that took place in Barnwell in December, 1889. Four Negroes were held in the county jail on suspicion of participation in the murder of a white man. Between two and four a.m. on the morning of December 28 a mob of about 100 masked men broke into the jail, took eight Negro prisoners out about three-quarters of a mile from town, tied them to trees, and shot them. One of those so lynched was charged with the murder and another

credence by a recognized newspaper or confirmed by a responsible investigator." Both sets of figures may be presumed to contain inaccuracies.

with being an accessory. Two were held as witnesses, although suspected of being accessories. Two were held only as witnesses. Another was charged with a different murder. The status of the eighth was not reported in the press. Two Negroes, held as accessories to the second murder, were left in the jail, unmolested.[20] A dispatch from Barnwell the following day reported that as a result of the lynching, "The condition on the part of the whites is now one of absolute safety; on the part of the blacks it is one of utter demoralization. The former is a consequence of the latter."

But there was in this case the almost invariable aftermath of a lynching—the rumor that Negroes in the surrounding countryside were gathering to attack the town. The safety of the whites was reported to depend upon the fact that two hundred armed whites were prepared to rendezvous on the town square at the first sign of an impending attack. A reporter, however, found that the "illusion" of impending attack "would . . . be soon dispelled by a glance at the faces of the negroes who came into the town from the interior today."[21] The white terror had taken its toll of suspicion and fear among both whites and blacks.

A spectacular and fantastic example of the double standard of morality frequently applied to such incidents can be found in the lynching of Willie Leaphart at Lexington in 1890. Leaphart, convicted of attempted rape, was sentenced to be hanged on April 11, 1890. The judge who had presided at the trial, however, later recommended a reprieve because of new evidence and also recommended that Leaphart be removed from the county jail in Lexington. Governor Richardson proceeded to remove the prisoner to Columbia. A protest meeting of white citizens in Lexington then declared that the removal was a reflection upon the law-abiding reputation of the county. A committee was appointed to go to Columbia and secure the return of Leaphart to the county jail. After the committee had called upon the judge he recommended that Leaphart be returned to the county jail because the members of the committee, fifteen in number, proposed "to pledge their honor as gentlemen for the personal safety of Willie Leaphart" as long as he was in the custody of the sheriff of Lexington. The judge expressed assurance that "no reproach upon Lexington

---

[20] Charleston *News and Courier,* December 29, 1889.
[21] *Ibid.,* December 30, 1889.

County was meant by the removal of Leaphart. . . ," but only that his safety was sought until certain legal questions could be settled.[22]

Early on the morning of May 5 a mob broke down the door of the jail, entered the sheriff's room and forced him to give up the keys. About half of the men wore masks, but the sheriff and his wife both recognized the voice of one F. Calhoun Caughman, and separately recognized four others. A white prisoner recognized another. The mob then proceeded to the door leading to the cells, where a white prisoner was confined with Leaphart. The white prisoner was not molested, except that someone fired a shot which inflicted a flesh wound in the arm. Leaphart then struck out with a stick at the lamp held by one of the mob and broke it, whereupon several of them departed and returned with two more lamps. Leaphart broke both of these, whereupon the lynchers began to fire into the cell. Leaphart jumped from corner to corner in a vain attempt to escape but finally fell to the floor, his body riddled with bullets. A placard found in Lexington after the lynching read: "Governor Richardson and Judge Wallace are responsible for lynch law in Lexington County. Our wives and daughters must and shall be protected at any and every hazard."[23]

The following morning Calhoun Caughman was heard on the streets of Lexington to declare that he was responsible for the murder. Two other whites later declared that they had been in the jail the night before. All the evidence as to persons recognized in the mob or overheard declaring that they had been in it was placed before a coroner's jury which took ten minutes to produce a verdict that "Leaphart had come to his death from gunshot wounds inflicted by persons unknown to the jury."[24]

On the day after the lynching the governor gave the press permission to copy the papers in his file which had led to the reprieve and removal of Leaphart from Lexington. These papers cast doubt upon both the nature of the crime with which he was accused and upon the identification of Leaphart as a participant. An affidavit collected by the defense attorney for Leaphart, from W. J. Miller, indicated that the victim of the alleged rape had stated that she did not believe that he had intended an assault upon her, but

---

[22] *Ibid.*, May 6, 1890.
[23] *Ibid.*, May 6, 7, 1890.
[24] *Ibid.*, May 7, June 14, 1890.

rather a robbery. The brother of the victim had been overheard to say that he did not believe Leaphart had attempted to assault her, but that she had been persuaded by certain persons to state that he had committed an assault in order to convict him. The signer of the affidavit also testified that the alleged victim was too strong for Leaphart to have committed an assault upon her by physical force, and that her reputation for virtue was not good. A corroborative story of the incident was related in an affidavit signed by the girl's brother. In this statement he said that Simeon Corley, in whose house the girl was living, would not permit her to go home after the alleged assault because "she might say something to some one that would injure the case or cause the negro to be released."[25]

Letters from the girl to her mother were also among the papers. In the first of these she told a story similar to that recounted above, and said "Some thinks he did not want to rob the house, that he was up to doing some meaness to me, but i don't think so, as he never tried to do anything but to keep me from hollering. . . . i did not no who it was, but it may have been Willie Leaphart, as he was seen on the streets soon after it happened. . . . Mr. Corley thinks it was Willie Leaphart, but i was scared so bad till i don't no positive who it was." Later she wrote that her brother "said that some one told you all that the negro done more than i wrote you he did. that was false. . . . i thought some one would be ready to try an say something to hurt my character or make out i am ruined. . . . Mr. Corley wants the boy punished an says it is Willie Leaphart an may have been, i don't say positive it is. . . ."[26]

On the day after the publication of these papers one of the prosecuting attorneys in the case declared the affidavits to have been "lies out of the whole cloth," and the letters to have been forgeries. Narciso G. Gonzales, a reporter covering the case, believed them to be genuine. The girl, however, signed an affidavit that she had not written the letters. Her brother swore that he had not signed the affidavit attributed to him, and W. J. Miller, the author of the first affidavit, testified that he had signed it at the behest of G. F. Graham, Leaphart's defense attorney, while

---

[25] *Ibid.*, May 7, 1890.
[26] *Ibid.*

drunk. Graham meanwhile told the reporter of the *News and Courier* that this statement "could only be attributed to the influence of fear of his own safety." The governor and assistant attorney general then stated that Miller had heard the affidavit read in their presence, had assented to it, and had promised later to get the letters from the alleged rape victim, which he did.[27] Calhoun Caughman, the leader of the lynch mob, swore that from "information and belief" he believed Graham to have been a party to the forgery of the girl's letters and the affidavit of her brother, whereupon Graham was arrested. Meanwhile warrants were also issued for the arrest of Caughman and two other members of the lynch mob.[28]

Miller, who had been arrested in Lexington, was removed to Columbia after a *habeas corpus* proceeding. He declared that his disavowal of the original affidavit had been made "while under arrest and in fear of his life, in jail at Lexington Court House, and while in fear of personal violence . . .," and that he would not have disavowed the affidavit had he not been forced to do so under duress.[29]

At a preliminary examination, the three men arrested for participation in the lynching were represented by three lawyers, two of whom had been members of the committee that had pledged their "honor as gentlemen" for the safety of Leaphart.[30] Early in June indictments were brought in against the three members of the lynch mob and they were put on trial on June 13. Three of the six defense attorneys and one of the members of the jury had been among the committee of fifteen that had pledged themselves to safeguard Leaphart. A feature of the trial was the presence of a number of white women in the courtroom who "had looked upon the defendants as their special champions and had maintained Mr. Caughman in luxury during his confinement in the jail. . . . From their hands bouquets were taken by little girls and placed on the lapels of the coats of the defendants." No evidence was introduced by the defense, but two of the defense attorneys spoke for about a half-hour each to the effect that Caughman had been

[27] *Ibid.,* May 9, 1890.
[28] *Ibid.*
[29] *Ibid.,* May 11, 1890.
[30] *Ibid.,* May 14, 1890.

"drunk and falsely boastful" when he admitted his part in the lynching. After deliberating an hour the jury returned a verdict of not guilty.[31]

It was rumored that the defense counsel had proposed a plea of insanity for Caughman, but he threatened, if they did, to take the stand and tell everything. "He has made no denial of his part in the lynching," it was reported, "but appears proud of it, and proposes to write a book on the subject, for which he has collected much data."[32]

The case was finally closed two years later when the lawyer who had defended Willie Leaphart was acquitted of a charge of perjury in connection with the alleged forging of the affidavits and letters that seemed to clear Leaphart. Ex-Governor Richardson and Assistant Attorney General W. K. Bachman both testified on behalf of the lawyer.[33]

Appointed in 1892 as "Tillman's Lord High Executioner of fish laws in Georgetown,"[34] Calhoun Caughman appeared as a delegate to the state Democratic convention of 1892 in which he took the floor to denounce Grover Cleveland for having invited to his wedding a Negro man who entered with a white woman on his arm.[35] In 1894 Caughman conducted an unsuccessful campaign for Congress, of which the Prosperity Press and Reporter complained, "It is all right about his having lynched a negro; . . . but we would rather for him to run on his merits and not on his record as a negro lyncher."[36] The white public, however, had turned its back on him and when Caughman appeared in Lexington to speak on behalf of his candidacy, three-quarters of the crowd walked out and then returned later to howl him down. Even Tillman, who had said of him two years before, "There is no blot or smirch on his record," seemed unsympathetic.[37]

Although lynching was generally accepted among whites as the proper punishment for rape and widely accepted as the proper punishment for the murder of a white, these were not the only

---

[31] Ibid., June 14, 1890.
[32] Ibid.
[33] Columbia State, February 19, 1892.
[34] Ibid., February 29, 1892.
[35] Charleston News and Courier, May 19, 1892.
[36] Ibid., July 2, 1894, quoting Prosperity Press and Reporter.
[37] Ibid., July 21, 1894.

causes of lynching. Between 1889 and the end of the century there are cases on record of Negroes lynched for quarrelling, burglary, larceny, incendiarism, highway robbery, horse stealing, violation of contract, and because of "racial prejudice."[38] For example, in Orangeburg County a Negro man was lynched in 1897 on suspicion of having burned a barn. His body was found hanging near a railway with a placard declaring that he had been killed in "protection of property."[39]

The practice was not confined to Negro victims altogether, for in some cases whites were the victims of lynch mobs. When a white man was lynched on suspicion of rape in 1879 the Spartanburg Grand Jury in its presentment said that the lynchers "acted in obedience to the law of the land."[40] Nor were all lynch mobs composed altogether of whites. Two Negroes were lynched for rape and murder near Prosperity in 1879 by a mob of both whites and Negroes, and a Negro member of the mob climbed a tree to pass over a limb the rope with which one of the victims was hanged.[41] In one unusual case a half-witted white suspected of the rape of a Negro girl was lynched by a Negro mob in Pickens County.[42] When members of the mob were brought to trial the jury was unable to agree, and the lynchers went free.[43]

Few Negroes charged with murder of whites were ever punished by the law, and practically none charged with the rape of white women. In 1897 a Negro rapist was duly convicted and hanged in Newberry, apparently the first legal execution of a Negro for rape under the law of 1879.[44]

Seldom before the nineties was it ever recognized by the press that most lynchings were for crimes other than rape. Press discussions of lynching for almost any crime usually concluded with a justification of lynching in cases of rape. Such cases were frequently headed, "Lynched for the Usual,"[45] indicating rape, ignoring the fact that the usual excuse for lynching was actually murder.

---

[38] *Thirty Years of Lynching in the United States,* pp. 88-91.
[39] Columbia *State,* January 7, 1897.
[40] Charleston *News and Courier,* June 27, 1879.
[41] *Ibid.,* January 20, 21, 1881.
[42] *Ibid.,* January 3, 5, 1888.
[43] *Ibid.,* July 12, 1888.
[44] *Ibid.,* August 21, 1897.
[45] *Ibid.,* January 1, November 4, 1894; March 1, 1896; February 18, 1900.

The inability of many whites to take the situation seriously is indicated by the air of tolerant humor that was sometimes adopted toward cases of lynching or the murder of Negroes. The Abbeville *Press and Banner* in 1885 noted that a young white man in Columbia had been fined $3.00 for the shooting of birds while during the same week two white men in Laurens who had killed a Negro, "sending the bullets through the right place—the back," were acquitted "as a matter of course." It suggested that a "close season" be declared on the killing of Negroes, at least between March and November, when they should be busy with the crops.[46]

The most articulate opposition to interracial violence naturally came from Negro leaders. One of the most impressive appeals of Negro leaders came in November, 1885, when a series of outbreaks was climaxed by the cold-blooded murder of "Democrat" Riley, a prominent Charleston Negro, by a white doctor of the town. A mass meeting of Negroes in Morris Brown Church called upon the ministers of the Negro churches to prepare and publish "an address to the races" on the subject of interracial violence.

The address was an impressively moving document which covered much broader aspects of interracial relations than the problem of violence. It began by pointing out that although Negroes had dwelt in the old slave states for two and a half centuries they were still completely unknown and misunderstood by their white brethren. "Of this ignorance," said the document, "the Southern whites are totally unconscious; they claim to understand the negro thoroughly." The appeal then recited what the ministers thought were some of the most serious misconceptions: that the Negro was not a man, but a higher order of beast; a statement in the *Encyclopaedia Brittanica*, based on information from Southern whites, that the Negro was dying out without the fostering care of slavery; assertions that the Negro was improvident, without a conscience, a born thief, liar, and sensualist, and that female chastity did not exist.

Then the Negroes cited evidences of progress since emancipation. Schools were dotted over the South:

> Colored lawyers, editors, clergymen, physicians, teachers, merchants, and artists show what the race has accomplished in

---

[46] Columbia *Daily Register*, February 26, 1885, quoting Abbeville *Press and Banner.*

every department of mental activity. The negro has built churches, parsonages, asylums, employed cultivated ministers and teachers, organized and conducted benevolent societies, and so proved his respect and veneration for morality and religion. Though slavery was not a good school for morals, yet there are men and women with characters clean and spotless. . . .

After declaring that colored people were "deprived of their rights to the protection of life, liberty, and property," the statement turned to a grim warning. "It is openly said that this is 'a white man's government,' and the negro must be kept down. We must warn the white people in time. They may go on depriving us of our rights until forbearance ceases to be a virtue. It may not be long before the revolutions of St. Domingo in the times of Toussaint L'Ouverture will be repeated in the South. . . ." Turning to a conciliatory tone, the ministers rested their case on a hope for the reassertion of a sense of justice among the whites.

. . . It cannot require a long time for a professedly Christian people to effect a reform in the administration of the laws and secure justice to all. We know that many deplore the existence of the things of which we herein complain, but action, early and positive action, is what is needed. Those in high places must take the initiative. And here we rest our cause.[47]

Simultaneously with the issue of their appeal the Negro ministers of Charleston preached sermons on a text from Judges, XVII, 6: "In those days there was no King in Israel, but every man did that which was right in his own eyes." Most of the sermons were characterized by forthright bitterness. The Reverend L. R. Nichols of Emanuel A. M. E. Church declared: ". . . I hate the mean, vacillating government which, if it finds that one or a part of the citizens are not wealthy or educated, throws her back on them when they cry for redress for their grievances, and says: 'Had you staid in your right place you would not need the arm of the law; those who are murdering you and cheating you are your best friends.' "[48] The sermon of another minister indicated his recognition of the desperate futility of his position.

---

[47] Charleston *News and Courier*, November 25, 1885.
[48] Columbia *Daily Register*, November 24, 1885.

Is it not time for somebody to say something? I do not say to do something. It is time for men to know that the 7,000,000 colored people of the country have rights. . . , and will enter a solemn protest against the existing state of society. We are law-abiding, as ignorant as we are, as oppressed as we have been, and as excitable as we are. A man's home is sacred, and no man should be allowed to trespass upon it.[49]

The white press, in reporting the sermons, noted that the ministers "closed their remarks with moral remedies for the state of affairs," but still feared that "the sermons will nevertheless have pernicious effect. . . ."[50] Violation of the taboo against open discussion of interracial difficulties was not to be taken lightly.

After the Barnwell lynching of eight Negroes a conference of Negro leaders was called in Columbia on January 2, 1890. This group issued a statement even more powerful than that of the Charleston ministers in its illumination of the sources of interracial violence. Three major indictments were stated against those responsible for the climate of opinion in which violence flourished. First,

Because of coveted advantages intended to be gained influential leaders among the whites of the State have either directly or indirectly advised or allowed to be taught that any treatment of the negro that would tend to impress him with the white man's superior power in a conflict of force is justifiable. From this irresponsible white men have obtained the notion that there are no rights for the negro which a white man, whether worthy or unworthy, is bound to respect, when the observance of these rights is judged by a white man as in any way contrary to his personal views or prejudices.

Second, there was complaint of "the untimely and ill-advised agitation of the separation of the races" in the daily white press, which had created unrest among Negroes and "emboldened the criminal classes of whites in their already thoroughly formed prejudices against us."[51] Third, "The hue and cry made by such white men after they have committed outrages against our people, to the effect that they are attempting insurrection against whites of

---

[49] *Ibid.*
[50] *Ibid.*
[51] This apparently had reference to the agitation of the emigration issue rather than the segregation issue.

such communities, is an additional outrage on us, and so intended. . . ." This statement, the address continued, "is not intended to convince those who stand convicted of these slanders against us, for we are sure they are conscious of the wrong they do us and the gravity of the evil thereof." The lynching of the eight prisoners in Barnwell was interpreted as "indicating the supremacy of the mob element of the Commonwealth over the law-abiding class." But the only remedies that the group saw were: first, the recommendation that Negroes "abandon such sections of the State wherein lawlessness prevails and life is unsafe . . .," and second, an appeal to all citizens, regardless of race or color, to unite in a common effort "in upholding the majesty of the law and the fair name of South Carolina."[52]

An indication of the beginnings of a shift in the prevailing white opinion, horrified by the brutality of the Barnwell massacre, was an editorial in the Charleston *News and Courier* which failed to note in an open discussion of the issue any possibility of a "pernicious effect" and had nothing but warm praise for the address of the Negro conference.[53]

The unusually unsavory circumstances surrounding the Barnwell massacre in 1889 and the lynching of Willie Leaphart in 1890 brought about an active revulsion in white opinion, and thereafter lynchings for causes other than rape, and sometimes even those for rape, were generally condemned by responsible whites. The editor of the *News and Courier*, upon first reading the affidavits in the Leaphart case, concluded that the case constituted "a most appalling commentary upon the blindness and lawlessness of lynch law. A horrible mistake has been made and the life of an innocent man has been taken to gratify the brutal passions of an irresponsible and unthinking mob."[54] Although further evidence convinced the editor that Leaphart deserved to be put to death, he still argued that his guilt could not be pleaded as justification for his murder by a mob.[55]

Even Ben Tillman, violent champion of white supremacy, was affected by the revulsion of feeling. In November, 1890, Governor

---

[52] Charleston *News and Courier,* January 3, 1890.
[53] *Ibid.,* January 4, 1890.
[54] *Ibid.,* May 8, 1890.
[55] *Ibid.,* May 10, 1890.

Tillman recalled in his first inaugural address the fact that the Negro was "a staunch friend and faithful servant during the war," and appealed to the whites of the state to listen to all reasonable complaints of the Negroes, to grant "all just, right and safe privileges" to the Negroes, and to give them equal protection under the law, and a guarantee of fair treatment.

> With all the machinery of the law in our hands; with every department of the government, Executive, Legislative and Judicial, held by white men; with white juries, white Solicitors, white Sheriffs, it is simply infamous that resort should be had to lynch law, and that prisoners should be murdered because the people have grown weary of the law's delay and its inefficient administration. Negroes have nearly always been the victims; and the confession is a blot on our civilization. Let us see to it that the finger of scorn no longer be pointed at our State because of this deplorable condition of affairs.[56]

He then suggested that one of the major justifications for lynching would be eliminated if measures were taken to hasten the processes of the state courts. And as a last desperate remedy, he called for executive power to remove any sheriff who failed to prevent violence after a prisoner had been taken in his hands.

> I have thought it wise to speak in emphatic terms on this subject because every Carolinian worthy of the name must long to see the time when law shall reassert its sway, and when our people will not be divided into hostile political camps, and all classes and colors shall vie with each other in friendly rivalry to make the State prosperous and happy.[57]

During the legislative session of 1891 a bill was introduced to give the governor the power, requested by Tillman in his inaugural address, to remove any sheriff who had permitted a prisoner once in his custody to be subjected to violence, but the bill was defeated in both houses.[58] Later during this session of the legislature Tillman indicated that he was genuinely sincere in his desire to take action on the problem of lynching. In the village of Edgefield the son of the sheriff was shot and killed by a Negro in December, 1891. The murderer, Dick Lundy, was locked up in the county jail. Tillman,

---

[56] *House Journal* (1890), pp. 132-33.
[57] *Ibid.*, p. 133.
[58] *Senate Journal* (1891), p. 288.

receiving reports of a threatened lynching, ordered the sheriff and the captain of the Edgefield Rifles, a militia unit, to protect the prisoner. The Edgefield Rifles were ordered out at six p. m., but between four and five in the afternoon, during the funeral of the sheriff's son, a mob broke into the jail and lynched Dick Lundy. Tillman, familiar with the jail as a former member of the Edgefield grand jury, reported to the legislature that it would have been impossible for the mob to have broken into the jail if the affair had not been arranged. Additional evidence that the lynching had been arranged was seen by Tillman in the fact that a coroner's jury had been convened and had rendered a verdict within an hour after the lynching. "The jailer is certainly responsible directly," Tillman said, "and Sheriff Ouzts indirectly, for the lynching; but can they be convicted of negligence or of being accessory to the murder of Dick Lundy? I am sure they cannot." In such a situation, the only effective measure, he argued, would be a law giving the governor power to remove the sheriff. Tillman expressed his sympathy for the sheriff, but pointed out that the sheriff of Chester County had recently defended the murderer of his father against a mob and let him be put to death by the processes of the law. "No Sheriff will lose his office to gratify his own or a mob's vengeance," said Tillman, "and he can always find friends to protect the jail rather than have him lose his place."[59]

Tillman was unable, however, to get any sort of anti-lynching measure through the legislature. There was, nevertheless, some indication that his strong stand on lynching had had some influence in the state. During the year 1891, after Tillman had indicated his position in his inaugural address, there had been no lynching until December, when the Dick Lundy affair occurred in Edgefield.[60] But Tillman, conscious of the political value of his general anti-Negro policy, undid much of the effect of his strong position during the campaign of 1892. Having always accepted the doctrine of lynching in cases of rape, he unequivocally stated more than a mere tolerance of lynching in such cases. Arguing that lynching was one of the principal reasons why capital feared to come into the state, he still said that there was "one crime which deserved lynching, and *Governor as I am, I'd lead a mob to lynch a man*

---

[59] *Ibid.,* pp. 285-88.
[60] *Thirty Years of Lynching in the United States,* p. 88.

who had ravished a white woman. . . . I justify lynching for rape, and, before Almighty God, I'm not ashamed of it."[61]

The press continued, during the nineties, to question the practice. In 1893 the *News and Courier* complained that while the governor claimed to approve of lynching for only one crime, he had taken no steps to punish lynching for any crime. Furthermore, it found "nothing in the laws he has sworn to uphold to warrant him [Tillman] in passing over mob murder, on any account, as a justifiable crime. It is his perverted personal opinion, not his official opinion, that 'there are some cases in which lynching is proper.' "[62] The remedies that were suggested were those already pointed out by Tillman: (1) measures to hasten the legal processes, especially in cases of rape; and (2) measures to punish persons participating in lynch mobs. In the first case, there was suggested the questionable procedure of "substituting for the mob court a special and regular Court to be convened as soon as the accused person is arrested and to try him and punish him within the week."[63] While this would probably have amounted in practice to a mere legalization of lynching, with few safeguards for the defendant, it was long advocated in the state and is still suggested occasionally as an effective deterrent to lynching. The second measure would have been the legal punishment of participants in lynch mobs. "If a half dozen or a dozen lynchers, in any county of South Carolina, were arrested and tried and punished severely, the law would resume its authority in all the counties. And they can be arrested and punished whenever the authorities see fit to undertake such work in earnest."[64] But there was the rub. Few of the authorities could be found willing to exert themselves to the prevention of a lynching, much less to the punishment of those guilty of one.

After its founding in 1891 the Columbia *State* was a persistent and potent source of propaganda against lynchings for whatever excuse. The relentless campaign of Narciso G. Gonzales was the pioneering effort in the white press at an editorial offensive against lynching. Carefully he pointed out the illogic of arguments "that it is justifiable and necessary to lynch men for one certain crime," when the press was full of lynchings for other reasons. He asked:

---

[61] Charleston *News and Courier*, July 11, 1892.
[62] *Ibid.*, October 3, 1893.
[63] *Ibid.*, August 1, 1893.
[64] *Ibid.*, September 29, 1893.

Does it not appear that the strenuous arguments used in favor of lynching for one offense are having their effect in inciting lynching for any offense? . . . It is for this very reason that the State and other papers have so steadfastly condemned lynching for any crime. No mob is reasonable. Once admit the righteousness of mob judgments and we give up the case of the law. If a mob be the proper judge of a man charged with rape, why not of one charged with murder, . . . or battery . . . ? You can draw the line between stern justice and cruel outrage in your mind, as you sit, impartial and cool, far from the scene; but can the mob do so, raging reckless, without responsibility? The answer is, the hanging of an innocent negro at Denmark and a crazy negro in Lancaster.[65]

However, no anti-lynching legislation was attempted until the meeting of the constitutional convention of 1895. The question of lynching was forcefully and repeatedly brought to the attention of the convention by the Negro delegates. I. R. Reed introduced a section to give the governor power to remove and replace any official who allowed personal harm to come to any prisoner in his custody, and also to give the governor specific authority to call out the militia in case of a threatened lynching. His proposal was recommitted.[66] James Wigg proposed to add to the oath of office in addition to the affirmation that one had not taken part in a duel the words "or in a lynching bee." His proposal was likewise lost.[67]

But more stringent anti-lynching proposals were introduced by white delegates. George D. Bellinger offered a motion to have any officer who permitted a prisoner to be seized "by force or strategy" removed from office and upon conviction become ineligible to hold any office unless pardoned by the governor.[68]

Opposition to Bellinger's proposal was strong. T. I. Rogers of Marlboro held that the proposal might cause the condemnation of an innocent sheriff who had been unable to prevent a lynching through no fault of his own. Bellinger, however, held that strict accountability of sheriffs might encourage a little shooting, and a

---

[65] Columbia *State*, June 4, 1894.
[66] *Convention Journal*, pp. 122-23.
[67] *Ibid.*, p. 316.
[68] *Ibid.*, p. 358.

little shooting would mean the end of lynching. D. J. Bradham, at that time sheriff of Clarendon County, agreed with Bellinger and argued that the sheriff should be held strictly responsible unless at least one member of the lynch mob were shot. He told of having stopped a lynch mob once by threatening to fire directly into it if it came any closer.[69]

In the convention, B. R. Tillman moved an addition to Bellinger's proposal in order to secure a heavy degree of punishment for the mobs themselves. Every member of the mob would be responsible for damages of $5,000 to the person injured or to his "personal representatives" in case of his death. Persons against whom judgment was found were to be imprisoned until the fine had been paid. The amendment was voted down 74-38.[70] Indicative of the temper of the times was Major T. G. Barker's statement that he voted against Tillman's amendment because "the provision is so extreme in its severity that it will defeat its own object, and . . . no conviction will be had under it."[71]

Bellinger's milder proposal was accepted, with the reservation that an officer to be removed must have been guilty of "negligence, permission, or connivance" in giving up his prisoner, but Tillman was able to add a provision that the county in which the lynching occurred should be liable to damages of not less than $2,000 to the legal representatives of the person lynched.[72]

The latter provision, however, was naturally extremely difficult to enforce. By 1900 there had been no case in which the requirement of pecuniary damages in the case of lynching had been enforced in the state. But in the field of public opinion, which was the basic factor that had to be changed in the elimination of lynching, there was abundant evidence in the press that gradual change was being brought about. Lynchings continued at a high rate into the first two decades of the twentieth century, but there was a tendency in the white press to cease the mild deprecation of lynching and to go on the offensive and to speak out boldly against "the condition of mind which renders the lynchers dangerous to their community. . . ."[73]

---

[69] Columbia *Daily Register*, November 10, 1895.
[70] *Convention Journal*, pp. 655-56.
[71] *Ibid.*, p. 656.
[72] *Ibid.*, pp. 527-28; *Constitution of 1895*, Art. VI, Sec. 6.
[73] Columbia *State*, January 7, 1897.

Intimidation had been since Reconstruction an accepted means of eliminating the political influence of Negroes. Intimidation was usually sufficient to achieve the ends of the whites, and since Negroes showed little interest in fighting fire with fire, there were few incidents in the state after 1876 that could be defined as riots, and almost none that were of major consequence. In 1880 one Negro had been killed and thirteen wounded in an election riot at Johnson's; and Lancaster saw an outbreak of violence in 1882 in which several Negroes were killed as the aftermath of a Greenback rally. A race riot which threatened in Bishopville in 1890 was prevented by the timely arrival of militia; and in a threatened riot in Georgetown in 1900 the citizens were calmed by the intervention of Negro county and town officials.[74] Isolated, unreported incidents, however, undoubtedly took a toll of life and limb.

Yet two outbreaks in 1898 demonstrated that the shift in white public opinion on the matter of violence was only in the first stages of a painfully slow metamorphosis. In February, 1898, a brutal murder showed the lengths to which some whites were prepared to go to prevent Negro officeholding. Early that year, Frazier B. Baker, a Negro Republican of Florence, was appointed postmaster of Lake City, a small community in Williamsburg County. Complaints were quickly made against Baker because he was a Negro and because he was not a resident of the county. Many whites, rather than deal with Baker, took their mail to Scranton, a small community nearby. A petition was circulated among the people of the town requesting the Postmaster General to remove him.[75] Then incidents commenced. An attempt was made to set the postoffice afire and shots were fired into Baker's home. On February 21, a mob of three to four hundred gathered outside Baker's home and set it on fire. As the members of the family tried to escape, they were shot down. Baker was killed inside the house and his body remained in the burning building. As his wife tried to escape she was shot through the arm. A baby of twelve months that she was carrying was killed, and three other children were wounded. A reporter on the scene wrote the next day that "the people of the whole United States ought to be made acquainted with the

[74] Columbia *Daily Register*, November 3, 1880; Charleston *News and Courier*, September 29, 1882, October 2, 1900; *Reports and Resolutions* (1891), I, 149.

[75] Charleston *News and Courier*, February 12, 1898.

fact that the postoffice authorities in Washington are largely responsible for the death of Frazier B. Baker."[76]

Narciso G. Gonzales of the Columbia *State,* in line with his persistent campaign against lynching, took a different view, and strongly protested an editorial in the Charleston *Evening Post* which sought to place the blame on federal authorities. Lynchings "for the usual crime" were "white-handed justice" compared with this murder. "A negro postmaster! Is that something to resent with assassination. Who are these people in Williamsburg County that they cannot endure that which the most refined, the most sensitive citizenship of the State has endured with patience and dignity in years gone by? . . . Dozens of South Carolina towns have had negro postmasters. . . ."[77]

No action was taken by state authorities. But the *News and Courier* warned the murderers that they had miscalculated in choosing a federal official as their victim, and expressed hope that federal officials would move into Lake City without delay and that "no guilty man will be suffered to escape."[78] There was delay, but in June several of the "leading citizens" of Lake City were taken into custody by federal officials.[79] In April of the following year, eleven men were put on trial in federal court for the murder. Two turned state's evidence, three were freed on directed verdicts of acquittal, and the jury was unable to agree on the others, it being reported that five members of the jury favored conviction.[80]

A far more bloody affair in November, 1898, resulted in the death of an undetermined number of Negroes. This riot grew out of an effort of Republican leaders in Greenwood County to secure evidence to be used in a contest for the congressional seat of that district. Acting on behalf of his brother, R. R. Tolbert, Republican candidate for Congress, T. P. Tolbert set up a box outside the regular polling place in the community of Phoenix. Negroes who were refused the right to vote were asked to fill out a form affidavit and drop it into a box which was in the possession of Tolbert. A white Democrat challenged his right to carry on

---

[76] *Ibid.,* February 23, 1898.

[77] Columbia *State,* February 25, 1898.

[78] Charleston *News and Courier,* February 23, 1898.

[79] *Ibid.,* June 29, 1898.

[80] *Appleton's Annual Cyclopaedia* (1899), p. 800; Charleston *News and Courier,* April 11-23, 1899.

this activity. This resulted in an altercation, then a general melee, and finally the firing of several shots. The Democrat who had challenged Tolbert was killed and Tolbert wounded. Tolbert and all the Negroes in the vicinity then fled the scene.[81]

The word spread rapidly over the countryside and a white mob immediately gathered in Phoenix. When John R. Tolbert, uncle of the candidate, unaware of the situation, rode up to his son's house he was fired upon and both he and a young nephew were injured. The idea of revenge was at first directed against the Tolberts, who had been holding meetings with Negroes "at weird places and unholy hours" to encourage them to vote, but it quickly took a racial turn when a group of whites approaching Phoenix were ambushed, presumably by Negroes who had gathered arms and banded together, and several of them wounded.[82]

For several days groups of whites ranged over the surrounding countryside, "mad with the lust of blood, and killed the men whom they thought they could kill with the least, or no risk to themselves."[83] Eleven Negroes were captured and brought to the grounds of Rehoboth Church, near Phoenix, for "trial." Persuasions such as a pistol at the ear or a rope around the neck were used to elicit "confessions." Four of the eleven were killed and the others permitted to escape. The following morning another Negro was brought to the scene by the mob and his body was riddled with bullets.[84] The precise number of victims of this mob violence will never be known because of the widespread area over which the mob ranged and because of conflicting and insufficient reports.[85]

Press opinion, however, generally condemned the Tolberts as responsible because they had encouraged Negroes to exercise their political rights.[86] The elder Tolbert, wounded on the scene by the white mob, escaped to Chester, where he was arrested and then released. Travelling on to Columbia he was again arrested and

---

[81] Columbia *State*, November 8, 9, 1898; James Allen Hoyt, *The Phoenix Riot, November 8, 1898*, Paper read before Cosmos Club of Columbia, South Carolina in May, 1935, n. p., n. d., p. 3.

[82] Columbia *State*, November 9, 1898; Charleston *News and Courier*, November 28, 1898, quoting New York *Independent*.

[83] Charleston *News and Courier*, November 12, 1898.

[84] *Ibid.*, November 11, 1898.

[85] *Appleton's Annual Cyclopaedia* (1898), p. 700.

[86] Charleston *News and Courier*, November 10, 1898; Columbia *State*, November 9, 1898.

charged with inciting riot, but the charges were so patently ridiculous that he was later released for lack of evidence.[87] But mass meetings in Greenwood, Phoenix, and Ninety-Six, and Senator Tillman individually declared the Tolberts guilty because they had encouraged Negroes to vote.[88] An aftermath of the massacre was a public meeting of white citizens in Abbeville which declared in "conservative resolutions" that it was the sense of the community that the continued presence of the congressional candidate, R. R. Tolbert, was undesirable and that, once he had transacted necessary business, he should move out of the county.[89]

Another aftermath in the following year was the terrorization of Negroes who had remained in the vicinity by groups of "white caps" who administered whippings to Negro men and criminally assaulted Negro women. The objective of their activities was reported to be the encouragement of Negro emigration so that whites could secure at low rent the lands occupied by Negro tenants. During these riots, it was reported that the "same masterly inactivity" which had characterized the sheriff's office during the massacre of the previous year once again hung over the office.[90] Ben Tillman, speaking in Greenwood, urged the whites to put down the "devilment" lest federal authorities seek to intervene. "If you want to uproot the snake and kill it," he said, "go and kill the Tolberts. . . . But don't bother poor Negroes who have nothing to do with the Tolberts."[91] Order was soon thereafter restored.

The Phoenix Riot was significant also in that it provided Negro citizens with evidence of the dangers involved in attempting to vote. The threat of violence was equally as potent a factor in disfranchisement as legalistic restrictions on the suffrage. The ending of Negro efforts to vote did, in fact, have a slight ameliorative effect upon interracial tensions in that it ended the occasion for incidents at the polling places. But this factor might be easily overestimated; on the other hand, white demagogues no longer felt the restraint, slight though it had been, of a Negro electorate.

Most Negroes, timid or discreet, escaped the direct threat of violence. But underlying the personal, economic, and political re-

---

[87] *Appleton's Annual Cyclopaedia* (1898), p. 700.
[88] Charleston *News and Courier*, November 14, 15, 1898.
[89] Columbia *State*, January 26, 1899.
[90] Yorkville *Enquirer*, August 19, 23, 1899.
[91] *Ibid.*, August 19, 1899.

lationships of the two races there was an unmistakable threat of potential violence if any Negro should forget his "place" and attempt to act independently or aggressively. "The intimidation of the negroes is a stern and awful fact," said a white man. "Yet what do Southerners say about it? It is the bloody shirt, the lying inventions of unscrupulous politicians, the last gasp of carpet-baggery and radical deviltry. So bitterly do Southerners hate to have the truth come out that it is at the risk of his life that any man dares to speak it." [92] Violence, while normally latent, was endemic. The fear of violence is a basic context in which the history of South Carolina Negroes during the period must be studied to be clearly understood.

---

[92] A South Carolinian, *Atlantic Monthly,* XXXIX (April, 1877), 471.

13

CRIME AND CONVICT LEASING

IN VIEW of the circumstances that surrounded the Negro population of South Carolina after Reconstruction, it would be difficult to draw from the statistics of crime conclusive evidence as to the extent of criminality among Negroes. Yet it was almost axiomatic among whites that Negroes had a high racial proclivity for crime. The Reverend W. H. Campbell of Charleston, drawing a contrast between the situation before and after the Civil War, put it thus:

> Then the negro was docile, peaceable and happy, and very seldom concerned in serious crime. Now, in by far the greater number of homicides the negro is involved either as the killer or the killed. Freed from the control of his owner, and wickedly put on civil equality with him, his natural lawlessness and savagery were asserted and constantly involved him in crime, and, besides, the rudeness, insolence, and aggressive self-assertion natural to his newly acquired freedom provoke collision with his white neighbor. Everybody knows that when freed from the compelling influence of the white man he reverts by a law of nature to the natural barbarism in which he was created in the hot jungles of Africa.[1]

This statement cannot be dismissed merely as an unusually prejudiced diatribe, for it expressed an important theory widely accepted among whites. The assumption by whites that a natural criminality and barbarism existed among the Negro population and the gen-

---

[1] The Reverend W. H. Campbell in Charleston *News and Courier*, January 11, 1898.

eral determination to repress that tendency goes far toward explaining why the prisons were crowded with Negroes. Statistics of crime demonstrate that the proportion of Negroes in state and county prisons was far above their proportion in the total population of the state. At one time in 1890, for example, in a total of 1,184 convicts in state and county penal institutions there were 1,061 Negroes.[2]

It was clearly recognized by informed Negroes that Negro crime constituted a real and peculiar problem. "We freely admit," said an editor in New York, "that the Negro population of South Carolina is given largely to indolence, thievery and mendacity." But, he argued, due consideration should be given the circumstances out of which this situation had arisen; and he expressed surprise that contemporary journals frequently gave currency to existing evils without contrasting them with "the infamous source from which they sprang." The source of evil was slavery. "For centuries the white people of South Carolina robbed the Negroes of their honest toil—put a premium upon thievery by denying just reward for labor, and filled the state with a race of mulattoes who have no father. . . ." Little wonder, then, that Negroes should be slow to develop a sense of morality or respect for the rights of property![3]

From different viewpoints both whites and Negroes recognized that most of the problem had arisen out of the transition from slavery to freedom. Under slavery most of the disciplinary problems had been handled by the owner. Public agencies were expected to handle only the problems of crime among the whites and a minor number of problems concerning Negroes. Slavery, so often described by its apologists as a "school of civilization," was a defective school insofar as training in civilization implied the development of a sense of property rights, of morality, or of personal responsibility. The slave, himself an item of property, seldom had clearly defined notions of property rights. Although some masters permitted slaves to possess minor items of personal property, the slaves seldom felt a sense of real ownership, for neither their cabins, their clothes, nor even their time was their own. Petty thievery to secure certain minor luxuries was so generally practiced, par-

---

[2] *Census* (1890), Vol. III, Part II, 3, 5, 17, 50.
[3] New York *Age,* January 13, 1883.

ticularly by household servants who had access to the master's larder, that it became almost an institution in itself. Marital relationships were so lax and indefinite that the development of a sense of the sanctity and permanency of marriage was a slow process in the days of freedom. Personal responsibility was a concept almost completely unknown to the slave who was worked under strict supervision and went through his motions by rote.

Nor were the circumstances surrounding Negroes in a state of freedom calculated to develop a sense of responsibility. Surrounded by poverty, paid low wages, and finding most of the property still in the hands of whites, Negroes saw that there was still a premium on thievery. Petit larceny most frequently brought Negroes into the toils of the law and either landed them in county jails or in a state of peonage to whites who were willing to pay their fines. Unprotected chicken coops and unfenced livestock proved irresistible lures to the Negro hungry for a change in his diet of hog and hominy. And the practice of petty thievery from the white pantry has down to the present day sometimes been advanced as an excuse for the low pay of domestic servants. Negro penchant for the chicken coop became a standing joke, and brought about a facetious scheme, attributed by the Aiken *Journal and Review* to a Mississippi editor, to make petit larceny grounds for disfranchisement and build hen roosts low to the ground.[4]

The development of a sense of personal pride and self-respect was extremely slow and difficult for Negroes. Even during his eight years of brief and dubious glory from 1868 to 1876 the Negro remained a subordinate element in society, and a sense of his subordination took precedence over any natural tendency toward pride that may have existed. "To arrive at a conclusion as to the opinion that the average American negro has of himself," a Negro minister lamented, "one has but to note a single expression which is in almost constant use among us, . . . 'He is nothing but a nigger like myself.' "[5] Slaves had been so frequently humiliated and whipped before each other that punishment came to be considered scarcely a disgrace. After the fall of slavery much the same attitude was shown toward imprisonment. The moment a Negro convict

---

[4] Clark, *The Southern Country Editor,* p. 207.
[5] Emancipation Day address by the Reverend I. S. Lee, Charleston *News and Courier,* January 2, 1892.

left the jail, a contemporary white noted, "he resumes the place in colored society that he left, finds himself for a week the object of general interest as he discourses on his adventures in the great 'pennytenshun' in the far-off city they have so often heard mentioned, begins life anew, and is treated as if nothing had happened."[6]

A genuine understanding of law in the abstract was naturally slow in developing. Negroes had little part in the framing of the law except during Reconstruction, and it appeared to be altogether an instrument of the white man's government and of his supremacy. The "law," as personified in the person of the white police officer, was all too often a matter of arbitrary enforcement.

Another serious law enforcement problem grew out of the prevalence of shootings and cuttings in the settlement of personal disputes or "insults." Violence, as the preceding chapter demonstrated, was confined neither to interracial difficulties nor to either race. The problem became especially concentrated and acute in the towns on Saturday afternoons and evenings. "Every Saturday afternoon," observed B. O. Townsend, "the negroes swarm into the towns from the country, and as far as their means will permit indulge in potations of poisonous whisky. Of these occasions street fights and riots are the invariable results." But even in this the Negroes were not without example. Intemperance, Townsend noted, had been as notorious a failing of white Carolinians "as of Kentucky itself." In drunken brawls he found that the whites rivalled the Negroes.[7]

The service of Negroes on juries was but gradually eliminated after Reconstruction. As late as 1885 a white editor professed surprise upon hearing that there was dissatisfaction with Negro jury service in Texas. No more was thought of seeing a Negro on a jury in South Carolina, he said, than of seeing Negroes on the police force in Charleston.[8] But it seems that care was taken in the counties outside of Beaufort and Georgetown that Negroes should not outnumber whites on the jury panel. Fairfield, a county with a Negro majority, had on its list of grand jurors for 1879

---

[6] A South Carolinian, *Atlantic Monthly*, XXXIX (April, 1877), 475
[7] *Ibid.*
[8] Charleston *News and Courier*, February 19, 1885.

the names of fifteen whites and three Negroes. The list of petit
jurors for one term of court had the names of twenty-seven whites
and nine Negroes.[9] But in Charleston the jury that acquitted Dr.
T. R. McDow of the murder of Francis W. Dawson in 1889 was
composed of seven Negroes and five whites.[10] By the end of the
nineties, however, Negroes were seen on juries only infrequently.
In 1897 the juries at the May term of court even in Beaufort
County had only three or four Negroes.[11] Soon after the turn of
the century the elimination of Negroes from practically all jury
service was complete.

Most Negroes executed by the state during the period from
1877 to 1900 were convicted of the murder of other Negroes, for
Negroes guilty of other capital crimes were considered fortunate
if they lived to appear for trial. Execution was carried out by
hanging in the county where the conviction took place. Public
hangings were extremely demoralizing performances. Seldom fewer
than six or seven thousand people attended them, even in the most
remote county. Prayers would be offered and hymns sung to "wild
airs" by the Negroes present. "A dead silence then ensues; this
is broken by the falling of the drop, and as the doomed man is
launched into eternity a piercing and universal shriek arises, the
wildest religious mania seizes on the crowd, they surge to and fro,
sing, and raise the holy dance."[12] Although these displays were
less demoralizing than the frenzied rite of lynching, it can be said
to the credit of the Democratic legislature that they were ended by
an act of 1878 which abolished public hangings. Hanging continued to be the form of capital punishment, however, until 1912,
when electrocution was substituted.[13]

The local and county lock-ups in which petty criminals served
their sentences were usually dismal affairs in which the dull
monotony of confinement was seldom relieved. A survey of nineteen county jails in 1880 revealed that no manual labor was required of the prisoners in any of the nineteen. Eighteen provided

---

[9] Columbia *Daily Register,* January 30, 1879.

[10] Port Royal *Palmetto Post,* June 27, 1889.

[11] Charleston *News and Courier,* June 1, 1897.

[12] A South Carolinian, *Atlantic Monthly,* XXXIX (June, 1877), 681-82.

[13] Albert D. Oliphant, *The Evolution of the Penal System of South Carolina
from 1866 to 1916* (Columbia, 1916), p. 5. Hereinafter cited as *The Penal
System of South Carolina.*

no prison clothes. In only six of the nineteen were there bath tubs for ordinary bathing, and in none of these were the prisoners required to use the bathing facilities. Cells and corridors were not heated in nine. In only ten were the accused separated from the convicted. In only six were the young separated from hardened offenders, and in three not even the sexes were segregated.[14]

Not until 1885 were the counties and municipalities authorized to use on the roads and streets convicts sentenced to less than ninety days.[15] Finally, in 1894, an act providing for a supervisor and board of road commissioners in each county vested the control of county convicts in the road supervisor. Courts were required to sentence all able-bodied male convicts whose sentences were for not over two years to hard labor on the public roads, although they might be sent to the penitentiary or county jail at the discretion of the presiding judge.[16] This act created the chaingang system virtually in the form that has since become the standard penal system of South Carolina.

Although the chaingang was perhaps an improvement over the dirty and unhealthful county jails where prisoners suffered the dry rot of enforced idleness, there was still little in the chaingang system that could be called reformative. Despite a provision in the Constitution of 1895 forbidding corporal punishment the most common mode of disciplinary punishment was whipping, usually administered in the presence of the other prisoners. Since the inception of the chaingang system, one writer has recently said, "Little has been done in South Carolina which can be associated with the methods of progressive penology; and from a penological point of view, South Carolina has remained one of the most backward states of the Union."[17]

Conditions in the state penitentiary were equally as lamentable as those in the county jails. When Theodore W. Parmele became superintendent under the Republican regime in 1875, he found the buildings still incomplete, although a total of $497,000 had been

---

[14] *Reports and Resolutions* (1880), pp. 438-39.

[15] Oliphant, *The Penal System of South Carolina*, p. 8.

[16] *Statutes at Large*, XXI, 486.

[17] Hilda Jane Zimmerman, "Penal Systems and Penal Reform in the South Since the Civil War" (unpublished Ph. D. dissertation, Department of History, University of North Carolina, 1947), p. 325.

appropriated for construction between 1867 and 1876. The prison
hospital, guards' quarters, commissary, and watchtower had been
blown down in a tornado. Prisoners slept on the stone floor. Some
of them were employed at making bricks and repairing the buildings, but most were left in idleness just as those in the county jails.[18]
Of the 350 convicts, 58 were minors, unsegregated from the older
men.

Despite reform efforts of Parmele and his successor, a Negro
minister who visited the state penitentiary in 1880 felt that "the
Democrats must think there is no hell for bad people, for they
make a hell of that prison." A keeper told him that he would
demonstrate "how we take niggers down." He began with a tread-
mill, which he said soon took "the stiffness and strength out of
the newcomers"; and then showed the minister men chained with
their necks in iron collars attached to ankle chains, and a fourteen
year old boy wearing handcuffs. The beds were of rotten straw, full
of vermin.[19] According to the annual report of the superintendent
in that year the straw was changed and the cells whitewashed only
once every two months, although prisoners were forced to bathe
once a week. Prisoners were confined in cells 5 x 7 x 8 feet, one
to a cell in the summer and two in the winter, with 250 cubic
feet of air. Ventilation was to be provided by a large iron pipe
running up the back part of each cell, although these were not
in use at the time of the 1880 report because the prison was incomplete.[20]

The drain on the public treasury that was caused by maintaining
prisoners in idleness brought a suggestion from Governor Chamberlain in the last year of his administration that the state adopt the
system of leasing prisoners to private contractors.[21] It was a system
already in effect in a number of Southern states, and had in fact
been adopted temporarily in South Carolina in 1873 when the
superintendent of the penitentiary had been forced to lease some
of the convicts in order to feed them when the legislature had cut
his appropriation in half.[22]

-----

[18] *Reports and Resolutions* (1875-1876), pp. 150-51.
[19] Holland (ed.), *Letters and Diary of Laura M. Towne*, p. 302.
[20] *Reports and Resolutions* (1880), pp. 440-41.
[21] Columbia *Daily Register*, February 2, 1876.
[22] *Reports and Resolutions* (1873-1874), pp. 115, 118.

Wade Hampton advocated in his first message to the special session of the legislature in 1877 measures to make the penal, charitable, and educational institutions of the state self-supporting.[23] On the very day of his message a bill "to Utilize the Convict Labor of this State" was introduced in the lower house of the legislature and was finally passed on June 8. This measure provided that the board of directors of the state penitentiary should have power to hire out any and all convicts in the penitentiary except those under sentence for murder, rape, arson, or manslaughter, under rules and regulations to be established by the board. Certain minimum regulations were laid down by the legislature, requiring that convicts be kept within the state and humanely treated; that food, clothing, lodging, and modes of punishment be prescribed in each contract; and that convicts should not be required to labor more than ten hours a day nor on Sundays and holidays. Provision was also made that contractors should be required to enter bond as surety of their good faith, and that contractors guilty of neglect, maltreatment, or cruelty toward prisoners should be punished by fine and imprisonment.[24]

The first contract was made with the Greenwood and Augusta Railroad, to which the board of directors leased one hundred convicts, for whom the railroad agreed to pay $3.00 a month per prisoner plus maintenance.[25] By the end of 1878 the board had leased 221 state convicts to work on railroads, in phosphate mines, and on private plantations.

From the beginning it was understood that the system of convict leasing was to be a method of utilizing Negro labor. Stating his approval of convict leasing, George Tillman said: "The negro has a constitutional propensity to steal, and in short to violate most of the ten commandments. The State should farm out such convicts even for only their subsistence, rather than compel taxpayers to support them in idleness."[26] The few whites who were sentenced to the state penitentiary were generally charged with serious crimes, for which they were kept within the walls of the penitentiary. But it would seem that little discrimination was shown in favor of the

---

[23] *Senate Journal* (1877, extra session), p. 24.

[24] *Acts and Joint Resolutions* (1877, extra session), pp. 263-64.

[25] *Reports and Resolutions* (1877-1878), p. 87.

[26] Columbia *Daily Register*, October 11, 1877, quoting Augusta *Chronicle and Constitutionalist*.

few who were available for leasing. They were housed and worked with Negro convicts and apparently received the same treatment.

Responsible officials early expressed doubt as to the wisdom of convict leasing, and evidence was soon available that prisoners in private hands suffered from maltreatment and exhaustion. Private contractors were naturally interested chiefly in the exploitation of the prisoners' labor, and there was little pressure on them to provide reasonably for the prisoners' welfare. In the summer of 1878 convicts were returned by the Greenwood and Augusta Railroad so disabled that they could not walk.[27] In his annual report later that year Superintendent Parmele said: "My opinion is that the proper protection of society and the necessity for punishment of crime require other ways of utilizing the labor of State prisoners."[28] A joint legislative committee which investigated the penitentiary in 1878 expressed approval of leasing only as a temporary expedient and advocated abolition of the system as soon as the state could use convicts in its own industries inside the penitentiary.[29] The first annual report of Parmele's successor, T. J. Lipscomb, in 1879 called attention to the fact that under the system of convict leasing, then but two years old, 153 prisoners had already died and 82 had escaped, "thereby proving that . . . the management of some of the contractors is very unsatisfactory." If the convicts had a property value, Lipscomb said, "then the contractors, having more interest in their lives and services, would look after them with greater zeal, and not leave them . . . to the ignorance, inattention, or inhumanity of irresponsible hirelings."[30]

The convict leasing system shortly after the writing of this report became a public scandal. W. N. Taft, white Republican from Charleston, introduced a resolution in the state senate calling for an investigation of conditions among leased convicts.[31] A substitute resolution by a Democratic senator was adopted. Under this measure the house and senate committees on the penitentiary were made a special joint committee to investigate the situation.[32]

---

[27] Yorkville *Enquirer,* December 11, 1879.

[28] *Reports and Resolutions* (1877-1878), p. 89.

[29] Zimmerman, "Penal Systems and Penal Reforms in the South Since the Civil War," p. 133.

[30] *Reports and Resolutions* (1879), pp. 296-97.

[31] *Senate Journal* (1879-1880), p. 7.

[32] *Ibid.,* pp. 47, 82.

In the middle of December Superintendent Lipscomb submitted papers dealing with his own investigation of conditions in a camp maintained by the Greenwood and Augusta Railroad in a remote sector of Edgefield County under the supervision of Captain J. J. Cahill, who doubled as an official of the railroad and of the state penitentiary.[33]

These papers included a report from the penitentiary physician, who had been dispatched to investigate the causes of a high mortality rate among prisoners leased to the road. The physician found in a log pen which constituted the camp hospital three prisoners, two Negroes and one white, lying on a shelf made of clapboards and covered with straw about two inches thick. One of the convicts was in the "last stages of exhaustion" and another suffering from general dropsy. The third was so weak that he was unable to leave the shelf and the doctor found the straw so full of vermin that he was unable to make a satisfactory examination. "The English language," he said, "does not possess words sufficiently strong to express the stench that arose from the place."

The quarters of the other prisoners were in two log pens, with sleeping accommodations of the same sort except that on some of the shelves there was no straw at all. The stench in these quarters was "sickening to the uttermost extent." From the stockade he went to where the convicts were at work and examined them separately. With the exception of nine, he found them to be infected with scurvy and with an eruption apparently caused by the vermin on their bodies. A neighborhood physician who had formerly attended the prisoners had refused to attend them any further because he felt that he could be of no possible service under the circumstances, and an associate engineer of the railroad reported that he had remonstrated time after time, with no effect.[34]

Shortly thereafter Superintendent Lipscomb made a personal investigation and verified the findings of the prison physician, discovering in addition evidence that prisoners had been subjected to beatings and that one had been shot to death for "revolt" while in shackles.[35] At the instigation of the prison physician the board of the penitentiary ordered twenty-six of the prisoners returned

---

[33] *Reports and Resolutions* (1879), pp. 889-947.
[34] *Ibid.*, pp. 891-92.
[35] *Ibid.*, pp. 889-90.

immediately. After some delay twenty-four of these were returned, along with the body of a twenty-fifth who had died en route.[36]

In a letter to the penitentiary board Cahill himself replied to the charges that had been made against his management of the stockade. In this letter he claimed that the prisoners' beds were without straw because the convicts did not want it in hot weather and kicked it off. As to the vermin he reminded the members of the board that they were "so common at every settlement in this part of the State at this time that no complaint is made of them." He suggested that "Superintendent Lipscomb must have gotten a portion of his stock of fleas at the residence of Hon. G. D. Tillman, where he spent the night."[37] To charges that the sick did not have sufficient treatment he replied that the attending physicians had been incompetent and had wrongly diagnosed many of the cases.[38] That all the prisoners were very dirty was attributed to the fact that they had been picking and shoveling dirt.[39] He denied having inflicted a scar on the head of the prisoner who had complained to the superintendent, but admitted that "I did tap him lightly on the head once with a small cane which I happened to have in my hand at the time, because he made me an insulting response when I upbraided him for cutting the stay chain in the stockade."[40]

To the even more damaging charge that a convict had been shot while in shackles and fastened to a chaingang, Cahill replied that the act had been carried out in compliance with a penitentiary regulation which permitted a guard to shoot a prisoner if necessary to quell revolt or attempted revolt. The revolt of which the prisoner had been guilty was that he had held up his shovel in front of a gang returning from work as a signal to halt and defied the order of a guard to move on.[41]

Cahill's explanation amounted, in effect, to so clumsy an admission of mismanagement and brutality that he was shortly afterward dismissed by the railroad.[42] Conditions, however, continued unsatisfactory and a doctor sent to investigate the stockade in October

---

[36] Oliphant, *The Penal System of South Carolina*, p. 6.
[37] *Reports and Resolutions* (1879), p. 894.
[38] *Ibid.*, pp. 895-96.
[39] *Ibid.*, p. 896.
[40] *Ibid.*, p. 897.
[41] *Ibid.*, pp. 897-99.
[42] Oliphant, *The Penal System of South Carolina*, pp. 6-7.

found very much the same conditions, the only improvement being that each prisoner had been provided with a blanket. He found that drinking water was kept in a tub near the door, and was passed down in a cup whenever any prisoner wanted a drink. Nearby there was an empty tub, without a cover, which was passed around so that the prisoners could relieve the calls of nature. Prisoners, both white and Negro, were still overworked, according to the testimony of disinterested persons.[43]

With this report in hand, the board ordered the return of the remaining convicts. When, after a month, they had still not been returned, the board instructed the attorney general to institute proceedings against the Greenwood and Augusta Railroad.[44] The convicts, however, were not finally returned until the board issued another order on January 15, 1880, after the railroad's contract had expired at the end of 1879.[45] The same resolutions also ordered back convicts on the Edgefield and Trenton Branch Railroad Company and convicts hired out in Spartanburg and Laurens counties.

Figures collected by the Superintendent of the Penitentiary on the mortality rate of prisoners leased to the Greenwood and Augusta Railroad are revealing of the conditions which prevailed.[46] The figures are as follows:

Date	No. Rec'd by R.R.	Total Deaths	Pct. of Deaths	Dis-charged	Es-caped	Par-doned	Ret. to Pen.	On Hand
Sept. 24, 1877	100	28	28.00	14	28	7	13	10
No date	3	0	0.00	0	2	0	1	0
No date	2	1	50.00	0	1	0	0	0
May 2, 1878	50	27	54.00	2	4	0	9	8
May 2, 1878	15	10	66.66	0	1	2	0	2
Dec. 6, 1878	40	25	62.50	2	2	0	1	10
Apr. 7, 1879	75	37	49.33	0	1	0	16	21
Total	285	128	44.91	18	39	9	40	51

Out of those prisoners returned to the penitentiary sixteen died within ten days after arrival, and if counted would make the death rate 50.52 per cent instead of 44.91.[47]

---

43 *Reports and Resolutions* (1880), pp. 426-28.
44 Oliphant, *The Penal System of South Carolina*, p. 7.
45 *Senate Journal* (1880, special session), pp. 113-14.
46 *Reports and Resolutions* (1880), p. 433.
47 *Ibid.*

Meanwhile, the special joint committee of the legislature moved slowly despite the fact that it already had before it the papers submitted by Superintendent Lipscomb. In the special session of 1880 an effort was made by Republican members of the senate to force a report out of the committee during February.[48] But their resolution to force the hand of the joint committee was indefinitely postponed, and a report was not made until the regular session of the legislature which began in November of the same year. In the regular session Thomas E. Miller sought the passage of a resolution instructing officials of the penitentiary to discontinue forthwith the leasing of convicts until the laws dealing with the convict lease could be repealed, but again the action sought by the Republicans was denied.[49]

The report, finally brought in well over a year after the first exposure of the miserable conditions in the Edgefield camp, tended to minimize the suffering of the prisoners and failed completely to place any blame for the situation. The recommendations made by the committee fell far short of the suggestions already made by Superintendent Parmele and Senator Miller that the situation could best be corrected by the complete abolition of convict leasing. The committee suggested first that the board of directors of the penitentiary make such definite conditions as to diet, clothing, and general rules of hygiene as might be necessary for the proper care of the convicts, a matter which the board was already responsible for handling. Second, it suggested competent medical inspection at regular intervals, a measure not formerly taken. Third, it suggested that all convicts taken out of the penitentiary should be worked under the supervision of a man appointed by and responsible to the Superintendent of the Penitentiary. This, too, was a new measure. J. J. Cahill had been primarily an officer of the railroad, and had simply been invested by the state with the authority to supervise the prisoners in line with his duties in connection with the railroad. And last, the committee suggested that all contracts for the hire of prisoners should be revocable by the governor whenever it appeared that prisoners were being cruelly treated.[50]

------

[48] *Senate Journal* (1880, special session), pp. 27-28.
[49] *Ibid.*, pp. 288-89.
[50] *Senate Journal* (1880), pp. 365-66.

The first recommendation involved the responsibility of the board of directors. On the last three the legislature had to act, and at the end of the 1880 session it adopted two of the committee's recommendations. The governor was given authority to require the return of convicts that were being ill-used, and the Superintendent of the Penitentiary was required to have all prisoners inspected by a physician of the penitentiary at least once a month.[51]

South Carolina was fortunate to have the evils of the convict lease system exposed within two years after its inauguration in the state, and the early exposure of brutality did bring a degree of amelioration through the requirement for regular medical examinations. However, white public opinion was never aroused to effective indignation over the system. In the first place, convict leasing was almost altogether a system for the leasing of Negro prisoners. It was but one of many indignities suffered by Negroes and few could become seriously aroused over it. Then, too, the stringent measure which was the only real solution—abolition of the system— seemed to involve expenses that the taxpayers of the state did not want to assume. It was also difficult for the public to become concerned over a problem with which it was not familiar, and convicts leased out on plantations, in phosphate mines, and in railroad camps did not frequently come to the public eye.

In 1883 a convention of Negroes, called to name delegates from the state to a national convention in Louisville on the general status of the Negro in the United States, declared that "it is proved conclusively that the system of hiring out convicts to corporations and individuals is productive of the most direful results . . . ," and called upon the legislature at its forthcoming session to repeal the law under which the system operated.[52] A committee sent to interview Governor H. S. Thompson found him sympathetic. He pointed out that he had instigated proceedings against a manager of the Seegers farm in Richland County where a convict had recently been severely whipped and had afterward died and that he had sent a special medical examiner to a camp in Laurens and, upon his recommendation, had directed better food and habitation for the convicts. He expressed doubt as to the advisability of con-

---

[51] *Acts and Joint Resolutions,* (1880), pp. 469-70.
[52] Columbia *Daily Register,* July 19, 1883.

tinuing the system and promised to see that criminals were properly treated as long as the law was on the books.[53]

In his message to the legislature that fall Governor Thompson expressed the belief that it was the lack of qualifications on the part of contractors that caused mistreatment rather than deliberate cruelty, but cited a statement of Superintendent Lipscomb: "The increase of revenue sinks into insignificance in comparison with the abuses which I believe will continue to exist while the convicts are hired to work beyond the control of the officers of the penitentiary."[54]

In 1884 an effort in the legislature to require guards responsible to state officials rather than to the contractors was successful. One member of the legislature expressed regret that it had been necessary "to lift the curtain upon one of the darkest pictures which has disgraced the history of our State Government," and quoted two judges as saying "that they shrank with horror from the duty of sentencing convicts to the Penitentiary" because of the lease system.[55] The new law, however, made it impossible for the penitentiary to lease prisoners because of the heavy expense, and after one year the legislature permitted reversion to the old system of permitting contractors to furnish the guards and overseers.[56]

In the year after the exposure of Cahill's mismanagement of the railroad camp, arrangements were made to hire convicts for the making of brooms and shoes within the walls of the penitentiary. Through the income from the hire of convicts for farming, phosphate mining, and manufacturing within the penitentiary, Lipscomb was able in 1881 to operate at a profit, turning $23,000 back into the treasury.[57] Adopting a policy of using convict labor for state projects the legislature in 1882 provided that the penitentiary should keep a minimum of two hundred convicts employed on the Columbia Canal. Other demands were then made on convict labor by the state from time to time: for completing the State House in 1884; for keeping its grounds in order, 1889; for erecting buildings at Clemson College, 1890; for erecting buildings at Winthrop College, 1891; for preparing brick to be used in a building for

[53] *Ibid.*
[54] *Ibid.*, December 20, 1883.
[55] *Ibid.*, December 10, 1884.
[56] Oliphant, *The Penal System of South Carolina*, p. 8.
[57] *Reports and Resolutions* (1881-1882), p. 67.

Negroes at the state insane asylum, 1894; and for erecting buildings at the Colored Normal, Industrial, Agricultural and Mechanical College, 1896.[58]

At the same time the state was experimenting with farming. In January, 1877, five months before the legal establishment of the leasing system, the penitentiary board had urged Superintendent Parmele to make arrangements with J. C. Seegers to work convicts on his Richland County farm and to provide for their maintenance in payment. In 1881, however, the penitentiary was able to get as much as $16.66 a month for convict labor; consequently the Seegers contract was terminated. Under a new contract Seegers got only twenty-five laborers and paid the State $5.00 a month each in addition to maintenance.[59] In 1883 a farm was purchased in the Dutch Fork section of Lexington, now Richland County, and the penitentiary was authorized to work convicts there under its own direction.[60] This practice was further extended in 1886, when three farms in the lower part of Richland County including one Seegers farm, were leased for five years.[61] On these farms, however, the penitentiary suffered a loss because of overflow in three successive years, and in 1888 the legislature refused to permit the working of the farms subject to overflow for reasons of health.[62] But in 1889 the legislature authorized the outright purchase of a farm at not more than $40,000 and forbade the working of convicts in phosphate mines.[63] The board then bought a farm on the Wateree River along the line between Kershaw and Sumter counties.[64] In the Constitution of 1895 it was provided that leased convicts should remain under officers appointed by the penitentiary.[65] Another blow was struck against the leasing system in 1896 when it was provided by the legislature that convicts could be leased only for legal money, except that convicts could do farm work under contracts that provided sharecropping arrangements with the state.[66] In 1896 the penitentiary cleared $58,000 from its farming operations and

---

[58] Oliphant, *The Penal System of South Carolina*, p. 8.
[59] *Reports and Resolutions* (1881-1882), p. 75.
[60] *Reports and Resolutions* (1883), II, 643; Oliphant, *The Penal System of South Carolina*, p. 8.
[61] *Reports and Resolutions* (1886), II, 279.
[62] Oliphant, *The Penal System of South Carolina*, p. 9.
[63] *Acts and Joint Resolutions* (1889), p. 320.
[64] Oliphant, *The Penal System of South Carolina*, p. 9.
[65] *Constitution of 1895*, Art. XII, Sec. 9.
[66] *Acts and Joint Resolutions* (1896), p. 379.

the legislature authorized the purchase of a farm in Sumter County adjoining the one already purchased. This brought the acreage owned by the institution, exclusive of its site, up to 5,116. Investments for farming purposes were $39,250.[67]

Thus, the state finally accepted farming as the solution to its convict labor problem. In 1897 it was made illegal to employ any other than convict labor on any state farm, or to employ convict labor on any private farm. The board of directors announced that as contracts for labor on private farms expired they would not be renewed.[68] The New York *Tribune* reported that those engaged on the state farms "seem more contented. . . . There are few attempts to escape and the health of the prisoners is better."[69] In 1901 the board of directors announced that all but one of the contracts for agricultural labor had expired, and that one was not to be renewed upon its expiration.[70] Thus, by a process of muddling through, the state had arrived at a solution which made its penal system self-supporting and at the same time ameliorated the inevitable evils of the "worse than Siberian system"[71] of convict leasing.

---

[67] Oliphant, *The Penal System of South Carolina*, p. 11.

[68] *Reports and Resolutions* (1897), p. 447.

[69] Zimmerman, "Penal Systems and Penal Reforms in the South Since the Civil War," p. 253, quoting New York *Tribune*, January 9, 1897.

[70] *Reports and Resolutions* (1902), I, 1855.

[71] New York *Nation*, XLI (July 16, 1885), quoting Charleston *News and Courier*.

14

CARE OF THE INDIGENT AND DEFECTIVE

THE condition of Negro indigents and defectives created a new and serious problem after the Civil War. The poverty of the state as a whole, and especially of its Negro population, made relief either by private philanthropy or state appropriation difficult, but public spirited citizens of both races recognized the situation as a problem to be faced rather than a nuisance to be deprecated.

Because of the general prevalence of poverty Negro indigence was scarcely recognized, although the *News and Courier* noticed that many Negroes regularly visited the Charleston city dump, taking therefrom scraps of meat, old ham bones, stale bread, or anything in the shape of food that could be found. The editor admitted that stern necessity drove people to such extremities, but assumed that the majority of them were old women, "who are either too feeble to work or do not care to do so."[1]

Amelioration of the problem was attempted through the admission of Negroes to county poor houses or by the distribution through the poor houses of meager rations to those living outside. Most of the county homes seem to have been institutions like that in Kershaw County which in 1886 consisted of a dilapidated building with two rooms for white and colored alike. "A glance into the place," said a Camden editor, ". . . is enough to sicken any one."[2] Apparently the only institution of the sort that approached adequacy was the Ashley River Asylum, maintained by the city of Charleston for Negro indigents, young and old, the lame, and the

[1] Charleston *News and Courier*, July 1, 1900.
[2] Columbia *Daily Register*, March 24, 1886, quoting the Camden *Messenger*.

blind under a board which included some of the leading Negro citizens. This institution owned a long two-story wooden building, containing fourteen rooms, which was used as a hospital, and smaller buildings for the use of the residents. There was a central kitchen, a laundry, a chapel, and a farm of fifteen acres on which fruits and vegetables were grown. In 1891 it had seventy-one inmates, one of whom was an infant in arms. During that year the city council spent $3,000 on its maintenance.[3]

Negro orphans, sometimes accepted or supported in part by the poor houses, seem to have been readily absorbed for the most part into neighboring families. The State Orphan Asylum, founded in Charleston by the Radical government about 1870,[4] fell victim to Democratic economy shortly after Wade Hampton's elevation to the Senate.[5] It was apparently operated exclusively for Negro children, and as late as 1878 housed forty-five children and had nineteen bound out under its care.[6] Organized private effort for the care of Negro orphans usually took the form of separate departments in the various small industrial schools, such as that in the Mather Industrial School in Beaufort.[7] Claflin University, in connection with its Quarto-Centennial celebration in 1894, laid the cornerstone of a colored orphanage to provide a "Christian home for friendless colored children." It was to be built on land donated by a wealthy resident of Orangeburg and with funds collected in Boston and in South Carolina.[8]

The Orphan Aid Society of Charleston was organized late in 1891 by D. J. Jenkins, a young Negro Baptist minister, after he had discovered on a raw, wintry morning a half dozen Negro orphans who had taken overnight shelter from the cold in some old dry goods boxes. Through the society he established an orphanage that was opened early in January, 1892;[9] by an effective fundraising campaign in Charleston and in the North, he was able to

[3] City of Charleston, *Year Book* (1880), p. 58; Charleston *News and Courier*. December 25, 1891.

[4] *Reports and Resolutions* (1873-1874), p. 520.

[5] It had a fund of $2,000.52 in 1877-1878, which dropped to $505.34 for 1878-1879. *Reports and Resolutions* (1878), pp. 179-80; *ibid.* (1879), p. 193. There is no record of any expenditures for 1879-1880.

[6] *Reports and Resolutions* (1878), p. 659.

[7] Pegues, *Our Baptist Ministers and Schools*, p. 621.

[8] Charleston *News and Courier*, May 25, 1894.

[9] *Ibid.*, June 16, 1892.

secure enough money to move the orphanage into the old Marine Hospital on Franklin Street where it had ample facilities.[10] By 1894 the Jenkins Orphanage had a farm several miles to the north of the city on which the children were trained in the methods of farming and was also offering vocational training in carpentry, bricklaying, tailoring, shoemaking, cooking, laundering, and dressmaking.[11] Jenkins was ingenious at devising methods of fundraising, but by 1895 the orphanage was largely supporting itself through the Jenkins Orphanage Band, which performed on the public streets for donations. In 1895 the band made a trip to England seeking support.[12] Another source of income was a job printing department that was in 1895 publishing the weekly Charleston *Messenger*.[13] In 1897 Jenkins convinced the Charleston city council that the orphanage was performing a valuable public service in keeping potential juvenile delinquents off the streets, and, beginning with that year, the city of Charleston contributed regularly to its support.[14]

The problem of the insane was one in which a greater degree of governmental responsibility was demonstrated. Negroes had been admitted to the state insane asylum since 1848. During the first decade thirty Negroes were admitted, but after the war the question of adequate care for the Negro insane became one of constantly increasing urgency.[15] Annual reports of the superintendents consistently demanded more space for the housing of the increased number of Negro inmates. In 1878 the superintendent warned the legislature that the "natural antagonism of the races" would require that steps be taken to domicile white and Negro patients in separate buildings.[16]

No steps were taken by the legislature, however, and as the number of Negro inmates grew rapidly from 101 in 1878 to 313 in 1889,[17] the officials of the asylum constructed new quarters out of savings from the regular appropriations for maintenance. These

---

[10] *Ibid.*, November 14, 1892; April 11, 1894.
[11] *Ibid.*, February 12, October 5, 1894.
[12] *Ibid.*, September 21, 1895.
[13] *Ibid.*
[14] City of Charleston, *Year Book* (1897), p. 285.
[15] *Reports and Resolutions* (1896), I, 365-66.
[16] *Ibid.*, (1877-1878), p. 460.
[17] *Ibid.* (1890), I, 209.

consisted of flimsy wooden buildings for the accommodation of Negro men and two pavilions annexed to the old Asylum building for the use of Negro women, who also occupied half of the old Asylum, built in 1822.[18] A committee of the state legislature investigated the situation in 1889 and concluded that strained relations between the races would be best relieved by the erection of a separate asylum, under the direction of the same board, but its recommendations were lost in a last-minute rush for adjournment.[19] Agitation for additional quarters for Negroes was continued by the Board of Regents in the following year when it urged the establishment of a separate institution in Lexington County; but nothing was done, and the superintendent was still reminding the legislature in 1893 that the wooden buildings were unhygienic and dangerous in case of fire.[20]

Finally a decision was reached that both economy and efficiency demanded the maintenance of a single institution for both races. In 1894 the legislature provided convict labor to make bricks and begin the construction of a new building for Negro men.[21] The Parker Building, a large three and a half story brick structure, was completed in 1897,[22] but at the turn of the century the Negro women were still quartered in part in the old building and in part in the two wooden pavilions, "in many ways inadequate for hospital purposes, besides being dangerous in case of fire."[23] Nevertheless, the state had accepted throughout the period a responsibility for the care of the Negro insane. It had provided facilities, inadequate though they were, to care for at least the worst cases and keep them off the public streets and out of the county jails.

The state was somewhat slower in accepting a responsibility for the deaf and dumb and the blind, except insofar as they were admitted to the county poor houses. Superintendent of Education Jillson in 1873 ordered the admission of Negroes to the State Institution for the Education of the Deaf, Dumb, and the Blind on the same basis as whites, but his action resulted in the resignation of the officers of the institution, after which it was closed for three

---

[18] *Ibid.* (1893), I, 258.
[19] *Ibid.*, p. 259.
[20] *Ibid.*, pp. 260-61.
[21] *Ibid.* (1896), I, 366.
[22] *Handbook of 1907*, p. 57.
[23] *Reports and Resolutions* (1901), II, 1427.

years.[24] Not until 1883 were Negroes admitted to the institution, and then on a completely segregated basis,[25] but by 1899 there were forty-nine Negroes, nine blind and forty deaf, under the care of the state at Cedar Springs.[26]

They were housed in an old frame building on the grounds of the institution until the end of the century, but an appropriation of $10,000 by the legislature in 1900 assured the erection of a new structure for the Negro students.[27] Thus, by the end of the century there was assurance that the state had accepted the same responsibility for the care of these unfortunates that it had accepted for the Negro insane since 1848.

---

[24] Thompson, *The Establishment of the Public School,* p. 14.
[25] *Reports and Resolutions* (1883), I, 741, 744.
[26] *Reports and Resolutions* (1900), II, 272-73.
[27] *Ibid.* (1901), II, 398.

15

SOCIAL LIFE

NEGRO social activities, like those of the whites, ranged all the way from the Saturday afternoon brawling of farm laborers filled with cheap and poisonous "joy juice" to the decorous high life that was affected by the prosperous few in the towns.[1] For great numbers of the race, especially in the rural areas, the center of social activity was in the church, the most universal and highly organized of Negro institutions. Church services provided a regular outlet for the spiritual, emotional, and social instincts of the people, and special events, like the singing convention and the camp meeting, brought people together from wide areas and provided relief from the monotony of isolated existence.

Picnics, sponsored by churches and other organizations, attracted Negroes by the hundreds during the summer months. An annual picnic, sponsored during the "lay-by" season by the Negro farmers of York township, attracted between six and seven hundred Negroes from various parts of the county. One of these was featured by the presence of three bands and a number of speeches by leading Negroes of the community. The speeches consisted chiefly of generalities and moral admonitions, one speaker congratulating his audience on the successful fight with "General Green" but warning of the coming battle with "General Frost" and exhorting them to be "honest, upright and fair, pay our debts, walk straight in the eyes of our fellow-men, do what we can to educate our children, give our attention to hard work, and . . . fit ourselves for all the

---

[1] Columbia *State*, January 4, 1899; Columbia *Daily Register*, August 10, 1883, April 10, 1890; Charleston *New Era*, August 25, 1883.

responsibilities of citizenship which may hereafter devolve upon us."[2]

A more elaborate variant of the picnic was the excursion. Religious groups, friendly societies, fire companies, militia organizations, and baseball clubs regularly hired excursion trains at special prices for transportation to conventions, informal gatherings with similar groups in other towns, or to various pleasure spots. The most popular destination of these groups was Charleston, whence they sometimes travelled by water to Remley's Point, a popular picnic site across the harbor, or over the Ashley River Bridge to St. Andrew's Parish, where there was another popular gathering place. Beaufort, in the midst of the picturesque sea island region, was another popular destination. The new-found delight in travel that slaves experienced after emancipation does not seem to have been quickly dissipated.[3] But toward the end of the eighties complaints began to be heard from Negroes who felt that their people were dissipating their money on expensive trips that benefitted chiefly the railroad corporations and from white farmers who sometimes found their labor forces depleted by the absence of workers at critical seasons. During the late eighties the excursion began to fade as a means of diversion.[4]

Outside the churches the most common Negro social organizations were the friendly societies. These began their growth during the Reconstruction period chiefly as a means of providing cooperative insurance funds from which their members could draw in case of sickness or death. One of the most successful was the Future Progress Society which had lodges scattered over the upper part of the state in the late eighties. The organization was described as strictly benevolent in its aims, ruling out all religious and political questions and seeking to harmonize all parties and creeds, to "bury the dead and aid the sick, and encourage industry and schools." One of its lodges, in Newberry County, purchased an engine, thresher, and cotton gin for the cooperative use of the members, and during 1887

---

[2] Yorkville *Enquirer,* August 11, 1897.

[3] Charleston *New Era,* August 25, September 29, 1883; Greenville *Enterprise and Mountaineer,* July 28, 1880; Port Royal *Palmetto Post,* August 25, 1887; New York *Age,* July 14, 1887.

[4] New York *Age,* July 30, 1887; Columbia *Daily Register,* September 14, 24, 1890.

paid out $1,200 on its policies, $375 for coffins and $250 for the relief of the sick.[5]

Organizations of this sort, frequently with bizarre names, proliferated in both the towns and rural areas. Among the friendly societies of Beaufort in 1883 were the Benevolent Society of the First Baptist Church, the Workers of Charity, the Shekinah Society, the Sons and Daughters of Zion, the Rising Sons and Daughters of Zion, the Rising Sons and Daughters of Benevolence, the Rising Sons and Daughters of Charity, the Mary and Martha Society, the Olive Branch, the Sisters of Zion, the Knights of Wise Men, and the Independent Order of Odd Fellows. With an aggregate membership of more than one thousand, they owned eleven buildings and lots, valued at over $12,000.[6] Charleston had at about the same time, among others, the Zion Travellers, Timothy Number One, Sons and Daughters of Sojourners, Ladies Christian Union, Followers ot Emmanuel, Sons and Daughters of Elders of the Throne, Banners of the Cross, Mary and Martha, Daughters of Meschech, Daughters of St. Joseph, Daughters of Noah, Sons and Daughters' Chariot, Sons and Daughters of Zion Number Two, the Gospel Harp's Band, Rising Sons and Daughters of Bethlehem Star, Brothers and Sisters of Charity, Sons and Daughters of St. Philip, Sons and Daughters of Abraham, the Widows' Union, and Daughters of Ezekiel.[7]

Membership in some of the friendly societies carried a degree of social prestige. This was especially true in Charleston where societies organized by ante-bellum free Negroes carried on useful careers enriched by long traditions. These included the Brown Fellowship Society, dating from 1790, the Friendly Union Society, in existence since 1813, and the Unity and Friendship Society, which celebrated its thirty-ninth anniversary in 1883.[8] The nature of the membership and the social outlook of these societies is indicated by the remarks of the president of the Brown Fellowship Society on the occasion of its 117th anniversary in 1911. Said he,

Fortunately there were the classes in society, and as our forefathers allied themselves with them, as a consequence they had their influence and protection and they had to be in accord

---

[5] Charleston *News and Courier*, March 13, 1888.
[6] *Handbook of 1883*, p. 667.
[7] Charleston *New Era*, September 2, 1882.
[8] Fitchett, *Journal of Negro History*, XXV (April, 1940), 144; Charleston *New Era*, August 18, September 22, 1883; Charleston *News and Courier*, April 17, 1883.

with them and stood for what they stood for. If they stood for high incentive so did our fathers. *If they stood for slavery so did our fathers to a certain extent. But they sympathized with the oppressed,* for they had to endure some of it. . . .[9]

Negro lodges, similar in nature to the friendly societies, but of wider organizational ramification, spread over the state during the period. They included the Masons, Odd Fellows, Good Templars, Pythians, and probably others.

The South Carolina Grand Lodge of Negro Freemasons had been formed in 1867. No statistics are available on its membership during the period under consideration, but it seems to have been sizable.[10]

The Grand Order of Odd Fellows in America already had a sizable organization by 1880, when 125 members from Charleston and 137 from Columbia gathered to celebrate the second anniversary of the Wayman Lodge, No. 1,339, of Columbia.[11] By 1890 the District Lodge No. 13 of South Carolina claimed 67 lodges and 17 chapters of the Household of Ruth, the women's auxiliary. Its total membership was 2,122 and during the year it paid $2,033 for the sick, $810 for funerals, and $532 in charity to widows and orphans of members. It claimed to have property and cash amounting to $21,440 in addition to real estate valued at $12,876.[12]

The Grand Lodge of the Independent Order of Good Templars had chapters scattered over all parts of the state. Officers elected at the annual sessions in 1883 and 1884 were from Charleston, Columbia, Greenville, Spartanburg, Anderson, Winnsboro, Florence, Sumter, Belton, and Marion. The meeting of 1884 selected a delegate to the 1885 meeting of the Grand Lodge of the World, which was scheduled to meet in Stockholm, Sweden.[13]

The first lodge of the colored Knights of Pythias in the state was Ionic No. 1, organized at Charleston in June, 1888, by S. H. Blocker of Augusta, Georgia. A controversy about the conduct of

---

[9] Fitchett, *Journal of Negro History,* XXV (April, 1940), 150, quoting The Holloway Scrapbook in the possession of Mrs. Mae Holloway Purcell, Charleston, S. C.

[10] Harold Van Buren Voorhis, *Negro Masonry in the United States* (New York, 1940), p. 109; Charleston *News and Courier,* March 7, 1891; Charleston *New Era,* August 25, 1883.

[11] Columbia *Daily Register,* January 13, 1880.

[12] Charleston *News and Courier,* August 14, 1890.

[13] Columbia *Daily Register,* May 13, 1883; Greenville *Enterprise and Mountaineer,* May 28, 1884.

the Endowment Department by the Supreme Lodge led in 1891 to the withdrawal of the Grand Lodge of South Carolina and its affiliation with a national group of secessionists from the parent body. As a result, the organization grew but slowly, and had a total of only eight lodges and 241 members in 1894. Its greatest growth came after the reorganization of the Grand Lodge and its reaffiliation with the parent body. Between 1907 and 1919 the Grand Lodge raised $203,543.26 for the mortuary department and paid to widows and orphans of deceased members $131,431.48. The women's auxiliary had an endowment fund of $10,000. In 1919 the order had a Uniformed Rank, comprising twenty-two companies and two cadet organizations which presented annual military displays.[14]

A love of military display and the tolerance of Democratic administrations kept alive until 1905 several companies of Negro militia. Hampton's Adjutant and Inspector General E. W. Moise recommended after the transfer of power to the Democrats that the colored troops be thoroughly reorganized, but that they not be disbanded. "Under careful and judicious management," he said, "a respectable colored militia can be established, and such a body will be an element of strength to the government and of value to the colored population."[15] This policy was followed by the state legislature in an act of June, 1877. The National Guard, comprising the Negro militiamen, was retained, but another group, the Volunteer State Troops, was organized. Into this group many of the Red Shirt companies and rifle clubs of 1876 were accepted as full-fledged components of the militia.[16]

The National Guard units were, of course, kept at a strength substantially smaller than the Volunteer State Troops, but their numbers remained about the same through the eighties and into the early nineties. In 1891, out of a total of 4,974 officers and enlisted men in the two organizations, there were 837 Negro National Guardsmen. In the neighborhood of Charleston they were organized into a brigade under the command of Samuel J. Lee, who held the rank of Brigadier General. Under him there were two regiments, one comprising nine companies in Charleston and the other, five

---

[14] Richardson (ed.), *The National Cyclopaedia of the Colored Race,* p. 441.
[15] *Reports and Resolutions* (1877-1878), p. 738.
[16] *Acts and Joint Resolutions* (1877, extra session), pp. 285-86; *Reports and Resolutions* (1890), I, 170.

companies in Berkeley County. In addition to these there were two unattached companies in Beaufort and two in Columbia.[17]

The function of the militia companies was altogether ceremonial and social. Excursions, parades, banquets, and picnics constituted their range of activities. The companies would frequently travel some distance from their homes to participate in ceremonies or meetings with companies in different towns and occasionally would entertain visiting companies from out of the state.[18] In 1898 the Capital City Guards of Columbia entertained at a banquet the First Rhode Island, a white unit.[19]

Emancipation Day, Decoration Day, and the Fourth of July were the usual occasions for parades, and the high point of the year for the First Brigade was an annual inspection in Charleston by the state Adjutant and Inspector General or his representatives. The inspection ceremony for 1883 was described by the Charleston *New Era* as follows:

> The streets were thronged, to witness the parade and inspection of colored troops . . . , indeed, the whole day partook of a holiday with the colored people, and the spirit of goodwill on the part of all classes and both races, was really delightful. The white business men left their desks and books of trade to see the troops pass, and people on the streets, stopped to get a view of the handsome spectacle. A Northern gentleman remarked that he was greatly surprised at such a fine display of colored soldiers, and much more so, at the interest and kind feelings of the Charlestonians therein. . . . The inspection and review lasted several hours and were enthusiastically observed by a dense throng of all colors and conditions of people. Gen. Manigault made a complimentary address, assuring the troops of State aid, and warmly referring to their appearance and evolutions, and general excellent deportment on parades, picnics, etc. Major-General McCrady did the reviewing with his full staff, all handsomely mounted and uniformed. A brilliant street parade and evening entertainment ended the fete, which has never been excelled.[20]

---

[17] *Reports and Resolutions* (1891), I, 177-81, 183-84, 195.

[18] Charleston *New Era*, July 29, 1882; Charleston *News and Courier*, May 19, 1894.

[19] Columbia *State*, December 17, 1898.

[20] Charleston *New Era*, May 12, 1883.

The Negro militia, however, rapidly declined during the nineties, and by 1903 the only units left were the two companies in Beaufort.[21] In a general reorganization in 1905, sixteen companies were disbanded, including the two Negro companies of Beaufort.[22]

Similar to the militia in their esprit and activities were the volunteer fire companies that existed in Charleston, Columbia, Greenville, and other towns before the organization of professional firefighting organizations. The fire companies enjoyed a healthy rivalry and holidays were frequently made the occasion for tournaments in which the companies competed to see which was fastest in getting to the scene of a supposed fire and putting its equipment into action.[23] The usefulness of the fire companies was far greater than that of the Negro militia companies, and when the city of Charleston proposed to retire two colored fire companies in 1881 as an economy measure, the *News and Courier* complained that the *Comet Star* and *Niagara,* steamers belonging to the companies, had not more than one equal among all the other companies. The editor suggested that white companies be retired if necessary in order to retain these two Negro companies and warned that the future "will be dark, indeed, when the color line is sharply drawn in this community."[24]

The holidays were given over particularly to the celebrations of the Negro citizens. On the first day of the year came the celebration of Lincoln's Emancipation Proclamation and on the Fourth of July the celebration of Independence Day, in which white citizens long failed to manifest interest because of its nationalistic connotations. Emancipation Day was usually the occasion for parades in which the social organizations of the towns joined. An Emancipation Day parade in Greenville that marched down Main Street from the African Methodist Church in West Greenville to the music of the Union Star Band was composed of the Palmetto and Neptune Fire Companies, the Odd Fellows, the Home Mission Benevolent Society, and colored citizens in general.[25] In Charleston, where the ceremonies were more imposing, one celebration began with a procession headed by the colonel commanding the National Guard,

---

[21] *Reports and Resolutions* (1900), II, 220; *ibid.* (1904), I, 214, 240.
[22] *Ibid.* (1906), I, 851.
[23] Greenville *Enterprise and Mountaineer,* January 7, 1880; July 6, 1881.
[24] Charleston *News and Courier,* January 7, 1881.
[25] Greenville *Enterprise and Mountaineer,* January 7, 1891.

two units of cavalry, and the Chicora Band, followed by the First
Regiment of the National Guard. These were followed by the
Liberian flag, borne by the Liberian Exodus Association and five
fire companies. One of the fire companies drew a wagon draped
with United States flags and decorated with evergreens and flowers.
Under an arch of evergreens was a little girl dressed to represent
the Goddess of Liberty. At the Battery, where the parade ended,
there was a speaking session which featured School Commissioner
J. E. Hayne, who urged Negroes to "Educate! Educate! Educate!"
and to keep their children in school "as long as you have a
nickel" or "as long as a bench or a desk or a teacher remains."
He was followed by B. F. Porter and Martin R. Delany, both of
whom spoke in favor of the Liberian Exodus scheme.[26]

No work was ever done by Negro farm laborers on the Fourth
of July. It was, said Elizabeth Allston Pringle, "a day of general
jubilation, . . . gorgeous costumes, little tables set about with
ice cream, lemonade, cakes; every kind of thing for sale—water-
melon above all." As late as two days after the holiday Mrs. Pringle
got word from the field hands that they could not work "so soon
after the Fourth."[27] Charleston became the center of jubilation on
the Fourth and attracted excursionists from as far away as Columbia, Savannah, and Augusta. The Battery was given over to Negro
celebrants on that day, and an observer in 1879 estimated that
10,000 were present. There was nothing approaching rowdyism or
violence, but "all their lungs seemed to be in constant exercise."
Their "rib-shaking laughter" rang out over the voices of extempor-
ized choirs and the general hubbub. The joy of the native colored
citizens was not unalloyed with the profit motive; tables covered
with food could be seen about the Battery and the chants of
hucksters could be heard in the general excitement.[28]

Beaufort made Decoration Day a similar occasion for celebration.
On Decoration Day in 1897 Negro military companies came from
Augusta and Columbia, steamers brought in excursionists from
Charleston and Savannah, and excursion trains brought Negroes
from as far away as Greenville until "ten to twelve thousand
strangers filled the streets, walking back and forth in sweltering

[26] Charleston *News and Courier*, January 2, 1878.
[27] Pennington, *A Woman Rice Planter*, pp. 86-87.
[28] Columbia *Daily Register*, July 16, 1879.

and purposeless confusion." The streets were lined with tables and booths with a profusion of pig, fowl, flesh and fish. "Barrels of pink, blue, and vari-colored tartaric acid iced lemonade slaked the thirst at three glasses for a nickel, and stomackache thrown in." The day's ceremony consisted of a parade to the National Cemetery, speechmaking at the cemetery, and the planting of small United States flags and flowers on the graves. At night the festivities were prolonged with dancing and other diversions.[29]

Christmas was the one holiday that was celebrated by white and colored alike, but was generally marked by rest and feasting instead of the strenuous activity that characterized the others. In Pendleton, William Pickens recalled, there was a quaint custom among the black folk who said that "there is no law for Christmas." The Negro men would catch the lone policeman in town and lock him in the calaboose for part of Christmas Day while one of the black men with star and club would strut about the town and play officer. The custom was an example of the tolerance that sometimes existed in patriarchal race relations. But by the second decade of the twentieth century, Pickens sadly observed, what had once been an act for laughter "would summon the militia from the four quarters of almost any state and be heralded the world over as ugly insurrection."[30]

Pickens' statement pointed up the gradual change in the social position of the Negro that had taken place during the period. But forced upon their own resources by the growing prevalence of racial segregation, Negroes demonstrated a vigorous capacity for developing fruitful social relationships within their own group. The development of social institutions and activities was another demonstration that emancipation had brought rights and privileges that would never again be taken away.

---

[29] Columbia *State*, June 2, 1897.
[30] Pickens *Bursting Bonds*, pp. 15-16.

16

THE COLOR LINE

AT the end of the Reconstruction
period the pattern of racial segregation had not been rigidly defined. The public schools were segregated, although some students
of the period have misinterpreted a provision in the Constitution
of 1868 as requiring mixed schools, and the mixed student body
of South Carolina University disbanded in 1877. The two races
for the most part attended separate churches. In personal relationships, involving the exercise of individual choice, Negroes and
whites had seldom intermingled on a basis of equality. Negroes
were seldom admitted to white homes on any basis other than a
servile relationship and whites seldom visited Negroes in their
homes for any other than business and philanthropic missions.
Wherever crowds collected there was a tendency for the two
races to gather in groups by themselves.[1]

There was no basis in law for segregation. It was then, as today,
enforced largely by social custom. The Supreme Court had not
yet discovered the doctrine of "separate, but equal" facilities, and
both the federal and state governments, in fact, had statutory pro-
hibitions against segregation on public carriers and in places of
public resort. The Republican state legislature had passed such
laws in 1869 and 1870. The second and stronger of the two established it as the policy of the state "that no person is entitled to
special privileges, or to be preferred before any other person in
public matters, but all persons are equal before the law. . . ." It
then proceeded to declare that it was unlawful for common carriers, or any person engaged in a business, calling, or pursuit for

---

[1] A South Carolinian, *Atlantic Monthly*, XXXIX (June, 1877), 676.

which a license or charter was required from the federal, state, or municipal government, to discriminate between persons on account of race, color, or previous condition. Persons guilty of violating the law were to be fined $1,000 and imprisoned five years, with an additional year if the fine were not paid. Persons in charge of any facility in which the discrimination took place were to be considered as aiding and abetting the offense, and with others who aided and abetted in discrimination, were to be liable to three years imprisonment, disfranchisement, and disqualification from holding office. In addition, the person or corporation under whose authority the offense should take place was subject to the loss of charter or license.[2]

The law was left on the statute books by the incoming Democratic administration, partly because of the conciliatory Hampton policy but largely because of the fact that it overlapped federal civil rights laws and no particular purpose would be served by its repeal. However, there is no case on record of anyone's ever having been convicted under the law.[3]

When the Supreme Court in 1883 declared provisions of the federal civil rights law of 1875 unconstitutional, Negroes expressed widespread chagrin and protest meetings were held all over the country. In South Carolina, however, the protest was discreetly held to a minimum. "Let us be patient," William Holloway advised his readers, "The objection to our commingling unreservedly with the whites, can be overcome, by education, and by such personal methods as will make us more presentable, than we could possibly be, under the degrading conditions of slavery, in its humanest administration. This cannot be done in a day, or in a year. It will take time. . . ."[4] Sam Lee cautioned the readers of the Charleston New Era not to rock the boat since the state of South Carolina had a civil rights law equally as strong as the invalidated federal law.[5] With this admonition Negroes "hauled in their horns, for fear that they might be sawed off at the next Legislature," as one white editor put it.[6] In Columbia an indignation meeting of Negroes

---

[2] Acts and Joint Resolutions (1869-1870), pp. 386-88.
[3] Charleston News and Courier, November 5, 1883.
[4] Charleston New Era, October 20, 1883.
[5] Ibid., November 3, 1883.
[6] Ibid., quoting Aiken Recorder.

was quietly called off after Wade Hampton, in a conversation with Postmaster Wilder, advised against it.[7]

Surprisingly, there was no clamor for the repeal of the state law. The *News and Courier,* in fact, advised its retention.

> The Democracy would be untrue to themselves and their pledges, and blind to their own interests, if, by repealing the State Civil Rights law at this time, they gave notice to the world that the law had only been allowed to remain on the Statute books because a United States law covered the same ground, and could be invoked by any persons who were discriminated against.[8]

The state civil rights law was left on the statute books until the end of the eighties. Its demise was made certain by the rise of the Tillman movement, and in 1888 a bill for its repeal was introduced by a young Tillmanite named John Gary Evans. The bill was referred to the Judiciary Committee of the House of Representatives but no action was taken until the following year.[9] In 1889, after several railroads had experimented with "separate but equal accomodations for passengers of the two races" travelling to the State Fair, Governor J. P. Richardson declared in his annual message that the experiment had been successful and that the state civil rights law should be amended so that carriers might be relieved of "disabilities under which they have been placed by those who no longer represent the state." Evans then reintroduced his bill, which passed the lower house without a record vote, but was defeated in the senate by a vote of 15-14. However, strong lobbying apparently pulled it through, for on the following day the senate voted 19-12 for reconsideration. Yet on a final vote, with the bill having been made a strong public issue, there were still four white senators who voted against it, three from Low Country areas of large Negro population and one, surprisingly, from the Up Country county of Laurens.[10] The difficulty in obtaining the repeal of the state civil rights law indicates that white unanimity on the issue of segregation was not complete, or at least that the partisans of Hampton were still willing to go far in the policy of adhering to the pledges of 1876.

---

[7] Charleston *News and Courier,* November 5, 1883.
[8] *Ibid.*
[9] *House Journal* (1888), p. 159.
[10] *Ibid.* (1889), pp. 49, 277; *Senate Journal* (1889), pp. 397-98, 416-17.

During the period of the effectiveness of the law Negroes frequently were admitted to places of public accommodation, not so much because of the law as because of accepted custom. B. O. Townsend noted at the end of the Reconstruction period that in Columbia Negroes were freely admitted to theaters, exhibitions, and lectures, although they were usually given a wide berth by the whites if the hall were not crowded.[11] When the New Orleans Jubilee Singers appeared at Columbia in 1880 to give a performance for the benefit of Howard School, the Opera House, "the resort of the fashion and elegance of the capital," was filled by an audience of both races.[12] The Charleston *New Era* frequently reviewed performances given at the Charleston Academy of Music, a practice indicating that Negroes were admitted there.[13] As late as 1885, and probably later, there was no formal discrimination in the theaters of Charleston.[14] In the rural areas and smaller towns Negroes did not generally gain admission to such places, but they were almost invariably admitted to circuses, although usually seated in a separate section while the clowns and other performers pointedly faced the whites. Minstrels usually made jokes on Negroes and the Republican party.[15]

In Columbia, at least, Negroes were served at the bars, soda fountains, and ice cream parlors.[16] This was still true as late as 1885, and T. McCants Stewart, who visited Columbia on a reporting mission for the New York *Age* in that year, reported rapturously:

> I can ride in first class cars on the railroads and in the streets. I can go into saloons and get refreshments even as in New York. I can stop in and drink a glass of soda and be more politely waited upon than in some parts of New England. Indeed, the Palmetto State leads the South in some things. May she go on advancing in liberal practices and prospering

---

[11] A South Carolinian, *Atlantic Monthly*, XXXIX (June, 1877), 676.

[12] Columbia *Daily Register*, March 8, 1880.

[13] For example: "The opera *Il Trovatore*, which was so superbly rendered by amateurs at the Academy of Music, will be repeated by request, next Tuesday evening." Charleston *New Era*, November 24, 1883.

[14] Charleston *News and Courier*, April 3, 1885. A Negro citizen of Charleston recalled that he was admitted to the Academy of Music without segregation until after the turn of the century. Conversation with Dr. J. A. McFall, July, 1951.

[15] A South Carolinian, *Atlantic Monthly*, XXXIX (June, 1877), 676, 681.

[16] *Ibid.*, p. 676.

throughout her borders; and may she be like leaven unto the South; like a star unto 'The Land of Flowers,' leading this our blessed section on and on in the way of liberty, justice, equality, truth and righteousness.[17]

However, Stewart was writing but one year before the inauguration of the farmers' movement by Ben Tillman. The movement, based on racial animosity as well as agrarian discontent, carried Ben Tillman into office as governor in 1890. Tillman's anti-Negro propaganda, which culminated after a decade in the disfranchising convention of 1895, also resulted in the hardening of the color line by the end of the century.

On the other hand, Negroes were invariably excluded from the hotels. The Charleston *News and Courier* explained with masterful evasion that at the hotels "the colored people are not received because their reception would interfere with the accommodation and comfort of the white people—especially of the visitors from the North and West. . . ."[18] In the larger towns Negroes could find accommodations in boarding houses maintained for them.[19]

There was in residential districts during this period no strenuous effort to achieve geographical segregation. A Northern reporter found it curious to notice both in the country and in the city "the proximity and confusion, so to speak, of white and negro houses."[20] In the older districts of coastal towns, such as Charleston and Beaufort, the absence of residential segregation is still noticeable.

In the subtle forms of personal address racial distinctions found frequent expression. Negroes were expected to address whites as Massa, Master, Boss, Miss, or Missis. The use of Mr. or Mrs. in addressing a white was by many considered an impertinence. Whites generally addressed Negroes by their first names, except the elderly ones, who were addressed as uncle, daddy, aunty, or mauma. It was extremely rare for whites to use Mr. before the name of a Negro except where they needed his vote in the legislature or had some other favor to seek. In formal relationships, however, Negro leaders or officeholders were given the courtesy title and newspapers occasionally referred to the leaders of the race as "Mr.," although

---

[17] New York *Age*, April 25, 1885.
[18] Charleston *News and Courier*, April 3, 1885.
[19] A South Carolinian, *Atlantic Monthly*, XXXIX (June, 1877), 676.
[20] Hogan, *International Review*, VIII (February, 1880), pp. 105-19.

they usually tried to avoid it by using some other title, as "Senator," "Sheriff," "Colonel," or "Professor."[21] As late as 1900 the practice had not faded, and the *News and Courier* referred to Booker T. Washington as "Mr. Washington."[22] Capitalization of the proper noun "Negro," a minor point of grammar that has since assumed major proportions as a symbol of attitudes, never became an issue during the period. Whites and Negroes alike wrote the word with an uncapitalized "n." Only one white paper, the Yorkville *Enquirer,* adopted the practice of capitalization, stating that it did so out of deference to the decision of a group of Negroes who had met in Memphis, Tennessee, in the early nineties, and after canvassing various terms for the race, as "nigger," "Afro-American," "colored man," and "freedman," had finally settled on the term "Negro."[23]

The question of miscegenation always created the most tense issue of race relations where the intimacy involved a Negro man and a white woman. Under the system of slavery there had sometimes been a degree of intimacy betwen the plantation owner, his sons, and the overseers and the female slaves. It was through relationships of this kind that the greatest portion of the mulatto population came into existence. After freedom such relationships continued, but in a less favorable atmosphere for their perpetuation. Nevertheless, relationships of this kind had never come into conflict with the widespread white fear of "amalgamation," since the children of such relationships followed the race of the mother and became Negroes.

The intimacies of white women with Negro men seem to have been rare, but some such cases, because they were unusual and because they attracted almost unanimous white disapproval, were more forcefully brought to the public eye. When legislation was introduced in the Democratic legislature of 1879 to outlaw interracial marriage, one of the most telling arguments in its favor was the statement by a member from York County that in Fort Mill township, where he resided, there were at least twenty-five or thirty white women living with colored men as husbands, most of them having come from North Carolina which already had a law against interracial marriage.[24] There was, on the other hand, a

21 A South Carolinian, *Atlantic Monthly,* XXXIX (June, 1877), 675-76.

22 Charleston *News and Courier,* July 19, 1900.

23 Yorkville *Enquirer,* September 6, 1893.

24 Columbia *Daily Register,* December 4, 1879.

surprising amount of opposition to the measure. One white Democrat held it to be "impolitic, unnecessary, unwise and unconstitutional both under the Federal and State constitution"; [25] another
argued that because of religious scruples he deemed it "preferable
that our people should enter the marriage relation rather than live
in concupiscence."[26] Negro members adopted the argument that
the measure interfered with individual liberty, and a Negro Democrat from Charleston argued,

> The prevention of the intermarriage of the races is not a polit-
> ical issue. This is a social question, which is regulated by the
> parties themselves. I object to this bill only on the ground
> that it is striking at the liberty of the colored man, while it
> is an indirect assault upon the white man's rights. Each in-
> dividual has the right to choose his own companion. Efforts
> have been made to show that inter-marriages injuriously affect
> the white race. You have so effectually held yourselves together
> in the past, that there seems but little prospect of our race
> affecting the white race now. This legislation is wholly un-
> necessary.[27]

The legislature, however, passed the bill making it "unlawful for
any white man to intermarry with any woman of either the Indian
or negro races, or any mulatto, mestizoe or half breed, or for any
white woman to intermarry with any person other than a white
man, or for any mulatto, half breed, negro, Indian or mestizoe
to intermarry with a white woman." Persons who violated the act
were guilty of a misdemeanor and subject to a fine of not less than
$500 or imprisonment for not less than twelve months. The person
who performed a marriage ceremony in violation of the act was
subject to a like penalty.[28]

A Northern reporter who observed the action of the legislature
could not see the objective as anything other than political, "as
legitimate miscegenation has never been a habit in South Carolina."[29] It would seem that his interpretation of the measure as
chiefly political in motivation was correct; certainly, only few cases

---

[25] *Ibid.*

[26] *Ibid.*, December 10, 1879.

[27] *Ibid.*

[28] *Acts and Joint Resolutions* (1879), p. 3.

[29] Hogan, *International Review*, VIII (February, 1880), 119

can be found of its application. A white woman charged with marrying a Negro in Kershaw County pleaded guilty in 1881 and was sentenced to twelve months in the county jail.[30] In York the same year a white woman and Negro man were convicted of living unlawfully in wedlock. The woman insisted that her family was generally regarded as being of mixed blood, but the presiding judge in the case charged the jury to decide all doubt as to her white ancestry "in her favor." It was so decided, and she was found guilty.[31] A white man of Union County was sentenced in 1882, although he pleaded in palliation of his case that he had married the Negro woman in question while drunk and had deserted her as soon as he became sober.[32]

Despite the law against interracial marriage there seems to have been no action taken against the illegitimate relationships of white men and Negro women. The Columbia *Daily Register* in 1879 complained of the "white male adulterers who more or less infest every community in our State," and urged that "White men living unlawfully with negro women must be taught that virtuous society will not endure the evil which the law has especially condemned and provided punishment for."[33] A Negro girl who worked during the nineties in a hotel patronized by travelling salesmen and construction workers building Clemson College complained that her job "meant constant battle against unwanted advances, a studied ignoring of impudent glances, insulting questions."[34] The informal relationships of white men and Negro women, however, received practically no mention in the press, and there seems to have been little will to bring the power of the law to bear against those who participated in such liaisons.

When it was sought in 1895 to write the law against interracial marriage into the new state constitution, Robert Smalls sought to back the white delegates into a corner by introducing an amendment providing that any white person guilty of cohabiting with a Negro should be barred from holding office, and further that the child of such a relationship should bear the name of its father and inherit property the same as if legitimate.[35] James Wigg, sharp-

---

[30] Columbia *Daily Register*, June 10, 1881.
[31] Charleston *News and Courier*, October 31, 1881.
[32] Charleston *New Era*, July 1, 1882.
[33] Columbia *Daily Register*, September 5, 1879.
[34] Hunter, *A Nickle and a Prayer*, p. 32.
[35] Columbia *State*, October 3, 1895.

tongued delegate from Beaufort, noting the consternation that Smalls had thrown into the white delegates, commented that the "coons" had the dogs up the tree for a change and intended to keep them there until they admitted that they must accept such a provision.[36] The Columbia *State* felt that the white delegates had no choice but to swallow the dose concocted by Smalls with the best grace they could muster.[37] Ben Tillman, not entirely unsympathetic with Smalls' proposal, introduced a substitute amendment to punish miscegenation as a crime in order to "protect negro women against the debauchery of white men degrading themselves to the level of black women," but the convention refused to accept either his substitute or Smalls' original motion.[38] It contented itself with a simple provision against intermarriage, leaving the punishment to the discretion of the legislature.[39]

The issue of miscegenation also posed for the convention the delicate question of defining "Negro." The legislative committee's report spoke of "one eighth or more" Negro ancestry. One delegate proposed that this be changed to read "any" Negro ancestry. George Tillman, with rare realism, opposed reducing the quota below one-eighth, pointing out that he was acquainted with several families in his Congressional District which had a small degree of Negro ancestry, yet had furnished able soldiers to the Confederacy and were now accepted in white society. He did not want to see such families needlessly embarrassed. In addition he made the astounding claim that there was not one pure-blooded Caucasian on the floor of the convention. He maintained that all had ancestors from at least one of the colored races, though not necessarily the Negro race. Therefore he called for a provision that would define "Negro" as a person with one-fourth or more Negro ancestry.[40] But as finally included in the constitution the provision was allowed to stand as reported by the committee, with the limitation set at one-eighth.[41]

The issue of segregation in public carriers was not early raised by Democratic politicians. Robert Smalls in 1884 found cause for pride in the fact that the state of South Carolina had a statute

---

[36] *Ibid.*, October 4, 1895.
[37] *Ibid.*
[38] *Ibid.*
[39] *Constitution of 1895*, Art. III, Sec. 33.
[40] Columbia *Daily Register*, October 17, 1895.
[41] *Constitution of 1895*, Art. III, Sec. 33.

providing that Negroes should get equal accommodations for equal fares on the railroads of the state.[42] T. McCants Stewart in the following year reported that "a colored lady or gentleman with a first-class ticket rides with Senator Hampton, and neither is hurt; nor, so far as I know, is amalgamation encouraged in my native State because Negroes dine with whites in a railroad saloon and ride with them in the same car."[43] As late as 1895 Ben Tillman rode from a station near Augusta to Columbia, side by side with a Negro reporter, while he explained to him his plans for the disfranchisement of Negroes.[44] Arguing against Jim Crow, the Charleston *News and Courier* found the *reductio ad absurdum* in the argument that if segregation were required on the railway cars it would have to be provided also in separate waiting rooms and separate eating facilities in the stations, a prohibitive item of expense.[45] Nevertheless, the absence of any formal provision for segregation did not prevent its occasional application. A Negro passenger complained in 1887 that he was unable to get a cup of coffee in the station at Florence because he was unable to produce his own cup from which to drink it.[46]

The repeal of the state civil rights law in 1889, removing the statutory prohibition against segregation was the signal for the introduction of legislation to give segregation the sanction of law. In the legislative session of 1889 the first bill was introduced providing for segregation on railways of the state.[47] Thereafter it became a perennial issue until passed in 1898. The inertia of white public opinion was one reason for the hesitation of the legislature to pass such a measure, but the strong opposition of the railway companies, made effective through conservative Low Country senators, was the greatest factor in preventing its passage.[48] The *News and Courier,* sympathetic to the railroad viewpoint, held in 1897 that the measure would increase "the burdens and troubles of the already over-burdened railroads without due cause," and expressed the opinion "that we have no more need for a Jim Crow car system this year

---

[42] *Congressional Record,* XVI (48th Congress, 2d Session), 316.
[43] New York *Age,* April 18, 1885.
[44] Charleston *News and Courier,* April 26, 1895.
[45] *Ibid.,* January 25, 1898.
[46] *Ibid.,* June 28, 1887.
[47] Columbia *Daily Register,* December 19, 1889.
[48] *Ibid.,* December 15, 1894.

than we had last year, and a great deal less need than we had twenty and thirty years ago."[49]

Jim Crow bills naturally found opposition among Negroes. The first measures provided for segregation only in first-class cars, and James Wigg pointed out that a poor man would have to seat his wife in a second-class car along with the Negroes. "If it is degrading to the rich," he asked, "why is it not degrading to the poor?"[50] In states that had already adopted similar Jim Crow provisions it had become customary for white men who wished to smoke, drink, or otherwise disport themselves to retire to the second-class cars. The members of the Claflin faculty, in an address to the legislature, asked:

> Why should you, who treasure the honor of your weaker sex more highly than life wish to subject our helpless children, our wives, our mothers, our daughters to the insults and vile actions of drunken and vulgar men and more vulgar women. . . .
>
> Think, gentlemen, that while we have no rights, we have at least feelings. Spare us this injustice. Follow the golden rule. Legislate, we pray you, for the whole people. Give greater police power, if you please, to the train officers; but save our mothers, our wives, our daughters from further humiliation and insults.[51]

In 1898 a bill finally got through the senate by one vote despite an unfavorable report by the senate's railroad committee. The measure became effective on September 1, 1898. It provided that separate first-class coaches or apartments, "separated by a substantial partition," should be provided for passengers on all railroads more than forty miles in length. It also provided that equal accommodations should be supplied to both races.[52] Shortly after its effective date one conductor noticed that Negroes generally preferred second-class accommodation to those in the Jim Crow apartments or cars. He suggested that the eventual solution would be elimination of the second-class cars and the provision of separate

---

[49] *Ibid.*, February 25, 1897.

[50] Columbia *Daily Register*, December 9, 1891.

[51] Address to the General Assembly, signed by seven members of the faculty of Claflin University, in Columbia *State*, January 17, 1898.

[52] *Acts and Joint Resolutions* (1898), pp. 777-78.

cars for white and colored.[53] In 1900 the law was amended to require separate coaches for the two races except on trains that did not require more than one coach. The law did not apply to extraordinary emergencies, nurses attending the children or sick of the other race, prisoners and guards, or to freight and through-vestibuled trains.[54]

Segregation rapidly became an established and unquestioned fact in all the institutions and relationships of the two races. Judge Christie Benet, presiding over a session of court at Beaufort in 1899, called attention to the fact that whites and Negroes were sitting together on the courtroom benches and directed that one side of the room be allotted to whites and the other side to Negroes. "God Almighty never intended," he said, "that the two races should be mixed. . . . "[55] Thus, by the end of the century a new social arrangement had been established by statute, by custom, by direction of the dominant whites, and by the institutional segregation of schools, churches, and private organizations. Slavery was replaced as an instrument of maintaining the subordination of the Negro by a caste system based on race under which white and black seldom came into personal contact except in the relationship of employer and laborer.

---

[53] Charleston *News and Courier*, October 11, 1898.
[54] *Acts and Joint Resolutions* (1900), p. 427.
[55] Yorkville *Enquirer*, January 11, 1899.

17

SOME EVALUATIONS

WHEN Walter Hines Page visited Charleston in 1899, he wrote to a friend that from his observation he would rather be "an imp in hades" than a Negro in South Carolina. "One decided advantage that the imp has is—personal safety." Observing the attitudes of people he met in Charleston he remarked.

> I can't find white men here whose view of the negro has essentially changed since slavery. Booker Washington told me last week that the result of his work of which he is proudest is the fast-changing attitude of the white man—the Southern white man. But he hasn't changed here—not a whit.[1]

To a sensitive and progressive-minded Southerner like Page there was ample cause for impatience. The general trend of events since 1877 had been in a reactionary direction. Emerging from Republican rule with race relations in a fluid and uncertain condition the whites had evolved a system of caste based on race. In the development of that system several dates stand out prominently in retrospect. Events marking the gradual movement of the whites to complete domination of the state's politics were the enactment of the Eight Ballot Box Law of 1882, Ben Tillman's disfranchising convention of 1895, and the establishment of the statewide white primary in 1896. The last election in which a Negro was sent to the legislature was in 1900. More rigid social attitudes brought about the repeal in 1889 of the state civil rights law and the enact-

---

[1] Walter Hines Page to Horace E. Scudder, 18 March 1899, in Hendrick (ed.), *The Training of an American: The Earlier Life and Letters of Walter H. Page. 1855-1913*, pp. 395-96.

[303]

ment in 1898 of Jim Crow legislation for the state's railroads. In other places of public resort, Negroes were increasingly segregated or excluded.

Yet in many ways, both tangible and intangible, emancipation and Reconstruction had wrought changes that could not be undone in the reaction of the eighties and nineties. These things were most clearly visible to Negroes whose lives had overlapped the eras of slavery, Reconstruction, and reaction. William Holloway, of Charleston, commenting on changed conditions since slave times, noted in 1883 that it excited no comment when a Negro smoked a cigar on Rutledge Street, rode in a street car, or even in his own carriage, or did "other things, only vouchsafed in the past few years, that would have caused sleepless nights and patrolling, had they been but hinted in the past. Yet, notwithstanding all this, the world still performs its physical and moral duties; the 'City by the Sea' is still where it was, and so on." He continued, "Far be it from us to crow over this changed condition of things, except to such a rational extent as affects the human heart. We rejoice that the white people around and about us are realizing their duty, and are looking upon us as they should. God knows as a race we sincerely desire peace, and freedom to live and enjoy as befits us—only these—nothing more."[2]

When T. McCants Stewart made one of his periodic visits to his home in Charleston, the changes were even more apparent to him. While at sea on his return from Charleston to New York he wrote for the New York *Age:*

> We Afro-Americans are restless and impatient because the march of progress is not fast enough for us. I do not complain against impatience; but I do contend that if in thought we should put ourselves in the Southern white man's place we would be astounded at our reflections. Think of it, when a boy, eight years of age, I had to dodge to go to school. Now, Charleston is full of public schools for colored children, and colored lawyers plead at the bar, physicians ride about the streets and the irrepressible Negro appears everywhere! Riding by the Court-House Square, in Charleston, my mind recalled the time when colored people were not allowed to enter the gates. If one were caught sitting on a bench, off to the station-

---

[2] Charleston *New Era*, September 22, 1883.

house to be beaten with stripes! Looking the other day into the square I saw the benches full of colored people and an apparently contented but weary colored man, fast asleep! Riding with a friend and observing the laborers, white and colored, returning from their work side by side on the same street cars, and seeing a white policeman and a colored policeman walking together in friendly converse, I said: Well, sir, these whites may continue to make fools of themselves, but they cannot build a dam strong enough to keep back the flood of democracy (I mean the rule of the people) which is sweeping the world. Everywhere the people are coming into greater rights and larger liberties. It is so even in autocratic Russia and despotic Germany and aristocratic England! The advancing tide of popular liberty will sweep away the puny levees of Mississippi prejudice and caste just as sure as God reigns.[3]

If Stewart misjudged the trend of his day it was still true that the bright thread of Negro progress that could be perceived in the dark tapestry of slavery could also be traced through the tapestry of post-Reconstruction history. Despite the fact that the trend of events from 1877 to 1900 brought violence, segregation, and political proscription, there was clearly evident progress among Negroes in fields not intimately associated with politics. The new dispensation of the Reconstruction period that had brought Negroes theoretical equality before the law was never again seriously challenged. Negro laborers secured an independent bargaining power with their employers, even though it was severely restricted because of their subordinate caste status. Small numbers became the owners of farms and homes, and some became independent entrepreneurs in business. The free public school system established by the Republican government was retained under the Democrats. While the Negro schools were neglected by Democratic administrators, they began to show some progress after the constitutional convention of 1895 made greater sums of money available through a new tax program. The Negro church grew into a permanent and solidly established institution, with all the major denominations represented by Negro members. By the end of the century the Baptist, Methodist Episcopal, and African Methodist Episcopal churches each had an institution of higher learning. In 1896 a state

---

[3] New York *Age*, September 6, 1890.

college for Negroes was established in Orangeburg. As the opportunities for education increased, Negroes in ever increasing numbers entered the professions which had formerly been closed to them.

The progress of South Carolina Negroes bore fruit during the twentieth century with the rise to leadership of many Negroes born in the state before the turn of the century: Ernest Everett Just, a biologist known especially for researches on marine eggs and the first recipient of the Spingarn Medal; Mary McLeod Bethune, educator; Kelly Miller, teacher and essayist; William Pickens, educator and leader in the National Association for the Advancement of Colored People; Benjamin Brawley, educator and author; Benjamin Elijah Mays, religious educator; Robert Shaw Wilkinson, educator and successor to Thomas E. Miller as president of the Colored Normal, Industrial, Agricultural, and Mechanical College at Orangeburg; and Jane Edna Hunter, social worker.[4]

However, in the two decades that followed the elevation of Wade Hampton to the Senate, the lessons of tolerance, moderation, and cooperation that he tried to inculcate were lost in the movement toward disfranchisement and segregation. In the new century white moderates of the Hampton tradition were overshadowed by leaders like Tillman himself, Coleman Livingstone Blease, and Ellison Durant Smith, who heaped abuse upon the voteless Negroes. By the mid-twentieth century Hampton's policies had been so completely forgotten that the charge was hurled at a political candidate that while governor he had appointed a Negro to a minor state office and had thereby ended "Wade Hampton's era of segregation" in the government of the state![5] This legendary Hampton was a far cry from the Hampton who in 1876 foresaw the day when all Negroes would become Democrats "because they will find that their rights will be better protected by that party."[6] Democratic politi-

---

[4] Writers' Program of the Works Projects Administration, *South Carolina: A Guide to the Palmetto State* (New York, 1941), p. 52; Hunter, *A Nickle and a Prayer.*

[5] Columbia *State,* June 25, 1950. The charge was inspired by Governor J. Strom Thurmond's appointment of Dr. T. Carr McFall to the Advisory Hospital Council.

[6] Hampton, *Free Men! Free Ballots!! Free Schools!!!,* p. 8. Quotation from a speech at Sumter, October 7, 1876.

[7] *Reports and Resolutions* (1879), p. 365.

cians, who were in the 1940's fighting a desperate rear-guard action against enforcement of the Fifteenth Amendment, had long since abandoned the policy of Hampton's Superintendent of Education "to elevate the negro and render him secure in his political rights . . ." through education in the responsibilities of citizenship.[7]

On the other hand, by the late forties a new trend was apparent even before South Carolinians began to rediscover the Hampton tradition in H. M. Jarrell's study of his policies.[8]

In 1942 there had been a movement among Richland County Democrats to permit the enrollment of qualified Negro voters for the primary.[9] The admission of Negro voters to the primary under a federal court order of 1947,[10] while not abrogating the disfranchising provisions of the Constitution of 1895, has now undermined the most effective instrument of disfranchisement—the white primary. But Negro voters have been generally accepted by whites without serious incident. While the Negro vote will probably continue to be a minor factor for some time, candidates already have demonstrated a noticeable unwillingness to antagonize Negro voters, and Negro candidates for public office have again appeared at party meetings.

A program for equalization of white and Negro school facilities has been instituted as the response to a suit challenging the constitutionality of segregation, which had given rise to gross inequalities in the public schools after the days of Hampton and Hugh S. Thompson. The state has authorized the issuance of bonds up to the amount of $75,000,000 for an equalization program, and a Negro has been appointed to the staff which administers the program.[11]

Under federal grants-in-aid and dollar-matching programs for education, welfare, and slum clearance projects, Negroes, by federal requirement, have received a considerable share in the benefits. The state has recently established an industrial school for delinquent Negro girls under the direction of a Negro staff. Negroes are eligible

[8] Jarrell, *Wade Hampton and the Negro.*
[9] Columbia *State*, May 5, 1942.
[10] *Elmore v. Rice*, 72 Federal Supplement 516.
[11] *Briggs v. Elliott*, 98 Federal Supplement 529; *Acts and Joint Resolutions* (1951), pp. 659-77.

to membership in such organizations as the Southern Regional Council, the state bar association, and the state association of social workers.[12] Daily newspapers give more serious coverage in news stories and pictures to Negro activities, and several have adopted the practice of giving Negroes the courtesy title of "Mr." and "Mrs." Seventeen towns and counties have appointed Negro policemen and policewomen.[13]

In these and in numerous other ways, even in the face of bitter controversy over civil rights, there has been demonstrated a profound shift of public sentiment which promises a revival of the spirit of interracial good will and cooperation that was lost in the aftermath of Governor Hampton's administration.

---

[12] *New South,* V (July, 1950), 1.
[13] *Ibid.,* VII (September, 1952), 7.

APPENDIX

NEGRO MEMBERS OF THE SOUTH CAROLINA GENERAL ASSEMBLY AFTER RECONSTRUCTION *

Year Elected	Senate (All Repub.)	House of Representatives	
		Republicans	Democrats
1878	Isaac Bird (Fairfield)	T. E. Miller (Beaufort)	S. C. Eckhard (Charleston)
	Bruce H. Williams (Georgetown)	Benjamin Simons (Beaufort)	W. T. Elfe (Charleston)
	S. L. Duncan (Orangeburg)	Hastings Gantt (Beaufort)	Rev. W. Smalls (Charleston)
			William Maree (Colleton)
			B. G. Frederick (Orangeburg)
			J. W. Westberry (Sumter)
1880	T. E. Miller (Beaufort)	Hastings Gantt (Beaufort)	Geo. M. Mears (Charleston)
	Bruce Williams (Georgetown)	Joseph Robinson (Beaufort)	W. A. Driffle (Colleton)
		J. C. Rue (Beaufort)	Joseph Parker (Charleston)
		Wm. Moultrie (Georgetown)	Paul B. Drayton (Charleston)
			Joseph Alexander Owens (Barnwell)
1882	Hamilton Robinson (Beaufort)	Hastings Gantt (Beaufort)	Geo. M. Mears (Charleston)
	Robert Simmons (Berkeley)	L. S. Mills (Beaufort)	B. G. Frederick (Orangeburg)
	Bruce H. Williams (Georgetown)	Joseph Robinson (Beaufort)	Caesar P. Chisolm (Colleton)
		W. G. Pinckney (Berkeley)	
		James Singleton (Berkeley)	
		Andrew Singleton (Berkeley)	
		W. W. Beckett (Berkeley)	
		Cain Ravenel (Berkeley)	
		W. J. Moultrie (Georgetown)	

* This list includes those who have been identified in contemporary documents as Negroes. Because of the difficulty involved in identifying the race of all members this list may be incomplete. It should be noted that senators were elected for terms of four years.

APPENDIX—Continued

		House of Representatives	
Year Elected	Senate (All Repub.)	Republicans	Democrats
1884	Robert Simmons (Berkeley) Bruce H. Williams (Georgetown) Thomas J. Reynolds (Beaufort)	W. H. Sheppard (Beaufort) F. S. Mitchell (Beaufort) Joseph Robinson (Beaufort) J. A. Baxter (Georgetown)	Geo. M. Mears (Charleston) Aaron Simmons (Orangeburg)
1886	Thomas J. Reynolds (Beaufort) Bruce H. Williams (Georgetown)	T. E. Miller (Beaufort) J. C. Rice (Beaufort) J. J. Washington (Beaufort) J. A. Baxter (Georgetown)	Geo. M. Mears (Charleston) Marshall Jones (Orangeburg)
1888	(None)	J. J. Washington (Beaufort) A. C. Reynolds (Beaufort) J. A. Baxter (Georgetown)	Geo. M. Mears (Charleston) Aaron Simmons (Orangeburg)
1890	(None)	James Wigg (Beaufort) T. R. Fields (Beaufort) Andrew Singleton (Berkeley) Mark P. Richardson (Berkeley) Thomas H. Wallace (Berkeley) R. B. Anderson (Georgetown)	Geo. M. Mears (Charleston)
1892	(None)	M. C. Hamilton (Beaufort) J. R. Rivers (Beaufort) R. B. Anderson (Georgetown)	(None)
1894	(None)	T. E. Miller (Beaufort) R. B. Anderson (Georgetown)	(None)
1896	(None)	R. B. Anderson (Georgetown)	(None)
1898	(None)	J. W. Bolts (Georgetown)	(None)
1900	(None)	J. W. Bolts (Georgetown)	(None)

BIBLIOGRAPHY

I. PRIMARY SOURCES

A. Manuscripts

Benjamin Allston Papers. Manuscript Collections, Duke University, Durham, N. C. Included in this small collection are several letters to "Ben" Allston from Bishop W. B. W. Howe regarding the status of Negroes in the Protestant Episcopal Church. These were written in 1877 and 1878.

American Colonization Society Papers. Manuscripts Division, Library of Congress, Washington, D. C. This large collection contains 540 volumes of letter books, letters received, account books, and reports, and also thousands of loose papers, dating from 1816 to 1908. Most valuable for this study are the letter books and the volumes of letters received, in which there are numerous items relating to South Carolina.

Dr. Peter Brockington Bacot Papers. Southern Historical Collection, University of North Carolina, Chapel Hill. These contain four small notebooks containing accounts and diary entries, 1866 to 1881, and receipts, notes, and other business papers enclosed in the volumes.

Borough House Papers. Southern Historical Collection, University of North Carolina. These papers include 20 volumes, with materials from 1815 to 1910, microfilmed at the Borough House, Stateburg, South Carolina, in April, 1949. They include accounts and plantation records of several individuals, but are valuable chiefly for the roll book of the Stateburg Democratic Club.

William C. and E. T. Coker Cotton Account Book, 1879-1884. South Caroliniana Library, University of South Carolina, Columbia. The Cokers were merchants and planters of Society Hill, Darlington County.

William C. and E. T. Coker Day Labor Account Book for 1880. South Caroliniana Library, University of South Carolina.

General Records, Department of Justice, 1790-1942. National Archives, Washington, D. C. These papers are valuable for the correspondence to and from federal attorneys and marshalls in South Carolina.

James B. and R. B. Heyward Papers. Southern Historical Collection, University of North Carolina. A small collection of miscellaneous plantation labor contracts, bills, and receipts, 1879-1897. The Heywards were rice planters in Colleton County.

William Godber Hinson Papers. Charleston Library Society, Charleston. These papers include a few clippings and pamphlets relating to South Carolina Negroes.

Mrs. C. A. Lawson to the Author, November 16, 1949. A letter from a former graduate student at Howard University identifying certain Negro members of the General Assembly.

[311]

William Lawrence Mauldin Diaries. Southern Historical Collection, University of North Carolina. These four volumes of the diaries, dated 1870 to 1912, of a businessman and local politician of Greenville, have occasional references to the role of Negroes in state politics.

Maham W. Pyatt to the Author, November 21, 1949. A letter from a white Democrat describing the workings of the fusion of Democrats and Republicans in Georgetown County, 1880-1902.

Richland Democratic Club. Minutes: Scrapbook, 1876-1880. South Caroliniana Library, University of South Carolina. This is the record of a Democratic ward club in Columbia.

Isaac Dubose Seabrook. "Before and After—or, The Relation of the Races in the South." South Caroliniana Library, University of South Carolina. This unpublished manuscript volume is valuable for an insight into the racial attitudes of a cultivated white conservative.

Yates Snowden Collection. South Caroliniana Library, University of South Carolina. These papers of a correspondent for the Charleston *News and Courier,* later professor of history at the University of South Carolina, contain one folder of correspondence from or about Negroes and another of clippings on the Negro.

Booker Taliaferro Washington Papers. Manuscripts Division, Library of Congress. This large collection contains a few letters from individuals in South Carolina, but is of only minor value to this study.

W. J. Whipper Papers. Moorland Foundation, Howard University. This small collection contains a typescript, "A Providential Revelation, Relationship with the Whipper Family," by Demps Whipper Powell, an orphan adopted by Whipper, and fifty-five legal papers pertaining to the legal practice of Whipper in Beaufort.

Carter Godwin Woodson Papers. Manuscripts Division, Library of Congress. This collection of materials on the history of the Negro in America was started by Carter G. Woodson but receives frequent additions from other sources. Most valuable is the correspondence of Whitefield J. McKinlay, a Negro who left South Carolina for Washington. Among his correspondents were Robert Smalls, W. D. Crum, and George Washington Murray.

B. Official Records and Documents

1. Publications of the United States Government

Biographical Directory of the American Congress, 1789-1927. Washington: Government Printing Office, 1928.

Bureau of the Census. *Negro Population,* 1790-1915. Washington: Government Printing Office, 1918.

——————. *Negroes in the United States,* Bulletin 8, 1904. Washington: Government Printing Office, 1904.

——————. *Negroes in the United States, 1920-1932.* Washington: Government Printing Office, 1935.

——————. *Religious Bodies,* 1906, 1916, 1926, 1936. Washington: Government Printing Office.

Census, 1870, 1880, 1890, 1900. Washington: Government Printing Office.

Congressional Record, 1876-1900. Washington: Government Printing Office.

Digest of Contested Election Cases Arising in the Forty-Eighth, Forty-Ninth, and Fiftieth Congresses. House Miscellaneous Document No. 63, 50th Congress, 2d Session. Washington: Government Printing Office, 1889.

Digest of Contested Election Cases in the Fifty-First Congress. House Miscellaneous Document No. 137, 51st Congress, 2d Session. Washington: Government Printing Office, 1891.

Jones, Thomas Jesse (ed.). *Negro Education. A Study of the Private and Higher Schools for Colored People in the United States,* Bureau of Education Bulletin No. 38, 1916. Washington: Government Printing Office, 1917.

Journal of the House of Representatives of the United States of America, 1876-1900. Washington: Government Printing Office.

Journal of the Senate of the United States of America, 1876-1900. Washington: Government Printing Office.

Mayo, Amory Dwight. "The Final Establishment of the American Common School System in North Carolina, South Carolina, and Georgia, 1863-1900," *Report of the Commissioner of Education for the Year Ending June 30, 1904.* Washington: Government Printing Office, 1906.

Recent Election in South Carolina. Testimony Taken by the Select Committee on the Recent Election in South Carolina. House Miscellaneous Document No. 31, 44th Congress, 2d Session. Washington: Government Printing Office, 1877.

Report of the Industrial Commission on Agriculture and Agricultural Labor. House Document No. 179, 57th Congress, 2d Session. Washington: Government Printing Office, 1901.

Reports of the Committees of the House of Representatives, 1876-1900. Washington: Government Printing Office.

Rowell, Chester H. *A Historical and Legal Digest of all the Contested Election Cases in the House of Representatives of the United States from the First to the Fifty-Sixth Congress, 1789-1901.* House Document No. 510, 56th Congress, 2d Session. Washington: Government Printing Office, 1901.

Russell, Charles W. *Report on Peonage.* Washington: Government Printing Office, 1908.

South Carolina in 1876. Testimony as to the Denial of the Elective Franchise in South Carolina at the Elections of 1875 and 1876. Senate Miscellaneous Document No. 31, 44th Congress, 2d Session. 3 vols. Washington: Government Printing Office, 1877.

Thorpe, Francis Newton (ed.). *The Federal and State Constitutions, Colonial Charters, and Other Organic Laws.* 7 vols. Washington: Government Printing Office, 1909.

2. Judicial Decisions

Briggs v. Elliott. 98 Federal Supplement 529.

Butler v. Ellerbe, Comptroller General, et al. 22 Southeastern Reporter 425.

Elmore v. Rice. 72 Federal Supplement 516.

Ex Parte Hollman. 79 South Carolina Reports 22.

Gowdy v. Green. 69 Federal Reporter 865.

Green v. Mills. 69 Federal Reporter 852.

Liberian Exodus Joint-Stock Steamship Company v. Rodgers. 21 South Carolina Reports 27.

Mills v. Green. 67 Federal Reporter 818.

3. Publications of the South Carolina State Government and Subordinate Units

Acts and Joint Resolutions of the General Assembly of the State of South Carolina, 1866-1900.

Annual Report of the State Superintendent of Education, 1910, 1912.

City of Charleston. *Year Book,* 1880-1900.

Code of Laws of South Carolina. Clinton: Jacobs Press, 1942.

The Constitution of South Carolina, Adopted April 16, 1868. Columbia: John W. Denny, 1868.

Constitution of the State of South Carolina, Ratified in Convention December 4, 1895. Columbia: R. L. Bryan, 1909.

Department of Agriculture. *The Cotton Mills of South Carolina. Their Names, Location, Capacity, and History.* Charleston: *News and Courier,* 1880.

Department of Agriculture, Commerce and Immigration. *Handbook of South Carolina.* Columbia: State Company, 1907.

Journal of the Constitutional Convention of the State of South Carolina. Columbia: Charles A. Calvo, Jr., 1895.

Journal of the House of Representatives of the General Assembly of the State of South Carolina, 1876-1900.

Journal of the Senate of the General Assembly of the State of South Carolina, 1876-1900.

Report of the Special Committee of the House of Representatives of South Carolina, Relative to the Organization of That Body and the Constitutional Validity Thereof. Adopted December 21, 1876. Columbia: Republican Printing Company, 1876.

Reports and Resolutions of the General Assembly of the State of South Carolina, 1876-1900. These include annual and special reports of the major departments and agencies of the state government.

Reports of Cases Heard and Determined by the Supreme Court of South Carolina, 1876-1907.

Revised Statutes of the State of South Carolina. Columbia: Republican Printing Company, 1873.

State Board of Agriculture, of South Carolina. *South Carolina. Resources and Population. Institutions and Industries.* Charleston: Walker, Evans and Cogswell, 1883.

Statutes at Large of South Carolina, 1866-1900.

C. Newspapers and Periodicals

Abbeville *Press and Banner,* 1878-1887.

The African Repository, 1876-1892.

*A. M. E. Church Review,** 1884-1900.

Appleton's Annual Cyclopaedia and Register of Important Events of the Year, 1876-1900.

Beaufort *New South,** March 7, 1895.

J. C. Calloway Scrapbook. Moorland Foundation, Howard University. This contains clippings chiefly from Philadelphia newspapers, especially the

---

* Negro Publications.

Philadelphia *Press*. Occasional clippings deal with South Carolina events and personalities.

Charleston *Afro-American Citizen*,* January 17, 1900.

Charleston *Monitor*,* May 26, 1888.

Charleston *News and Courier*, 1876-1900.

Charleston *New Era*,* 1880-1884.

Charleston *Recorder*,* November 6, 1886; August 27, 1887.

Columbia *Daily Register*, 1876-1897.

Columbia *People's Recorder*,* March 19, 1898.

Columbia *Record*, May 6, 1948; February 10, 1950.

Columbia *State*, 1891-1900.

The Friend (Philadelphia), March 11, 1876.

Georgetown *Advocate*,* 1902-1903.

Greenville *Democrat*, May 31, 1893.

Greenville *Enterprise and Mountaineer*, 1875-1891.

The Nation (New York), 1876-1900.

New South, October, 1949; September, 1952.

New York *Age*,* 1883-1900.

New York *Daily Tribune*, 1876-1900.

North American Review, July, 1865.

Outlook, March 2, 1901.

Port Royal *Palmetto Post*, 1882-1896.

Rock Hill *Messenger*,* January 26, 1900.

Washington (D. C.) *Bee*,* 1882-1900.

Yorkville *Enquirer*, 1876-1900.

D. Travel Accounts, Reports, and Miscellaneous Writings

An Address to the People of the United States, Adopted at a Conference of Colored Citizens, Held at Columbia, S. C., July 20, and 21, 1876. Columbia: Republican Printing Company, 1876.

Allen, Walter. *Governor Chamberlain's Administration in South Carolina: A Chapter of Reconstruction in the Southern States.* New York: Putnam, 1888.

Archer, William. *Through Afro-America, An English Reading of the Race Problem.* London: Chapman and Hall, 1910.

American Newspaper Directory. New York: George P. Rowell, 1884.

Arnett, Benjamin William. *The Annual Address Delivered Before the Faculty, Students and Friends of Claflin University and the Claflin College of Agriculture and Mechanical Institute, May 22nd, 1889, Orangeburg, S. C.* Columbia: William Sloane, 1889.

——————(ed). *Proceedings of the Quarto-Centennial Conference of the African M. E. Church, of South Carolina, at Charleston S. C., May 15, 16, and 17, 1889.* Xenia, Ohio: Aldine Printing House, 1890.

---

* Negro Publications.

Azor. Edward Willis Pamphlets, South Carolina Historical Society, Charleston. This is a volume of clippings, broadsides, and other materials dealing with the Liberian Exodus Association and its vessel, the *Azor.*

Bellinger, E. E. *Counter Statement: A Reply to the "Statement" by the Deputies who Withdrew from the Late Diocesan Convention of South Carolina.* Charleston: Lucas, Richardson, and Company, 1888.

Campbell, George. *White and Black; The Outcome of a Visit to the United States.* London: Chatto and Windus, 1879.

Chamberlain, Daniel Henry. *Dependent Pension Bills; and the Race Problem at the South. Speech of ex-Governor D. H. Chamberlain before the Massachusetts Reform Club at Boston, February 8, 1890.* New York: Albert B. King, n. d.

——————. "The Fourteenth and Fifteenth Amendments," New York *Nation,* LXXVII (August 20, 1903), 151.

——————. *Present Phases of Our So-Called Negro Problem. Open Letter to the Right Honorable James Bryce, M. P., of England.* n. p., 1904.

——————. "The Race Problem at the South," *New Englander,* LII (June, 1890), 507-27.

——————. "Reconstruction and the Negro," *North American Review,* CXXVIII (February, 1879), 161-73.

Childs, Arney Robinson (ed.). *The Private Journal of Henry William Ravenel.* Columbia: University of South Carolina Press, 1947.

Christensen, Neils. "Fifty Years of Freedom: Conditions in the Sea Coast Regions," *Annals of the American Academy of Political and Social Science,* XLIX (September, 1913), 58-66.

——————. "The Negroes of Beaufort County, South Carolina," *Southern Workman,* XXXII (October, 1903), 481-86.

Constitution and Canons of the Protestant Episcopal Church in the Diocese of South Carolina. Charleston: Walker, Evans, and Cogswell, 1897.

Dixon, William Hepworth. *White Conquest.* London: Chatto and Windus, 1876.

DuBois, William Edmund Burghardt (ed.). *The Negro Artisan.* Atlanta: Atlanta University, 1902.

——————. *The Negro in Business.* Atlanta: Atlanta University, 1899.

——————. *The Negro Church.* Atlanta: Atlanta University, 1903.

Evans, Maurice Smethurst. *Black and White in the Southern States: a Study of the Race Problem in the United States from a South African Point of View.* London and New York: Longmans, Green, 1915.

Fairly, John S. *The Negro in His Relations to the Church.* Charleston: Walker, Evans, and Cogswell, 1889.

Haley, James T. *Afro-American Encyclopedia.* Nashville, Tennessee: Haley and Florida, 1895.

Hampton, Wade. *Free Men! Free Ballots!! Free Schools!!! The Pledges of Gen. Wade Hampton, Democratic Candidate for Governor to the Colored People of South Carolina, 1865-1876.* Charleston: Charleston County Democratic Executive Committee, 1876. [Dawson Pamphlets, University of North Carolina Library.]

——————. "The Race Problem in the South," Extract from *Forum Extra,* I (March, 1890). [Dawson Pamphlets, University of North Carolina Library.]

―――――――. "What Negro Supremacy Means," *Forum*, V (June, 1888), 383-95.

Hayne, Joseph Elias. *Are the White People of the South the Negroe's Best Friends? or, The Only Just Human Methods of Solving the Race Problems.* Philadelphia: A. M. E. Book Concern, 1903.

―――――――. *The Negro in Sacred History, or Ham and his Immediate Descendants.* Charleston: Walker, Evans, and Cogswell, 1887.

Hendrick, Burton Jesse. *The Training of an American: The Earlier Life and Letters of Walter H. Page. 1855-1913.* Boston and New York: Houghton Mifflin, 1928.

Herbert, Hilary Abner (ed.). *Why the Solid South? or, Reconstruction and Its Results.* Baltimore: R. R. Woodward, 1890.

Higginson, Mary Thatcher (ed.). *Letters and Journals of Thomas Wentworth Higginson, 1846-1906.* Boston and New York: Houghton Mifflin, 1921.

Hogan, Edward. "South Carolina To-Day," *International Review*, VIII (February, 1880), 105-19.

Holland, Rupert Sargent (ed.). *Letters and Diary of Laura M. Towne, Written from the Sea Islands of South Carolina, 1862-1884.* Cambridge: The Riverside Press, 1912.

Hunter, Jane Edna. *A Nickle and a Prayer.* Cleveland: Elli Kani, 1940.

Journal of the Annual Convention of the Protestant Episcopal Church, in the Diocese of South Carolina, 1876-1900. In 1895 the Annual Convention changed its title to Annual Council.

Kershaw, John. "The Issue in South Carolina," *Church Review*, L (October, 1887), 385-412.

Lawrence, W. H. *The Centenary Souvenir, Containing a History of Centenary Church, Charleston, and an Account of the Life and Labors of Rev. R. V. Lawrence, Father of the Pastor of Centenary Church.* Philadelphia: Collins Printing House, 1885.

McClure, Alexander Kelly. *The South: Its Industrial, Financial, and Political Condition.* Philadelphia: Lippincott, 1886.

McCrady, Edward. *The Necessity of Education as the Basis of Our Political System, An Address Delivered before the Euphemian Society, Erskine College, June 28, 1880.* Charleston: Walker, Evans, and Cogswell, 1880. [Dawson Pamphlets, University of North Carolina Library.]

―――――――. *The Necessity for Raising the Standard of Citizenship and the Right of the General Assembly of the State of South Carolina to Impose Qualifications upon Electors.* Charleston: Walker, Evans, and Cogswell, 1881. [Dawson Pamphlets, University of North Carolina Library.]

―――――――. *The Registration of Electors.* Charleston: 1880. [Dawson Pamphlets, University of North Carolina Library.]

McKinley, Carlyle. *An Appeal to Pharaoh: the Negro Problem and its Radical Solution.* Columbia: State Company, 1907. First edition, New York: Fords, Howard, and Hulbert, 1890.

Memorial from St. Mark's Church, Charleston, S. C. to the Bishops, Clergy and Laity of the Protestant Episcopal Church in the U. S. asking the Wisdom and Love of the Church to Devise Some Method of Relief and for Direction as to their Duty in their Painful Position. Charleston: 1886. [Dawson Pamphlets, University of North Carolina Library.]

Miller, Mary J. *Suffrage Speeches by Negroes in the Constitutional Convention.* n. p., n. d.

Miller, Thomas Ezekiel. *Address Delivered on Negro Day in the South Carolina Interstate and West Indian Exposition, January 1, 1902.* Orangeburg: W. P. Cannon, 1901 [*sic*]. [Moorland Foundation, Howard University.]

Minutes of the First, Second and Third Sessions of the Abbeville Singing Convention of the A. M. E. Church, held in St. Peter's Church, 1887, 1888, and 1889, to which is Appended a Sketch of the Life and Work of Rev. James T. Baker. Abbeville: Hugh Wilson, 1889. [South Caroliniana Library, University of South Carolina.]

Minutes of the General Assembly of the Presbyterian Church in the United States of America. New York: S. W. Green, 1877.

Minutes of the General Assembly of the Presbyterian Church in the United States of America. Philadelphia: MacCall, 1894.

Minutes of the Seventy-sixth Session of the South Carolina Annual Conference of the Methodist Episcopal Church for 1882. Greenville: John C. Bailey, 1882. [Dawson Pamphlets, University of North Carolina Library.]

Minutes of the Twenty-fourth Session of the South Carolina Annual Conference of the African Methodist Episcopal Church, held in Mt. Zion Church, Charleston, S. C., February 8th to February 14th, 1888. Charleston: Kahrs, Stolze, and Welch, 1888. [Dawson Pamphlets, University of North Carolina Library.]

O'Connor, Mary Doline. *The Life and Letters of M. P. O'Connor.* New York: Dempsey and Carroll, 1893.

Payne, Daniel Alexander. *History of the African Methodist Episcopal Church.* Nashville, Tennessee: Publishing House of the A. M. E. Sunday School Union, 1891.

Penn, Irvine Garland. *The Afro-American Press and Its Editors.* Springfield, Massachusetts: Willey and Company, 1891.

Pennington, Patience [Pringle, Elizabeth Waties Allston]. *A Woman Rice Planter.* New York: Macmillan, 1913.

Pickens, William. *Bursting Bonds.* Boston: Jordan and More, 1923. [Enlarged edition of *The Heir of Slaves*, 1911.]

Poor's Manual of Railroads. New York: H. V. and H. W. Poor, 1900.

Porter, Anthony Toomer. *Led On! Step by Step, Scenes from Clerical, Military, Educational and Plantation Life in the South, 1828-1898.* New York: Putnam's, 1898.

Prospectus and Appeal of the Industrial Mission School Society. Charleston: Walker, Evans, and Cogswell, 1888. [Yates Snowden Pamphlets, South Caroliniana Library, University of South Carolina.]

A Reply to the Statement of Messrs. Memminger, McCrady, and Others, as to the Causes of the Withdrawal of Certain Deputies from the Diocesan Convention of South Carolina, of 1887. Charleston: Walker, Evans, and Cogswell, 1888.

Republican Party. South Carolina. State Central Committee. *An Address Upon the Election Law of South Carolina, and the Methods Employed to Suppress the Republican Vote.* Columbia: W. Sloane, 1889.

Rhett, Robert Barnwell(?). *The Code of Honor; its Rationale and Uses, by the Tests of Common Sense and Good Morals, With the Effects of its Preventive Remedies.* Charleston: Parry, Cooker, 1878.

Rollin, Frank A. *Life and Public Services of Martin R. Delany.* Boston: Lee and Sheppard, 1883.

Seabrook, E. M. *The Law and the Gospel as Applied to the Questions before the Diocesan Convention of the Episcopal Church of the Diocese of South Carolina.* Charleston: Walker, Evans, and Cogswell, 1887.

Smith, Samuel M. *The Negro in Ecclesiastical Relations.* Extract from Presbyterian *Quarterly,* No. 10 (October, 1889). [Dawson Pamphlets, University of North Carolina Library.]

South Carolina in 1884. Charleston: *News and Courier,* 1884.

South Carolina in 1888. Charleston: Walker, Evans, and Cogswell, 1888.

A South Carolinian [Belton O'Neall Townsend]. "The Political Condition of South Carolina," *Atlantic Monthly,* XXXIX (February, 1877), 177-94.

——————. "South Carolina Morals," *ibid.* (April, 1877), 467-75.

——————. "South Carolina Society," *ibid.* (June, 1877), 670-84.

Statement of the Causes which Led to the Withdrawal of the Deputies from the Diocesan Convention of South Carolina, Prepared by the Committee Appointed for that Purpose. Charleston: Walker, Evans, and Cogswell, 1887.

Straker, Daniel Augustus. "The Negro in Science, Art, and Literature," *A. M. E. Church Review,* I (July, 1884), pp. 56-60.

——————. *Negro Suffrage in the South.* Detroit: The Author, 1906.

——————. *The New South Investigated.* Detroit: Ferguson Printing Company, 1888.

Taylor, Rosser Howard and McDavid, Raven I. (eds.). *Memoirs of Richard Cannon Watts, Chief Justice of the Supreme Court of South Carolina, 1927-1930.* Columbia: R. L. Bryan, 1938.

Trapier, R. S., *et al.* (compilers). *A Protest Against the Admission of any Other than the White Race in the Councils of the Protestant Episcopal Church of the Diocese of South Carolina.* Charleston: Lucas and Richardson, 1890.

Williams, Alfred Brockenbrough. *The Liberian Exodus. An Account of Voyage of the First Emigrants in the Bark "Azor," and Their Reception at Monrovia With a Description of Liberia—Its Customs and Civilization, Romances and Prospects. (A Series of Letters from A. B. Williams, the Special Correspondent of the News and Courier.)* Charleston: *News and Courier,* 1878.

II. SECONDARY SOURCES

A. General Works and Special Studies

Andrews, Columbus. *Administrative County Government in South Carolina.* Chapel Hill: University of North Carolina, 1933.

Bailey, Thomas Pearce. *Race Orthodoxy in the South.* New York: Neale, 1914.

Baker, Ray Stannard. *Following the Color Line.* New York: Doubleday, Page, 1908.

Ball, William Watts. *A Boy's Recollections of the Red Shirt Campaign in South Carolina. Paper Read Before the Kosmos Club of Columbia, S. C.* Columbia: State Company, 1911.

——————. *The State That Forgot: South Carolina's Surrender to Democracy.* Indianapolis: Bobbs-Merrill, 1932.

Berry, Lewellyn L. *A Century of Missions of the African Methodist Episcopal Church,* 1840-1940. New York: Gutenberg, 1942.

Bragg, George Freeman, Jr. *History of the Afro-American Group of the Episcopal Church*. Baltimore: Church Advocate Press, 1922.

Brawley, Benjamin Griffith. *Negro Builders and Heroes*. Chapel Hill: University of North Carolina, 1937.

——————. *A Short History of the American Negro*. 4th Revised Edition. New York: Macmillan, 1939.

——————. *A Social History of the American Negro*. New York: Macmillan, 1921.

Bruce, Philip Alexander. *The Rise of the New South*. Philadelphia: George Barrie and Sons, 1905. [*The History of North America*, Vol. XVII.]

Cable, George Washington. *The Negro Question*. New York: American Missionary Association, 1888.

——————. *The Silent South, Together with The Freedmen's Case in Equity and The Convict Lease System*. New York: Scribners, 1907.

Caldwell, Arthur Bunyan (ed.). *History of the American Negro: South Carolina Edition*. Atlanta: A. B. Caldwell Publishing Company, 1919.

Calhoun, William Patrick. *The Caucasian and the Negro in the United States. They Must Be Separate. If not, then Extermination. A Proposed Solution: Colonization*. Columbia: R. L. Bryan, 1902.

Christensen, Mrs. A. M. H. *Afro-American Folk Lore, Told Round Cabin Fires on the Sea Islands of South Carolina*. Boston: The Author, 1898.

Clark, Thomas Dionysius. *The Southern Country Editor*. Indianapolis: Bobbs-Merrill, 1948.

——————. *Pills, Petticoats, and Plows; The Southern Country Store*. Indianapolis: Bobbs-Merrill, 1944.

Coan, Josephus Roosevelt. *Daniel Alexander Payne: Christian Educator*. Philadelphia: A. M. E. Book Concern, 1935.

Coleman, James Karl. *State Administration in South Carolina*. New York: Columbia University Press, 1935.

Cooley, Rossa Belle. *School Acres, an Adventure in Rural Education*. New Haven: Yale University Press, 1930.

Crum, Mason. *Gullah: Negro Life in the Carolina Sea Islands*. Durham: Duke University Press, 1940.

Cutler, James Elbert. *Lynch-Law: An Investigation into the History of Lynching in the United States*. New York: Longmans, Green, 1905.

Daly, Louise Porter Haskell. *Alexander Cheves Haskell: The Portrait of a Man*. Norwood, Massachusetts: Plimpton Press, 1934.

Drake, Joseph Turpin. "The Negro in Greenville, South Carolina." Unpublished Master's thesis, Department of Sociology, University of North Carolina, 1940.

Education Division, Works Progress Administration of South Carolina. *70 Years of Progress, 1866-1936*. Mimeographed, n. p., n. d.

Evans, Matilda Arabelle. *Martha Schofield, Pioneer Negro Educator*. Columbia: DuPre, 1916.

Fortune, T. Thomas. *Black and White: Land, Labor and Politics in the South*. New York: Fords, Howard, and Hulbert, 1884.

Franklin, John Hope. *From Slavery to Freedom: A History of American Negroes*. New York: Knopf, 1948.

Garlington, J. C. *Men of the Time, Sketches of Living Notables in South Carolina.* Spartanburg: Garlington, 1902.

Gordon, Asa H. *Sketches of Negro Life and History in South Carolina.* Hammond, Indiana: W. B. Conkey, 1929.

Greene, Evarts Boutell and Harrington, Virginia Draper. *American Population Before the Federal Census of 1790.* New York: Columbia University, 1932.

Hamphill, James Calvin. *Men of Mark in South Carolina.* 4 Vols. Washington: Men of Mark Publishing Company, 1907-1909.

Henry, Howell Meadoes. *The Police Control of the Slave in South Carolina.* Emory, Virginia: The Author, 1914.

Heyward, Duncan Clinch. *Seed from Madagascar.* Chapel Hill: University of North Carolina, 1937.

Hicks, John Donald. *The Populist Revolt.* Minneapolis: University of Minnesota, 1931.

Hoffman, Frederick Ludwig. *Race Traits and Tendencies of the American Negro.* New York: Macmillan Company, 1896.

Hone, Mildred. *The Former Charleston Normal and Industrial Institute, now Dart Hall.* n. p., n. d. [Dart Hall Branch, Charleston Free Library.]

Hood, James Walker. *One Hundred Years of the African Methodist Episcopal Zion Church.* New York: A. M. E. Zion Book Concern, 1895.

Hoyt, James Allen. *The Phoenix Riot, November 8, 1898. Paper Read Before Kosmos Club of Columbia, S. C., in May, 1935.* n. p., n. d. [South Caroliniana Library, University of South Carolina.]

Irvine, E. Eastman (ed.). *The World Almanac and Book of Facts for 1949.* New York: New York World Telegram Company, 1949.

Jarrell, Hampton M. *Wade Hampton and the Negro: The Road Not Taken.* Columbia: University of South Carolina Press, 1949.

Jervey, Theodore Dehon. *The Slave Trade: Slavery and Color.* Columbia: The State, 1925.

Johnson, Guion Griffis. *A Social History of the Sea Islands, with Special Reference to St. Helena Island, South Carolina.* Chapel Hill: University of North Carolina, 1930.

Johnson, Guy Benton. *Folk Culture on St. Helena Island, South Carolina.* Chapel Hill: University of North Carolina, 1930.

Jones, Frank Dudley and Mills, W. H. (eds.). *History of the Presbyterian Church in South Carolina since 1850.* Columbia: R. L. Bryan, 1926.

Jordan, Lewis Garnett. *Negro Baptist History, U. S. A., 1750, 1930.* Nashville: Sunday School Publishing Board, N. B. C., 1930.

Klingberg, Frank Joseph. *An Appraisal of the Negro in Colonial South Carolina.* Washington: Associated Publishers, 1941.

Lawton, Samuel Miller. The Religious Life of South Carolina Coastal and Sea Island Negroes. Unpublished Ph.D. dissertation, Department of Religious Education, George Peabody College for Teachers, 1939. Abstract of this is available in *Contributions to Education,* No. 242. Nashville: George Peabody College for Teachers, 1939.

Leiding, Harriette Kershaw. *Street Cries of an Old Southern City.* Charleston: Daggett Printing Company, 1910.

Lewinson, Paul. *Race, Class, and Party: A History of Negro Suffrage and White Politics in the South.* London and New York: Oxford University, 1932.

Lewisohn, Ludwig. *Up Stream: an American Chronicle.* New York: Boni and Liveright, 1923.

Loescher, Frank. *The Protestant Church and the Negro. A Pattern of Segregation.* New York: Association Press, 1948.

Mabry, William Alexander. "The Disfranchisement of the Negro in the South." Unpublished Ph.D. dissertation, Department of History, Duke University, 1933.

Mangum, Charles Staples. *The Legal Status of the Negro.* Chapel Hill: University of North Carolina, 1940.

McCrady, Edward. "Slavery in the Province of South Carolina, 1670-1770." *Annual Report of the American Historical Association for the Year 1895.* Washington: Government Printing Office, 1896. Pp. 631-73.

————— and Ashe, Samuel A. *Eminent and Representative Men of the Carolinas.* 2 vols. Madison: Brant and Fuller, 1892.

Mitchell, Broadus. *The Rise of Cotton Mills in the South.* Baltimore: Johns Hopkins, 1921. [*Johns Hopkins University Studies in Historical and Political Science,* Series XXXIX, No. 2.]

Moore, Burchill Richardson. "A History of the Negro Public Schools of Charleston, South Carolina, 1876-1942." Unpublished Master's thesis, Department of Education, University of South Carolina, 1942.

Murphy, Edgar Gardner. *The Basis of Ascendancy.* New York: Longmans, Green, 1910.

—————. *Problems of the Present South.* New York: Macmillan, 1904.

Murray, George Washington. *Race Ideals: Effects, Cause, and Remedy for the Afro-American Race Troubles.* Princeton: Smith and Sons, 1914.

Myrdal, Gunnar. *An American Dilemma: The Negro Problem and Modern Democracy.* New York: Harper, 1944.

Nicholson, Alfred William. *Brief Sketch of the Life and Labors of Rev. Alexander Bettis.* Trenton, South Carolina: The Author, 1913.

Odum, Howard Washington. *Social and Mental Traits of the Negro.* New York: Columbia University Press, 1910.

Oliphant, Albert D. *The Evolution of the Penal System of South Carolina from 1866 to 1916.* Columbia: The State, 1916.

Parsons, Elsie Clews. *Folk-Lore of the Sea Islands, South Carolina.* Cambridge: American Folk-Lore Society, 1923.

Patton, James Welch. "The Republican Party in South Carolina, 1876-1895," in Green, Fletcher Melvin (ed.), *Essays in Southern History.* Chapel Hill: University of North Carolina, 1949.

Pegues, Albert Weitherspoon. *Our Baptist Ministers and Schools.* Springfield, Massachusetts: Willey and Company, 1892.

Phillips, Charles Henry. *History of the Colored Methodist Episcopal Church in America: Comprising its Organization, Subsequent Development and Present Status.* Jackson, Tennessee: C. M. E. Publishing House, 1898.

Reynolds, John Schreiner. *Reconstruction in South Carolina, 1865-1877.* Columbia: The State, 1905.

Rice, John Andrew. *I Came Out of the Eighteenth Century.* New York: Harper, 1942.

Richardson, Clement (ed.). *The National Cyclopedia of the Colored Race.* Montgomery, Alabama: National Publishing Company, 1919.

Sheppard, William Arthur. *Red Shirts Remembered: Southern Brigadiers of the Reconstruction Period.* Atlanta: Ruralist Press, 1940.

Shufeldt, Robert Wilson. *The Negro: A Menace to American Civilization.* Boston: Gorham, 1907.

Simkins, Francis Butler. *Pitchfork Ben Tillman: South Carolinian.* Baton Rouge: Louisiana State University, 1944.

——————— and Woody, Robert Hilliard. *South Carolina During Reconstruction.* Chapel Hill: University of North Carolina, 1932.

Smith, Reed. *Gullah.* Columbia: University of South Carolina Bulletin No. 190, 1926.

Smith, Samuel Denny. *The Negro in Congress, 1870-1901.* Chapel Hill: University of North Carolina, 1940.

Smith, Septima Chappell. "The Development and History of Some Negro Churces in South Carolina." Unpublished Master's thesis, Department of Education, University of South Carolina, 1942.

Spero, Sterling Denhard and Harris, Abram Lincoln. *The Black Worker: The Negro and the Labor Movement.* New York: Columbia University Press, 1931.

Stackhouse, Mrs. Addie. *The Negro and his Progenitors, Abraham, Isaac and Jacob.* Columbia: Palmetto Leader, n. d.

Stephenson, Gilbert Thomas. *Race Distinctions in American Law.* New York: Appleton, 1910.

Stone, Alfred Holt *Studies in the American Race Problem.* New York: Doubleday, Page, 1908.

Taylor, Alrutheus Ambush. *The Negro in South Carolina During the Reconstruction.* Washington: Association for the Study of Negro Life and History, 1924.

Thirty Years of Lynching in the United States, 1889-1918. New York: National Association for the Advancement of Colored People, 1919.

Thomas, John Alexander William. *A History of Marlboro County with Traditions and Sketches of Numerous Families.* Atlanta: Foote and Davies, 1897.

Thomason, John Furman. *The Foundations of the Public Schools of South Carolina.* Columbia: The State, 1925.

Thompson, Edgar Tristram. "The Natural History of Agricultural Labor in the South," in Jackson, David K. (ed.), *American Studies in Honor of William K. Boyd.* Durham: Duke University, 1940.

Thompson, Henry Tazewell. *The Establishment of the Public School System of South Carolina.* Columbia: R. L. Bryan, 1927.

——————, *Ousting the Carpetbagger from South Carolina.* Columbia: R. L. Bryan, 1926.

Tillman, Benjamin Ryan. *The Struggle of '76, Speech at Anderson, S. C., 1909.* n. p., n. d. [South Caroliniana Library, University of South Carolina.]

Tindall, George Brown. "The South Carolina Constitutional Convention of 1895." Unpublished Master's thesis, Department of History, University of North Carolina, 1948.

Voorhis, Harold Van Buren. *Negro Masonry in the United States.* New York: Henry Emerson, 1940.

Wallace, David Duncan. *The History of South Carolina.* 3 vols. New York: American Historical Society, 1935.

Weatherford, Willis Duke. *Negro Life in the South, Present Conditions and Needs.* New York: Young Men's Christian Association, 1910.

Webster, Laura Josephine. *The Operation of the Freedmen's Bureau in South Carolina.* Northampton, Massachusetts: Department of History of Smith College, 1916. [Smith College Studies in History, Vol. I.]

Wesley, Charles Harris. *Negro Labor in the United States, 1850-1925.* New York: Vanguard, 1927.

Wharton, Vernon Lane. *The Negro in Mississippi, 1865-1890.* Chapel Hill: University of North Carolina, 1947. [*James Sprunt Studies in History and Political Science,* Vol. XXVIII.]

Williams, George Washington. *History of the Negro Race in America from 1619 to 1880.* New York: Putnam, 1883.

Woodson, Carter Godwin. *A Century of Negro Migration.* Washington: Association for the Study of Negro Life and History, 1918.

——————. *The History of the Negro Church.* Washington: Associated Publishers, 1921. Second edition, 1945.

——————. *The Negro in Our History.* Washington: Associated Publishers, 1931.

——————. *Negro Orators and their Orations.* Washington: Associated Publishers, 1925.

——————(ed.). *The Works of Francis James Grimke.* 4 vols. Washington: Associated Publishers, 1942.

Woodward, J. Herbert. *The Negro Bishop Movement in the Episcopal Diocese of South Carolina.* Savannah: Braid and Hutton, 1916.

Woody, Robert Hilliard. *Republican Newspapers of South Carolina.* Charlottesville, Virginia: Historical Publishing Company, 1936.

Woofter, Thomas Jackson. *Black Yeomanry.* New York: Henry Holt, 1930.

Wright, Richard Robert, Jr. *Centennial Encyclopedia of the African Methodist Episcopal Church.* Philadelphia: A. M. E. Book Concern, 1916.

——————. *The Encyclopaedia of the African Methodist Episcopal Church.* Philadelphia: Book Concern of the AME Church, 1947.

Writers' Program of the Works Projects Administration. *South Carolina: A Guide to the Palmetto State.* New York: Oxford University, 1941.

Zimmerman, Hilda Jane. "Penal Systems and Penal Reforms in the South Since the Civil War." Unpublished Ph.D. dissertation, Department of History, University of North Carolina, 1947.

B. Periodical Articles

Abramowitz, Jack. "The Negro in the Agrarian Revolt," *Agricultural History,* XXIV (April, 1950), 89-95.

Berry, Brewton. "The Mestizos of South Carolina," *American Journal of Sociology,* LI (July, 1945), 34-41.

Birnie, C. W. "The Education of the Negro in Charleston, South Carolina, Prior to the Civil War," *Journal of Negro History*, XII (January, 1927), 13-21.

Carroll, Richard. "The Industrial Education of the Negro," *The Educational*, I (December, 1902), 227-29.

Fitchett, E. Horace. "The Origin and Growth of the Free Negro Population of Charleston, South Carolina," *Journal of Negro History*, XXVI (October, 1941), 421-37.

——————. "The Role of Claflin College in Negro Life in South Carolina," *ibid.*, XII (Winter, 1943), 42-68.

——————. "The Status of the Free Negro in Charleston, South Carolina, and His Descendants in Modern Society," *ibid.*, XXXII (October, 1947), 430-51.

——————. "The Traditions of the Free Negro in Charleston, South Carolina," *ibid.*, XXV (April, 1940), 139-51.

Frazier, Edward Franklin. "The Booker T. Washington Papers," *The Library of Congress Quarterly Journal of Current Acquisitions*, II (February, 1945), 23-31.

Gilbert, William Harlen, Jr. "Memorandum Concerning the Characteristics of the Larger Mixed-Blood Racial Islands of the Eastern United States," *Social Forces*, XXIV (May, 1946), 438-47.

Jackson, Luther Porter. "The Educational Efforts of the Freedmen's Bureau and Freedmen's Aid Societies in South Carolina, 1862-1872," *Journal of Negro History*, VIII (January, 1923), 1-40.

Knight, Edgar Wallace. "Reconstruction and Education in South Carolina," *South Atlantic Quarterly*, XVIII (October, 1919), 350-64, and XIX (January, 1920), 55-66.

Mabry, William Alexander. "Ben Tillman Disfranchised the Negro," *South Atlantic Quarterly*, XXXVII (April, 1938), 170-83.

Mendenhall, Marjorie Stratford. "The Rise of Southern Tenancy," *Yale Review*, XXVII (September, 1937), 110-29.

Meyers, Frederick. "The Knights of Labor in the South," *Southern Economic Journal*, VI (April, 1940), 479-87.

Simkins, Francis Butler. "Ben Tillman's View of the Negro," *Journal of Southern History*, III (1937), 161-74.

——————. "The Problems of South Carolina Agriculture After the Civil War," *North Carolina Historical Review*, VII (January, 1930), 46-57.

——————. "Race Legislation in South Carolina Since 1865," *South Atlantic Quarterly*, XX (January-April, 1921), 61-71, 165-77.

——————. "The Solution of the Post-Bellum Agricultural Problems in South Carolina," *North Carolina Historical Review*, VII (April, 1930), 192-219.

Taylor, Alrutheus Ambush. "Negro Congressmen a Generation After," *Journal of Negro History*, VII (April, 1922), 127-71.

Tindall, George Brown. "The Campaign for the Disfranchisement of Negroes in South Carolina," *Journal of Southern History*, XV (May, 1949), 212-34.

——————. "The Question of Race in the South Carolina Constitutional Convention of 1895." *Journal of Negro History*, XXXVII (July, 1952), 277-303.

Wallace, Henry A. "Names of Negro Delegates from South Carolina to National Republican Conventions," *Journal of Negro History*, VII (October, 1922), 420-24.

Woodson, Carter Godwin. "Robert Smalls and His Descendants," *The Negro History Bulletin*, XI (November, 1947), 27-33.

Woody, Robert Hilliard. "Jonathan Jasper Wright, Associate Justice of the Supreme Court of South Carolina, 1870-1877," *Journal of Negro History*, XVIII (April, 1933), 114-31.

Work, Monroe Nathan. "Some Negro Members of Reconstruction Conventions and Legislatures and of Congress," *Journal of Negro History*, V (January, 1920), 63-125.

Zeichner, Oscar. "The Legal Status of the Agricultural Laborer in the South," *Political Science Quarterly*, LV (September, 1940), 412-28.

INDEX

Abbeville, 28, 39, 104, 114, 119, 155, 201, 206-7, 225
Abbeville *Journal of Enterprise,* 149, 150
Abbeville *Medium,* 28
Abbeville *Press and Banner,* 135, 183, 246
African Methodist Episcopal Church, 5, 49, 59, 155, 161, 178, 186, 187, 190-91, 193-94, 202, 206, 207, 232, 305
African Methodist Episcopal Zion Church, 187, 191, 202
African Repository, 158
Agricultural Society of Newberry, 24
Agriculture: general conditions, 92-95; land tenure, 10, 96-98, 100-5, 120-22, 171, 173-74; labor, 10, 24, 95-96, 98-100, 120, 121, 124; labor contracts, 7, 111-14, 120, 179; successful Negroes in, 104-5; lien system, 105-11, 120; organizations, 114-20
Aiken, 75, 104, 130, 155, 158, 171, 189
Aiken, D. Wyatt, 183
Aiken *Journal and Review,* 262
Aiken *Little Observer,* 150
Alabama, 176, 190
Allen University, 145, 151, 191, 206, 231, 232
Alliance Aid of South Carolina, 118
Alston, Mrs. Carolina, 143
American Baptist Publication Society, 188, 205
American Colonization Society, 154, 156, 158, 159, 163, 164
Anderson, 130, 144, 285
Anderson, G. W., 81, 151
Anderson, Robert B., 61, 61n., 81, 84, 85, 180, 221, 229
Andrews, W. T., 147
Arkansas, 92, 170, 171, 174, 175, 176, 177, 184
Arnett, Bishop Benjamin William, 178
Ashley River Asylum, 277-78
Atlanta University, 59, 204, 205, 225
Atlantic Coast Lumber Company, 127
Augusta, 172, 177
Avery Normal Institute, 205, 224
Azor, 160-67, 169, 189, 190, 203

Bachman, John, 4
Bachman, Assistant Attorney General W. K., 243, 244
Baker, Frazier B., 255-56
Ball, William Watts, 41, 66
Bamberg, 28, 131
Bampfield, S. J., 44, 62, 78, 81, 151
Banks, 144
Baptist Home Mission Board of Atlanta, 205
Baptist Home Mission State Convention of South Carolina, 189
Baptist Church, 4, 171, 187-90, 202, 204, 205, 224, 229, 231-32, 305
Barbadian Code, 2
Barbering, 129
Barker, Major T. G., 254
Barnwell, 23, 66, 104, 114, 127, 155, 159, 170, 175, 205, 239-40, 248-49
Baxter, Jonathan A., 23, 60
Beaufort, 1, 6, 23-24, 25, 85, 44, 51, 53, 55-56, 58, 59, 60, 61, 62-63, 64, 80, 81, 84, 88, 92, 100-3, 109, 125, 127, 136, 143, 145, 146, 147, 151, 155, 159, 170, 172, 182, 204, 214, 218, 220, 223, 226, 263, 264, 283, 284, 287, 288, 289, 295, 302
Beaufort Knitting Mills, 132
Beaufort *New South,* 78, 81, 150, 151
Beaufort Normal and Industrial Academy, 151
Beaufort *Sea Island News,* 151
Beaufort *Tribune,* 34, 151
Becker, C. E., 232
Beldock, 175
Bellinger, George D., 253-54
Belton, 136, 285
Benedict, Bethesba A., 231
Benedict, Stephen, 231
Benedict College, 205, 231-32
Benet, Judge Christie, 302
Bennettsville, 151
Bennettsville Graded School, 151
Bennettsville *Pee Dee Educator,* 150
Berkeley county, 53, 58, 59, 63, 92, 106, 190, 287
Bethune, Mary McLeod, 306
Bettis, Rev. Alexander, 187-88, 189, 207, 225
Betts, C. H., 138, 139
Birnie, Richard, 144
Bishop, Rev. H. C., 197
Bishopville, 255

[327]

EAU CLAIRE STATE TEACHERS COLLEGE
LIBRARY RULES

No book should be taken from the library until it has been properly charged by the librarian.

Books may be kept one week but are not to be renewed without special permission of the librarian.

A fine of two cents a day will be charged for books kept over time.

In case of loss or injury the person borrowing this book will be held responsible for a part or the whole of the value of a new book.

DUE	DUE	DUE	DUE
Oct 7 '54			
Jan 6 '55			
Jan 12 '55			
Feb 25 '55			
Feb 7 '58			
Dec 3 '58			
‑12 '59			
Feb 18 '59			
Apr 7 '59			
My5 '60			
Mar 26 62			